European Business Law

European Business Law

Legal and Economic Analyses on Integration and Harmonization

Edited by

Richard M. Buxbaum, Gérard Hertig,
Alain Hirsch, Klaus J. Hopt

Associate Editor

Marina Hertig

1991

Walter de Gruyter · Berlin · New York

♾ Printed on acid-free paper which falls within the guidelines of the ANSI to ensure permanence and durability.

Library of Congress Cataloging-in-Publication Data

European business law : legal and economic analyses on integration and harmonization / edited by Richard M. Buxbaum ... [et al.].
p. cm.
Based on a colloquium held Sept. 1–3, 1988 in Lugano. Switzerland.
Includes bibliographical references and index.
ISBN 0-89925-469-1 (alk. paper)
1. Commercial law – European Economic Community countries – Congresses. 2. Trade regulation – European Economic Community countries – Congresses. 3. European Economic Community – Congresses. 4. Europe 1992 – Congresses.
I. Buxbaum, Richard M.
KJE2044.95 1988
346.4'07–dc20
[344.067] 90–26910
CIP

Deutsche Bibliothek Cataloging-in-Publication Data

European business law : legal and economic analyses on integration and harmonization / ed. by Richard M. Buxbaum ... – Berlin ; New York : de Gruyter, 1991
ISBN 3-11-011648-0
NE: Buxbaum, Richard M. [Hrsg.]

Typesetting: Knipp Textverarbeitungen, Wetter
Printing: Ratzlow-Druck, Berlin
Binding: Lüderitz & Bauer, Berlin
Printed in Germany.

Preface

In 1988, Professor Richard M. Buxbaum (University of California at Berkeley) and Professor Klaus J. Hopt (University of Munich) published their book *Legal Harmonization and the Business Enterprise – Corporate and Capital Market Law Harmonization Policy in Europe and the USA* (Berlin/New York 1988).

In September 1987, I had the privilege of discussing some of the issues presented in the book with the authors. It appeared to me that these issues were of great importance. I suggested that it would be very worthwhile having a broader discussion of them with a number of specialists, from different countries and of different expertises. The authors welcomed this idea with enthusiasm and we agreed that such a discussion could take place in a closed colloquium to be organized in Switzerland in the Summer of 1988.

Each participant at the colloquium was asked not only to read the book and present his general observations, but more specifically to present a report in writing upon a specific issue. The reports were sent in advance to all participants.

The colloquium took place as envisaged in Lugano, from September 1st to September 3, 1988. The discussion was very free and interesting. Consequently, we decided to publish not only the written contributions presented by each participant but also a full report of the discussion.

The colloquium was extremely well organized by Professor Gérard Hertig, Director of the Centre d'Etudes Juridiques Européennes of the University of Geneva Law School. Thanks to him and to his wife, Mrs. Marina Hertig, the participants enjoyed not only very stimulating intellectual discussion, but also moments of friendly contact in lovely surroundings. Moreover, Professor Gérard Hertig has accepted the very difficult task of editing the discussion and we are greatly indebted to him. EC changes of law have been taken into account as of January 1, 1991.

Professor Klaus J. Hopt and Professor Richard M. Buxbaum wrote the final conclusion of this book. Our thanks are also due to them and Professor Buxbaum's assistants for their contribution towards the editing of the written reports.

I hope that the readers of this book will have some of the pleasure which the participants had in our discussion together in Lugano.

Alain Hirsch

Contents

List of Participants

Austin Robert P., Visiting Professor in Corporation and Securities Market Law, University of Sydney; Partner, Minter Ellison, Australian Solicitors

Buxbaum Richard M., Jackson H. Ralston Professor of International Law and Director, Center for German and European Studies, University of California at Berkeley; Editor-in-chief, *American Journal of Comparative Law*

Fitchew Geoffrey E., Director-General, Directorate-General XV, Financial Institutions and Company Law, Commission of the European Communities, Brussels

Gower, L.C.B., Formerly Cassel Professor of Commercial Law, University of London; Commissioned by the UK Government to undertake a review of investor protection (see *Review of Investor Protection, A Discussion Document,* London 1982) and to advise on new legislation, which recommendations led to the Financial Services Act 1986

Guillod Olivier, Professor, University of Neuchâtel School of Law; Deputy Director, *Centre d'études juridiques européennes*, University of Geneva School of Law

Hertig Gérard, Professor, University of Geneva School of Law; Visiting Professor, Catholic University of Louvain School of Law; Director, *Centre d'études juridiques européennes*, University of Geneva School of Law

Hirsch Alain, Professor, University of Geneva School of Law; Chairman, Commission for Regulation of the Asso ciation of Swiss Exchanges; Formely Vice-Chairman, Swiss Banking Commission

Hopt Klaus J., Professor, University of Munich School of Law; Director, *Institut für internationales Recht*, University of Munich School of Law; Formerly Judge at the Court of Appeals, Stuttgart

D'Illiers Bertrand, Chief, Accounting Division, *Commission des opérations de Bourse*, Paris

Kitch Edmund W., Joseph M. Hartfield Professor of Law, University of Virginia; Member of the bars of the United States Supreme Court, various federal courts, and States; Formerly Professor of Law, University of Chicago, and Special Assistanto, the Solicitor General of the United States

McComb Desmond, Formerly Professor, Department of Accounting and Management Science, University of Southampton, now retiered but continues to be associated with Southampton University and to engage in research on the international harmonisation of corporate financial reporting

Meier-Schatz Christian, Professor, University of St. Gallen School of Law; Partner, Pestalozzi Gmuer and Heiz, Attorneys, Zurich

Schmidt Hartmut, Professor, University of Hamburg; Director, *Institut für Geld- und Kapitalverkehr*, University of Hamburg; Co-editor of the *Zeitschrift für Bankrecht und Bankwirtschaft;* Member of the board of the Hanseatic Stock Exchange Hamburg and of the recently established *Deutsche Terminbörse*

Timmermans Christian W.A., Deputy Director-General, Legal Service, Commission of the European Communities, Brussels; Formerly Professor, University of Groningen School of Law

Tunc André, Professor Emeritus, University of Paris I (Panthéon Sorbonne); Author of *Le droit anglais des sociétés anonymes* (3d ed., Paris 1987) and *Le droit américain des sociétés anonymes* (Paris 1985)

Wymeersch Eddy, Professor, University of Gent School of Law; Director, Department of Commercial and Business Law, University of Gent

European Community Acts and Proposals

The Commission of the European Communities has published three brochures containing the acts and proposals in the areas of banking, securities and company law:

- *Credit Institutions – Community Measures Adopted or Proposed* (situation as at May 1990) (Office for Official Publications of the European Communities, Luxembourg 1990).
- *Securities Markets – Community Measures Adopted or Proposed* (situation as at June 1989) (Office for Official Publications of the European Communities, Luxembourg 1989).
- *Harmonization of Company Law in the European Community – Measures Adopted and Proposed* (situation as at 1 January 1989) (Office for Official Publications of the European Communities, Luxembourg 1989).

See also:

- *Compendium of EC Financial Services Law* (London/Dublin/Edinburgh/Munich 1990).
- *Compendium of EC Company Law* (London/Dublin/Edinburgh/Munich 1990).

Abbreviations

A.2d	Atlantic Reporter, Second Series (USA)
ABA	American Bar Association (USA)
Acc. Rev.	The Accounting Review (USA)
A.C.L.C.	Australian Company Law Cases (Australia)
A.C.L.R.	Australian Current Law Review (Australia)
AG	Aktiengesellschaft, stock corporation; Die Aktiengesellschaft (Germany)
AICPA	American Institute of Certified Public Accountants (USA)
ALI	American Law Institute (USA)
A.L.J.R.	Australian Law Journal Reports (Australia)
All E.R.	All England Law Reports (UK)
Am. Econ. Rev.	American Economic Review (USA)
AMEX	American Stock Exchange
Am. J. Comp. L.	The American Journal of Comparative Law (USA)
Am. J. Leg. Hist.	The American Journal of Legal History (USA)
APB	Accounting Principles Board (USA)
Art.	Article(s)
ASC	Accounting Standards Committee (UK & Ireland)
B.C.L. Rev.	British Columbia Law Review (Canada)
B.F.L.R.	Banking & Finance Law Review (Canada)
BFuP	Betriebswirtschaftliche Forschung und Praxis (Germany)
BGBl.	Bundesgesetzblatt, Official Gazette (Germany)
BIS	Bank for International Settlements
Bost. Coll. L. Rev.	Boston College Law Review (USA)
Bull.	bulletin
Bull. EC	Bulletin of the European Communities (Luxembourg)

Bus. Law.	The Business Lawyer (USA)
c.	chapter
Cal. L. Rev.	California Law Review (USA)
Can. L.T.	Canadian Law Times (Canada)
Cardozo L. Rev.	Cardozo Law Review (USA)
CBI	Confederation of British Industry (UK)
CEN	Comité Européen de Normalisation
CENELEC	Comité Européen de Normalisation Electrotechnique
cf.	confer
CFTC	Commodity Futures Trading Commission (USA)
Ch(s).	chapter, chapters
CICA	Canadian Institute of Chartered Accountants (Canada)
C.M.L.R.	Common Market Law Reports (UK)
C.M.L. Rev.	Common Market Law Review (The Netherlands)
Cmnd	Command Papers (HMSO) (UK)
COB	Commission des Opérations de Bourse (France)
Co. Law	The Company Lawyer (UK)
Colum. L. Rev.	Columbia Law Review (USA)
CONSOB	Commissione Nazionale per le Società e la Borsa (Italy)
Creighton L. Rev.	Creighton Law Review (USA)
Ct.	Court
DB	Der Betrieb (Germany)
Del. Ch.	Delaware Court of Chancery (USA)
Del. J. Corp. L.	Delaware Journal of Corporate Law (USA)
Den. L.J.	Denver Law Journal (USA)
Doc.	document
Doc. COM	Commission Document (EC)
DTI	Department of Trade & Industry (UK)
EC	European Community/Communities
ECJ	European Court of Justice
Economica	Economica (UK)

ECOSOC	United Nations Economic & Social Council
E.C.R.	European Court of Justice, Official Reports (Luxembourg)
ECSC Treaty	Treaty Establishing the European Coal and Steel Community
ed(s).	editor(s), edition
EEC	European Economic Community
EEC Treaty	Treaty Establishing the European Economic Community (Treaty of Rome)
EEIG	European Economic Interest Grouping
e.g.	exempli gratia, for example
Emory L.J.	Emory Law Journal (USA)
EuZw	Europäische Zeitschrift für Wirtschaftsrecht (Germany)
EWS	Europäisches Wirtschafts- & Steuerrecht (Germany)
F.2d	Federal Reporter, Second Series (USA)
FASB	Financial Accounting Standards Board (USA)
Fed	Federal Reserve Board of Governors (USA); Federal Reserve System
FEE	Fédération des Experts Comptables Européens
FIW	Forschungsinstitut für Wirtschaftsverfassung und Wettbewerb e.V. Köln (Germany)
F. Supp.	Federal Supplement (USA)
GAAP	Generally Accepted Accounting Principles (USA)
GATT	General Agreement on Tariffs and Trade
GDP	Gross Domestic Product
Geo. L.J.	The Georgetown Law Journal (USA)
Geo. Wash. L. Rev.	George Washington Law Review (USA)
GmbH	Gesellschaft mit beschränkter Haftung, limited liability company (Germany)
Harv. L. Rev.	Harvard Law Review (USA)
Hastings L.J.	The Hastings Law Journal (USA)
HGB	Handelsgesetzbuch, Commercial Code (Germany)
HMSO	Her Majesty's Stationary Office (UK)
IASC	International Accounting Standards Committee

ibid.	ibidem
id.	idem
i.e.	id est
IFAC	International Federation of Accountants
Int'l Fin. L. Rev.	International Financial Law Review (UK)
Int'l J. of Account.	International Journal of Accounting (USA)
Int'l Rev. Law & Econ.	International Review of Law & Economics (USA)
IOSCO	International Organization of Securities Commissioners
IPC	Investment Protection Committees (UK)
J. Acc. & Econ.	Journal of Accounting & Economics (USA)
J. Acc. & Pub. Pol.	Journal of Accounting & Public Policy (USA)
J.B.L.	The Journal of Business Law (UK)
J. Bus.	Journal of Business (USA)
J. Comp. Bus. & Cap. Mkt. L.	Journal of Comparative Business & Capital Market Law (USA)
J. Corp. L.	The Journal of Corporation Law (USA)
J.C.P.	Jurisclasseur périodique (France)
J. Econ. Hist.	Journal of Economic History
J. Econ. Lit.	Journal of Economic Literature (USA)
J. Fin. Econ.	Journal of Financial Economics (USA)
J. L. & Econ.	The Journal of Law & Economics (USA)
J. Law, Econ. & Org.	Journal of Law, Economics & Organization (USA)
J. Leg. Studies	Journal of Legal Studies (USA)
J. Nat. Educat. Ass.	Journal of the National Educational Association (USA)
J. Pol. Econ.	Journal of Political Economy (USA)
J.T.	Journal des Tribunaux (Belgium)
KG	Kommanditgesellschaft, limited partnership (Germany)
KGaA	Kommanditgesellschaft auf Aktien, limited partnership on shares (Germany)
Kyklos	International Review for Social Sciences (Switzerland)
Law & Contemp. Prob.	Law & Contemporary Problems (USA)

L.Q.R.	Law Quarterly Review (UK)
Mich. L. Rev.	Michigan Law Review (USA)
M.L.R.	Modern Law Review (UK)
NASD	National Association of Securities Dealers (USA)
NASDAQ	National Association of Securities Dealers Automated Quotations (USA)
NCSC	National Companies & Securities Commission (Australia)
No.	number(s)
N.S.W.L.R.	New South Wales Law Reports (Australia)
Nw. U. L. Rev.	Northwestern University Law Review (USA)
OCAM	Organisation Commune Africaine, Malgache et Mauricienne
OECD	Organisation for Economic Co-operation & Development
Ohio St. L.J.	Ohio State Law Journal (USA)
O.J.	Official Journal (of the EC unless otherwise stated)
para(s)	Paragraph(s)
Pub. Ad. Rev.	Public Administration Review (USA)
RabelsZ	Rabels Zeitschrift für ausländisches und internationales Privatrecht (Germany)
repr.	reprinted
Rev. Prat. Soc.	Revue Pratique des Sociétés (Belgium)
Riv. soc.	Rivista delle Società (Italy)
RIW	Recht der Internationalen Wirtschaft/Außenwirtschaftsdienst des Betriebs-Beraters (Germany)
RPB	Recognised Professional Body (UK)
R.T.D.E.	Revue trimestrielle de droit européen (France)
SA	société anonyme, stock corporation
SARL	société à responsabilité limitée, limited liability company
Sched.	Schedule
S. Comm.	société en commandite, limited partnership
S. Ct.	Supreme Court Reporter (USA)
SEA	Single European Act

SEAQ	Stock Exchange Automated Quotations (UK)
SEC	Securities & Exchange Commission (USA)
SIB	Securities & Investments Board (UK)
SRO	Self-Regulating Organisation (UK)
Stat.	United States Statutes at Large (USA)
Supr.	Supreme
TASC	Tripartite Accounting Standards Committee (The Netherlands)
Tenn. L. Rev.	Tennessee Law Review (USA)
Tex. L. Rev.	Texas Law Review (USA)
TNC	Transnational Corporation
TNE	Transnational Enterprise
U. Chi. L. Rev.	The University of Chicago Law Review (USA)
UCITS	Undertakings for Collective Investment in Transferable Securities
UDC L. Rev.	University of California at Davis Law Review (USA)
UEC	Union Européenne des Experts Comptables Economiques et Financiers
UK	United Kingdom
UN	United Nations
UNCITRAL	United Nations Commission on International Trade Law
U.S.	United States Supreme Court Reports (USA)
USA	United States of America
U.S.C.	United States Code (USA)
USM	Unlisted Securities Market
v.	versus
Va. L. Rev.	Virginia Law Review (USA)
Vand. L. Rev.	Vanderbilt Law Review (USA)
VAT	Value-Added Tax
Vol(s)	Volume(s)
WM	Zeitschrift für Wirtschaft- und Bankrecht (Wertpapier-Mitteilungen) (Germany)
Wpg	Die Wirtschaftsprüfung (Germany)
WuR	Wirtschaft und Recht (Switzerland)

Yale L.J.	The Yale Law Journal (USA)
ZfbF	Zeitschrift für betriebswirtschaftliche Forschung (Germany)
ZGR	Zeitschrift für Unternehmens- und Gesellschaftsrecht (Germany)
ZHR	Zeitschrift für das gesamte Handelsrecht und Wirtschaftsrecht (Germany)
ZIP	Zeitschrift für Wirtschaftsrecht (Germany)
ZSR	Zeitschrift für Schweizerisches Recht (Switzerland)

Chapter One

Political Choices

A. Report: Geoffrey Fitchew

I. Introduction

In this comment, I will respond to the criticism that there is no clear theory, whether economic or judicial, underlying the Commission's view of what needs harmonizing at the Community level, what can be left to national legislation, and what does not need regulation at all. I shall briefly comment on the EEC Treaty provisions relating to harmonization. I shall comment more extensively on the Commission's 1985 White Paper on Completing the Internal Market and the proposed approach to harmonization and how it is being applied to *regulation of capital markets and company law*. I will conclude by addressing specific criticisms and suggestions made in the book by Prof. *Buxbaum* and *Hopt*,[1] and by some of the other contributions to this Symposium.

II. Theory of Harmonization

I have to confess that I find myself cheerfully unrepentant in face of the criticism that the Commission has not made any serious attempt to develop a theory of harmonization.

This is, I believe, not merely a consequence of my nationality and profession – though both Englishmen and administrators are notorious pragmatists. Nor is it simply that none of the theories discussed in Chapter 1 of the *Buxbaum* and *Hopt* book[2] are altogether satisfactory, though that also seems to be the case. Rather, I would argue, it is in principle simply not possible to construct such a theory at all, at least if one defines harmonization as a set of principles derived from some economic model that would enable all reasonable men to agree that such a subject should be regulated at

[1] R.M. BUXBAUM & K.J. HOPT, *Legal Harmonization and the Business Enterprise* (Berlin/New York 1988).

[2] *Id.* at 1-23.

the federal or Community level while another should be regulated at State level. One can apply the same argument and conclusion to the question of whether any particular economic activity needs to be regulated and how it is to be regulated.

The justification for this apparently agnostic conclusion lies in the elementary distinction between positive and normative economics. The best that economics as a science can do, is to identify (but by no means always quantify) the costs and benefits likely to arise from regulating or failing to regulate a particular economic activity and from doing so at one governmental level rather than another. But each choice depends on the personal and social preferences of those making the decisions (or, one might add, of the economists who offer particular prescriptions). The choice to be made in each case depends on political judgments that can and will vary from place to place and from time to time. A rather striking example is that of insider dealing, which has only quite recently become regarded as offensive; and even then, not by all members of OECD or even by all economists.

This is certainly not to say that economic analysis has nothing to offer to those having to make these judgments. Economic analysis is useful in illuminating the type of costs and benefits which should enter into the calculus. Both the *Scitovsky* theory of economic integration[3] and the theory of public choice[4] certainly do so. In this context, I was surprised by one omission from Chapter 1 of *Buxbaum* and *Hopt*. Two pieces of economic analysis which seem to me to have quite a lot to offer to those taking regulatory decisions are the theory of pure public goods and the theory of externalities or spillovers.

Both these theories (which date back to the 1930s and which some have traced back to Adam Smith) shed light on the problem of *when* governmental intervention or regulation may be necessary to correct for deficiencies in the operation of market mechanisms. Specific examples are the case of "pure public goods" (e.g. defense, the rule of law, stability of the financial system) which the market simply cannot produce at all, or the case of externalities where there are social costs and benefits which the private sector and the market process ignore (e.g. many forms of economic infrastructure such as irrigation, roads, health, education, environmental pollution).

Moreover, the theory of externalities can, at least in some cases, offer guidance as to which level of government public intervention should occur. Ideally, it should be the lowest level of jurisdiction at which all or at least most of the social costs and benefits are captured.

The utility of these two theories is qualified by two factors. First, the weighing to be given to the externalities – particularly where they cannot be quantified – will be a matter of subjective political judgement and may be regarded by some of the participants in the negotiation as being offset by the intrinsic merits of diversity and of retention of national sovereignty or

[3] See *id.* at 10.
[4] See *id.* at 8.

by the benefits of "competition between rules." Second, there is no particular reason why the boundaries of the "optimum regulatory area" in any particular case (which captures all the externalities in question) need necessarily to coincide either with the boundaries of the federation/Community or with those of its constituent States. Some "public goods," for example protecting the ozone layer or saving the whale, clearly demand at least some degree of intervention at global level, and the same conclusion is increasingly becoming accepted for at least certain aspects of regulating banking and securities markets. For the moment the only conclusion I want to draw from this part of the argument is that it will usually be a mistake to ask whether the Community (or for that matter the USA) is the "optimum regulatory area" for a particular problem, since it will not be. The more practical questions to ask will be whether it is a *feasible* regulatory area and whether the regulatory objectives in question can be more efficiently achieved at Community level than at Member State level.

III. EEC Treaty Provisions Relating to Harmonization

The EEC Treaty provisions relating to harmonization of laws are thoroughly discussed in Chapter 3 of the *Buxbaum* and *Hopt* book,[5] and I will therefore only add one brief comment.

I agree with *Buxbaum* and *Hopt* that the Treaty has proved to be a remarkably flexible and open-ended instrument, capable of accommodating diverse, and perhaps even contradictory interpretations by the different Community institutions, including the European Court. The two main sources of that flexibility are, first, as the authors indicate, the broad meaning given to the apparently limiting clause "to the extent necessary for the functioning of the Common Market" in the various Articles dealing with harmonization; second, the possibility of recourse to Article 235 to achieve the objectives of the Treaty where other more specific Articles of the Treaty prove insufficient. There is also, of course, the possibility of Treaty amendment. The passage of the Single European Act (SEA),[6] which made major changes to the Treaty, demonstrates that even this apparently cumbersome process can be completed with surprising rapidity when a sufficient political will exists.

The SEA:

- substantially extends the area of majority voting;
- enlarges the legislative role of the European Parliament;
- creates specific Articles for new Community policies (e.g. on environment, R and D, health and safety at work);
- allows Member States to adapt to Community policies at different rates.

[5] *Id.* at 167-269, 194 ff.
[6] *Bull. EC*, Supp. 2/1986.

Negotiations on the SEA began in June 1985 and the Treaty amendments entered into force in July 1987, despite a delay of several months while their constitutionality was challenged before the Irish courts.[7]

The flexibility described, which closely parallels that in the US Constitution, is absolutely essential to allow Community policy to reflect the changing political and social preferences.

IV. The 1985 White Paper on Completing the Internal Market

I have been asked to speak about the political aspects of harmonization. The 1985 White Paper on Completing the Internal Market[8] is the expression of the policy aims of the Commission then in office over a very large area of Community life. Indeed it was intended to lay down much of the agenda for the subsequent Commission as well, since the target date for completing the program is December 31, 1992.

The analysis or theory on which the White Paper is founded seems to me to be close to the economic integration approach of *Scitovsky*. The diagnosis made by the Commission which entered office in 1985 was that Europe had been falling seriously behind the United States and Japan in both economic performance and potential and that this gap could not be bridged unless the remaining barriers to the freedom of movement of *goods*, *services*, *capital* and *persons* (both natural and legal) were removed. Contrary to the suggestion in *Buxbaum* and *Hopt*,[9] there is, in my view, no disagreement that this is what a common market means. The definition given to the internal market in the SEA is perfectly clear on this point.

The clear expectations of the White Paper are that the removal of these barriers will lead not only to sharper competition and hence to a general improvement in factor productivity, but ultimately to increased investment by industry and services in order to take advantage of the economies of scale offered by a genuinely unified market. It is clear, however, that the beneficiaries of this integration process are the final consumers rather than producers. There is indeed a net loss of producer surplus as a result of this increased competition.

Two criticisms of the economic integration theory have been made by other contributors to this Symposium, which I will try to refute at this point.

Buxbaum and *Hopt* argue that:[10]

> "The unjustified optimism of this model is evidenced by the more than 10 million unemployed workers in the European Community, and the discrepancies in regional development shown by the extremes of Hamburg and Sicily."

[7] Crotty v. An Taoiseach, Judgment of 9 April 1987, [1987] 2 *C.M.L.R.* 666.
[8] Doc. COM(85)310 (14 June 1985).
[9] BUXBAUM & HOPT, *supra* note 1, at 200.
[10] *Id.* at 200.

This criticism seems to be misconceived for the following reasons:

- It is on the contrary the *failure* of the Community to achieve a genuinely unified market in goods and services, which has contributed to the relative stagnation of European economic performance in the late 1970s and early 1980s and thus to high levels of unemployment.
- The programme of measures contained in the 1985 White Paper is, to use the current economists' jargon, aimed at improving the "supply-side" of the economy. The full benefits in terms of increased employment will depend also on sensibly-constructed and coordinated policies for demand management. Current unemployment levels in Europe to some extent reflect the strong efforts made by most Member States to squeeze out the inflationary excesses of the 1970s.
- It has never, so far as I am aware, been claimed that economic integration *by itself* will solve problems of structural adjustment whether in the labor market, in general, or, in particular, in less developed regions. Certainly the Commission has not made such a claim. On the contrary, it has got the Member States to agree to a doubling of the structural funds precisely in order to alleviate these problems.

A second argument advanced against the Community's efforts to promote economic integration through harmonization is the proposition in Prof. *Kitch*'s paper[11] that the economic gains to be made are small, essentially on the grounds that international trade is sufficiently liberalized to capture most of the worthwhile gains offered by the application of the principle of comparative advantage. This leads him to the conclusion that it may not matter whether authority "over these matters is exercised at the federation or the constituent state level."[12] As I understand the argument, "these matters" are not just company law and the regulation of capital markets, but all matters relating to the free movement of goods, services and the factors of production.

This is a judgement which may well be valid for interstate trade within the USA (though there are relatively restricted sectors, such as insurance). But it is one which, I suspect, would strike most impartial observers of the European scene as surprising and probably erroneous.

It is true that the Community made major advances in the 1960s in removing all quotas and tariffs on trade in manufactured goods between Member States. But a host of non-tariff barriers, often in the form of different technical standards, remained and have multiplied over the years. In the case of services, until recently, there has been little progress towards a genuinely integrated market and until recently, a majority of Member States maintained elaborate and extensive systems of control over capital movements.

The Commission's *a priori* expectation that there are worthwhile gains to be made from the achievement of the single market has been supported by a

[11] See *infra* at 36 ff.
[12] See *infra* at 37.

recently published economic study entitled the *Cecchini Report*[13] which suggests that if the entire programme is achieved, there should be a gain to Community GDP of the order of 5%. Now this may not be enormous by historical standards, but it is certainly not trivial. The 5% gain is in terms of a once-and-for-all increase in the *level* of GDP. But if the integration process leads to an increase in both the level and efficiency of investment, there should also be a good prospect of an increase in the trend rate of productivity. Given that the Community's present rate of growth is of the order of 2.5% to 3%, even an 0.5% gain in the rate of productivity would be substantial.

The 1985 White Paper describes three types of barriers to the creation of the single market:
- physical barriers;
- fiscal barriers;
- technical barriers.

The category of technical barriers covers not only the obstructions to trade, which can arise from divergencies in standards applied to manufactured goods, but differences in the regulatory and prudential standards applied in particular to operators and providers of services in the capital and financial markets.

In discussing the removal of these technical barriers, the White Paper proposes an explicit move away from the highly-detailed harmonization efforts which characterized the 1960s and 1970s, to a three-step approach consisting of:
- harmonization of essential or key standards (the White Paper uses the term "minimum standards," but it has subsequently been made clear that "key standards" is meant);
- control of the application of key standards by the home country;
- mutual recognition of the way in which these standards are applied in each Member State.

In some cases, such as banking, the concept of home country control leads naturally to the idea of a single banking licence, issued by the home country authorities, which, on the basis of mutual recognition, is valid for the entire Community.[14]

In support of the objectives I have described, the White Paper contains a programme of 300 measures aimed at removing the barriers to the exercise of the four economic freedoms.

Since 1985, the sifting and refining of this programme has been carried forward. In this process some of the original 300 proposals have been dropped and some important new ones added; but the bulk of them have been retained. Before looking in more detail at those parts of the programme relating to capital markets and company law, a word about the

[13] EC COMMISSION, *Research on the Cost of "Non-Europe"* (Cecchini Report, 16 vols., Brussels 1988).

[14] See the Second Banking Directive adopted in 1989: O.J. L 386/1 (1989).

progress of the programme is appropriate. Over 200 of the measures have been tabled by the Commission and we expect to get up to 90% by the end of 1989. More importantly, the Council has reached agreement on some 100 proposals, including a number of measures that are crucial to the success of the programme as a whole and were highly contentious.

In the first six months of 1988, agreement was reached on:

- the complete liberalization of capital movements; this will take effect by mid 1990 for eight Member States and by end 1992 for the rest;
- the liberalization of a large part of the market in non-life insurance;
- the complete dismantling of road haulage quotas;
- the mutual recognition of diplomas and other professional qualifications.

While there is a substantial amount still to be done, the progress already made justifies a much more optimistic view than that expressed by *Buxbaum* and *Hopt*.

The Commission's confidence that the programme can be completed is underpinned by the strong support it is getting from the twelve Member governments and from industry and commerce. The "announcement effect" of the programme has already been considerable, evidenced by the spate of cross-frontier takeovers and cooperative ventures and initiatives by Member governments to anticipate future Community legislation.

I now turn to consider how the approach set out in the White Paper applies to the two main subjects of this Symposium – the regulation of capital markets and the harmonization of company law.

V. Capital Market Regulation

The 1985 White Paper clearly states that the Commission's principal objective in relation to capital markets is the liberalization of financial services. To quote from Paragraphs 102 and 109 of the White Paper:[15]

> "The accent is now put increasingly on the free circulation of 'financial products.' ... The Commission considers that it should be possible to facilitate the exchange of such 'financial products' at a Community level, using a minimal coordination of rules (especially on such matters as authorisation, financial supervision and reorganisation, winding up, etc.) as the basis for mutual recognition by Member States of what each does to safeguard the interests of the public. Such harmonisation ... should be guided by the principle of 'home country control'."

The White Paper compared this approach to the strategy the Commission was already following with respect to industrial and agricultural products following the "*Cassis de Dijon*"[16] approach, namely that products lawfully

[15] See *supra* note 8.

[16] Case 120/78, Rewe-Zentral AG v. Bundesmonopolverwaltung für Branntwein, [1979] E.C.R. 649.

manufactured and marketed in one Member State should circulate in another.

Clearly a *sine qua non* of liberalizing financial services is the complete liberalization of capital movements. Now that this has been agreed upon, some people may wonder why any other action is needed to ensure the free cross-frontier supply of financial services and more specifically why any harmonization of the regulation of financial institutions is required.

The main answer to this question is that the directives which provide for freedom of capital movement are a necessary, but not sufficient, condition for freedom of financial services. They grant the investor the right to purchase any financial product circulating on Community markets and to approach, on his own initiative, any supplier of financial services or products for that purpose. But the directives do not guarantee the supplier of financial services the unrestricted right to approach the customer and to market his product or services. While the *Van Binsbergen* judgement of 1974[17] decided that the rights of establishment and of freedom to supply services are directly applicable simply as a consequence of the provisions of the Treaty, in practice important obstacles have remained in existence in most Member States, which have seriously inhibited the exercise of these rights, in particular the right to supply services across frontiers.

In the case of *capital markets* these obstacles can be classified into three types:

- Access to markets can be subject to twelve different authorization requirements and to associated rules of supervision and conduct of business. Indeed, until a judgement given by the European Court in December 1986,[18] several Member States held that they were entitled to require insurance companies to be established on their territory in order to conduct business with their residents. And several Member States still restrict advertising for deposits by foreign banks.
- There are significant differences in national rules as to the types of business which different financial institutions can carry out in different markets. For example, in some Member States banks cannot undertake securities business or some types of securities business. Again, there are widely differing rules relating to stock exchange membership.
- There are restrictions in some Member States relating to the types of financial product which may circulate; for example, some Member States prohibit variable interest rates or indexed loans.

The major objective of our capital markets legislation is to remove these remaining obstacles. In general, the approach we are adopting is to introduce the idea of a single license or authorization issued by the home country authority, which will be valid either for setting up a branch or providing cross-frontier services throughout the Community. This is the approach we have already adopted for unit trusts (UCITS), for non-life

[17] Case 33/74, [1974] E.C.R. 1299.

[18] Case 205/84, Commission v. Germany, [1986] E.C.R. 3755.

insurance and for banks and which we will be proposing for broking and dealing and other investment services. It is, I think, more or less self-evident that the single license concept depends on at least some degree of harmonization of the key supervisory and prudential rules. Member States will understandably be reluctant to drop their own authorization requirements and prudential rules and grant mutual recognition to licenses issued by other Member States, unless they are assured that their own residents in their capacities as depositors, investors or policy holders will receive adequate protection. In this sense, there will usually be a necessary link between Commission's actions to remove barriers to trade in financial services and proposals to harmonize national legislation aimed at the protection of investors and depositors or at other "public goods." The crucial questions the Commission has to decide are:

- what are the key supervisory or prudential rules which should be harmonized;
- how specific should the harmonization be;
- how should responsibilities be divided between the home country and host country supervisors.

Since the answers vary from sector to sector, I will only highlight the conclusions which have emerged from our work over the last few years.

The first point is the central importance of the *capital adequacy* or solvency of banks and operators in securities in the list of key rules to be harmonized at the supranational level. The prime objective of the regulation is to strengthen the stability of the banking and financial system as a whole. Financial stability is a pure "public good" in that it will not be produced by the operation of market forces. On the contrary, unrestrained competition in the banking sector is likely to lead to instability. In the banking sector it is widely accepted that common rules on solvency must be set at the international level. This is not so much to ensure a "level playing field" for the competitors, desirable though that is; more important, it is to avoid a competition in laxity between the supervisors themselves. In an international market-place systemic stability can only be achieved at the international level.

So a Directive on an harmonized solvency ratio, which does not even appear in the White Paper list, is at the heart of our proposals for the banking sector.[19] That proposal, however, only deals with *credit risk*. Further rules will be needed, to be applied by both banks and non-bank operators, to deal with "*market risk*" arising on securities transactions.[20]

The second point relates to what we mean by "*minimum regulation*." This does not mean regulation at the level of the lowest common denominator. But "minimum regulation" does mean that individual Member States can apply tougher standards, but only to their own domestic enterprises. This gives rise to the possibility of "reverse discrimination." For

[19] Directive adopted in 1989: see O.J. L 386/14 (1989).
[20] See the proposal published in 1990: O.J. C 152/6 (1990).

example, our proposals for the banking sector[21] envisage that the single banking license can, in principle, be valid for a wide range of activities on the universal bank model. A bank licensed in one Member State to carry out the full range of activities must be allowed to do them throughout the Community. But the banking supervisors in one Member State can restrict the authorization of their own domestic banks to traditional banking, if they so wish.

Third, the division of responsibility between home and host country supervisors. Although the White Paper sets out "home country" supervision as an ideal, it is clear that some subjects can be more effectively handled by host country supervisors and, second, that cooperation between supervisors both bilaterally and multilaterally will be essential. There are some difficult borderline cases, notably in respect of securities market regulation. We are at present discussing with Member States a wide ranging investment services directive.[22] At one end of the spectrum it is clear that authorization and capital adequacy should be a home country responsibility and, at the other end, that at least in the first instance marketing and advertising rules should be a host country responsibility. But how about compensation schemes and reporting requirements?

Fourth, a word about the free circulation of "financial products." The White Paper's approach implied that duly authorized banks or securities firms should be free to market all their financial products and use their full range of technologies throughout the Community. Life will unfortunately not be quite so simple. We have encountered resistance to this proposition both from Member States and the European Court. Under our current proposals, while there is a presumption that any financial product may circulate freely, this will still be subject to the right of Member States to impose restrictions justified on grounds of "public good." My reference to the Court arises from the judgement in the insurance case against Germany at the end of 1986,[23] which in effect rejected the application of the "*Cassis de Dijon*" principle to insurance. Here the Court ruled that, in the absence of Community harmonization, Member States remained free to impose rules governing the policy conditions of insurance policies, at least where they were being sold to the mass market.

Potential problems of this nature relating to specific financial products cannot be solved by prior harmonization at this stage. The only sensible prescription is *solvitur ambulando* though whether the solutions will be found in the market place or the Court remains to be seen.

Before leaving the subject of capital market regulations, I will comment on our policy on disclosure, particularly with respect to issues in the primary market. Our proposals here are again clearly linked with the

[21] See *supra* note 14.
[22] Amended proposal published in 1990: see O.J. C 42/7 (1990).
[23] See *supra* note 18.

objective of economic integration. We want to encourage the creation of an integrated European securities market in two ways:

- ensuring that investors are supplied with comparable and full information about all new securities issues and about all listed shares on Community markets;
- making it easier for companies to get listings and make issues simultaneously on all Community markets.

We have already got agreement to the *mutual recognition* of listing particulars,[24] so that a multiple listing can be made on the basis of a single listing document.[25] We are still in the middle of difficult negotiations in the Council of Ministers on the contents of a single public offer document for new issues. In fact the Council reached a "common position" on this directive on December 12, 1988.[26]

VI. Company Law Harmonization

The company law harmonization programme also has to be judged largely, though not exclusively, by the contribution to the objective of economic integration.

There are two aspects to this: first, the removal of specific barriers to cross-frontier operations such as mergers and takeovers. Second, and more generally, it is argued, not only will it be easier for companies to operate across frontiers in twelve different Member States if the legal environment is broadly the same, but also third parties (notably shareholders, employers and creditors) need to know that they have broadly the same rights in their dealings with companies in order to create the confidence needed for a much wider network of cross-frontier trading relations.

The company law directives, which have already been adopted, are clearly directed at these two objectives. The two accounting directives (the Fourth and the Seventh)[27] in particular already seem to have made a useful contribution to raising the average standard of disclosure in Europe and seem likely to assume increasing importance as the remaining restrictions on capital movements are dismantled. Disclosure requirements are not justified solely by considerations of investor protection. The optimal allocation of investment resources depends on adequate information being available. I have to say that I simply find completely unconvincing (at least in a European context) the argument that market forces themselves would suffice to bring about adequate disclosure.

There are reasons for arguing that harmonization of accounting requirements may need to be taken further in the Community. As noted in

[24] See O.J. L 66/2 (1979) and O.J. L 62/22 (1982).
[25] O.J. L 100/1 (1980) and O.J. L 185/81 (1987). See also O.J. L 112/24 (1990).
[26] Directive adopted in 1989: see O.J. L 124/8 (1989).
[27] O.J. L 222/11 (1978) and O.J. L 193/1 (1983).

Buxbaum and *Hopt*,[28] the Fourth and Seventh Directives are not very detailed and contain a fair number of options. As far as listed companies are concerned, the directives are much less detailed than those of the US SEC. If we are to move towards mutual recognition of accounting standards at the global level for listed companies, the Community may need to move towards more detailed standards. Perhaps more seriously, there is a risk of divergent standards and interpretations emerging in different Member States because of lacunae in the Fourth and Seventh Directives; the treatment of off-balance sheet financing for example. Finally, Europe needs to play its full part in the developing discussions in global accounting standards in the IASC and elsewhere. These are problems to which the Commission will need to give its attention in the not too distant future.

At the same time, however, we are already having to accommodate pressure, particularly from Germany, for changes in the opposite direction, namely to lighten accounting requirements on small and medium-sized companies. Amendment proposals to the Fourth and Seventh Directives are expected in early autumn.[29]

In the case of the Fifth Company Law Directive[30] one must look beyond the goal of economic integration for the motive. The provisions on workers' participation clearly reflect a political choice made by the Commission on social as much as economic grounds. They are aimed at giving salaried employees a stronger voice in the running of the enterprises for which they work. The Commission believes that such arrangements should indeed improve labor relations and thus the efficiency of the enterprises concerned, but they are primarily put forward as the broader political argument of the need to involve organized labor in the process of creating the single market. But it is difficult to argue that the Fifth Directive is strictly necessary to the achievement of the four economic freedoms in the White Paper.

Unfortunately, the Member States currently remain equally divided on the issue of workers' participation.[31] This disagreement is holding up not only the Fifth Directive, but the Tenth Directive on cross-frontier mergers[32] as well. It is obvious that where a cross-frontier merger takes place, in which the workers in the company being absorbed enjoy legal rights of participation in the supervision of that company, the treatment of those rights after the merger is a sensitive matter.

The Commission has recently taken a new initiative, aimed at bypassing the difficulties just described, and at making progress on both cross-frontier mergers and on workers' participation, by a different route. We have proposed the reopening of negotiations on a revised and simplified European Company Statute. In contrast to the original version, enterprises

[28] BUXBAUM & HOPT, *supra* note 1, at 275-278.
[29] See O.J. C 287/5 (1988).
[30] O.J. C 240/2 (1983).
[31] For a survey, see BUXBAUM & HOPT, *supra* note 1, at 259-262.
[32] O.J. C 23/11 (1985).

incorporating under the Statute would have a choice between several different forms of workers' participation. A feature of this approach is that it does not automatically impose the controversial requirements of the Fifth Directive on major enterprises in all Member States. The Statute instead offers an *option* to those enterprises, which judge that it is to their advantage to make use of it, as in the earlier more limited case of the European Economic Interest Grouping (EEIG).[33] The discussions in the Council of the Commission's proposal for reviving the *Societas Europaea* by the Council of Ministers were positive, we are now aiming to have a revised version of the Statute in the first half of 1989.[34]

I propose to complete my observations on company law by making a few remarks on *group law* and on *takeovers*.

Group law presents an awkward problem. As *Buxbaum* and *Hopt* indicate,[35] Germany is the only Member State that has legislated on group status, though the legislation has not been a conspicuous success. On the other hand, there is a risk that judge-made law in the Member States will begin to get further and further apart. If the rights and obligations between parent companies and their subsidiaries and between parent companies and minority shareholders in their subsidiaries take widely different forms, that could clearly discourage economic integration in the Community. The Commission has not made a decision on legislation in this area, so I can only give you my personal viewpoint. When a draft Directive on groups (the Ninth)[36] was circulated informally to Member States, reactions were lukewarm or hostile and it seems unlikely this proposal will be maintained in its present form. A survey of recent developments in jurisprudence on groups in seven Member States has been commissioned which may result in a revised proposal at a later date.

The Commission was, however, committed to producing a draft Directive on *takeovers* before the end of 1988. In fact a draft proposal was adopted by the Commission on 22 December.[37] The need for some Community wide general rules on this subject has grown much stronger over the last few years with an increase both in contested cross-frontier takeovers in preparation for 1992 and in cross-frontier shareholding.

The draft directive lays down a set of minimum procedural rules to be followed as regards the conduct of takeover bids, concentrating in particular on disclosure. In addition it contains a number of provisions to protect the interests of the shareholder of the target company. In particular, it requires that all shareholders be treated equally.

[33] O.J. L 199/1 (1985).

[34] See the amended proposals published in 1989: O.J. C 263/41 (1989) and O.J. C 263/69 (1989).

[35] BUXBAUM & HOPT, *supra* note 1, at 222.

[36] Doc. No. III/1639/84, reprinted in 14 *ZGR* 444 (1985).

[37] O.J. C 64/8 (1989) amended O.J.C 240/7 (1990).

There is, however, increasing concern within the Community at the absence of a truly "level playing field" for takeovers both within the Community and outside. Hostile takeovers can be more easily blocked by the target companies in some countries than others. The directive goes some way towards tackling this problem, by requiring that certain defensive measures, e.g. on issue of new shares, can only be made with the agreement of the shareholders' meeting. But major inequalities in the different markets still exist and may well call for further action under the new Commission.

VII. Conclusion

Instead of summing up I want to touch briefly on three more general issues raised by *Buxbaum* and *Hopt* and by other contributors.

First, why institute *directives* rather than codes of conduct, or recourse to the ECJ, etc.? There are two straightforward answers to this. First, experience has shown that only legally binding instruments are effective. In general, recommendations and codes of conduct have simply not been observed by Member States. The 1977 Code of conduct on securities markets transactions[38] is a case in point. Second, only legally binding directives create the legal certainty which enterprises and individuals need to take full advantage of the benefits of a single market.

This is not to say that we wholly rule out other methods. Cases are and will obviously continue to be taken to the European Court. But piecemeal and highly specific judge-made law cannot generally be a substitute for a coherent legislated framework. Non-binding recommendations can sometimes also be useful particularly in defining subsequent legislation and can be used to develop a more detailed set of accounting standards out of the principles of the Fourth and Seventh Directives. Finally, the European Economic Interest Grouping and the European Company Statute can be viewed as a kind of "model law."

The price for legal certainty is, however, the risk of petrification, to which *Buxbaum* and *Hopt* rightly draw attention.[39] On the whole, I agree with Prof. *Gower*[40] that this has not so far proved too serious a problem. I can confirm that not only in the UK but in several other Member States, Community directives are often welcomed as a means of carrying national legislation which has been held up because of resistance from domestic pressure groups or for lack of Parliament time.

There are two further ways in which the risks of petrification will be reduced. First, the emphasis on key or minimum harmonization will leave Member States quite a lot of freedom of manoeuvre to experiment. Second, it is intended that in the new legislation to create the single market there

[38] O.J. L 212/37 (1977).
[39] BUXBAUM & HOPT, *supra* note 1, at 239.
[40] See *infra* at 320.

should be greater use of the Commission's "powers of implementation." This is made clear in an amendment to Article 145 of the EEC Treaty in the Single European Act. The Commission's powers of implementation enable technical changes to be made to the details of harmonizing directives by a procedure of secondary legislation, which does not require consultation of the European Parliament. Obviously, if the fundamental principles of a directive were to prove wrong or out of date, then an amending directive would be required. But the wider use of the Commission's implementing powers will impart an additional element of flexibility to the Community's legislation.

Finally, on the question of implementation and enforcement. *Buxbaum* and *Hopt* assert that:[41]

> "[T]he traditional neat division between the EC competence for enacting ... substantive law and the Member States competence for sanctions and enforcement is a dated model. Thought should be given to the problem of how to overcome this division politically and, as far as possible, legally. Europe needs less law in the books and more law in action."

Rather surprisingly this proposition is simply asserted without argument at the end of a section on self-regulation. Granted that the process of enforcing Community law falls short of perfection, the conclusion apparently drawn that responsibility for enforcement should be taken at Community level seems to be wide of the mark on both theoretical and practical grounds. Indeed, it is not clear that there is a general problem about *sanctions* as such. Member States are required by the Treaty to ensure that directives are *effectively* implemented and the Commission can certainly challenge the relevant national legislation if it does not contain effective sanctions. Contrary to *Buxbaum* and *Hopt*'s suggestions,[42] our draft Insider Trading Directive would certainly require Member States to apply effective civil or criminal sanctions to any breach of the implementing national legislation.[43]

At the theoretical level, given that directives have to be translated into national law and that in many cases they will be "minimum standards" directives, it is difficult to see how responsibility for *enforcement* can rest elsewhere than with the Member States. At the practical level, as *Buxbaum* and *Hopt* recognize elsewhere,[44] the Commission has neither the machinery, the manpower nor the expertise to take on the responsibility for enforcement. Where it is recognized that there is a problem is in the obstructions and delay which can impede the bringing of actions before the European Court.

[41] BUXBAUM & HOPT, *supra* note 1, at 250.
[42] *Id.* at 250.
[43] See Art. 13 of the directive, adopted in 1989: O.J. L 334/30 (1989).
[44] BUXBAUM & HOPT, *supra* note 1, at 247.

B. DISCUSSION

I. Introductory Remarks

Geoffrey Fitchew

The first point I would like to make is that the Commission is a rather peculiar political institution and one for which it is rather difficult to construct a coherent political programme or philosophy. In the first place, the Commission is not an elected body. The members may not even have had any contact with each other until they come together for the first time at the beginning of their four-year period of office in January. Moreover, in many cases, but not all, they do not stay in Brussels much longer than four years. The appointment of President Delors for a second period as President of the Commission is the first time that has happened since Hallstein. They are also obviously both in politics and in nationality a disparate group and they do not arrive in office with any manifesto or programme other than what is in the EEC Treaty.

One consequence of the character of the Commission, as I have described it, is that there is a risk of there being a vacuum as far as their political programme is concerned. If such a vacuum occurs, there is then likely to be a strong influence of the permanent officials in the Commission on the contents of the programme of each succeeding Commission. At the lower levels within the services of the Commission, i.e., from heads of division downwards, it is customary for officials to remain in the same area of work for very long periods of time, very often for periods of 15-20 years.

Despite these obstacles, I would nevertheless want to argue that in the White Paper on Completing the Internal Market[1] the present Commission has produced a coherent programme which is clearly aimed at the goal of economic integration and which is generally based on a philosophy of economic liberalism, and also on the method of minimum or key organization. As evidence of the proposition that the 1985 White Paper is based on a philosophy of economic liberalism, I would simply like to quote the definition which has been given to the internal market and written into the Treaty through the amendments in the Single European Act.[2] Article 8A of the Amended Treaty says:

[1] Doc. COM(85)310 (14 June 1985).
[2] *Bull. EC*, Supp. 2/1986.

> "The internal market shall comprise an area without internal frontiers in which the free movement of goods, persons, services and capital is ensured in accordance with the provisions of this Treaty."

I would suggest that that is perhaps more clearly based on a philosophy of economic liberalism than the Commerce Clause in the United States Constitution. I think perhaps the reason why there is a clearer statement of a philosophy of economic liberalism in the Community Treaty than in the American Constitution is perhaps linked with the fact that it is more difficult to achieve within the Community than in the United States.

To turn to the politics of the Council rather than the Commission, the programme in the White Paper has acquired a considerable momentum since 1985 and at least up to the present has the strong backing both of the Member States and of the business community. Each of the succeeding Presidents of the Member States acting as Presidents of the Council has seen it as their duty over the last two or three years to make as much progress as possible in fulfilling the White Paper programme and it has almost become a question of competitive prize to get as many directives adopted by the end of each six-month period as possible. This has been reinforced by the informal so-called troika system of cooperation between the outgoing presidency and the presidency in office and the next succeeding presidency. And the result of this commitment and momentum, a number of notable successes have been scored over the last two years, some of which I have mentioned in the paper.[3] Having said that, we are all very conscious that there is still a long way to go and that there are very many difficulties to be overcome.

One should perhaps pause to ask why is there this degree of support from both the Member States and the business community, and I think some part of the answer lies in the two normal motives which underlie economic progress, namely fear and greed. But probably mainly fear. Fear in this case of being outstripped not only by the United States and Japan but by the newly industrializing countries as well, a fear reinforced by the economic difficulties of the 1970s following the first oil shock. Of course this general support for the White Paper programme is perfectly consistent with Member States continuing to fight their corner in the Council negotiations as toughly as they always have, and the normal expectation that Member States support those proposals which they see as bringing economic advantage to themselves and resist those which do not is generally met.

I should, before leaving the White Paper, say that economic integration is certainly not the only goal being pursued in the Community in the current programme of legislation. The negotiations on the Single European Act led the Member States to introduce into the Treaty, in some cases for the first time, a number of specific provisions dealing with various public goods which it is considered appropriate to pursue at Community as well as

[3] See *supra* at 6 f.

national level, notably for example the protection of the environment and the protection of consumers. The new Article 100A(3) of the Treaty states for example that the Commission in its proposals concerning health, safety, environmental protection and consumer protection will take as a base a high level of protection. It is fairly obvious that conflicts can and will arise between the basic goal of economic integration and the setting of high standards for the environment and consumer protection and so on. But it is obviously the job of politicians to seek to reconcile competing goals of that kind. Nevertheless, one is bound to bear in mind from time to time Isaiah Berlin's well-known statement that not all good things are consistent with each other.

Just to complete these remarks I want to comment on two questions. First of all: what is the fundamental explanation as to why harmonization in the Community needs to be done from the top down rather than from the grass roots up? I think the main and most convincing explanation is the following: that in the United States, as is evident from Chapter 3 of *Buxbaum* and *Hopt*,[4] the starting point for legislation and regulation of economic activity was a frontier society in which the main economic freedoms – that is free movement of goods, free movement of persons and free movement of capital – were already there to a very large extent and the legislation and regulation have developed to deal with problems and conflicts arising from the exercise of those economic freedoms, whereas in the Community the starting point was exactly the opposite one, namely we start from a position in which there are a very large number of barriers to the exercise of those economic freedoms between the Member States. Having said that, I think that nevertheless the present Commission is conscious of the desirability in many areas of competition between rules, and that is evidenced by the approach based upon minimum rather than highly detailed harmonization.

The second point I wanted to comment on is the question of how company law and capital market regulation does fit into the framework of economic integration which I have been emphasizing, and I think on that I would say simply that I in general agree with the message in the *Buxbaum* and *Hopt* book that capital market regulation fits very easily into the framework of economic integration and the pursuit of the goal of that economic integration. I think the same is true to a considerable extent for the accounting directives.

Turning to the more traditional area of company law, had I had the benefit of reading Prof. Timmermans' excellent paper before I wrote mine, I would, I think, have entirely endorsed what he says about the relationship between Article 54(3)(g) and Article 58,[5] namely that the provisions of Article 54 were always seen as a *quid pro quo*, as a compensation, for the

[4] R.M. BUXBAUM & K.J. HOPT, *Legal Harmonization and the Business Enterprise* 167 ff (Berlin/New York 1988).

[5] See *infra* at 132 ff.

basic freedom of the incorporation in Article 58. What then is the objective of the company law proposals? It is clearly to pursue what are regarded as the public goods of assuring an equivalent level of protection to shareholders, creditors and other third parties who have dealings with companies and enterprises, and I think it is clear that over the years, that has led in some cases to the Commission making proposals of a perfectionist and idealistic character. That was not always the case. I understand that when the Commission started off in the 1960s, its original proposal was that there should be only one company law directive setting out basic principles and that Member States should be left free to fill in details, and it was the Member States themselves who insisted upon a highly detailed approach to company law regulation. The wheel now seems to be coming round, towards a more minimalist approach to company law regulations as well. The example of our approach to capital market regulation is increasingly influencing the company law side as well.

The final remark that I would like to make, which is very strongly reinforced by reading all the reports, is the need for humility in economic regulators, and I think on that I can do no better than quote a remark by Kenneth Galbraith in his book on the great crash, in which he remarks that economic regulators daily confess their inadequacy which in any case is all too painfully apparent.

II. Policy and Theories of European Integration

Christian Timmermans

I have listened with much interest to the introductory remarks of Mr. Fitchew. I have also read with much interest his paper and particularly read with pleasure the remark[6] that he is cheerfully unrepentant on not having a particular economic theory of harmonization. I must say that I agree on that.

Nevertheless, I think Mr. Fitchew and all of us will agree that – and setting aside capital market harmonization because there is no problem there as far as goals, necessity and justification are concerned – with regard to company law there is a problem that has to be solved because the ambition to harmonize company law is, as has sometimes been said, really coming into the inner circle of national sovereignty and if we are to allow it to do so it will require, I think, quite a clear view on necessity, goals and scope.

I have heard your hesitation in your introductory remarks. I think that hesitation is also clear in your paper and in the recent documents from the Commission. My personal impression is that the Commission is getting

[6] See *supra* at 1.

somewhat lukewarm, if that is the right expression, as to harmonization of company law.

When I read the justifications you are giving, Mr. Fitchew, in your paper,[7] the first point concerns solving the problems of international mergers. There is no doubt that that is really necessary and I think in that respect the proposed Tenth Directive[8] and particularly the European Company Statute[9] are appropriate proposals. However, the second more general justification given which covers the whole field of company law in my view is really too vague. It is somewhat like saying: the economic actors on the Common Market must feel at home with the company law of other Member States because that will facilitate the cross-frontier trading within the Common Market. Personally I think feeling at home with laws of other Member States is something that could apply also to private law in general, the law of obligations or the law of torts. I think we should try to be a bit more specific in this respect. To give two examples, I think for instance that with regard to private companies a clear concept must be developed whether to exclude them from further harmonization, which I do not think is justified, or to include them and why. And secondly with regard to groups of companies I have read with great interest that both Prof. Gower[10] and Prof. Tunc[11] have emphasized the need for harmonization in that respect.

Geoffrey Fitchew

Is the Commission becoming lukewarm about company law harmonization? The answer to that is no. There are a number of areas where I think on the contrary we see an increasing need to go forward in the company law area. One is certainly the takeovers question. Until relatively recently, hostile takeovers, contested takeovers, have been almost exclusively a United Kingdom phenomenon, for a variety of reasons which I won't go into, but that is clearly changing and there are an increasing number of cross-frontier takeovers in the Community and pressure for the Commission to intervene.[12]

The group question, as I tried to indicate in my paper,[13] is one which I find very difficult. At present very few Member States have legislated in this area. I think Germany and Portugal are the only examples and the German legislation has, as I understand it, not been very successful. Very few German companies have actually opted for group status and Commission

[7] See *supra* at 11.

[8] O.J. C 23/11 (1985).

[9] See the new proposals published in 1989: O.J. C 263/41 (1989) and O.J. C 263/69 (1989).

[10] See *infra* at 323 ff.

[11] See *infra* at 212.

[12] Proposal for a directive: see O.J. C 64/8 (1989) amended O.J. C 240/7 (1990).

[13] See *supra* 13.

services' earlier attempt at a directive in this area[14] which follows the German model pretty closely would neither be acceptable to Member States, nor would make much sense in the current atmosphere of deregulation. Nevertheless, there is a potential problem of diverging jurisprudence in different Member States and therefore, not least in the financial sector, of groups being faced with quite different obligations in relation to their subsidiaries in different Member States which we will have to look at. As I said in the paper,[15] we have commissioned a study of what is happening in the jurisprudence of the Member States and the first phase of that has been completed, and I suppose we may well try to publish it at some point.

Second, I would like to emphasize that the Commission remains committed to the social dialogue, that is to say trying to strengthen the position of salaried employees in the company sector. The progress on the Fifth Directive,[16] as I said,[17] has been blocked and it seems unlikely that the block will be removed; we are therefore trying to get around that by reviving the European Company Statute proposal.[18]

Richard Buxbaum

I am not competent, in both senses of the word, to react to those fascinating comments from the inside, so I will provide some external comments, one general and one specifically on company law.

Let me start the general comment with the aphorism of Justice *Frankfurter* which we quote somewhere in the book.[19] In the American situation, as he once remarked, so far as the individual States are concerned, if the National Congress has not regulated then *laissez faire* is the regulator. That suggests to me an important linkage between economic philosophy and federalism issues. For the European Community to lock in economic liberalism at the central level suggests that there will develop, in time and in certain circumstances, an inherent tension between the centralizing opportunities and the Member States. Somewhere there has to be a location for the appropriate regulatory intrusion that, in the Musgrave terminology, provides the stabilization norms or the redistributive norms, and not only the allocative efficiency support norms. I do not think one can put all this simply under the label of public goods and externalities. There has to be clear political and constitutionally based location for that necessary right of intervention. Of course it will exist somewhere, but to the degree that you develop a constitutional philosophy of liberalism – and I appreciate that the European Community's organic acts in a soft sense raise economic

[14] See Doc. No. III/1639/84, reprinted in 14 *ZGR* 444 (1985).
[15] See *supra* at 13.
[16] O.J. C 240/2 (1983).
[17] See *supra* at 12.
[18] See *supra* note 9.
[19] See BUXBAUM & HOPT, *supra* note 4, at 50.

liberalism to that level, as contrasted with the American Constitution – there has to be a different vision about the degree of autonomy left to the Member States. It seems to me that you cannot have it both ways. You cannot lock out the Member States under a strong commerce clause or other centralizing norm, and yet have only a one-legged constitutional structure. Now I am being provoking of course; this is not, as the Germans say, a soup that is eaten as hot as it is cooked. But since Mr. Fitchew has emphasized this economic liberalism constitutional perspective,[20] I would just like to say that economic liberalism is no less contingent and no more transcendent than is any other political philosophy. It seems to me that at least from the American experience one has to recognize that fact.

A brief comment on the company law point. It seems to me that a lot of the accepting approach to economic liberalism that I heard in this first discussion and that one does hear in Europe rests, consciously or not so consciously, on a kind of corporatist discipline that the current economic organization of Europe, not in all countries but in some, provides. There is a degree of banking or financial-sector and of large-enterprise control of the overall economy not in an industrial organization (concentration) but in the more soft philosophical sense. There is a corporatist discipline, I would, perhaps provocatively, assert, that justifies this confidence in an economic liberalism approach. But as you move towards extremely free movement of capital of juristic persons and especially of financial services, that discipline will dissipate. I think it stands to reason that with more competition in these areas you cannot count on preexisting – I would call them, in the soft sense, ideological – underpinnings to this debate to persist. So in time there may be more rather than less tension around that first question of liberal versus regulatory structures. That ties to some comments we can save for later, but I am interested in this question of company law as a candidate for harmonization. With increasing liberalism of movement of services and units it seems to me that company law, and here I look at the American experience, more or less will harmonize itself. That is, I do not think, quite apart from the aberration that the Court of Justice recently delivered itself of[21] – if I may say that as an outsider – that the seat philosophy can long be a bulwark against the mobility of legal orders that the mobility of capital will bring with it. Thus in a sense I think one can expect a company law harmonization from below as distinct from the capital market harmonization.

Finally, however, that ties to a last problem: much company law is moving into the area of public law. I do not mean so much the worker-management or owner conflict or even the creditor-owner conflict. I mean, for example, the question of takeovers. We will have some focused

[20] See *supra* at 17.

[21] The case-law of the European Court is discussed by TIMMERMANS, at 134 ff.

discussion of the takeover problem later,[22] but I do not believe one can comfortably look at the takeover field without seeing its close linkage to capital market regulation and of course also its close linkage to public law structures generally – which completes my circle of bringing it back to the question of liberalism versus regulation.

Geoffrey Fitchew

The fundamental and difficult question raised by Prof. Buxbaum is whether we do not need to have a clear philosophy which extends beyond the resource allocation problem into the other two areas in the Musgrave approach to public finance of stabilization and distribution. I think I agree with the proposition that progress in opening up markets, that the allocation question on the basis of economic liberalism is already posing questions to the Community on the problems of stabilization in particular.

I think on the question of distribution, it is certainly implicit, if not explicit, in the EEC Treaty that the main responsibility on distributional questions will rest with the Member States rather than with the Centre. That is implicit in the provisions of the Treaty relating to taxation. Nevertheless, the fact that the Community is seeking to intervene in harmonizing indirect taxes to the purpose of removing fiscal frontiers and that we are also committed to make proposals in the area of corporation tax is clearly going to impose a further constraint on Member States' room for maneuver, both in the area of responsibility for the distribution and stabilization. The Commission is again following up the philosophy, if you like, of minimum harmonization in this area, in the sense that we are on the VAT and excise duties proposing quite wide bans of taxation and I think the same would be true of corporate tax. But there are no plans to intervene to any significant degree in the area of personal taxation except insofar as one cannot avoid doing that because of the interface between personal taxation and corporate taxation.

Stabilization policy. I think the debate is really just beginning with the setting up of the Delors Committee to study the question of a central bank.[23] The essential problem that the Community faces is: can it combine total freedom of capital movements with a regime of relatively fixed exchange rates which is what the present exchange rate mechanism is? And the answer that the Commission is giving to that question is that the dilemma of freedom of capital movements and relatively fixed exchange rates can only be resolved by stronger cooperation on monetary management. But the discussions on that are only just beginning.

[22] See *infra* 375 ff.

[23] See EC COMMITTEE FOR THE STUDY OF ECONOMIC AND MONETARY UNION, *Report on Economic and Monetary Union in the European Community* (Luxembourg 1989).

Edmund Kitch

As a distant observer, I must say that I am struck by what seems to me a fairly clear and strikingly powerful theory of European economic integration, which seems to be one of political liberalism. It will have very important and profound effects for the politics of the Community and of the Member States. I am a little confused myself about the political dynamic of this and how this has come about.

Dick Buxbaum was saying last night that the *Buxbaum* and *Hopt* book had some of the quality of a time warp, that it had been written not too long ago at a time when there was a sense of plodding technical progress towards an objective of economic integration, and in the period of the book's gestation this has been transformed into a suddenly accelerated and exciting programme which seems to be moving swiftly to completion. Why that has come about and what has happened to cause it is not clear to me, although we have had resonant political developments in the United States.

If you open up these markets in the Member States, through this rather odd centralized bureaucratic truncated political process in Brussels, you are also setting forth a process of very important political transformation within the Member States. I think I differ from Dick in my view about the prospects for that to work in positive ways. I think I am probably much more comfortable than Dick with the actual implementation of that programme, but it seems to me a programme with a rather clear political purpose and rather predictable political consequences, which is striking in the radicalness of its likely effects. It will force the political processes of the Member States to focus much more on the problem of how to bring about a lot of internal change. I think that will unleash a period of great creativity in Europe, which in turn would have very beneficial effects upon the United States. If European culture and economic organization become much more competitive and dynamic than in the United States, we in turn will have to confront that challenge and adapt.

André Tunc

As I have nothing important to contribute, I will only say that I found Mr. Fitchew's paper extremely interesting, convincing, instructive. Perhaps on some points of detail I may not fully agree or slightly disagree, but it is not serious.

There is only a point on which I may say a few words: it is the pragmatic approach. Some criticism has been made of this approach. I fully approve of it. For many years, I have been inclined to take a pragmatic approach to problems and I distrust – at least to a certain extent – economic theories. Economic theories of course are changing and I am slightly frightened when they are taken as a basis for decisions. I prefer to try to see – perhaps I am somewhat English educated now except for the language – the problems as they arise, to try to make a cost-benefit analysis, but using economic facts rather than economic theories. I do not reject economics, of course, but I do not like to start from an economic theory. So I fully subscribe to the pragmatic approach which has been taken.

Christian Meier-Schatz

My position is somewhat similar to Prof. Kitch's in the sense that I, too, do not come from a EC country and that I am not a specialist on EC law itself. Yet I have also listed with great interest to these comments by an insider. The main thing I, from my perspective, can probably do is to ask two questions which seem to me particularly relevant with respect to the present optimism and enthusiasm about European integration. Before doing so, however, I have two specific short remarks.

First, I was very glad that Mr. Fitchew introduced in his paper, as far as economic theories are concerned, some additional approaches.[24] I think that the book of *Buxbaum* and *Hopt* itself did not make many comments (maybe even too few) on the question as to whether some microeconomic insights could be used in answering the question of the optimal allocation of regulatory authorities. Personally, I believe that, for instance, the externalities and public good theories could be used – we may discuss that afterwards[25] – to show that mandatory disclosure rules are necessary, and why. Even more importantly, spillover effects indicate that disclosure rules should be enacted at a federal level. All this reveals that additional economic theories can eventually be used to support the harmonization effort in this field.

The other point I would like to make with respect to company law is that we have a good chance of getting many enabling, harmonized rules from below. Mr. Fitchew's counterargument[26] that the public good consists in an increased confidence of all Memberd States in an equal (or at least similar) protective environment is not entirely compelling. It appears to be overinclusive since with such an argument you can legitimize almost any kind of harmonization rules. And reading the examples in his paper of why and where to harmonize company law rules, only two topics are mentioned[27] to prove the point. The first relates to disclosure. But this subject, although historically in Europe a company law issue, is probably functionally more appropriately located within the capital market law field. The other topic is the codetermination issue (*Mitbestimmung*). Yet this is, as he admits himself, a subject which certainly transcends the traditional domain of company law and touches upon the public law field.

Let me finally add two questions which I deem to be very important. First, you made a very optimistic overall assessment of what is going on

[24] See *supra* at 2 f.
[25] See e.g. *infra* at 95 f.
[26] See *supra* at 19.
[27] See *supra* at 11 ff.

now.[28] I asked myself how persistent this positive, almost enthusiastic recent trend would be. Historically, we always had the kind of wave movement with respect to the dominance of centralization versus decentralization forces within the EC. Is this now really a definitive shift of trends which will persist? The second question may even be more important: are the direction and especially the pace realistic? Is the enactment of 300 regulations within an extremely complex regulatory framework politically and institutionally feasible and do not we risk getting regulations which are not sufficiently informed and mature? I would, for instance, be very interested to hear more details about the Directive on takeovers[29] which is obviously very ambitious in the sense that it does not only aim to introduce some type of structurally relatively simple Williams Act provision, but intends also to integrate rules on defensive measures. Finally, I am somewhat skeptical with respect to the infrastructural possibilities and limits of implementing such a complex regulatory structure before the end of 1992.

Christian Timmermans

I would say that the remarks of Mr. Fitchew with regard to the momentum of the internal market 1992 movement[30] are particularly useful. Lawyers, and particularly European lawyers, have been in general I think too skeptical and too negative with regard to the Single European Act and have particularly underrated the political spillover of the European Act. And I think also with regard to harmonization in the field of which we are talking, and particularly company law, it is now time to come out with a clear concept, because the political climate is much more propitious and favorable than it has been for quite a number of years.

Gérard Hertig

If I may just be provocative and brief, I would say that aims do not matter that much. We are going to harmonize. What aims are we following? That is for lawyers or for economists to judge afterwards. So what are the constraints? Probably worldwide developments and what the Member States are going to do.

Hence, when one considers the White Paper, there is one main thing: marketing. That is what it is all about. It is to sell the idea of an integrated market. That is why everybody speaks about it and that is why things are starting to go faster. You have sold it very well; but otherwise the White Paper is not all that special and I am not trying to buy it.

[28] See *supra* at 17.
[29] See *supra* note 12.
[30] See *supra* at 4 ff.

Geoffrey Fitchew

Prof. Hertig is quite right of course, I was making propaganda on behalf of the Commission. Nevertheless, even administrators like to have some idea of where they are going.

Eddy Wymeersch

I was very much struck by the enthusiasm and the optimistic tone of Mr. Fitchew, both in his paper and in his presentation. I may add that I share his enthusiasm. This state of mind clearly reflects the present state of opinion in the EC as the White Paper has launched a tremendous thrust towards the full realization of the internal market, whether in 1992 or later.

I will take up two points at this stage.

The first one deals with the need for fundamental thinking with respect to the formation of Community regulations. It seems that progress is being made in many fields. But this progress is not the result of any fundamental analysis or study of the situation. In the accounting field the Commission is harmonizing rules without any general framework to put the rules in an overall perspective. The same remark can be made about the rules on financial disclosure. This is the more striking as precisely in the same period a very large debate was going on in the United States about the usefulness of the disclosure policies and rules. In the 1970s the EC was harmonizing disclosure rules with no or very little regard to what was a fundamental discussion on the purpose of its activity.

The three directives that have been enacted therefore are not based on a clear policy view: it is not clear whether they view disclosure as an instrument for market transparency, or as an instrument for the protection of investors, or even as a soft technique for regulating company conduct. This implicit diversity in regulatory objectives may explain why there remain some complaints about the usefulness of some of the rules these directives contain. One can of course understand the Commission's position in this matter: the Commission does not legislate, it harmonizes pre-existing legislation. But this should not be a sufficient reason not to be worried about future harmonization directives. Suppose the Commission started harmonization proceedings with respect to defenses in the matter of takeovers.[31] The subject is rather controversial in many of the States and nowhere has a clear philosophy emerged. Could the Commission stay out of the controversy and wait until the States have reached a sufficient level of harmonizable regulation, at the risks of creating very unbalanced situations, or would it not be preferable that some more fundamental study be made of the long-term industrial policies to be developed in this matter? I may be too optimistic, certainly in the light of Prof. Meier-Schatz's contribution.[32]

[31] See *supra* note 12.
[32] See *infra* at 74 ff.

The second matter to be brought up relates to the kind of self-discipline, or of self-regulation that Prof. Buxbaum rightly referred to.[33] It seems that the German situation to which he alluded does not prevail, or prevails less and less, in the other States. Moreover, and as he stated, the time for this type of regulating company or financial conduct is over, as has been visible in cross-border transactions for several years, but is clearly illustrated by the raw practices that have recently developed in several of the States. Up until a couple of years ago, the use of strong defensive measures against takeovers would have been considered morally abject. Today they tend to become a regular part of the company structure. This development will put new pressure on the legislators to enact explicit rules, and often to protect national industries or national interests.

We will certainly have the opportunity to discuss those issues later during the Symposium. But one can but stress at this stage the need for harmonized regulation, preferably at the Community level. Otherwise, the internal market will come about very painfully, and only after very prolonged negotiations. The time to act on these subjects is now.

Hartmut Schmidt

I do not share the optimism of my good friend, Prof. Wymeersch. He seems to think that all you need to do is to study a topic thoroughly and then you will come up with the right answers. These may be right answers for the moment but economics and I think law are social sciences, and you will always have competing models. And there will be new and better models. Even if you do a lot of study and if you are at the state of the art, you may find a few years later that some other regulator comes up with a better mousetrap. This process, I think, lends some support to the idea of restricting regulation to a minimum.

I understand of course the view that one should not trust economic models too much, but there are some economic models which have stood the test of time, and I think the liberalistic approach has done just that. One can expect that 1992 will be a day when services can move freely throughout Europe and we can be sure that this will break up anticompetitive practices in various countries and bring about a gain in efficiency. I still do not believe that the day will come, but if it comes we certainly will learn that it has a great impact not just on the Member States but also on countries in other parts of the world.

Desmond McComb

I find it extremely difficult to determine what the accounting directives were designed to achieve, because there does not seem to be any coherence about the way in which they are either being implemented or indeed how

[33] See *supra* at 22 f.

they were formulated in the first place, in the sense that no one seemed to have sat down at the very beginning and said: "Do we need a directive on company disclosure equivalent to the Fourth[34] and what do we want it for? Is the objective to provide information for government economic planners or is it for capital market purposes?" Indeed the recent Bank of Accounting Information that the Commission has put together seems to me to have more macroeconomic orientation than capital market orientation.

Geoffrey Fitchew

What the purpose of the accounting directives should be seen as being? I think that the answer that we would give is that the main purpose is disclosure, but not just for the purpose of capital markets regulation. Certainly disclosure to protect investors and shareholders is an important feature, but I think we would equally regard disclosure as desirable for the purposes of creditors and competitors of the companies concerned. I think the question of using the accounting information for macroeconomic purposes, I would regard as being a by-product rather than the essential objective. Whether the accounting directives as they stand at present achieve these objectives, I think is perhaps a matter for a later session.[35] But I do think the purpose is as I have described it.

III. Various Other Topics

Klaus Hopt

Mr. Fitchew, you mentioned fear and greed as basic motivations.[36] I agree on that. But I am astonished that fear and greed came up just in time for the White Paper in 1985 and were not there before or at least did not have these effects before. The question is therefore: why did that just happen in 1985? You made already some suggestions: the American challenge, the challenge by the Japanese, the depression in the 1970s. However the 1970s were quite a time ago, and one would have expected these movements to go quicker. Maybe there are (also) other factors and explanations. The phenomenon is probably to be explained not only as an economic drive but also and more as a political act: but then the political act of whom? Was it more a personal or more an institutional act? One may say it was the accomplishment of the Commission as such, getting the right time and using the opportunities for further development. But again: why was it the right time? And what was the role of the law in it? Did the law, i.e. the Treaty provisions, particularly the freedoms established there, develop their own political impact?

[34] O.J. L 222/11 (1978).
[35] See *infra* at 287 ff.
[36] See *supra* at 17

Another context: I have problems with the concept of "minimum harmonization."[37] Probably you do not really mean minimum harmonization but something else, so that minimum harmonization is just a convenient word to get better acceptance on the political stage. But if you mean "the right harmonization" or however you want to put it, then this is an empty formula, I would say, because since the very beginning of European integration we have striven for the right harmonization, i.e. for the right mix, and I wonder whether that means anything. It is true that this formula may mean something in a concrete case for harmonization or non-harmonization. But even this formula shows at the most some vague direction and does not give a real answer since the right answer would follow only from a discussion case by case. The question is therefore: would the Commission generalize "right harmonization" at least a little bit more?

You mentioned just very briefly the "*Europe à deux vitesses.*"[38] I would be very interested to hear your personal view on that. Of course, as far as the European Act was concerned (Art. 15 SEA), this "*Europe à deux vitesses*" is a fact. But is it a concept to be used also later on, for example in the currency debate, in the national bank debate and so on, or does it have more negative consequences overall than positive ones?

Finally, this distinction between so-called public laws and other ones[39] is of course a little bit difficult. Take the group example. According to your logic, if I am not mistaken, this would belong to the public law area. Certainly I do not see any movement of harmonization of group law from below. Of course you may say: "It is right that there should be no harmonization impetus." In this case we would end up with a political debate on whether specific rules in this field are needed or not. But this goes already into tomorrow's topic.[40]

Geoffrey Fitchew

Prof. Hopt's main question, I think, is: why 1985? Why did all this process get going in 1985? I think like any important historical phenomenon there has to be a multicausal explanation of this.

I think that the two factors that I would single out are first of all that during the 1970s the Community had been preoccupied with a number of other problems, in particular the absorption of the new Member States from the first enlargement in the early 1970s. Then there was the second enlargement at the beginning of the 1980s. The enlargement negotiations themselves were extremely time-consuming. Superimposed on top of all that, were the two oil shocks of the beginning of the 1970s and then again at

[37] See *supra* at 9.
[38] See *supra* at 3.
[39] See *supra* at 2 f, 9.
[40] See *infra* at 238 ff.

the end of the 1970s. So first of all I think the Community's energies were otherwise engaged.

But secondly, and I come back to the fear and greed motivations,[41] I think that during the 1970s it is not that these two motives were not operating, but they were operating in the opposite direction, that is to say that Member States continued to be preoccupied with protecting their national markets to a large extent and believed that that best served their economic interests. The recessions, first the recession following the first oil shock and then the recession following the second oil shock and the very sharp rise in structural unemployment, combined with the perceived threat from the USA-Japan and the newly industrializing countries, I think, changed people's perceptions in a very marked way.

Perhaps the third phenomenon which is worth mentioning and particularly relevant to capital markets, is the breakdown of exchange controls on a worldwide basis. Even in those countries which still maintain the exchange controls, they are becoming increasingly ineffective; and the development of new technology has led to globalized financial markets. It became increasingly evident to those Member States which had nevertheless maintained controls, that they were going to lose market share in important areas of financial business. And I think that has certainly been an important factor.

So I think that 1985 marked a point at which the Community got the business of the second enlargement off its plate and the new Commission came into office, first of all looking for something to do, but secondly faced with the economic problem of a Europe which appeared to be in relative decline and the White Paper was its response to that.

"*Europe à deux vitesses.*" I think Prof. Hopt asked about Article 15 of the Single European Act. It does provide for different Member States to proceed at different speeds, but subject to an important constraint which I think is actually contained in the text of the Single European Act. It is Article 8C of the Amended Treaty, where it is said in the second paragraph:

> "*Si ces dispositions prennent la forme de dérogations, elles doivent avoir un caractère temporaire et apporter le moins de perturbations possibles au fonctionnement du marché commun.*"

So the basic proposition is that the less developed Member States have ultimately got to accept the objective of economic integration on a sector-by-sector basis and have got to come into line with the harmonizing requirements, but they may be given temporary derogations to do so, and the experience so far is that that is actually proving a very useful negotiating tool along with the qualified majority voting. It is helping to get directives through the Council which had previously been blocked, for example non-life insurance.

[41] See *supra* at 17.

Olivier Guillod

I would like to point out first that I am not a specialist on company law and capital market regulations. I am more interested in the process of harmonization at the European level. I will, therefore, make only one brief comment after all that has already been said.

The political choice was framed mainly as one between harmonization from below or harmonization from above. I think that another issue which is as important relates to the substantive, rather than formal, level: should not the Commission look outside the Community and try to spell out Community directives that are compatible with what is happening, for example, in the United States or in Japan? A very nice example is the takeover of Rowntree by Nestlé: surely the reverse could not happen, quite apart from the power and the wealth of each company, simply because of the Swiss regulation.

Geoffrey Fitchew

Your question is related to the compatibility of Community directives with the external developments, and I think that is something that we are increasingly conscious of in probably all areas of Community life. One important legal factor which the Commission is always well aware of is that under the *AETR* judgement of the Court[42] adoption of a directive gives the Community and therefore the Commission external competence to negotiate, so that that aspect is already in our minds. But more specifically, it is clear that we need to take account of regulatory developments at a global level and that is being done. To give two examples of that: there has been and will, I hope, continue to be very close cooperation between the Commission and the Cooke Committee in Basle in relation to capital adequacy of banks, and the proposal that we in the Commission produced for a harmonized solvency ratio[43] is very close to the proposal that has come out of the Cooke Committee. That is not very surprising because seven members of the Cooke Committee are Member States of the Community. We in the Commission have been invited to take part in the discussions in the Cooke Committee and there has been a continual interflow of ideas between the two centres. In the products markets, the standard is being set at Community level and generally also tries to take account of ISO standards. So I think that that is certainly well accepted and will become increasingly important not least in the area of financial market regulation.

[42] Case 22/70, [1971] E.C.R. 263.

[43] Directive adopted in 1989: see O.J. L 386/14 (1989).

Alain Hirsch

I would be very interested to hear some more comments from Mr. Fitchew on the last paragraph of his paper.[44] Obviously the Commission cannot have the main and the full responsibility for enforcement of Community law in all twelve Member States; that would just be an impossible task. However, I have often felt that, for the European civil servants, once a regulation is adopted by the Council of Ministers, it is finished for them. I often had the impression that they were not interested in receiving information about how it was implemented. Possibly it was fear of having that information and knowing the difficulties of implementation... My question is: should not the Commission be informed about implementation and, especially, about differences of implementation in the Member States and how different authorities in the Member States are applying European regulations?

Geoffrey Fitchew

You raise the question of implementation and enforcement. The same comment was made in Prof. *Hopt*'s Chapter in the book,[45] namely the lack of emphasis given to the process of implementation and enforcement and I think there is a criticism in the book that the Commission has been reluctant to take this on. I do not think that is right. I think there is a problem of priorities, that is that at the moment in particular we have got a heavy programme of legislation to put forward and as to the 1992 timetable the priority is being given to that. And we are faced with the problem of scarce administrative resources. The Council has imposed additional personnel. But I think throughout the Commission directorates which are concerned with the internal market, there is increasing consciousness that we will have to devote more resources to the question of implementation and enforcement, and that is beginning to take place. We do automatically follow the process of a national implementing legislation through the national legislators and we do carry out the process of checking that it is in conformity with the directives that are adopted. But is a very time-consuming business and I think it is possible that in this area we will want to make more use of external resources, that is use outside consultants for the purpose of checking conformity, and we are already beginning to do that. We commissioned an outside study[46] for example on the implementation of the Fourth Accounting Directive.[47] It is likely that we will want to hold a conference towards the beginning of 1990 on the implementation of the Fourth Directive.

[44] See *supra* at 15.
[45] BUXBAUM & HOPT, *supra* note 4, at 250.
[46] Research compiled by the *Fédération des Experts Comptables Européens*, reported in the *Financial Times* of 20 October 1989.
[47] See *supra* note 34.

L.C.B. Gower

Watching what is going on, to see whether there has been adequate implementation in the various States etc., does it extend further so that you actually monitor how the harmonized regulations that you have introduced are in fact working? I mean, the great weakness in England is that we constantly are engaging in what we like to call law reforms, and having done so it is very rare that anybody bothers to monitor what is going on to see whether they are in fact working in the way that was intended.

Geoffrey Fitchew

On Prof. Gower's question, I think essentially for the same reason of the resource constraint we do not do as much as we should on monitoring the actual effects of legislation once it has been implemented by the Member States. I think the contact committees that are provided for in most directives do provide a forum in which that can and should be done, and in quite a lot of directives as well there is usually a clause which says that the Commission will make a report after five years to the Council and the European Parliament on the impact of that. But I suspect that as progress is made we will have to develop a capacity for monitoring the implementation and effects of legislation which we do not have at present.

Chapter Two

Economics and the Law

A. Report No. 1: Edmund Kitch

Business Organization Law: State or Federal?

An Inquiry Into the Allocation of Political Competence in Relation to Issues of Business Organization Law in a Federal System

Prof. *Buxbaum* and *Hopt*[1] refrain for nearly 300 pages from offering answers untrue to the complexity of the materials they so skillfully and concisely describe. I sense that their self-discipline is not easily won, and that they hunger to offer answers as a reward for an inquiry diligently pursued. I find their presentation careful and self-disciplined. They find my essay *Regulation and the American Common Market*[2] tantalizing. There they see an argument for a simple proposition: leave these matters to the constituent states where the "invisible hand" of jurisdictional competition will lead to the optimal mix of uniformity and diversity, to freedom for experimentation and adaptation, and, miracle of miracles, the "correct" rules. But, alas, after caressing my essay for all it is worth, they cannot embrace it. It must be used with "caution."[3] So it is with many simple, even beautiful things.

My assignment is to bring economic models to bear on the topic which *Buxbaum* and *Hopt* address. Should matters of business enterprise law be the subject of national law in a federal system or should they be left to the constituent states? This is a daunting assignment for a relatively brief comment. As the extensive bibliographic reach of *Buxbaum* and *Hopt*

[1] R.M. BUXBAUM & K.J. HOPT, *Legal Harmonization and the Business Enterprise* (Berlin/New York 1988).

[2] KITCH, "Regulation and the American Common Market," in *Regulation, Federalism, and Interstate Commerce* 9 (A.D. Tarlock ed., Cambridge, Mass. 1981).

[3] BUXBAUM & HOPT, *supra* note 1, at 278.

illustrates, it is not a topic on which there is an extensive literature. The topic falls between the theoretical vision of the economists and the detailed institutional focus of the lawyers.[4] Without the assistance that a richer literature would provide, I shall outline the basic analysis of the problem that economics suggests.

I. The Economic Magnitudes

One reason that the issues are difficult from an economic perspective is that the magnitudes are small. This is for two reasons. First, there is relatively free international trade, at least among the peoples of those countries who permit their people to trade, as even a cursory review of world trade statistics suggests. And second, both the Common Market and the United States are committed to the principles of free movement and non-discrimination, principles which when implemented obtain almost all of the objectives of free trade, without more. The remaining economic gains to be realized from the "correct" resolution of issues of business organization law are comparatively minute.

(1) International trade is relatively free. Adam Smith's intellectual case against mercantilism was based upon an appeal to the self-interest of nations. Mercantilism was a mistake because it harmed the interests of the country that pursued it, not because it was contrary to some broader world interest. The correctness of his arguments are widely accepted today, and nations have pursued their self-interest to accommodate and facilitate the international movement of goods, services and capital.

This was the heart of the argument I offered in *Regulation and the American Common Market*.[5] Because the states in a federal union will each benefit from trade within the union, we can rely upon them to pursue policies which facilitate that trade. I was there arguing in the context of a claim by the United States Supreme Court that its negative commerce clause doctrine is necessary to protect the American "common market" against the inevitable predations of the states. The Supreme Court is not needed to protect the market, I argued, because every state has an interest in protecting that market in order to share in its benefits. Indeed, I argued, the greater long-term enemy of free internal trade is the national government, acting under the affirmative commerce power and less subject than the

[4] In particular, the public choice literature, which has pioneered the use of economic models to analyze political problems, has not addressed this issue. It has suggested, however, that one can think of political markets as analogous to product markets, and analyze issues in terms of competition and market share. The suggestion that one can think of a local government as a firm competing to offer a product composed of its laws and their administration is credited to TIEBOUT, "A Pure Theory of Local Expenditures," 64 *J. Pol. Econ.* 416 (1956).

[5] KITCH, *supra* note 2, at 9.

states to the pressures generated by harmful economic policies. Such American follies as price controls were available to make my point very nicely.

The point is more general. Indeed, *Buxbaum* and *Hopt* offer this as a criticism. Pointing out that these forces apply everywhere, to "Albania and Zimbabwe," to "not only company laws ... [but to] the tariff walls themselves," they assert that:[6]

> "The model claims too much, and if cut down to more modest claims by reasons of judgment or expediency, itself reopens the original issue of fixing the division of powers on the basis of other, typically and explicitly more political, independent variables."

This criticism, however results from the desire to find more guidance than the argument contains. The position I took in *Regulation and the American Common Market* was not that this line of argument could provide clear criteria for the allocation of powers in a federal system, but only that a national market was not automatically threatened by local authority. Indeed, the strongest conclusion that can be drawn from the argument is that it does not matter very much one way or the other whether authority over these matters is exercised at the federation or the constituent state level. *Both* jurisdictions are subject to international competitive pressures, although the pressure will be greater on the local jurisdiction if the movement of goods, capital and persons in and out of the constituent state to other constituent states is less costly than movement between the federation and the rest of the world.

Because the point is general, and because it is largely right, international trade is relatively free. And since it is relatively free, the actual magnitudes of the economic gains to be realized by departing from past practice, and the changes to be made to realize those gains, are relatively small and difficult to identify.

Tariffs and customs procedures survive at international borders but not within nations, and shortly, not within the Common Market. That leads the casual observer to conclude that international trade is less free than internal trade. But the conclusion does not necessarily follow from the phenomenon. First of all, a tariff is a tax, and a tax upon imports can be viewed as the equivalent of an internal transfer tax with different collection arrangements to allow for the extraterritorial position of the principals. Although there is no "first best" tax, there is a general consensus that taxes with uniform rates applied to a broad base are the least harmful. Thus at least some component of tariffs can be viewed as a "second best" tax.[7] And

[6] BUXBAUM & HOPT, *supra* note 1, at 9, and generally at 8-9.

[7] It is clear, however, that the second best component may be small. Theory suggests that in order to minimize the economic distortions of a tariff, the rate of tariff should vary depending upon the elasticity of the supply of the import – the less the elasticity the higher the tariff. But a tariff with different rates on every good is extremely complex to administer and creates an opportunity for political manipulation

if we introduce the further complexity of possible inequalities in tax burdens between internal and external firms, it becomes even more difficult not to allow tariffs some role in an economically sensible system of national taxation.

Furthermore, nation states have tax, subsidy and regulatory policies whose effects can be every bit as disruptive of free trade and efficiency as can tariffs. A high tariff may shield a domestic producer from the international price level, but so can a subsidy. The internal trade of a nation state is not completely free, and whether the distortions of internal or international trade are relatively greater is difficult to measure.

It is because of this relative freedom of international trade that economists have long agreed that the welfare effects of a customs union are indeterminate as a matter of theory. The gains from freedom of trade *within* a union can be offset by losses in the trade between the union and the rest of the world.[8]

(2) The free access and non-discrimination principles. The United States and the Common Market share a commitment to principles of non-discrimination and free access. A federation whose constituent states are bound to honor these principles will have already obtained most of the benefits of free trade among its states. A non-discrimination rule means that each state cannot, in its law, explicitly disfavor the goods, commerce or persons of the other states. Although it remains possible for each member state to in fact favor its own through manipulation of taxes, subsidies, or regulation, a non-discrimination principle makes such maneuvers more difficult and much more subject to leakage as persons and activities the state does not want to favor slip into the qualifying class. And a free access rule means that no member state can protect the economic activity of its own citizens from the competition of citizens of other states. The combination of a free access rule with non-discriminatory application of simple agency principles provides commercial enterprises with the legal basics necessary to compete throughout the federation.

Although both the United States and the Common Market are in form committed to these principles, the United States is far ahead of the Common Market in their actual implementation. The national government in the United States has controlled immigration from its inception, and there have been no internal legal barriers to the movement of citizens. Tariffs applicable to imported goods violate the non-discrimination principle, and have never existed between states in the United States. The national US government has had exclusive power over the currency from its

of the rates to favor particular domestic producers. The value added tax with a flat rate applied to base computed by means of a uniform procedure applicable to all goods solves these problems. I am indebted to Robert D. Cooter for this point.

[8] KRAUSS, "Recent Developments in Customs Union Theory: An Interpretive Survey," 10 *J. Econ. Lit.* 413 (1973), traces this position to J. VINER, *The Customs Union Issue* (New York 1950).

inception, while the Common Market continues to have separate currencies, with recognition of the power over capital transactions that are considered an appropriate aspect of the modern power over the currency.

The fact that the United States has from its inception been more strongly committed to the principles of a free internal market than is the Common Market at present does not mean that the issues have been entirely free from doubt. With the decision not to renew the charter of the Second Bank of the United States, the banking system in the United States was organized along state lines until after the Civil War, when a parallel system of nationally chartered and regulated banks emerged. Even these national banks, however, were required to conform to the geographic limitations of state banking laws, a system of market segmentation that survived inviolate nearly to the present day. As a result all American banks (until very recently) have been limited to operating banking offices in a single state, and many to a single location. The financially important insurance industry has been exclusively subject to state regulation, complete with separate regulatory requirements for entry into each state. The most economically important nineteenth century issue was the free national movement of corporations, an issue whose esoteric metaphysics *Buxbaum* and *Hopt* describe.[9] That was settled as a matter of practice in favor of free movement, although even this rests upon no very solid constitutional foundation.

There is no reason to think that Europe will not shortly achieve an implementation of these principles nearly as complete as that of the United States. Tariffs and entry controls are scheduled for elimination in 1992. The Common Market is committed to the free movement of workers rather than persons, and although the difference is not unimportant it is not economically significant. The Common Market is committed more clearly than is the United States to the free movement of business establishments. The major difference that will remain is the existence of separate national currencies. Even here the Community can achieve nearly the same result as a common currency if the member states permit free market exchange and eschew exchange controls with their accompanying restrictions on the free movement of capital.[10]

II. The Basic Economic Analysis

An economic analysis of the issue of national versus constituent state competence identifies the costs and benefits of each strategy, and then attempts to compare the net gain (or loss) of one against the other. The factors are neatly symmetrical, that is the benefits of one strategy are the costs of the other, and vice versa. The critical factors are (1) the gains and

[9] BUXBAUM & HOPT, *supra* note 1, at 30-40.

[10] And, of course, the Community has done even better by coordinating exchange rate shifts among its members with the "snake in the tunnel" concept.

losses from uniformity versus diversity and (2) the gains and losses from centralization versus decentralization of the law making power.[11] The matrix looks something like this.

Option 1: A strategy of federal competence

A. Benefits
   1. Mandated uniformity, or more generally "economy of scale."
   2. Maximize sovereign "leverage," or more generally, "political market power."

B. Costs
   1. Reduces opportunity for diversity.
   2. Reduces competitive invisible hand phenomena.

Option 2: A strategy of constituent state competence

A. Benefits
   1. Diversity, permits laws to be tailored to "market."
   2. Competitive pressure on political abuse, i.e. eliminates dominant "political firm."

B. Costs
   1. Diversity, i.e., loss of economy of scale.
   2. Reduces leverage of law makers, i.e. all constituent states face competition.

This matrix is only in a metaphorical sense "economic" since it is really a compendium of basic arguments for and against rather than a measure of costs and benefits in standard, measurable units. Indeed, it does not even imply a consistent methodology for measuring those costs and benefits since the importance of any particular "cost" or "benefit" will depend upon the value that an observer places upon them.

The fact that a national strategy is automatically uniform does not mean that it is the only strategy that produces uniformity, or that such mandated

[11] There is a similarity between the analysis here and the concept of "optimal currency areas" once discussed in the literature. See MUNDELL, "A Theory of Optimum Currency Areas," 51 *Am. Econ. Rev.* 657 (1961), and McKINNON, "Optimum Currency Areas," 53 *Am. Econ. Rev.* 717 (1963). The topic, once thought important enough to merit treatment in introductory texts such as C.P. KINDLEBERGER, *International Economics* 424-426 (5th ed., Homewood 1973), has dropped from sight, probably because it has been rendered unimportant by the success of floating rates. See the prescient essay by SOHMEN, "Currency Areas and Monetary Systems," in *Trade, Balance of Payments and Growth; Papers in International Economics in Honor of Charles P. Kindleberger* (J.N. Bhagwati & R.W. Jones eds., Amsterdam 1971). Similarly, worldwide acceptance of the free access and non-discrimination principles would render many issues about the allocation of competence within the EC unimportant. Predictably, the economics profession was never able to decide what would be an "optimal currency area." I am indebted to Saul X. Levmore for pointing out this similarity.

uniformity is preferable to voluntary uniformity. Because there are gains from uniformity, autonomous constituent states will have incentives to coordinate their laws with those of other jurisdictions. Students of commercial and business law are aware of strong similarities that run through the law of these areas in many countries, similarities that reflect the needs of the international community of merchants whose history predates that of many modern nations. The Commissioners on Uniform State Laws have enjoyed considerable success in the United States encouraging such voluntary harmonization. But the substance of the rules adopted under such a scheme of voluntary harmonization may be quite different than the rules of a uniform national law because no constituent state can urge uniformity around a rule that disfavors businesses in the state that adopts it.

What are the benefits of uniformity? Uniformity means that businesses can use standardized forms, compliance procedures, contract terms, etc. across all of the jurisdictions in which they operate. Personnel trained and expert in these uniform procedures can function in any of the jurisdictions.

What are the benefits of diversity? The diversity which localism permits enables laws to reflect the preferences of the locality. If one locality prefers a policy of investor protection in the sale of securities, and another *caveat emptor*, both preferences can be honored if each can make its own law on the subject. The existence of competition between jurisdictions does not mean that jurisdictions cannot adopt costly social policies, it only means that their citizens must be prepared to bear the cost. If, for instance, a jurisdiction wishes to decree that every employer should provide its employees two fine cakes at Christmas time, it must be prepared to see the cost of those cakes reflected in the local wage structure. If the workers of the jurisdiction prefer the cakes to the equivalent (tax-adjusted) wages, they will be pleased by the requirement and have no incentive to seek employment elsewhere.

Because the economic magnitudes involved are small, and because both diversity and uniformity have their advantages, the historical "starting" point may be a very important, if not controlling, factor in the allocation of competencies. Whatever the existing arrangements are, businesses will have adjusted to those arrangements. A host of existing arrangements, personnel and practices will be based upon them. Any change will impose transition costs. For instance, the procedures required for a corporation to "qualify" to do business in a state of the United States are archaic, but American businessmen have gotten so used to complying with them that they would probably think it a waste of time to even think about changing them. When a jurisdiction has an established area of decisional competence, its past practices and decisions create a stability of expectation that cannot be quickly duplicated by the replacement jurisdiction.

The American states developed bodies of statutory and decisional law in the area of business association law in the course of the nineteenth century. Although it has been argued that the constitutional draftsmen envisaged a more active federal role, it was not to be realized until the twentieth century. The pattern of national participation in this area has been episodic and occasion-specific. When there were perceived crises or failures that the states were deemed unable to handle, Congress would enact specific legislation (usually, at first, very narrow) to address the problem at hand.

A similar pattern will probably emerge in the Common Market, given the strength of the reliance interests built into existing practice and the costs of change. Because the Common Market emerges at a time when each of the constituent states have already developed elaborate bodies of law in this area, the assertion of federal competence will probably face even more substantial resistance than federal initiatives in these areas did in the early American experience.

The importance of the path of historical development explains why neither the American nor European arrangements display any evident coherence. Indeed, as I read *Buxbaum* and *Hopt*'s intricate description of the American law, I thought to myself: "How wonderful this work is, to so concisely describe this sprawling material." But then I thought: "How many readers are there who have a background that will enable them to understand it?" And as I read on: "My, won't this all seem strange to a European reader? Who could think that it even works!" Then, when I got to the European materials, which I am much less well equipped to understand, I found myself thinking: "My goodness, their rules are just as strange and arbitrary as ours are." Businesses are able to operate with tolerable efficiency within these rules because they have learned to adapt to them. Any change imposes the cost of new adaptations, and thus requires a justification based upon demonstrable improvement.

III. Applications to Particular Subjects

Because an economic analysis requires an estimate of costs and benefits, it must be conducted in relation to issues more specifically defined than "business association law" if it is to have any persuasive bearing on the issue of federal versus constituent state competence. An economic analysis dictates neither that business association law should all be federal nor that it should all be state. It is necessary to know what is at stake, in a functional sense. The company or business enterprise law that *Buxbaum* and *Hopt* discuss touches on (A) Corporation or business organization law, including agency; (B) Securities law; (C) Antitrust law; (D) Labor law; (E) Creditor's rights; (F) Bankruptcy law and (G) Conflict of laws.

A. Corporation Law

There are two basic views as to what the law in this area is, or should be, about, and each has important implications for the federal versus state question. The older and more venerable view is that corporation law is about the public regulation of businesses carrying on their activities in corporate form. This is a public law view of corporation law. The corporate charter is a regulatory document granted by the sovereign to prevent corporations from doing things they would otherwise do in response to market forces. The alternative view is that corporation law is nothing more than an area of complex, multiparty contracts, and that its purpose is to make enforceable and administer the contractual relationships entered into among shareholders, creditors, management, workers and suppliers, all essential components of a coalition necessary to make a business function.

Each of these visions of corporation law has articulate defenders in American legal scholarship, and each has been identified with a view on the issue of federal versus state competence. In American terms the issue is this: does current Delaware corporation law represent the outcome of an evolutionary process that has been "a race to the bottom," or a "race to the top?"

The leading statement of the race to the bottom position is that of *William Cary*, Columbia University law professor and President Kennedy's choice as Chairman of the Securities and Exchange Commission. In his *Federalism and Corporate Law: Reflections Upon Delaware*,[12] he argued:

> "Delaware is both the sponsor and the victim of a system contributing to the deterioration of corporation standards. This unhappy state of affairs, stemming in great part from the movement toward the least common denominator, Delaware, seems to be developing on both the legislative and judicial fronts. ... Perhaps now is the time to reconsider the federal role."

Cary's complaint was that Delaware law unduly favored management at the expense of shareholders, a characteristic he explained by the interaction of Delaware's desire for franchising revenue with the ability of managements to control the choice of the state of incorporation. *Cary* made it clear that he, at least, would favor a national corporation law, but because that was politically unfeasible, argued for minimum federal standards.

The direct response came from *Ralph Winter*, then a Yale University law professor and now a Reagan-appointed Judge of the United States Court of Appeals for the Second Circuit. In his *State Law, Shareholder Protection, and the Theory of the Corporation*,[13] he argued that *Cary*'s claim that Delaware law was injuring corporate shareholders was "implausible on its face." According to *Winter*:[14]

> "The plausible argument runs in the opposite direction: (1) If Delaware permits corporate management to profit at the expense of shareholders and other states do not, then earnings of Delaware corporations must be less than earnings of comparable corporations chartered in other states and shares in the Delaware corporations must trade at lower prices. (2) Corporations with lower earnings will

[12] 83 *Yale L.J.* 663 (1974).
[13] 6 *J. Leg. Studies* 251 (1977).
[14] *Id.* at 256.

be at a disadvantage in raising debt or equity capital. (3) Corporations at a disadvantage in the capital market will be at a disadvantage in the product market and their share price will decline, thereby creating a threat of a takeover which may replace management. To avoid this result, corporations must seek out legal systems more attractive to capital. (4) States seeking corporate charters will thus try to provide legal systems which optimize the shareholder-corporation relationship."

Winter's view that Delaware incorporation did not have a negative impact on share prices was later confirmed by finance economists. Shareholders, at least, do not appear to believe that Delaware law impairs the value of their shares because it places insufficient constraints on management, leaving them free to operate the corporation to the detriment of shareholder interests.

The *Winter* side of the *Cary-Winter* debate has won wide acceptance among American legal scholars, in part because the *Winter* position is compatible with the development of a law and economics literature which views the corporation, and indeed any business organization, as a web of interrelated contracts designed to deal with problems in the efficient mobilization and management of the resources necessary for the business.[15] Contractual arrangements which work to solve these problems are adopted by successful firms and the problem for the law is to understand and enforce these arrangements in a manner compatible with their purpose. This is a view which eliminates the public law component from corporation law altogether.

Recently *Roberta Romano* has returned to the topic of the role of Delaware in American corporation law in *Law as a Product: Some Pieces of the Incorporation Puzzle*.[16] There she brilliantly explores empirically the question of why Delaware has been so successful in attracting corporations. She not only replicates with a more sophisticated methodology earlier results that showed that shareholders are sometimes helped and never hurt by a move to Delaware incorporation, but she identifies two aspects of Delaware's comparative advantage in the competition for corporate charters. First, since incorporation revenues are important to Delaware, Delaware has a continuing interest in pleasing its corporate clientele. Because Delaware is "hostage" to this continuing source of revenue, users of Delaware corporation law have greater assurance that present policies will continue. Second, Delaware's specialization has enabled it to develop specific "assets" such as a rich body of case-law and experienced practitioners and judges,[17] and to offer specialists in Delaware law economies of scale

[15] The now classic works in this school are COASE, "The Nature of the Firm," 4 *Economica* (n.s.) 386 (1937), and JENSEN & MECKLING, "Theory of the Firm, Managerial Behavior, Agency Costs and Ownership Structure," 3 *J. Fin. Econ.* 305 (1976).

[16] 1 *J. Law, Econ. & Org.* 225 (1985).

[17] One unusual feature of Delaware law is that it has preserved the distinction between law and equity, which means that all actions seeking temporary restraining

because of the large number of corporations they can service with their expertise.

On the subject of federal versus state competence, *Romano* concludes:[18]

> "[T]hese characteristics ... suggest how a centralized system could impose a welfare loss on firms, to the extent that it would be difficult to duplicate the important transaction-specific assets that serve to safeguard the interests of the parties. For given the size of the federal budget, there is no revenue incentive to constrain the national government from acting opportunistically by installing high franchise fees without delivering the laws that corporations prefer, while there are not many options for firms (except to become unincorporated or expatriated) in retaliation against such behavior."

The *Winter*-organizational economics-*Romano* position is critically dependent on accepting their view of the appropriate domain of corporation law. In the *Cary-Winter* debate this was not in issue, because *Cary* defined the issue as one of the allocation of rights and duties *within* the corporation. But, if corporation law is considered to be the equivalent of public regulation of the business corporation, then the arguments for state competence do not flow with such syllogistic ease.

One reason it seems sensible to define corporation law as dealing only with the internal allocation of rights and duties as between officers, directors and shareholders is that if the subject is public regulation of *business*, then it is odd to limit the subject only to businesses conducted in the corporate form. Although the corporation has been the dominant form of large business organization in western capitalist economies in the twentieth century, there are other available forms that can be used. The choice of corporate form is based upon tax and regulatory considerations often quite separate from corporation law. For instance, in the last few years in the United States there has been a move to the limited partnership form as the result of federal income tax changes that have made that form of business relatively more attractive. Another example is the rise of the GmbH in Germany in recent years in order to avoid codetermination and other requirements.[19] Any scheme of public regulation that is applied to a business based upon its form encourages movement to other forms. If the regulation has substantive objectives, basing it upon the legal form of the business makes little sense.

orders or injunctions will be heard by the Chancellors. These remedies are likely to be sought in transaction situations where litigation holdup problems are acute. There are only a few Chancellors and because of the substantial corporation litigation business, they develop expertise in these subjects. The Delaware Chancellors have a professional reputation for ability and promptness. In other American states these issues will be litigated before a judge of general jurisdiction, one of many, whose familiarity with business law and problems is likely to be small.

[18] ROMANO, *supra* note 16, at 281.

[19] BUXBAUM & HOPT, *supra* note 1, at 171.

The definitional issue does not dispose of the substantive questions. No matter how the appropriate domain of corporation or even business association law is defined, the issue of federal versus state competence in the areas of public regulation of business remains.

I now turn to the areas that are touched upon in the *Buxbaum* and *Hopt* book.

B. Securities Law

Securities law can be functionally divided into two components. First, the regulation of the sale of securities to investors. And second, the regulation of securities markets.

American law provides for a parallel state and federal regulation of securities sales. From the inception of the twentieth century securities have been viewed as "inherently dangerous" instruments which require special regulation to protect purchasers. The dangerousness stems from the difficulty purchasers have separating good securities from bad ones since the quality of a security cannot be ascertained by inspecting it, and from the fact that the large amounts of money typically involved in securities purchases make their sale a comparatively attractive domain for swindlers. The states supplemented their common law style civil and criminal fraud law with specialized regulatory statutes called "blue sky laws" at the beginning of this century. These laws provided for seller licensing, administrative supervision, and disclosure filing. In the 1930s the federal government entered the area with a non-exclusive system of civil and criminal fraud remedies, a system of disclosure filings, and the creation of a specialized administrative agency, the Securities and Exchange Commission. The emergence of specialized administrative agencies reflects in part the fact that securities swindlers are often highly sophisticated, with access to substantial resources, and present problems of investigation and enforcement that would tax the generalist law enforcement agencies.

This parallel and duplicative scheme has continued for over fifty years without any dramatic harm, its theoretical potential for unnecessary duplicative regulatory filings ameliorated by cooperation between federal and state regulators. In practice, the Securities and Exchange Commission focuses on nationally syndicated securities whose sellers are headquartered in the major financial centers while the state regulators focus on local financial promotions.

Aside from the fact that interstate operations are common in the securities area on the part of both legitimate and illegitimate enterprises, each state could have its own system of investor protection. Today, however, large scale securities frauds are operated not only at the national but the international level, a fact that requires cooperation among the national securities enforcement agencies for effective enforcement. Some kind of effective federal securities swindle control agency is likely to be an aspect of any modern integrated securities market.

The governance of markets was historically conducted by private organizations in the United States, the most notable being the New York Stock Exchange. The New York Stock Exchange regulated such matters as trading rules and conventions, membership, member solvency, and customer relations. Since 1934 the federal government has in turn regulated the exchanges through the Securities and Exchange Commission to ensure that these powers were used in the "public interest," although in fact the Commission has been deferential to the Exchange, and the Exchange has had strong influence upon the Commission.

There is no reason why in a federal system the constituent states cannot regulate their own exchanges as to these matters, each exchange then offering its services throughout the federation. The exchanges would then compete for business in the areas of price, transaction cost, execution and financial reliability, and so on. This competition would overcome the tendency of this type of regulation to protect the incumbent exchanges against competition and to deter entry by newcomers. For instance, in the United States there have been no new securities exchanges formed since the enactment of the Securities Exchange Act of 1934, and the major innovations in securities trading have come from the National Association of Securities Dealers (who sponsored the computerized over-the-counter facility known as "NASDAQ") and the commodities exchanges (who pioneered futures trading in securities). A federal regulator of securities exchanges is more likely to freeze existing business practices and to be hostile to innovation than would a state system.

C. Antitrust Law

The federal Sherman Antitrust Act was passed in 1890, partly in response to complaints that business corporations were engaging in practices beyond the reach of state governments. Those practices such as the formation of national holding companies with numerous different state subsidiaries in a position to do business everywhere seem inoffensive today. By my reading the debate has echoes of the "devil as multinational corporation" arguments one hears today. But the problem thus defined, a national solution was clearly necessary. The federal statute was accompanied by the enactment of state antitrust laws, and this parallel system of antitrust has endured ever since. The federal role has been dominant and the state statutes dormant. Because the statutes rely upon judicial enforcement and critical terms that are quite ambiguous, the whole program continues to be obscured in an unending fog of judicial procedure. To the extent that antitrust law is viewed as a system of public restraint on business practices that firms would otherwise regularly engage in, then a federal program is appropriate. To the extent it is viewed as a harmful program of ideology masquerading as law, state competence is preferable, but only because it is less powerful.

D. Labor Law

If the problem of the relationship between a firm and its employees is viewed as a problem of contract law, then state competence is appropriate. Contract approaches, however, are not congenial to the formation of labor unions because of the difficulty of avoiding unanimity requirements that paralyze effective organization. (Similar issues of shareholder unanimity requirements bedeviled early corporation law.)

In the United States, the labor unions had a national organizing vision from their beginning, and sought confirmation and legitimation of that strategy from the federal government. That they obtained in the Wagner Act of 1935 which regulates the procedures for union organization and collective bargaining throughout the United States, with strong preemption of state law. The functional reason for the national focus of the unions was a concern that some states would resist the adoption of laws supportive of union organization, and that those states would in turn attract firms and business away from states with effective unions. It seems likely that the emergence of vigorous competition across national borders within the European Community will turn the attention of European labor leaders to the Community level.

Labor economists in the United States have tended to view unions as a device for monopolizing the labor supply to a firm in order to extract wages in excess of the competitive level for their members. Indeed, it has frequently been suggested that one effect of unions will be to lower wages for nonmembers, as those seeking employment without the benefit of union membership seek a reduced number of jobs. If that is the purpose of unions, then it can be more effectively achieved through federal law which extends union power throughout the market.

This traditional view, however, has difficulty explaining such phenomena as the stable coexistence in the same market of unionized and nonunionized firms. Recently, another view, analogous to the organizational economics view of corporations, has begun to emerge, which views labor unions as specialized intermediaries with a comparative advantage in the administration of certain kinds of labor contracts.[20] If this view better reflects what labor unions really do, then state competence would be appropriate, just as in the corporation case.

E. Creditor's Rights

These are state law matters in the United States, and are governed by principles equally applicable to all debtors, whether corporate or otherwise. It is possible for one jurisdiction to function as a debtor's haven, offering release from obligations enforceable in other jurisdictions. Apparently, this

[20] The leading work articulating this view is R.B. FREEMAN & J.L. MEDOFF, *What Do Unions Do?* (New York 1984).

was a possibility feared by the drafters of the Constitution, who empowered Congress to enact uniform bankruptcy laws. But this has never in fact been a problem in the American system, and the allocation of this competence to the states in the commercial area has not occasioned any dissatisfaction.

F. Bankruptcy Law

Bankruptcy law in the United States is federal. The Constitution confers power to enact uniform bankruptcy laws on the Congress. The origins of this clause are obscure.[21] It resulted in part from concern about the ability of state courts to discharge indebtedness of citizens of other states. This was remedied in the Constitution by the Full Faith and Credit Clause. The Bankruptcy Clause in turn emerged from the discussion of this issue. My guess is that the recognition of state power to discharge debts by judgments effective everywhere led to a concern that a state might emerge as a "debtor's haven," with bankruptcy laws favorable to debtors. The power, in any case, was not utilized by Congress until 1890.

Although the bankruptcy law is federal, it incorporates by reference most of the standards of state law. It has recently been pointed out that this is necessary in order to avoid creating incentives for parties to move disputes into the bankruptcy forum in order to change their rights.[22]

G. Conflict of Laws

Many of the problems in this area are affected by the rules relating to applicable law and deference to foreign judgments. For instance, states can effectively administer bankruptcy if other states recognize the effect of their judgments of discharge. The American Constitution contains a Full Faith and Credit Clause that requires the states to recognize the judgments of the others, and empowers Congress to implement it through legislation. Congress has not done so, largely because there have not been any problems sufficiently acute to lead to demands for legislation.

One can imagine a scheme of rules so bizarre that it would make impossible a regime of state law in any commercial area. For instance, if a jurisdiction took the position that it would always apply its own law to any dispute in its courts, no matter what its connection to the underlying transaction, the effective extraterritorial application of that law could create serious difficulties. In fact, however, courts throughout the western world have been sensitive to these problems, and the ability of parties through

[21] NADELMANN, "On the Origin of the Bankruptcy Clause," 1 *J. Am. Leg. Hist.* 215 (1957).

[22] Th.H. JACKSON, *The Logic and Limits of Bankruptcy Law* 21-27 (Cambridge, Mass. 1986).

choice of law, arbitration and forum clauses to shape the applicable law and forum further eases the way.

The system of Delaware dominated public corporation law in the United States has been aided by a rule of conflict of laws under which internal corporate matters are governed by the law of the state of incorporation. The European seat of business approach does not preclude the operation of similar forces, but would make them more costly for businesses to exploit because they would be required to actually move the required activities to the jurisdiction whose law they wished to embrace. To the extent it is desired to give these forces full play at minimum economic cost, the American rule is preferable.

IV. Conclusion

The basic American approach to the issue of state versus federal competence in the area of business association law has been a presumption of state competence combined with a power of federal intervention addressed to problems in cases where a failure of state competence is identified. These failures have occurred in situations where policies are desired which will impose costs on firms greater than the benefits that will be realized in the jurisdiction that enacts the policy, so that competition between the constituent states will deter if not prevent its implementation. This can occur in two quite different situations. First, when the real costs of the policy exceed its benefits. And second, when the value of the policy is not correctly appreciated by the citizens of the jurisdiction so that they are unwilling to absorb its costs themselves. In other cases, the United States has left these matters within the competence of the states, and has enjoyed the benefits of competition and opportunity for experimentation and diversity such decentralization facilitates.

Such an approach appears to this reader to be consistent with the relevant clauses of the Treaty of Rome.

Report No. 2: Hartmut Schmidt
Economic Analysis of the Allocation of Regulatory Competence in the European Communities

I. The Problem

Buxbaum and *Hopt* want economics to provide a rational dividing line between European and member country regulation of company and capital market law[1]. They would like to know which enterprise activities can be safely left to local regulation and which ought to be subjected to Community regulation[2]. Economic theory should provide, in their view, a model for the appropriate reach and, moreover, the appropriate intensity of Community legislation on enterprises[3]. Most desirably, economics should prescribe guidelines for the ranking of a legal agenda[4].

This paper explores the extent to which economics provides guidance as to scope, intensity and order of legal harmonization. *Buxbaum* and *Hopt* may ask for more than economics has to offer.

II. Economics and Law

If people would find everything equally pleasant, there would be no need for economics. But people strive to overcome poverty and hardship, and they tend to pursue their goals by using the least expensive means available. It is this vast and interdependent process that economics describes, explains, and predicts.

A substantial part of this process is the production of private and public goods[5]. As to private goods – goods that a person may produce or obtain at a price for exclusive use – the economist is in a position to explain and, to a lesser extent, predict what goods will be offered. This task is much more

[1] R.M. BUXBAUM & K.J. HOPT, *Legal Harmonization and the Business Enterprise* 15, 21 f (Berlin/New York 1988).

[2] *Id.* at 2.

[3] *Id.* at 7.

[4] *Id.* at 7.

[5] For a precise delineation, see R.D. GRASS & W. STÜTZEL, *Volkswirtschaftslehre* 41-45 (Munich 1983).

difficult if a good is readily available to many people and if it may be used simultaneously by a number of persons at zero marginal cost (public good). Thus, though many economists perceive law as a public good, it appears that it is impossible even to come close to the problem addressed by this paper by following the public goods branch of economic theory. It may be worth noting, however, that public goods may be made available by bodies both public and private. This is in line, for example, with capital market regulations promulgated by the exchange and other private bodies in the United Kingdom.

If law is seen as a public good, changing the legal system is a part of the dynamic economic process. Changes in law reflect shifts in needs. This may become quite visible if the judicial role dominates in adjusting law[6]. Some economists, however, view law differently: they see the legal system as a part of the given framework within which the economic process functions[7]. Certain parts of the law, which provide for private property and the corresponding liability, for freedom of contract, and for free access to trade, are deemed to contribute to the foundation on which the market economy rests[8]. All other regulation, as well as the values and morals of society, should in this view be stable, so as to relieve economic decision makers of as much uncertainty as possible.

This static view may provide some economic guidance as to what a constitution should contain, but the focus here is on enterprise law and harmonization.

III. Economics and Integration

A. Methodological Aspects

By its very nature the economic process brings about an increase in welfare. In a strict sense, this means that whenever a change occurs at least one person is better off thereafter, and no one is poorer (Pareto criterion). It is thus legitimate for an economist to use welfare as a criterion for judging the merits of economic, legal and political proposals or measures. To prove an increase in welfare may be very simple in transactions involving only two persons. This calculation, however, becomes an intractable task if many

[6] *Cf.* BUXBAUM & HOPT, *supra* note 1, at 5.

[7] BERNHOLZ & FABER, "Überlegungen zu einer normativen Ökonomie der Rechtsvereinheitlichung," 50 *RabelsZ* 35-60 (1986), seem to hold both views simultaneously. They postulate a *Versorgungsstaat* to provide public goods and, apart from that, a *Rechtsstaat* (at 38 f), yet at 41 they make it a point that law has the properties of a public good.

[8] W. EUCKEN, *Grundsätze der Wirtschaftspolitik* 163-174 (Reinbek 1962; repr.). For a discussion of earlier views, see MESTMÄCKER, "Die sichtbare Hand des Rechts," in E.J. MESTMÄCKER, *Recht und ökonomisches Gesetz* 118-135 (2d ed., Baden-Baden 1984).

persons are involved. The most troublesome aspect is that measures which increase the output of goods with no change in input will in many cases leave some people worse off than before. Of course, the gain in efficiency is always sufficient to compensate the losers, but a redistribution may never occur. Thus, interpersonal comparisons of income changes would be necessary to make a judgment on the welfare effect. Since interpersonal comparisons, however, are impossible, no judgment can be rendered.

Faced with this dilemma, the purist economist may abstain from evaluating policy proposals. But the more common approach is to treat a gain in efficiency as an increase in welfare, distributional (or equity) issues being neglected.

B. Efficiency of Integration

This is the way economists have looked at European integration. The first task in any welfare-effect or efficiency analysis is to establish the basis of comparison. Should this basis be the war torn economies of the forties or the inward looking national economies of the thirties? Most economists obviously have thought that neither is appropriate. In their judgment the people of Europe, since about the end of the war, have held that a higher standard of living would be within reach if governments removed impediments to international trade. Thus, perceiving the increasing political momentum of this popular belief, economists have tended to choose a Europe within a free or liberalized trade environment as the proper basis of comparison[9].

The second task in the efficiency analysis of integration is to subdivide the main question conveniently, and to look at the various sources from which welfare changes may flow, such as a customs union, factor mobility, specialization in a large market and a monetary union.

In the analytical process of establishing the various welfare changes, the economist may gladly or grudgingly have to pass judgment as to which additional assumptions are appropriate and as to how a proper balance between negative and positive welfare effects can be struck.

[9] For some economists a liberalized trade environment is tantamount to integration. According to RÖPKE, international integration is characterized by free trading, convertibility and factor mobility (at least capital mobility). European integration is, in his view, merely undoing the international economic disintegration that occurred after 1914; RÖPKE, "Integration und Disintegration in der internationalen Wirtschaft," in *Wirtschaftsfragen der freien Welt, Festschrift für Ludwig Erhard* 494 f, 500 (E. von Beckerath *et al.* eds., Frankfurt 1957) [hereinafter cited as von BECKERATH]. A similar view is expressed by PREDÖHL, who stresses that disintegration did much more harm in Europe than elsewhere because national particularism cut off what from an American view amounted to European interstate or to domestic European trading; PREDÖHL, "Von der alten zur neuen Weltwirtschaft," in von BECKERATH, at 517-520.

C. Efficiency of Harmonization

It appears that the harmonization of enterprise law has not been explicitly considered in any extended analysis as a source of efficiency gains. One may, however, be tempted to glean the welfare change of harmonization from a bold overall judgment on integration. *Scitovsky*, in summing up the results of his analysis, states[10]:

> "Few economists expect integration to bring about very great improvements in Western Europe's organization; and while many consider its effects on investment the most important, even these effects are bound to be very limited and gradual."

If the efficiency advantage of integration over a liberal trade environment is rather limited, then legal harmonization also is of limited importance, since integration implies harmonization whereas liberalization of trade does not.

How might harmonization nevertheless improve efficiency?

(1) Doing business under more uniform regulations may result in some savings, particularly for smaller companies, which have to give up relatively more resources to cope with an international legal environment than do larger ones. The resultant competitive effects may cause additional efficiency gains.

(2) The harmonization process will in due course bring about a review of national regulation. Anticompetitive regulations seem to have less chance of remaining untouched if change can be initiated at the Community level. At the national level the anticompetitive forces may still be firmly entrenched. This should encourage entrepreneurs to invest and to encroach on the markets of their competitors throughout the Community[11].

(3) In a free trade environment any country may fall victim to protectionist pressure from within. Since investment is a long-run decision it must be based on long-run considerations. Therefore, much depends on the confidence of entrepreneurs in the enduring nature of their access to the international market on unchanging or improving terms[12]. The harmonization process, by producing a reasonably steady flow of Community directives, is well suited to build and to maintain this confidence, since it testifies to the commitment of governments to the common market.

(4) Particularly in the financial sector, regulatory moves may have the effect of shifting business and employment to an extent that may give rise to protectionist measures or even hostility. Shifts to a country like Luxembourg, due to its limited overall resources, may not threaten an

[10] T. SCITOVSKY, *Economic Theory and Western European Integration* 133 (London 1958; repr. w./intro. 1984). For a more skeptical view, see HABELER, "Die wirtschaftliche Integration Europas," in von BECKERATH, *supra* note 9, at 526-530.

[11] SCITOVSKY, *supra* note 10, at 133.

[12] *Id.* at 135.

existing balance of powers, but shifts to a larger country might do so. Harmonization may assure a "level playing field" and prevent such shifts even if the contents of the directives or cooperation agreements makes little sense economically. Therefore, harmonization is useful to dispel fears of disruptive developments in the supranational market. This effect seems to be closely related to the size criterion[13].

Before one rushes to the conclusion that efficiency may be improved by steadily expanding the scope of compulsory Community law, the substantial cost of the services of the Community ought to be considered. It is also important to deal with the question of who is going to review and revise Community law. In other words, are independent competing legislatures more conducive to progress in law than the approach taken by the European Community[14]?

IV. Evaluating Harmonization Projects

The economist is committed to the welfare goal. If he abstains from value judgments, he is likely to be taciturn on the overall effects of integration and harmonization. What then is the use of an economist? Has he anything to offer concerning the scope, intensity and order of harmonization?

A. Evaluation by the Market

The job of the economist is to describe, explain and predict the economic process. Here, predictions of the effects of harmonization projects are needed. Those who are familiar with predictions of stock prices and exchange rates by economists may not want to rely on them, since they are based on vast array of assumptions that often prove incorrect. The predictions needed here, however, are of a different type; they are based on reliable and known data, and on the knowledge that people will act according to the economic principle[15].

Economists who render predictions of the second type can be of great use. Consider the following: in the United States credit card loans by commercial banks increased by $72.4 billion between 1980 and 1987. Delaware accounted for $25 billion and South Dakota for $12.3 billion of that increase. In Delaware the loans grew 100 times as fast as in the United States on average, in South Dakota 855 times the national average. State and

[13] BUXBAUM & HOPT, *supra* note 1, at 2.
[14] *Cf. id.* at 13.
[15] *Cf.* GRASS & STÜTZEL, *supra* note 5, 12-17.

local income taxes paid by banks also increased much faster in these two states, as did commercial bank employment[16].

South Dakota was the first state to act on a 1978 Supreme Court decision that a national bank may charge interest rates to out-of-state credit card customers at the rate permitted by the law of its home state. In 1980, South Dakota removed all usury ceilings on credit card loans and permitted out-of-state bank holding companies to establish a single *de novo* bank in the state for credit card operations. Obviously, South Dakota economists knew that usury ceilings cut off the supply of loans to certain high risk borrowers, that even less risky borrowers must be cut off as market interest rates rise and that these ceilings disrupt customer relationships and complicate the credit card business. Consequently, they predicted that eliminating the ceiling would, given the banking environment in the United States, attract banks to the state. The state regulations after the change would provide the flexibility needed for consistent credit card lending.

The letter of the Federal Reserve Bank of Chicago puts this in proper perspective[17]:

> "Early and aggressive, South Dakota and Delaware have captured a significant share of the credit card market by creating a regulatory environment that has attracted financial services organizations. The marketing strategies and experiences of these states may serve as a warning to others that a failure to maintain a competitive banking environment will lead to a loss in jobs."

Since the South Dakotas and the Luxembourgs come in many shapes and sizes to capitalize on the accepted free-world principle of competitive legal systems[18], it may be appropriate to view them in the light of generalizing theses:

(1) The hunger for employment and taxes, combined with the predictive skills of economists and the ability of enterprises to shift operations

[16] ERDEVIG, "Small States Teach a Big Banking Lesson," in FEDERAL RESERVE BANK OF CHICAGO, *Chicago Fed Letter* 1 (No. 10, June 1988).

[17] *Id.* at 1.

[18] In a speech before industrialists, the President of the Federal Republic of Germany, Richard von WEIZSÄCKER, called attention to the fact that entrepreneurs can internationally choose the business environment that appears to be on balance the most favorable and that consumers can choose from competing domestic and foreign products. This is bound to limit or correct actions taken by politicians or interest groups. Thus the time has passed when reforms mirrored national preferences and national interest group conflicts. In the future, reform will reflect the pressures of internationalization, since whichever party is in power, it will have to pay tribute to the fact that the Germans' economic livelihood is internationally based and rooted. As von WEIZSÄCKER pointed out, it is both the quality of the product and the quality of the business environment that count in international competition, which governs the allocation of jobs. R. von WEIZSÄCKER, "Ansprache bei der Jahrestagung des Bundesverbandes der Deutschen Industrie in Bonn am 7. Juni 1988," in DEUTSCHE BUNDESBANK, 41 *Auszüge aus Presseartikeln* 5-6 (June 8, 1988).

across borders, is a strong force in adapting regulatory environments to current business needs.

(2) Adaptations that have met with a favorable market response are likely to be copied by other regulators. This process may be viewed as harmonization by the market[19], as opposed to harmonization by bureaucracy[20]. It gains momentum as technological advances facilitate transport and communications.

(3) A regulator, aware of the dynamic welfare effects of adapting regulations, will want to effect desirable regulatory changes as early as possible.

(4) A single large national or supranational regulator tends to be slow in adapting regulation. Progress in regulation may be speeded up by introducing some sort of regulatory competition. To achieve this, closely related fields may have different regulators[21]. For example, official stock exchange markets are subject to Community law, while unofficial markets are not; securities market financing and investing in the United States are regulated by one federal agency, financing and investing through banks by others.

B. Evaluation by Economists

Predictions require the analysis of the related economic processes. The potential impact of any regulatory or harmonization proposal is anticipated, and can be judged against the objective relevant in the given situation. These objectives, e.g., tax receipts, employment, protection of the depositor or of the environment, will merely reflect the preferences of the decision makers and may be only loosely related to the welfare goal. If the economist is allowed independence in evaluating harmonization proposals, he will stick to the welfare goal, or use as close a proxy for welfare as possible. Frequently, the procedure for evaluation of legal or institutional arrange-

[19] L.C.B. GOWER in his paper herein on the British experience (see *infra* at 307 ff) describes the Big Bang and the Financial Services Act as results of market pressure and of borrowing solutions from the well tried American system. This example provides an excellent illustration of harmonization by market.

[20] MÜLLER-ARMACK, "Fragen der Europäischen Integration," in von BECKERATH, *supra* note 9, at 534, has already pointed out that harmonization by bureaucracy is a dangerous approach to integration since it may lead, if unanimity is required, to a buildup of tensions since more and more regulations then rest on unsatisfactory compromise. This is likely to strengthen centrifugal forces. Therefore, it may be desirable to respect regional preferences and accordingly to allocate regulatory competence to the member states or to their subdivisions. *Cf.* KIRSCH, "Über zentrifugale und zentripetale Kräfte im Föderalismus," in *Beiträge zu ökonomischen Problemen des Föderalismus* 14-34 (K. Schmidt ed., Berlin 1987).

[21] *Cf.* H. GIERSCH & H. SCHMIDT, *Offene Märkte für Beteiligungskapital: USA, Großbritannien, Bundesrepublik Deutschland* 65-69 (Stuttgart 1986).

ments is developed on an *ad hoc* basis. In many cases, however, a formalized approach is used, cost-benefit analysis being probably the best known.

Other approaches use as proxies for welfare increases such items as the reduction of transaction and coordination costs, the reduction of market organization determined costs, or the reduction of agency costs. Because of the heterogeneity of the advantages and disadvantages, the economist cannot avoid value judgments in arriving at an overall evaluation. The quality of the evaluation, however, critically depends on the extent to which the deliberations leading up to these judgments are conclusive or, alternatively and less strongly, are shared by others.

This evaluation process is suitable to rank and to modify given harmonization proposals. Of course, the analysis of existing regulations will often generate proposals as a by-product. In a static world one could imagine that analysis of this type carried out by economic experts committed to serve the public would also delineate the desirable scope of regulation.

Since the economic process is dynamic, however, there is one value judgment relevant to harmonization that is very difficult to pass. This troublesome element comes into play whenever the competence to adapt regulations is transferred from a number of countries, agencies, market organizers, or associations to a single authority. In any given situation, the new central regulation doubtlessly may improve welfare and be clearly superior to alternative regulations. Yet, for many reasons, the situation will change, and this may, from an economist's point of view, require the adaptation of regulations. If adaptation is slow, substantial welfare losses will accrue. Since centralization of regulatory competence tends to slow future adaptation processes, it is likely to require a kind of value judgment that an economist should pass only if forced to; this judgment rests, like stock price predictions, on uncertain assumptions.

Whether to centralize regulatory authority is a question quite similar to that of whether we should have one truck factory in Europe instead of 12 in order to avoid duplication costs, to utilize fully economies of scale and to deliver a superb product. Conventional wisdom has it that technology and needs change fast enough to make the duplication costs and the scale losses that are inextricably linked to any competitive effort worthwhile. Harmonization by mandatory Community law, therefore, seems to rest on the implicit assumption that relevant change and the potential for progress are negligible, or that independent regulators within the Community would not act if the opportunity to progress arose[22].

[22] Past behavior of independent regulators may not be a reliable indicator as to future activities. A case in point are the European stock exchanges. They did not compete for centuries and were slow to react to technological changes. Therefore, the Community intended to regulate exchanges and to lead the way to a technologically advanced European stock exchange. In analyzing the policy options of the Community the present writer pointed to probable future developments and recommended reliance on exchange competition. *Cf.* H. SCHMIDT, *Advantages and Disadvan-*

V. Conclusion

Buxbaum and *Hopt* look to economics for guidance as to scope, intensity and order of legal harmonization. As this article has shown, harmonization should advance and intensify until no further positive welfare effects accrue. Those harmonization projects have priority that will generate the highest welfare effects.

Unfortunately, this answer does not provide the guidance *Buxbaum* and *Hopt* have asked for. Welfare effects of regulatory change are difficult to measure even in a static environment. Their measurement in the dynamic real world environment requires clairvoyance if regulatory authority is to be centralized. Therefore, the economist is inclined to accept compulsory Community enterprise law only if there is strong and proven reason to believe that this law is well devised to meet permanent needs.

Even if there is a reasonable degree of doubt as to the enduring nature of this law, however, harmonization may still be worth considering, though some mechanism that assures speedy adaptation should be installed. One such mechanism is already in place, i.e., the approximation pressure from abroad. But it tends to work with substantial friction. Therefore, mechanisms other than the international competition of legal systems should be devised, which would, as pointed out above, give enterprises a domestic choice as to the regulatory regime under which they pursue their business. It may be the choice between various sets of mandatory regulations provided by a single central regulator[23], a choice between a mandatory central regime and various sets of member country regimes[24], or the choice between the regimes or sets of regimes of two or more central regulators[25]. Moreover, the regulatory objective may be accomplished by regulations with few or even no mandatory elements: non-mandatory regulation sets a standard; it also allows and encourages competitive private regulation to develop[26]. A regulatory system that provides for domestic choices takes advantage in a subtle way of the principle of competitive legal systems, since perceptive regulators are in a better position to observe shifts in choice, to become aware of new demands on the system, and to effect regulatory changes early.

tages of an Integrated Market Compared with a Fragmented Market 401-407 (Luxemburg 1977). Today, European exchange competition works as witnessed by new listing regulations for smaller companies, by new markets for options and futures, and by changes in trading and settlement techniques.

[23] Examples would be the choice between various forms of business organization (such as AG, GmbH or KG) or between obtaining a quotation on the Official Market, the Unlisted Securities Market or the Third Market.

[24] E.g., the choice between primary market disclosure requirements of the SEC and those of the states set forth in the blue sky laws; this choice exists for flotations that could be made either interstate or strictly intrastate.

[25] E.g., the Bank of England and the Securities and Investments Board (SIB).

[26] *Cf.* GIERSCH & SCHMIDT, *supra* note 21, at 70-73.

No clear-cut dividing line between Community and member country regulation emerges. Superficially, this may be attributed to the economist's inability to anticipate and authoritatively measure welfare effects accurately. In addition, it is the dynamic economic process that blurs the dividing line, since the desirable degree of centralization depends on the rate of change, which varies with time and among different areas of regulation. Finally, the questions as to the dividing line between Community and member country regulation, and as to the intensity of regulation, turned out to be parts of a more general question: what mechanisms are conducive to regulatory progress? It appears promising to pursue these questions in the context of regulatory system design.

Report No. 3: Christian Meier-Schatz*
American Legal Harmonization from a European Perspective

I. Introduction

The topic and title assigned to this contribution comprise two elements. One is descriptive and promises at least a fragmentary report on legal and theoretical developments of harmonization in the United States of corporate and capital market law. The other is analytical and indicates an exterior (almost Aristotelian) viewpoint from which to interrogate that American experience. The second element calls for a delineation of this peculiarly European perspective.

Comparative legal research may be most illuminating when it focuses on essential structural differences as well as historical and socioeconomic backgrounds. Somewhat deviating from the excellent study of Prof. *Buxbaum* and *Hopt*,[1] this paper perceives two main differences between European and American evolution. The first relates to status quo and recent trends in the allocation of regulatory authorities in the field of corporate and capital market law. A second lies in the influence of modern economic theory on the legal debate over the federalist question as on other crucial issues of corporation law and securities regulation.

The comparative status quo of harmonization and federalization is so familiar and so well outlined in the work of *Buxbaum* and *Hopt*, that it is entirely unnecessary to reiterate it here.[2] The to some extent opposite trends, however, with respect to centralization and decentralization of corporate and capital market law, deserve special remark. While the legal harmonization in the EC, with widespread support in the academic community, steers away from national towards federal rules, a reverse tendency appears to prevail in the United States. On the one hand, important Supreme Court decisions have restricted federal intervention or

* I am grateful to Prof. Uriel PROCACCIA, Faculty of Law, The Hebrew University of Jerusalem, for critical and helpful comments.

[1] R.M. BUXBAUM & K.J. HOPT, *Legal Harmonization and the Business Enterprise* (Berlin/New York 1988).

[2] *Cf. id.*, especially at 111 ff and at 250 ff.

granted states an extended latitude in the area of corporate and capital market law.[3] On the other hand, current legal and economic thought has initiated an impressive movement for the deregulation or at least regulatory decentralization of the field. This influential school may already have had an impact on recent administrative rules.[4]

The role of economic theory in legal discourse is a second (and probably even more significant) difference between recent American and European developments. Analysts of EC law still bemoan the little advanced theoretical and empirical foundation of European efforts towards harmonization.[5] In the United States the whole legal discussion of federalism as well as of corporate and capital market law has been reshaped by new economic theories, in particular by neoclassical microeconomics and modern theory of finance. Two American hypotheses are of particular interest for this article. The first alleges that a competitive decentralized system of corporate laws produces rules maximizing shareholder wealth.[6] A second maintains that federal securities regulation, especially mandatory federal disclosure rules, are needless and socially wasteful.[7]

This article explores the history and status quo of the American distribution of regulatory competencies. In addition, it questions the persuasive power of modern economic theory regarding the benefits of a federalist corporation law and the value of federal disclosure rules. The article hereby attempts to consider both elements suggested by its title. Despite some summary introductory information, it concentrates on a critical analysis of the two crucial issues.

The first paragraph (A) of section II reviews the historical genesis of American corporate law and securities regulation. It emphasizes in particular economic and political background, theoretical underpinnings and regulatory alternatives. Analysis will reveal that the status quo is much more the result of particular (almost accidental) economic and political factors than of a conceptual outline. Paragraph (B) then portrays the newer theoretical discourse in corporate and capital market law. It concludes that such an advanced economic research is quite a recent phenomenon which nevertheless generates extremely far-reaching analytical and normative demands. This discourse invites, in section III, closer examination of the relevant neoclassical hypotheses with respect to a decentralized corporate law and a federal disclosure regime. It summarily reviews theoretical arguments as well as empirical evidence and concludes that neither can live

[3] In Santa Fe Industries, Inc. v. Green (430 U.S. 462 (1977)), the Court held that federal Rule 10b-5 does not provide a cause of action for breach of state law fiduciary duty. In CTS Corp. v. Dynamics Corp. (107 S. Ct. 1637 (1987)), it upheld a particular form of a state takeover statute ("control shares acquisition statute").

[4] *Cf.* text accompanying notes 52-68 *infra.*

[5] See, e.g., BUXBAUM & HOPT, *supra* note 1, at 200 ff.

[6] *Cf.* text accompanying notes 55-61 *infra.*

[7] *Cf.* text accompanying notes 62-66 *infra.*

up to its (excessive) explicative and normative claims regarding the optimal structure and regulatory level of corporation and capital market law.

II. Historical Development and Theoretical Discourse

A. Status Quo and Historical Development

1. Corporation Law

The fundamental features of the present American corporate law regime are widely known.[8] Corporations are legally creatures of an individual state; their formation requires only the fulfillment of some formal requirements. State corporate codes essentially regulate the internal governmental structure of private firms. As a matter of principle, the rules are fairly uniform among the states, and enable private parties to shape their firms' internal affairs.[9] Under a political perspective, US corporation codes are characterized by the concept of regulatory division of power.[10] They mainly address shareholder concerns and have "no tradition of internalizing within corporation law public policy and public law elements."[11]

These structural features of modern American corporation law are hardly self-evident given their historical evolution. Early on in the Union, corporations still had a quasi-public status. The states' concession system required a special charter granted by the government.[12] The process of

[8] For similar short overviews see ROMANO, "The State Competition Debate in Corporate Law," 8 *Cardozo L. Rev.* 709 (1987); SCHWARTZ, "Federalism and Corporate Governance," 45 *Ohio St. L.J.* 545, 551 ff (1984); WINTER, "State Law, Shareholder Protection and the Theory of the Corporation," 6 *J. Leg. Studies* 251, 252 (1977). For a broader analytical study *cf.* CONARD, "An Overview of the Laws of Corporations," 71 *Mich. L. Rev.* 623 (1973).

[9] For a listing of major components of enabling acts see BUXBAUM & HOPT, *supra* note 1, at 119 ff.

[10] For the term and a more elaborate comparative discussion, see Ch.J. MEIER-SCHATZ, *Wirtschaftsrecht und Unternehmenspublizität* 66 ff (Zurich 1989).

[11] BUXBAUM & HOPT, *supra* note 1, at 128. This harks back to the belief that broad social effects have to be controlled by "external" regulation and not by "internal" corporate law. See BUXBAUM, "Juridification and Legitimation in Enterprise Law," in *Contract and Organization: Legal Analysis in the Light of Economic and Social Theory* 241 ff (T. Daintith & G. Teubner eds., New York 1986); MANNING, "Thinking Straight About Corporate Law Reform," 41 *Law & Contemp. Prob.* 3, 11 ff (1977); KRIPKE, "The SEC, Corporate Governance, and the Real Issues," 37 *Bus. Law.* 173, 184 (1981). A commentary on this "dualist view" can also be found in R. CLARK, *Corporate Law* 677 ff (Boston 1986).

[12] See generally J. DAVIS, *Essays in the Earlier History of American Corporation Law* Chs. 3 and 4 (Cambridge, Mass. 1917); E.M. DODD, *American Business Corporations Until 1860* 196 (Cambridge, Mass. 1954); BUTLER, "Nineteenth Century Jurisdictional Competition in the Granting of Corporate Privileges," 14 *J. Leg. Studies* 129, 138 ff (1985).

conceptual change was gradual and transition towards a general incorporation law relatively long.[13] This change of the legal system, and the perseverance of exclusive state domain in corporation law were based neither on explicit deliberations nor on articulated thoughts of economic theory. A technological breakthrough in transportation and communication,[14] for example, when it led to the formation of a national market, was a primary step in the evolutionary process. Or the Supreme Court's decision in *Paul v. Virginia*,[15] and the following drastic decrease of rents for the traditional state monopolies in corporate charters[16] generated a current of change. Moreover, the egalitarian philosophy of the Jacksonian age strongly urged equal access to incorporation rights.[17] The infamous "charter mongering" process which led to the well-known "race to the bottom"[18] with respect to the regulatory stringency of corporate law, was clearly carried out by political opportunists in state legislatures. After small states (New Jersey, Delaware) had taken an early lead in a competitive market for corporate control, others followed the trend in order to curb migration and

[13] See, e.g., the three stages outlined in BUTLER, *supra* note 12, at 138 ff. *Cf.* also SHUGHART & TOLLISON, *Corporate Chartering: An Exploration in the Economics of Legal Change, Economic Inquiry* 585 ff (1985).

[14] UROFSKY, "Proposed Federal Incorporation in the Progressive Era," 26 *Am. J. Leg. Hist.* 160, 161 ff (1982); BUTLER, *supra* note 12, at 138 ff; R. NADER, M. GREEN & J. SELIGMAN, *Taming the Giant Corporation* 38 ff (New York 1976). *Cf.* generally A.E. CHANDLER, *The Visible Hand, The Managerial Revolution in American Business* 79 ff (Cambridge, Mass. 1977); V.S. CLARK, *History of Manufactures in the United States* 449 ff (New York 1929; repr. 1949).

[15] 75 U.S. (8 Wall.) 168 (1868). See also BUXBAUM & HOPT, *supra* note 1, at 36 ff; BUTLER, *supra* note 12, at 155 ff.

[16] After the court had made interstate competition for corporate charters constitutionally possible, foreign general incorporation laws instantly became a cheap legal substitute. For a good description of this process in an economic perspective see BUTLER, *supra* note 12, at 152 ff.

[17] W. GOUGE, the leading egalitarian economist, provided the following political statement (quoted in J. HURST, *The Legitimacy of Business Corporations* 30, Charlottesville 1970):
"Against corporations of any kind the objection may be brought that whatever power is given to them is so much taken from either the government or the people. As the objective of charters is to give to members of companies power which they would not possess in their individual capacity, the very existence of monied corporations is incompatible with equality of rights."
The statements of Justice BRANDEIS on the Jacksonian mistrust of corporate power are in *The Unpublished Opinions of Mr. Justice Brandeis* 142 ff (A. Bickel ed., Cambridge, Mass. 1957).

[18] The term is, of course, borrowed from CARY, "Federalism and Corporate Law: Reflections upon Delaware," 83 *Yale L.J.* 663, 664 ff (1974). *Cf.* also A. CONARD, *Corporations in Perspective* 11 ff (Mineola 1976); NADER, GREEN & SELIGMAN, *supra* note 14, at 43 ff. The three major steps of this enabling law concept are listed in BUXBAUM & HOPT, *supra* note 1, at 112 ff.

to save at least some income from corporate taxes and fees.[19] Attempts to develop an alternative concept based on more articulated policy goals proved short-lived and unsuccessful.[20]

Nor is today's federal absence in corporate law historically compelling. As early as the Constitutional Convention, James Madison presented a proposal for federal incorporation, which was rejected on exclusively political grounds.[21] More recently, three strong and influential movements favored federal licensing or chartering.[22] A first appeared during the Progressive Era around the turn of the century, when "populism" gave vent to concerns about the enormous rate of economic concentration and fears of the political and economic power of trusts.[23] The theoretical discourse of the progressive movement was spoken in the language of populism.[24] Barely more substantiated were the opponents' *laissez-faire* arguments stressing again and again the benefits of legally unrestricted "natural causes."[25] The concept of federal incorporation itself had the astonishingly broad political support of three presidents, various Democratic and Republican party platforms, the financial press (*Wall Street Journal*), major industry associations, and many top managers.[26] Between 1905 and 1914, twenty bills were

[19] There is a broad consensus today that economic income motives were behind the states' efforts to attract corporations by liberal rules. See, e.g., CARY, *supra* note 18, at 664 ff; FISCHEL, "The 'Race to the Bottom' Revisited: Reflections on Recent Developments in Delaware's Corporation Law," 76 *Nw. U. L. Rev.* 913, 921 ff (1982); ROMANO, *supra* note 8, at 709. *Cf.* generally ROSE-ACKERMAN, "Does Federalism Matter? Political Choice in a Federal Republic," 89 *J. Pol. Econ.* 152 (1981).

[20] A good example is the ABA Code of 1946. For a short description of those countertrends see, e.g., BUXBAUM & HOPT, *supra* note 1, at 116 ff. *Cf.* generally EISENBERG, "The Model Business Corporation Act and the Model Business Corporation Act Annotated," 29 *Bus. Law.* 1407 (1974).

[21] See Note, "Federal Chartering of Corporations: Constitutional Challenges," 61 *Geo. L.J.* 123, 124 ff (1972) (citing the original sources). *Cf.* also NADER, GREEN & SELIGMAN, *supra* note 14, at 66.

[22] For a brief historical summary of federal chartering movements, see SCHWARTZ, *supra* note 8, at 567 ff; SELIGMAN, "The Historical Need for a Mandatory Corporate Disclosure System," 9 *J. Corp. L.* 1, 19 ff (1984); Note, *supra* note 21, at 126 ff; NADER, GREEN & SELIGMAN, *supra* note 14, at 66 ff; WATKINS, "Federalization of Corporations," 13 *Tenn. L. Rev.* 89 (1935).

[23] An excellent analysis of the Progressive Era is provided by the newer study of UROFSKY, *supra* note 14.

[24] A prominent and typical example is the speech of Judge S.D. THOMSON, "Abuse of Corporate Privileges," *Proceedings of the Kansas State Bar Association* 42 (vol. 9, 1892).

[25] *Cf.* the quotes in G. KOLKO, *The Triumph of Conservativism: A Reinterpretation of American History, 1900-1916* 13 (1963).

[26] See WATKINS, *supra* note 22, at 94 ff; UROFSKY, *supra* note 14, at 164 ff; NADER, GREEN & SELIGMAN, *supra* note 14, at 67 ff; Note, *supra* note 21, at 126 ff. *Cf.* also the examples given by L. LOSS, *Fundamentals of Securities Regulation* 31 (Boston 1983).

introduced in Congress.[27] The time, in short, appeared ripe for some form of federal corporation law. Its implementation finally failed only because the large support for the general principle could not be transformed into a consensus on specific workable rules. Moreover, many concerns of the reformers were appeased by the enactment of alternative economic regulations, in particular of antitrust laws.[28]

The second round, arguably the "most sustained drive for federal licensing,"[29] developed in the New Deal period of the 1930s. The market crash of 1929 and the following depression spread mistrust of the securities and banking industry. Again proponents of a federal corporation law implemented arguments of social and economic reform; this time the different strands of thought were largely depression-related.[30] Between 1915 and 1932, eight congressional bills were introduced, and a very powerful popular movement emerged shortly before the war.[31] These facts demonstrate the political significance and popularity of the issue. During the debates on a new federal securities regulation, many prominent participants preferred a system of federal chartering or licensing.[32] The war efforts, however, broke the momentum of reform. Later, the federal securities laws enacted in the early Roosevelt presidency approached some of the same goals.[33]

In the 1970s, for a third time, reformers called for a federal incorporation system or at least federal minimum standards. The postulates in this case did not arise out of economic difficulties as they had before. Rather, a legitimacy crisis of political and entrepreneurial institutions, influenced considerably by Watergate and the questionable payment scandals of many leading firms, gave rise to the debate. What developed then was a broad social reform movement transcending by far the corporation law issue in its

[27] SELIGMAN, *supra* note 22, at 20; Note, *supra* note 21, at 126 (both with many sources).

[28] UROFSKY, *supra* note 14, at 181 ff. The most important statutes were the Clayton Act and the Federal Trade Commission Act, both supplementing the earlier Sherman Act.

[29] NADER, GREEN & SELIGMAN, *supra* note 14, at 69.

[30] SCHWARTZ, *supra* note 8, at 547. *Cf.* also comment and sources on the federal securities laws *infra* para. 2. A good example of a populist background is the movement started by Senator O'MAHONEY resulting in a bill covering a broad agenda of social issues. See for a short survey NADER, GREEN & SELIGMAN, *supra* note 14, at 69. *Cf.* generally O'MAHONEY, "Federal Charters and Licenses for Corporations," 22 *J. Nat. Educat. Ass.* 27 (1938).

[31] NADER, GREEN & SELIGMAN, *supra* note 14, at 66. The most influential movement emerged in the second half of the 1930s and was led by Senator O'MAHONEY. See the sources in note 30 *supra*.

[32] *Cf.* text accompanying notes 44-46 *infra*.

[33] Influential advisors of President Roosevelt evaluated a federal incorporation law early on. See, e.g., J. SELIGMAN, *The Transformation of Wall Street* 51 (1982).

traditional conception.[34] Consumer and environmental activists emphasized a connection between modern business behavior and a wide range of social problems like product safety, pollution, sex and race discrimination.[35] The volume of political support as well as the congressional echo may have been somewhat lower in this third round. But many still believed federal intervention in the corporate law to be imminent.[36] The movement finally lost its impetus after a remarkable change of political climate in the 1980s. In addition, some of the mentioned problems had been addressed by special public law regulations.[37]

2. Capital Market Law

Unlike corporation law, a dual legal regime delineates American capital market law. All states have their blue sky laws in one form or another and with differing degrees of regulatory strictness. The federal securities regulation is an extremely complex and dense legal network whose central pieces, i.e., the Securities Act and the Securities Exchange Act, are dominated by a disclosure approach. Like the structural rules of corporation law, these information provisions were meant to provide material data for shareholders and investors, and not to serve other constituencies (e.g., workers) or a general, more inclusive public interest.[38]

[34] Much emphasis was given to a new concept of "social responsibility" of corporations. *Cf.* for important contributions of the day SCHWARTZ, "Towards New Corporate Goals, Coexistence with Society," 60 *Geo. L.J.* 57 (1971); NADER, GREEN & SELIGMAN, *supra* note 14; C.D. STONE, *Where the Law Ends: The Social Control of Corporate Behavior* (New York 1975). For a comprehensive restatement and analysis of the debate see ENGEL, "An Approach to Corporate Social Responsibility," 32 *Stan. L. Rev.* 1 (1979).

[35] With a similar diagnosis LOSS, *supra* note 26, at 32; SCHWARTZ, *supra* note 8, at 558, and the book of NADER, GREEN & SELIGMAN, *supra* note 14, with its broad and amorphous reform program. See also R. NADER & M. GREEN eds., *Corporate Power in America* (Washington, D.C. 1973). For an interesting treatment of corporate law reform in a broader regulatory context see WEISS, "Social Regulation of Business Activity: Reforming the Corporate Governance System to Resolve an Institutional Impasse," 28 *UCLA L. Rev.* 343 (1981).

[36] Some observers argued that the indirect pressure of a potential federal incorporation legislation was strong enough to provoke a more shareholder-oriented approach of state court decisions. See COFFEE, "The Future of Corporate Federalism: State Competition and the New Trend Towards De Facto Federal Minimum Standards," 8 *Cardozo L. Rev.* 759, 764 (1987). *Cf.* also the extensive analysis of FISCHEL, *supra* note 19, at 924 ff.

[37] Helpful overviews of these external economic law regulations are provided in M. WEIDENBAUM, *The Future of Business Regulation, Prioritization and Public Demand* 7 ff (New York 1979); A. STONE, *Regulation and Its Alternatives* 32 ff (Washington, D.C. 1982).

[38] *Cf.*, with many sources, MEIER-SCHATZ, "Disclosure Rules in the United States, Germany and Switzerland," 34 *Am. J. Comp. L.* 271, 274 (1986).

Historically, many similarities exist between the respective evolutions of corporation and of capital market law. They share political factors of influence, standards of economic discourse, and imminent actuality of regulatory alternatives. The state blue sky laws were a response to a seemingly widespread increase in securities fraud cases.[39] At least the initial codifications had their roots in populist philosophy and economics, and were intended, to use a famous quote, to prevent the sale of "building lots in the blue sky in fee simple."[40] These developments were founded on underlying paternalistic assumptions about capital markets which exposed innocents to the greed of financial professionals.[41] The enactment of the federal securities laws and the market crash of 1929 and the following depression[42] were, of course, closely interrelated. They were again a reaction to a perceived or real wave of large-scale frauds, and to enormous losses to the investing public.[43] A broad spectrum of reform proposals, ranging from a pure antifraud rule to a far-reaching governmental market control, were discussed.[44] Although a relatively "mild" disclosure concept was finally adopted,[45] there had been remarkable political support for a substantive

[39] For a discussion of the historical roots of blue sky law see NASH, "Government and Business: A Case Study of State Regulation of Corporate Securities, 1850-1933," 38 *Bus. Hist. Rev.* 144 (1964); M. PARRISH, *Securities Regulation and the New Deal* 5 ff (New Haven 1970).

[40] MULVEY, "Blue Sky Law," 36 *Can. L.T.* 37 (1916). The characterization as an "era when an 'agrarian West' was bled by a 'monied East'" is another typical statement. LOSS, *supra* note 26, at 8. This populist background is also emphasized in SELIGMAN, *supra* note 33, at 44; LOSS, *supra* note 26, at 8; SARGENT, "Report on State Merit Regulation of Securities Offerings," 41 *Bus. Law.* 785, 791 ff (1986).

[41] SARGENT (*supra* note 40, at 792) speaks of a "strong sense of victimization associated with populist unrest."

[42] Shorter commentaries on the legislative history are MEIER-SCHATZ, *supra* note 38, at 273 ff; ANDERSON, "The Disclosure Process in Federal Securities Regulation: A Brief Review," 25 *Hastings L.J.* 311 (1974); MORTON & BOOKER, "The Paradoxical Nature of Federal Securities Regulation," 44 *Den. L.J.* 479 (1967). For a more comprehensive presentation see SELIGMAN, *supra* note 33, at 1 ff; R. DE BEDTS, *The New Deal's SEC* 1 ff (New York 1964).

[43] DE BEDTS, *supra* note 42, at 11 ff; R. STEVENSON, *Corporations and Information* 80 ff (New York 1980). There is no consensus about the empirically established degree of securities fraud cases. See, e.g., G. BENSTON, *Corporate Financial Disclosure in the UK and the USA* 104 ff (Lexington, Mass. 1976) on one side, and SELIGMAN, *supra* note 22, at 18 ff on the other side.

[44] *Cf.* DE BEDTS, *supra* note 42, at 4 ff (reviewing the most important legislative proposals); MORTON & BOOKER, *supra* note 42, at 483 ff (distinguishing three historical approaches of securities regulation). See for the "battle of the philosophies" also LOSS, *supra* note 26, at 33 ff.

[45] The leading historian of the SEC calls it "more remarkable, considering the sentiments of the day, for the powers it did not grant than for the limited powers it did." SELIGMAN, *supra* note 33, at 70.

regulatory scheme.[46] Also surprising is the relative modesty of the economic analysis on which this politically highlighted legislation was built.[47] Systematic empirical studies were very rare,[48] and a coherent and conclusive theoretical approach towards securities regulation did not exist.[49] Nor did the federal aspect of the functional relationship between state and federal rules provoke much debate. Although the Securities Act and the Securities Exchange Act were never intended to replace the blue sky laws,[50] it is, in the words of a modern commentator,[51]

> "not clear from the legislative history ... whether anyone in Congress or anyone otherwise connected with the bills had any systematic understanding of what the relation of state and federal securities regulations should be [and] how regulatory responsibilities should be allocated."

B. Theoretical Discourse

1. Corporation Law

An exacting economic debate on US corporation law is a relatively recent phenomenon, which has taken place essentially during the last two decades. Initially, the studies of neoclassical economists resulted in a new theory of the firm. This theory perceives the corporation as a nexus of contractual relations. The separation of ownership and control, then, represents an efficient form of functional specialization. Specialization, however, induces the problem of agency costs. Yet that agency problem appears not to be so

[46] *Cf.* SELIGMAN, *supra* note 33, at 40 ff (citing promoters within Roosevelt's own "brains trust"). A first proposal submitted to both Houses of Congress was basically a substantive regulatory concept. See DE BEDTS, *supra* note 42, at 33 ff.

[47] Accord, e.g., DE BEDTS, *supra* note 42, at 83; COOPER & KEIM, "The Economic Rationale for the Nature and Extent of Corporate Financial Disclosure Regulation, A Critical Assessment," 2 *J. Acc. & Pub. Pol.* 189, 200 ff (1983); SOMMER, Comment, in *Economic Policy and the Regulation of Corporate Securities* 88, 88 (H. Manne ed., Washington, D.C. 1969). Partly responsible for these shortcomings were certainly the relatively low standard of serious capital market research at that time and the focus of economic analysis on the broader background of the market crash itself. See STEVENSON, *supra* note 43, at 80.

[48] This has been stressed early by economists like BENSTON, *supra* note 43, at 160; MANNE, "Economic Aspects of Required Disclosure Under Federal Securities Laws," in *Wall Street in Transition, The Emerging System and Its Impact on the Economy* 21, 24 (H. Manne & E. Solomon eds., New York 1974). But also a former SEC commissioner has emphasized that the legislative history was "singularly free of any sort of empirical economic analysis." SOMMER, *supra* note 47, at 88.

[49] *Cf.* also LOSS, *supra* note 26, at 7; COOPER & KEIM, *supra* note 47, at 201.

[50] They even contain language expressly excluding a preemption of state regulation. See Securities Act § 18, 15 U.S.C. § 77r (1982).

[51] SARGENT, *supra* note 40, at 793. *Cf.* for a more elaborate discussion WARREN, "Reflections on Dual Regulation of Securities: A Case Against Preemption," 25 *Bost. Coll. L. Rev.* 495, 515 ff (1984).

disruptive since, as many empirical studies agree,[52] the management of large firms is effectively monitored by various market mechanisms.[53] This microeconomic theory has influenced the legal doctrine of corporation law considerably, especially in the field of corporate governance.[54]

A separate branch of the contemporary theoretical movement addresses the federalist question. Partly in connection with the new economics of federalism,[55] this school defends the status quo of a dual system and of primarily state responsibility. The pioneering advocate of this theory was Judge *Winter*, who attacked Prof. *Cary*'s famous call for federal minimum standards. *Winter* argued that states competing for corporate charters will provide legal rules optimizing shareholder wealth.[56] He based his conclusion on the assumption that corporate law rules injuring shareholders lead to lower securities prices. Lower prices, in turn, have negative impacts on financing policies and invite hostile takeovers. Various markets, moreover, acting as control institutions, should monitor the efficiency of management's (re)incorporation decision.[57] *Winter*'s hypotheses triggered an elabo-

[52] Empirical studies have been undertaken especially with respect to the market of corporate control and the manager market. Studies on the control market are summarized in EASTERBROOK & FISCHEL, "The Proper Role of a Target's Management in Responding to a Tender Offer," 94 *Harv. L. Rev.* 1161, 1187 ff (1981). A review of recent studies is given by JENSEN & RUBACK, "The Market for Corporate Control," 11 *J. Fin. Econ.* 5, 9 ff (1983). A survey of the (rarer) studies on the manager market can be found in BRUDNEY, "Corporate Governance, Agency Costs, and the Rhetoric of Contract," 85 *Colum. L. Rev.* 1403, 1423 (1985).

[53] See JENSEN & MECKLING, "Theory of the Firm: Managerial Behavior, Agency Costs and Ownership Structure," 3 *J. Fin. Econ.* 305, 308 ff (1976); FAMA, "Agency Problems and the Theory of the Firm," 88 *J. Pol. Econ.* 288 ff (1980); FAMA & JENSEN, "Separation of Ownership and Control," 26 *J. L. & Econ.* 301 (1983); FAMA & JENSEN, "Agency Problems and Residual Claims," 26 *J. L. & Econ.* 327 (1983).

[54] See, for representative restatements, FISCHEL, "The Corporate Governance Movement," 35 *Vand. L. Rev.* 1259, 1261 ff (1982); BAYSINGER & BUTLER, "Race for the Bottom v. Climb to the Top: The ALI Project and Uniformity in Corporate Law," 10 *J. Corp. L.* 431, 436, 448 ff (1985); GILSON, "A Structural Approach to Corporations: The Case Against Defensive Tactics in Tender Offers," 33 *Stan. L. Rev.* 819, 837 ff (1982); N. WOLFSON, *The Modern Corporation* 45 ff (New York 1984).

[55] ROSE-ACKERMAN, *supra* note 19; KITCH, "Regulation and the American Common Market," in *Regulation, Federalism and Interstate Commerce* 9 (A.D. Tarlock ed., Cambridge, Mass. 1981).

[56] WINTER, *supra* note 8; R. WINTER, *Government and the Corporation* (Washington, D.C. 1978).

[57] This nonlegal management control by markets has been stressed again and again by proponents of a market for corporate charters. See FISCHEL, *supra* note 19, at 918 ff; BAYSINGER & BUTLER, *supra* note 54, at 448 ff; WINTER, *supra* note 8, at 262 ff; WINTER, *supra* note 56, at 16 ff. *Cf.* also ROMANO, *supra* note 8, at 711; MACEY & MILLER, "Toward an Interest-Group Theory of Delaware Corporate Law," 65 *Tex. L. Rev.* 469, 477 (1987).

rate debate. Some authors attempted to establish empirically the social benefits of the federalist system.[58] Others situated themselves in the "gray area" between the extreme poles of *Winter* and *Cary*.[59] These theorists delivered many important insights not only into the economic background of corporate migration[60] but also into the political mechanism of corporate legislation, particularly in the state of Delaware.[61]

2. Capital Market Law

During approximately the same two decades, another advanced economic discussion evolved in the field of capital market law. It was based partly on similar analytical approaches, yet influenced essentially by modern theories of finance. This debate did not, unlike that over corporate law, take a defensive stand as to the status quo, but launched an attack against current federal disclosure rules. After prominent authors had questioned empirically the effectiveness of the Securities Act and the Securities Exchange Act,[62] three major critical arguments evolved. Some theorists developed a private information model and stressed that voluntary disclosure incentives guarantee a sufficient information flow among private firms.[63] Others, relying on a rich body of empirical research, argued that data released in mandatory documents are redundant since securities prices of efficient capital markets already reflect them.[64] A third group of critics questioned the informational value of traditional accounting data and maintained that governmental disclosure rules, based on a historical cost approach, require the release of only marginally relevant information.[65] These economic

[58] DODD & LEFTWICH, "The Market for Corporate Charters: 'Unhealthy' Competition v. Federal Regulation," 53 *J. Bus.* 259 (1980); ROMANO, "Law as a Product: Some Pieces of the Incorporation Puzzle," 1 *J. Law, Econ. & Org.* 225 (1985); BAYSINGER & BUTLER, *supra* note 54, at 456 ff.

[59] ROMANO, *supra* note 8; ROMANO, *supra* note 58; COFFEE, *supra* note 36; BAYSINGER & BUTLER, *supra* note 54; MACEY & MILLER, *supra* note 57; WEISS & WHITE, "Of Econometrics and Indeterminacy: A Study of Investors' Reactions to 'Changes' in Corporate Law," 75 *Cal. L. Rev.* 551 (1987).

[60] ROMANO, *supra* note 8, at 717 ff; ROMANO, *supra* note 58, at 225; BAYSINGER & BUTLER, *supra* note 54, at 456 ff.

[61] MACEY & MILLER, *supra* note 57, at 483 ff; ROMANO, *supra* note 8, at 720 ff. *Cf.* the earlier analysis of CARY, *supra* note 18, at 686 ff.

[62] STIGLER, "Public Regulation of the Securities Markets," 37 *J. Bus.* 117 (1964); BENSTON, *supra* note 43; BENSTON, "The Value of the SEC's Accounting Disclosure Requirements," 44 *Acc. Rev.* 515 (1969); BENSTON, "Required Disclosure and the Stock Market: An Evaluation of the Securities Exchange Act of 1934," 63 *Am. Econ. Rev.* 132 (1973).

[63] For a review of the relevant literature of both agency and signaling theory see MEIER-SCHATZ, *supra* note 10, at 162 ff.

[64] Many important sources are quoted in MEIER-SCHATZ, *supra* note 10, at 204 ff.

[65] The most influential book was probably H. KRIPKE, *The SEC and Disclosure*

analyses, again, had a considerable influence on the legal literature which questioned more and more the social value of governmental disclosure rules.[66]

Surprisingly, the attack focused almost exclusively on the federal regulatory scheme, respectively on disclosure regulation as such. Not much attention was paid to state law.[67] More importantly, no economic theory paralleling that in corporate law emerged on federalism in securities regulation. An economic model of a capital market law based on state regulation and competition is lacking, and no reform programs for a decentralized federalist scheme are forthcoming.[68]

C. Conclusion

The status quo of the overall regulatory structure in the fields of US corporation and capital market law is less the product of a rational conceptual outline than of particular settings and developments in economic and political history. The outcome, under this perspective, appears quite accidental as to the allocation of regulatory authorities, and as to the content of the rules themselves. Historically, political opportunism and interest group policy were arguably more at work than theoretical and strategic projections directed towards a general public interest.[69] Major political factors shaped the American history of corporation and capital market law,

(New York 1975); but see also BENSTON, *supra* note 43, at 123 ff. The problem is also discussed (with a review of the relevant literature) in MEIER-SCHATZ, *supra* note 10, at 182 ff.

[66] See, e.g., KRIPKE, *supra* note 65; S. PHILLIPS & J. ZECHER, *The SEC and the Public Interest* (Cambridge, Mass. 1981); WOLFSON, "A Critic of the Securities Exchange Commission," 30 *Emory L.J.* 118 (1981).

[67] Some discussion, it is true, evolved with respect to decentralized systems covering certain aspects of securities regulation. But it focused rather on competition among *stock exchanges*, not state legislators. Moreover, it was mainly concerned with the (corporate law) issue of dual voting rights. See, e.g., FISCHEL, "Organized Exchanges and the Regulation of Dual Class Common Stock," 54 *U. Chi. L. Rev.* 119 (1987); *cf.* also the sources quoted in note 82 *infra*.

[68] It is symptomatic that even authors who heavily criticize the present federal regime don't propose an alternative state law scheme. See, e.g., KRIPKE, *supra* note 65, at 106 ff; EASTERBROOK & FISCHEL, "Mandatory Disclosure and the Protection of Investors," 70 *Va. L. Rev.* 669, 700 ff (1984); Note, "The Efficient Capital Market Hypothesis, Economic Theory and the Regulation of the Securities Industry," 29 *Stan. L. Rev.* 1031, 1070 ff (1979).

[69] One is, hence, not surprised by the preference of some commentators to explain the current state and federal rules rather in terms of interest group analysis than of economics of corporate and capital market law. The literature on interest group constellations around state corporate law legislators has been quoted in note 61 *supra*. A similar analysis, also based on economic theory of regulation has, with considerably less convincing power, been attempted at the federal level as well. See PHILLIPS & ZECHER, *supra* note 66, at 17 ff; WOLFSON, *supra* note 54, at 122 ff.

such as significant macroeconomic changes or crises, and popular (perceived or real) concerns about certain business practices of corporations, or about the economic and social effects of corporate activity. This high degree of historical contingency may also explain the fact that the rules which were finally enacted (as well as those which were not) always faced imminent regulatory substitutes whose rejection, again, often appears quite random. A particularly illustrative example is the federal incorporation which was, in three major rounds, narrowly "circumvented" by other ("alternative") laws.[70]

Generally speaking, sophisticated economic theory had, and still has, no immediate impact on the implementation of the basic regulatory schemes.[71] While this may have changed during the last decade as far as particular regulatory provisions or judicial decisions are concerned,[72] the fundamentals of the status quo remain more a product of historical contingency than of theoretical conception.[73] For a long time, corporate and capital market law reform was influenced politically by populist thinking and other (broader) social reform programs. Thus, the debate focused almost entirely on some general economic and social policy issues and not on the federalist aspect of an optimal division of regulatory competencies.

An advanced economic discussion represents a relatively late and recent phenomenon in the history of American corporation and capital market law. Theoretically, the debate was promoted and dominated by neoclassical microeconomics and modern theories of finance. Its novelty, however, did not prevent it from making extremely high explicative and normative claims. One strand delivered a vigorous *ex post* legitimation of the current federalist corporate law system; the other vigorously attacked the present federal securities regulation scheme. The obvious tension between "old" historically contingent rules and "new" theoretical wisdom invites, particularly from a European point of view which so often rests on loose

[70] See also the historical conclusion of NADER, GREEN & SELIGMAN, *supra* note 14, at 70.

[71] Accord, e.g., COOPER & KEIM, *supra* note 47, at 200 ff.

[72] Some influences have been diagnosed by SELIGMAN, *supra* note 22, at 3 ff (with examples). *Cf.* also the relatively large space a special SEC report on disclosure reserved for the modern theory of finance. Report of the Advisory Committee on Corporate Disclosure to the Securities and Exchange Commission XVIII ff (1977). An impact of neoclassical theory on Supreme Court decisions has been shown by BUXBAUM & HOPT, *supra* note 1, at 49 ff.

[73] More recent historical studies of federal securities regulation have repeatedly stressed that the Securities Act and the Securities Exchange Act were much more the result of a political compromise to save the traditional market structure than a true legal innovation. COOPER & KEIM, *supra* note 47, at 200 ff; MERINO & NEIMARK, "Disclosure Regulation and Public Policy: A Socio-Historical Reappraisal," 1 *J. Acc. & Pub. Pol.* 33 (1982). With a similar conclusion already MORTON & BOOKER, *supra* note 42.

theoretical grounds,[74] an assessment of the reach and limits of the respective analytical power of these theories. Such an endeavor is justified by the remarkable impact the whole economic movement had on the recent academic as well as judicial and legislative debates on US corporation and capital market law. Considerable skepticism appears to be appropriate both towards overoptimistic analytical expectations and towards overinclusive normative implications.

III. Corporation and Capital Market Law and Economic Theory

A. Theoretical Arguments

1. Corporation Law

a. Market for Corporate Charters

The influential argument of corporate federalists that regulatory competition among state law regimes leads necessarily to corporate law rules maximizing shareholder welfare raises doubts under at least four important aspects:

(1) While we understand quite well how competition among private firms works, we know much less about regulatory rivalry among legislators.[75] Serious doubts emerge about even the alleged motivational motor of the competitive race. It is generally believed that states try to cause or to prevent corporate migration in order to gain or to save income from taxes and fees.[76] Such an assumption appears to overestimate the tax motivation.[77] In many states corporate fees are simply not important enough financially to produce significant competitive pressure. After all, other factors are at work as well,[78] and internal political dynamics rather than tax-driven competition models more reliably explain legislative outcomes.[79]

In addition, the competitive mechanism seems to suffer from structural deficiencies. Procedure as well as outcome have the features of an oligopolis-

[74] *Cf.*, e.g., BUXBAUM & HOPT, *supra* note 1, at 197 ff. Even American participants at the Lugano Symposium stressed that there is not much general theoretical literature on the issue of optimal allocation of regulatory authorities in federal systems. *Cf.* KITCH, *supra* at 36.

[75] This is also admitted by convinced proponents of corporate federalism. See EASTERBROOK, "Antitrust and the Economics of Federalism," 26 *J. Law & Econ.* 23, 44 (1983).

[76] *Cf.* sources quoted in note 19 *supra*.

[77] Accord COFFEE, *supra* note 36, at 761 ff; BUXBAUM & HOPT, *supra* note 1, at 274.

[78] One may be the preference of enabling rules for judicial and administrative reasons. *Cf.* BUXBAUM & HOPT, *supra* note 1, at 274.

[79] *Cf.* text sub 2 *infra*. With a similar conclusion COFFEE, *supra* note 36, at 762 ff.

tic market. A few small states dominate the corporate charter market, with a proportionately high income rate at stake.[80] Interaction among state legislators does not appear truly competitive. The trend-setters, especially Delaware, dictate path and direction as market leaders, while the others strive only "to stay within a hailing distance."[81] An astonishing uniformity among state corporate rules also reveals the oligopolistic character of market results.

Finally, some counterevidence further challenges the calculable and beneficial effects of competition among various regulatory bodies. Experiences in the fields of banking law and stock exchange rules indicate that a competitive process may weaken regulatory authority, thus harming those whom the regulation meant to protect.[82]

(2) Important new insights have appeared lately into competition among corporate law provisions. Both the demand and the supply side of the market for corporate charters have been the objects of theoretical study. Yet this fresh information still leave unanswered the crucial public policy question: who benefits in fine from competitive incorporation decisions?

Seen in the demand perspective of the market for corporate charters, a transaction-cost approach shows reincorporation in connection with three transactions (public offerings, mergers and acquisitions programs, defensive tactics); firms also migrate to reduce litigation costs which are potentially high in these transactional settings.[83] Such an analysis remains obviously inconclusive as to the beneficiary question. If firms reincorporate merely to lower litigation costs, particularly in judicial procedures which harm shareholders, migration promotes management's interests exclusively.[84] Even if the law of the new domicile lowers the cost of the basic transaction,

[80] See, in a historical perspective, BUTLER, *supra* note 12, at 156 ff. MACEY & MILLER (*supra* note 57, at 483) speak also of a market dominance of Delaware which allows an adoption of certain rules which are not optimal for shareholders as long as the overall package of corporate law provisions is more attractive than that of other states.

[81] CONARD, *supra* note 18, at 11 ff. Accordingly, he characterizes the competition process as a "chase" and not a "race." *Cf.* also COFFEE, *supra* note 36, at 764.

[82] See, citing the relevant sources, COFFEE, *supra* note 36, at 769 ff. Lately, skepticism has risen especially with respect to the beneficial effects of competitive stock exchange rules on shareholder protection. There are at least some (although controversial) indications of a risky race to the bottom, for instance in the area of shareholder voting. *Cf.* SELIGMAN, "Equal Protection in Shareholder Voting Rights: The One Common Share, One Vote Controversy," 54 *Geo. Wash. L. Rev.* 687 (1986); DENT, "Dual Class Capitalization: A Reply to Professor Seligman," 54 *Geo. Wash. L. Rev.* 725 (1986).

[83] ROMANO, *supra* note 8, at 718 ff.

[84] MACEY & MILLER, *supra* note 57, at 482. This is also regularly admitted by the leading figure of the transactional approach herself. *Cf.* ROMANO, *supra* note 8, at 719 ff.

the transaction itself, e.g., a defensive tactic, may be detrimental to shareholders.[85]

Similar conclusions can be drawn from supply-side analyses of the internal political dynamics of the market for corporate charters.[86] Here a public interest group approach reveals that there is no political equilibrium in the process of corporate law reforms. This regulatory process is distinctly dominated by the corporate bar, while other interest groups remain relatively powerless.[87] Such an insight, again, says nothing about the ultimate winners in corporate migration. The corporate bar's interests, however, do not necessarily coincide with those of shareholders. Given that the management decides over reincorporation, and that corporate lawyers' clients are mostly managers (and not shareholders), it is equally plausible that legal rules are enacted with a pro-managerial bias.[88]

(3) The management's factual authority to make migration decisions has important consequences in an institutional perspective as well.[89] Today's corporations are characterized by a structurally inherent conflict of interests between management and shareholders, leading to significant agency costs for the firm.[90] This conflict of interests is just as prevalent in (re)incorporation as in any other strategic decision. Management may very well speak out for migration to have a better litigation position, or against migration to remain under protection of a state takeover law; in either case their argument is backed by selfish reasoning.[91] This agency cost problem of incorporation decisions is theoretically recognized but significantly underestimated by proponents of corporate federalism.[92] Their counterargument holds that markets guarantee a coordination of shareholder and management interests.[93] The next section shows that market mechanisms have only

[85] *Cf.* also ROMANO, *supra* note 8, at 720.

[86] See the studies quoted in note 61 *supra*.

[87] MACEY & MILLER, *supra* note 57, at 498 ff; with similar results ROMANO, *supra* note 8, at 725 ff. See also the case study on state takeover laws in ROMANO, "The Political Economy of Takeover Statutes," 73 *Va. L. Rev.* 111 (1987). A still partly valid earlier diagnosis making similar suggestions is CARY, *supra* note 18, at 686 ff.

[88] State legislators' inclination to enact rules which please managers is often stressed. See, e.g., SCHWARTZ, *supra* note 8, at 557; MACEY & MILLER, *supra* note 57, at 478, 485. *Cf.* also COFFEE, *supra* note 36, at 771.

[89] That managers (and not shareholders) determine *de facto* the corporation's legal domicile is notorious. See WINTER, *supra* note 8, at 252; MACEY & MILLER, *supra* note 57, at 485; SCHWARTZ, *supra* note 8, at 557.

[90] *Cf.* text accompanying notes 52-54 *supra*.

[91] BUXBAUM, *supra* note 11, at 285; MACEY & MILLER, *supra* note 57, at 485. It is also emphasized that management hardly moves firms away from protective states. See COFFEE, *supra* note 36, at 770 (with an illuminating example).

[92] Accord ROMANO, *supra* note 8, at 753; MACEY & MILLER, *supra* note 57, at 479.

[93] It has been rightfully stressed that probably the most significant difference

a marginally relevant impact on management control and agency costs in modern firms.

(4) Finally, there is a theoretically inexplicable and not sufficiently distinguishable model case in which, even ardent defenders of the market of corporate charters admit, regulatory competition does not lead to optimal results for shareholders. The case in point is, of course, state takeover laws, which have constantly been attacked by corporate federalists.[94] These regulations prescribe procedural and substantive rules which, in the federalists' view, even shareholders should not be allowed to adopt.[95] Early attempts to distinguish takeover statutes from other corporation laws by their extraterritorial effects have failed.[96] Some corporation codes include "pseudo-foreign" firms as well and, more importantly, the second generation of takeover laws now has a much narrower jurisdictional reach.[97]

The impact of state takeover statutes on shareholder wealth remains an open question indeed. Quantitative studies have not yet brought conclusive results.[98] While such rules may lead to higher shareholder premiums, they almost certainly reduce the number of hostile bids.[99] In addition, management can use them for selfish purposes, thereby raising agency costs. It is well-known that shareholders increasingly resist defensive tactics of target companies. Depending upon the ownership structure, management may try to circumvent a shareholder vote on certain defensive maneuvers by pushing a state takeover law with the same effects.[100] State takeover statutes

between federalists and their opponents lies exactly in their opposite views of the effectiveness of market constraints. MACEY & MILLER, *supra* note 57, at 477.

[94] WINTER, *supra* note 8, at 286 ff; WINTER, *supra* note 56, at 42 ff; FISCHEL, "Efficient Capital Market Theory, the Market for Corporate Control and the Regulation of Cash Tender Offers," 57 *Tex. L. Rev.* 1 (1978); JARRELL & BRADLEY, "The Economic Effects of Federal and State Regulations of Cash Tender Offers," 23 *J. L. & Econ.* 371 (1980).

[95] See, e.g., EASTERBROOK & FISCHEL, *supra* note 52; GILSON, *supra* note 54.

[96] WINTER maintained that takeover statutes apply to more than domestically incorporated firms and thereby enable states to restrain the competition in corporate charters. WINTER, *supra* note 8, at 268. Accord KITCH, *supra* note 55, at 41 ff.

[97] ROMANO, *supra* note 8, at 726 note 48. *Cf.* also the critical statements of BUXBAUM, *supra* note 11, at 286 ff; BUXBAUM & HOPT, *supra* note 1, at 52.

[98] *Cf.*, e.g., the studies of DODD & LEFTWICH, *supra* note 58; ROMANO, *supra* note 58; JUSTICE DEPARTMENT, ANTITRUST DIVISION, "State and Federal Regulation in the Market for Corporate Control," Economic Analysis Group Discussion Paper 86-4 (1986).

[99] See, with a presentation of various empirical results, ROMANO, *supra* note 8, at 737 ff. *Cf.* also COFFEE, *supra* note 36, at 771; COFFEE, "Regulating the Market for Corporate Control: A Critical Assessment of the Tender Offer's Role in Corporate Governance," 84 *Colum. L. Rev.* 1145, 1181 ff (1984).

[100] ROMANO, *supra* note 8, at 728 ff.

(at least in their present form) thus remain an enigma in the market for corporate control.[101]

b. Management Control by Markets

Corporate federalists commonly discount the agency cost problem with the argument that managers' reincorporation decisions are effectively supervised by various market mechanisms. Once again they overestimate the social and economic steering function of markets. The four markets listed as control techniques suffer from substantial deficiencies.[102]

As to *product markets*, one may even ask whether a functional relationship exists between the agency problem and product competition. Agency theory argues convincingly that managers even in monopoly firms have incentives to diverge from the value-maximation goal, and that their owners have incentives to limit this divergence.[103] Furthermore, the long interval between management failure and the reaction of the product market, along with other imperfections in the competitive process, severely limit the monitoring capacity of this institution.[104] Crucial barriers exist also in *capital markets* since large corporations are now able to meet most of their capital needs with internal financing or with external lines of credit through banks and other financial institutions. These alternative financial tools lower management's dependence upon the capital market, and thereby decrease its sanctioning power at the same time.[105]

[101] It is difficult to argue that the takeover legislation is not indicative of anything in this debate because legal rules may also promote takeovers as an efficiency mechanisms (i.e., by outlawing poison pills). Although the assumption may theoretically be correct, it is simply not supported by the factual legislative developments. All state takeover laws make takeovers, in one form or another, more difficult.

[102] A much more detailed and elaborate discussion of what follows can be found in MEIER-SCHATZ, "Über die Notwendigkeit gesellschaftsrechtlicher Aufsichtsregeln," 107/I *ZSR* 191 ff (1988).

[103] See especially JENSEN & MECKLING, *supra* note 53. *Cf.* also C. RIDDER-AAB, *Die moderne Aktiengesellschaft im Lichte der Theorie der Eigentumsrechte* 125 ff (Frankfurt/M./New York 1980).

[104] See M. EISENBERG, *The Structure of the Corporation* 168 (Boston 1976); STONE, *supra* note 34, at 88 ff; WEISS & SCHWARTZ, "Using Disclosure to Activate the Board of Directors," 41 *Law & Contemp. Prob.* 63, 70 ff (1977). These problems are also well-known among representatives of the neoclassical school. See, e.g., EASTERBROOK & FISCHEL, "Corporate Control Transactions," 91 *Yale L.J.* 698, 701 (1982).

[105] For a classical statement on the problem see W. BAUMOL, *The Stock Market and Economic Efficiency* 76 (New York 1965). *Cf.* also EISENBERG, "Corporate Legitimacy, Conduct and Governance, Two Models of the Corporation," 17 *Creighton L. Rev.* 1, 15 (1984); WEISS, "Disclosure and Corporate Accountability," 34 *Bus. Law.* 575, 585 (1979). Accord in the European literature. *Cf.* HOPT, "Self-Dealing and the Use of Corporate Opportunity and Information: Regulating Directors' Conflicts of Interest," in *Corporate Governance and Directors' Liabilities* 285,

Manager markets and labor markets share the same general imperfections, namely high transactions costs, geographical and functional immobility, and irrational employment decisions. In addition, markets for managers have trouble fitting individual managers into particular positions, and face the common practice of filling vacancies from within. A wide variance in executive pay, and the considerable impact of meta-monetary criteria in management decisions further destabilize the manager market.[106]

Markets for corporate control face three essential functional shortcomings. Firstly, many bad management decisions do not lead to a stock price decline that can justify the high premiums of today's tender offers. Secondly, the corporate control market is distorted by excessive transaction costs which are structurally inherent and not rooted only in regulatory burdens. Thirdly, transactions often feature motifs which have simply nothing to do with "pruning deadwood," i.e., the replacement of inefficient management.[107]

2. Securities Regulation

Neoclassical economic theory has criticized the federal securities regulation scheme by alleging the sufficiency of private information incentives and the redundancy of disclosure rules in efficient capital markets. The following sections question the validity of these arguments.

317, (K. Hopt & G. Teubner eds., Berlin/New York 1985); BRESSER & KIRCHNER, "Reformansätze für eine Verwaltungskontrolle von Grossunternehmen," 22 *AG* 145 (1977).

[106] For more details see VAGTS, "Challenges to Executive Compensation: For the Markets or the Courts?," 8 *J. Corp. L.* 231, 236 ff (1983); BRUDNEY, *supra* note 52, at 1421 ff; COFFEE, "Shareholders v. Managers: The Strain in the Corporate Web," 85 *Mich. L. Rev.* 1, 74 ff (1986). But see also FISCHEL, "Labor Markets and Labor Law Compared with Capital Markets and Corporate Law," 51 *U. Chi. L. Rev.* 1061, 1065 ff (1984).

[107] The most profound analysis of corporate governance and the control market is still COFFEE, *supra* note 99, at 1199 ff. See also W. KLEIN & J. COFFEE, *Business Organization and Finance* 165 ff (3d ed., New York 1990); BUXBAUM, "Corporate Legitimacy, Economic Theory and Legal Doctrine," 45 *Ohio St. L.J.* 515, 526 ff (1984). For a critical review of the "pruning deadwood" thesis see E. HERMAN, *Corporate Control, Corporate Power* 98 ff (New York 1981); BEBCHUK, "The Case for Facilitating Competing Tender Offers," 95 *Harv. L. Rev.* 1028, 1033 ff (1982); LOWENSTEIN, "'Pruning Deadwood' in Hostile Takeovers: A Proposal for Legislation," 83 *Colum. L. Rev.* 249, 288 ff (1983). A European restatement and assessment can be found in MEIER-SCHATZ, "Managermacht und Marktkontrolle," 149 *ZHR* 76, 95 ff (1985); MEIER-SCHATZ, "Unternehmenszusammenschlüsse mittels Übernahmeangebot," 39 *WuR* 16, 33 ff (1987).

a. Voluntary Disclosure

It is true that management, especially that of capital market oriented firms, has remarkable incentives for a voluntary disclosure policy.[108] Nevertheless, corporate data are not a normal private good; no market can produce an optimal output of this material. Two external factors distort private information production. Firstly, investors can use data about a firm without finally investing in it. This may occur in connection with broader shopping activities[109] or with the use of general information on the industry itself.[110] Secondly, firms' specific data may be helpful for the production decisions of competitors.[111] Both forms of externalities produce free-rider effects: not all beneficiaries of the firm's data have to pay for them.[112] These free-riders, as always, have a negative impact on private information production. Individual corporations do not disclose enough data on a voluntary basis as long as no mandatory disclosure rules guarantee that *all* firms have to make the same information available.[113]

In addition, the arguments of the dominating signaling and agency theories are seriously flawed. Because of "proprietary costs," firms may have rational motives to retain even positive information. If investors don't interpret "no news" always as "bad news," the crucial stimulus for an ongoing voluntary disclosure becomes questionable.[114] Accordingly, the private incentive mechanism of the signaling theory breaks down. The agency theory underestimates the realm of discretion left to management by accounting practices. Management may, at least in a short-term perspective, rationally be inclined to manipulate the information along the lines of own interests.[115]

[108] They go back to its professional as well as personal interest in high securities prices. See, e.g., KRIPKE, *supra* note 65, at 123 ff; WOLFSON, *supra* note 54, at 132; STEVENSON, *supra* note 43, at 87 ff.

[109] See STEVENSON, *supra* note 43, at 87; BEAVER, "The Nature of Mandatory Disclosure," in SEC Disclosure Report, *supra* note 72, at 627 ff.

[110] See also CLARK, *supra* note 11, at 758 ff; EASTERBROOK & FISCHEL, *supra* note 68, at 685 ff.

[111] Some authors qualify these externalities as "spillover" effects. *Cf.* EASTERBROOK & FISCHEL, *supra* note 68, at 686. See (with a similar analysis) BENSTON, *supra* note 43, at 142; MANNE, *supra* note 47, at 37; STEVENSON, *supra* note 43, at 87; SELIGMAN, *supra* note 33, at 251; CLARK, *supra* note 11, at 759.

[112] The fundamental theoretical argument that the theory of externalities and spillovers may be helpful to determine necessity and level of governmental regulation has also been supported by FITCHEW, *supra* at 2.

[113] BEAVER, *supra* note 109, at 626 ff; STEVENSON, *supra* note 43, at 87; EASTERBROOK & FISCHEL, *supra* note 52, at 686; BENSTON, *supra* note 43, at 142.

[114] Such a "proprietary cost" approach has been developed by VERRECCHIA, "Discretionary Disclosure," 5 *J. Acc. & Econ.* 179 (1983). With similar thoughts EASTERBROOK & FISCHEL, *supra* note 68, at 687 ff.

[115] For a more detailed critique see MEIER-SCHATZ, *supra* note 10, at 175 f.

b. Disclosure and Efficient Capital Markets

The argument that efficient capital markets make mandatory federal disclosure rules redundant can be questioned on two grounds. On the one hand, only about 10% of the corporations registered under the Securities Exchange Act are regularly followed by analysts; for the remaining 90% the market is presumably less efficient.[116] The widely cited studies of market efficiency rely largely on the New York Stock Exchange. Whether their efficiency assessments can be extended to other "submarkets," in particular to the over-the-counter market and other stock exchanges, seems doubtful.[117] Federal disclosure requirements may improve the allocation of capital resources in these submarkets because public information does not always reach them in advance of the mandatory disclosure data.[118]

On the other hand, there are good reasons to believe that disclosure regulation has a beneficial impact even on efficient capital markets. It reduces the costs for information intermediaries (especially analysts), and thereby increases the aggregate amount of securities research.[119] The regulation also collectivizes securities data and diminishes wasteful duplication of parallel search activities in the market.[120] Overall costs of information gathering and analysis are reduced when legally required standards allow investors or intermediaries a quicker and less expensive evaluation of securities and increase the informational value of (comparable) financial statements.[121] Mandatory disclosure rules may also operate as a check on previously disseminated data, thereby enhancing the quality of corporate

[116] See COFFEE, "Market Failure and the Economic Case for a Mandatory Disclosure System," 70 *Va. L. Rev.* 717, 731 ff (1984). *Cf.* also SEC Disclosure Report, *supra* note 72, at XVIII ff. What follows is a summary of MEIER-SCHATZ, "Objectives of Financial Disclosure Regulation," 8 *J. Comp. Bus. & Cap. Mkt. L.* 219, 224 ff (1986).

[117] BARRY, "The Economics of Outside Information and Rule 10b-5," 129 *U. Pa. L. Rev.* 1307, 1348 ff (1981). FIFLIS, "Economic Analysis as One Phase of Utilitarianism," in *Corporations at the Crossroad: Governance and Reform* 70, 93 (New York 1980). *Cf.* also W. BEAVER, *Financial Reporting: An Accounting Revolution* 154 ff (Englewood 1981).

[118] *Cf.* BARRY, *supra* note 117, at 150 ff.

[119] See the excellent analysis of COFFEE, *supra* note 116, at 725 ff (with review of the relevant literature).

[120] See, e.g., EASTERBROOK & FISCHEL, *supra* note 68, at 681 ff; STEVENSON, *supra* note 43, at 87 ff; COFFEE, *supra* note 116, at 733 ff.

[121] The advantages of standardized financial statements are frequently stressed in the European literature. See, e.g., SCHMIDT, "Rechnungslegung als Informationsproduktion auf nahezu effizienten Kapitalmärkten," *ZfbF* 728, 746 ff (1982). For the American literature *cf.* BENSTON, *supra* note 43, at 142.

information.[122] Finally, disclosure rules can promote the capital formation process itself by increasing investor confidence in the capital market.[123]

c. Disclosure Rules and Federalism

So far, no serious call for a federalist concept of securities regulation or of disclosure rules has arisen. This may not surprise anyone who is familiar with the history and status quo of state disclosure schemes. Corporation codes never had and still haven't any significant information and accounting provisions.[124] Only blue sky laws require firms selling securities in the state to disclose material data. Yet they have since faced endless enforcement problems with respect to nonresidents.[125] All this has led to an universal consensus that, if mandatory governmental disclosure rules are beneficial to investors, they need to be established at federal level. Stringent theoretical arguments for such a conclusion, however, remain hardly articulated, although the reasons are quite obvious. The interstate nature[126] of modern securities markets, and the inability to confine the effects of disclosure rules to the enacting state elicit the need for federal regulation.[127]

Depending upon the implementation concept, a state competition system may under- or overproduce disclosure provisions. If they are prescribed for firms incorporated in the state, burdens weigh exclusively on resident corporations (inviting them to migrate) while benefits are reaped by all investors including nonresidents. Those third party effects produce a regulatory disincentive for states which may only be overcome by federal intervention.[128] If information requirements are established for securities sold in the state, then the situation becomes exactly inverse. All resident

[122] This confirmation effect is discussed in the United States as well as in Europe. See MENDELSON, "Economics and the Assessment of Disclosure Requirements," 1 *J. Comp. Corp. L. & Sec. Reg.* 49, 55 (1978); SEC Disclosure Report, *supra* note 72, at XLVI; SCHMIDT, *supra* note 121, at 746; REUTER, *Aktienmarkt und Aktieninformationsmarkt* 148 ff (Göttingen 1980).

[123] The argument still plays an important role in the European capital market law debate. See KOCH & SCHMIDT, "Ziele und Instrumente des Anlegerschutzes," 33 *BFuP* 231, 236 (1981); KÜBLER, "Transparenz am Kapitalmarkt," 22 *AG* 85, 88 (1977). For the contemporary American debate *cf.* EASTERBROOK & FISCHEL, *supra* note 68, at 692 ff; SELIGMAN, *supra* note 22, at 51 ff.

[124] See, e.g., the critical assessment of CONARD, *supra* note 18, at 66 ff.

[125] Historical comments stress again and again that state rules were (and are) ineffective because states are unable to reach residents of other states. SELIGMAN, *supra* note 22, at 21; SELIGMAN, *supra* note 33, at 45 ff; SARGENT, *supra* note 40, at 793.

[126] EASTERBROOK & FISCHEL, *supra* note 68, at 697.

[127] It is self-evident that the effectiveness of state competition depends, *inter alia*, upon the extent to which consequences of one jurisdiction's rules are felt within that jurisdiction. See EASTERBROOK, *supra* note 75, at 34. Generally on the role of spillover effects ROSE-ACKERMAN, *supra* note 19, at 154 ff.

[128] The connection between third party effects and state competition is also emphasized by EASTERBROOK & FISCHEL, *supra* note 68, at 697.

investors are protected while the costs are born by nonresident firms and shareholders alike. This disequilibrium induces excessive state disclosure regulation; a federal regime may indeed be the only way "to prevent states from engaging in exploitation of securities transactions."[129]

B. Empirical Studies

Empirical studies have become an influential factor in the American debate on federalism in corporate and capital market law. Quantitative data are referred to support at least four relevant hypotheses. With respect to corporation law, empirical evidence is relied upon to show both the beneficial effects of state law competition and the effectiveness of management control by markets.[130] Securities regulation and disclosure rules have come under attack by both empirical stock price studies and market efficiency tests.[131]

Many of these sophisticated analyses have been instructive and illuminating, but on the whole they lack consistency and harbor severe methodological problems. This can be shown on the basis of the our most influential test topics.

1. Corporation Law

a. Empirical studies of the *market for corporate charters* did not achieve homogeneous results. While an early test diagnosed generally beneficial effects,[132] a more recent study found statistically relevant positive outcome for only a specific corporate transaction.[133] Other studies produced plain counterevidence.[134] The methodology of these studies is undercut by the phenomenon of noise. If reincorporation decisions are indeed made in view of certain transactions, then stock prices may be influenced by the market's evaluation of these transactions rather than of the migration itself.[135] Moreover, often the public does not know in advance why management wants to change the corporate domicile. Some shareholders then may view reincorporation, whether rightly or wrongly, as a positive sign (e.g., anticipation of an acquisition), while colleagues can read it as a negative symptom (e.g., anticipation of a defensive maneuver). "Either way, they may overreact and the result could be statistical noise if other shareholders

[129] EASTERBROOK & FISCHEL, *supra* note 68, at 698.
[130] *Cf.* the literature quoted in notes 52 and 58 *supra.*
[131] *Cf.* the literature quoted in note 62 *supra.*
[132] DODD & LEFTWICH, *supra* note 58.
[133] ROMANO, *supra* note 58, at 265 ff.
[134] WEISS & WHITE (*supra* note 59, at 602) read their empirical results as allowing the overall conclusion that investors do not care about corporate law regimes at all.
[135] Similarly MACEY & MILLER, *supra* note 57, at 482.

view the reincorporation differently."[136] Additional methodological flaws include skewed samples[137] and uncertain relative measurement standards.[138] Such variables lead to a strong warning against overinclusive normative deductions. Most advanced transactional research does not allow the systematic determination of the beneficiary of an entire legal regime changed by migration.[139] Furthermore, a disaggregated analysis and a prediction as to whether *specific* rules are good or bad for shareholders are even more difficult.[140]

b. Empirical research supporting the sufficient effectiveness of *management control by markets* suffers from similar deficiencies. Particularly illuminating flaws mark the stock price tests underlying the "pruning deadwood" hypothesis and the theory of the market for corporate control.[141] Alternative accounting and other studies have brought conflicting results.[142] The supposed takeovers of firms under bad management by firms under good management face remarkable counterevidence.[143] Noise problems reappear in the methodology, since the price tests are unable to isolate external factors relevant for certain sectors and industries.[144] As to a normative assessment, the conclusion seems inevitable that the sources of financial gains and hence the motives of hostile takeovers cannot be

[136] COFFEE, *supra* note 36, at 767.

[137] The sample may be skewed because firms which reincorporate have probably growth rates and earnings above average which make them more ambitious and takeover oriented. Moreover, the studies conducted in the early 1980s may not be representative since during this period the Delaware case law appeared to be relatively stringent while the statutory law was still very lax. With more details COFFEE, *supra* note 36, at 768.

[138] All empirical studies suffer from the fact that they measure only the relative difference between Delaware and other states. They can, therefore, only determine this margin and not "the total distance that this state competition took us from the legal regime that would result without such competition." COFFEE, *supra* note 36, at 768.

[139] Accord ROMANO, *supra* note 8, at 719; MACEY & MILLER, *supra* note 57, at 482.

[140] See also WEISS & WHITE, *supra* note 59, at 560 ff.

[141] The same is basically true for the manager market. Advanced quantitative analyses were unable to show a systematic connection between success of the enterprise and managerial changes. See BRUDNEY, *supra* note 52, at 1423 (surveying the most recent empirical studies). With a similar conclusion VAGTS, *supra* note 106, at 273.

[142] See the survey in COFFEE, *supra* note 99, at 1207 ff. *Cf.* also the analytical results of LOWENSTEIN, *supra* note 107, at 289 ff.

[143] An analysis of the available empirical evidence is provided by HERMAN, *supra* note 107, at 100; HERMAN, "The Limits of the Market as a Discipline in Corporate Governance," 9 *Del. J. Corp. L.* 530, 536 (1984).

[144] COFFEE, *supra* note 99, at 211 ff. *Cf.* also the methodological reservations in LOWENSTEIN, *supra* note 107, at 289 ff; JENSEN & RUBACK, *supra* note 52, at 23 ff.

identified empirically. Accordingly, it is far from certain that these acquisitions indeed occur to sanction inefficient management.[145]

2. Securities Regulation

The empirical evidence which grounded the theoretical redundancy of mandatory disclosure rules is likewise insufficient. The stock price studies on the *effects of disclosure rules* produced ambiguous results which have been invoked by both proponents and opponents of a governmental information regime.[146] An exclusive reliance on statistical figures of financial returns restricts their explanatory power.[147] When such tests compare pre- and post-1933/34 markets, they are not compelling because the institutional structures of capital markets have changed considerably since the enactment of the securities acts.[148] Those interpretive and methodological problems have caused recent commentators to balk at hasty normative implications. While some doubt any direct relationship between price effects and the value of information provisions,[149] others go so far as to maintain that[150]

> "there may not be any accurate method to ascertain the gross benefits of mandatory disclosure today other than by abandoning some or all of the disclosure system and observing the long term effects."

Finally, the *efficient capital market hypothesis* itself, which had an undisputedly strong empirical support within its own conceptual premises, is plagued by analogous problems. While some previous studies had presented disturbing counterevidence,[151] more recent and more important research has

[145] These empirical uncertainties and inconsistencies are even admitted by commentators sympathetic to the neoclassical school. See, e.g., JENSEN & RUBACK, *supra* note 52, at 24 ff. *Cf.* in addition HERMAN, *supra* note 143, at 536; HERMAN, *supra* note 107, at 100.

[146] An overview of the conflicting literature can be found in MEIER-SCHATZ, *supra* note 10, at 201 ff. A comprehensive restatement of the discussion is provided by MENDELSON, *supra* note 122, at 49 ff.

[147] See the extensive comments of EASTERBROOK & FISCHEL, *supra* note 68, at 709 ff; GILSON & KRAAKMAN, "The Mechanism of Market Efficiency," 70 *Va. L. Rev.* 549, 636 ff (1984). *Cf.* also CLARK, *supra* note 11, at 759 ff; COFFEE, *supra* note 116, at 734 ff.

[148] Some of the relevant factors are listed in GILSON & KRAAKMAN, *supra* note 147, at 640 ff. *Cf.* also COFFEE, *supra* note 116, at 744.

[149] "In sum, the absence of price effects is not necessarily an indictment of a regulation, and the presence of price effects is not sufficient to confirm the value of the regulation." BEAVER, *supra* note 117, at 169 ff.

[150] GILSON & KRAAKMAN, *supra* note 147, at 641. A skeptical assessment of the potential of empirical studies can also be found in STEVENSON, *supra* note 43, at 86.

[151] They are presented in BEAVER, *supra* note 117, at 157 ff; GORDON & KORNHAUSER, "Efficient Markets, Costal Information and Securities Research," in University of Toronto School of Law, Working Paper 1983, 37 ff.

revealed a series of new anomalies difficult to reconcile with the basic hypothesis.[152] Furthermore, the unreliability of the underlying Capital Asset Pricing Model impairs the methodology in these studies.[153] The whole hypothesis (in its semi-strong form) also remains open-ended and circular as long as there is no precise perception of what information is publicly available.[154] Reservations against premature normative implications are again more significant than all the cracks in the conceptual framework. As has been shortly sketched, disclosure rules may indeed have a beneficial impact even in efficient capital markets. Such an assessment corroborates the work of Prof. *Beaver* who concludes[155] that even

> "the concept of market efficiency [is] by itself not sufficiently rich to warrant inferences regarding institutional structure."

C. Conclusion

The US experience elucidates the relationship between economic theory and legal doctrine in general and in the particular field of corporate and capital market law. This relationship is now one of the focal issues of modern economic law in which factual settings, as the regulatory substratum, have become increasingly differentiated and complex. To reduce precisely this complexity, legislators and courts alike search continuously for explicative models which offer theoretically "plausible" and normatively "applicable" solutions.[156] Modern neoclassical economic theory, with its persistent efficiency goals and its straightforward *laissez-faire* approach, offers such solutions, and thereby appears especially attractive for implementation into the legal doctrine.[157]

Yet American developments teach an important lesson about the limits of such a direct application of economic theory to legal doctrine in federalism

[152] See the studies listed in COFFEE, *supra* note 116, at 719 note 10; GILSON & KRAAKMAN, *supra* note 147, at 551 note 10. *Cf.* also generally WANG, "Some Arguments that the Stock Market Is Not Efficient," 19 *UCD L. Rev.* 34 (1986).

[153] Some pretend that this model is simply not testable while others criticize the questionable figure to assess efficiency. See, for the German literature, e.g., SCHMIDT, *supra* note 121, at 733; D. SCHNEIDER, *Investition und Finanzierung* 552 (Opladen 1980). *Cf.* also GORDON & KORNHAUSER, *supra* note 151, at 41 ff. Relevant literature of financial theory can also be found in BARRY, *supra* note 117, at 1349 note 160; COFFEE, *supra* note 116, at 719 note 10.

[154] See for more details SCHNEIDER, *supra* note 153, at 555 ff; BEAVER, *supra* note 117, at 146. *Cf.* also GILSON & KRAAKMAN, *supra* note 147, at 557 ff.

[155] BEAVER, *supra* note 117, at 169.

[156] For similar conclusions in another context see MEIER-SCHATZ, *supra* note 10, at 207 ff.

[157] See also the critical comments by BUXBAUM, *supra* note 11, at 280; BRUDNEY, *supra* note 52, at 1427 ff. *Cf.* also (more explicitly and with examples) BUXBAUM, *supra* note 107, at 517 ff.

and corporate as well as capital market law.[158] An exclusive efficiency-oriented model cannot capture the richness and complexity of institutional realities of market mechanisms, political processes, and business entities.[159] The inherent boundaries of economic theory and empirical evidence underline these limitations.

Regarding the federalist question,[160] competition between state rules has had from the outset a relatively narrow suitability framework. Regulatory rivalry promises to work only when effects of rules can be well confined to the individual states. As the US experience in the field of disclosure rules shows, significant spillover effects may lead to a suboptimal over- or underproduction of state provisions. But as may be the case with enabling structural rules under an incorporation principle, even when the congruence between enacting state and territorial impacts may be substantial, four important limits of the market for corporate charters remain. Firstly, the functioning of the competitive process itself is uncertain. Secondly, no evidence defines whether shareholders are always the beneficiaries of the competitive outcome. Moreover, there are obvious agency problems also with respect to management's reincorporation decisions. Finally, recent experiences with state takeover laws offer a model case of strong anecdotal counterevidence.

A European point of view necessitates further discussion of the connection between state law competition and regulatory goals. If, as in the United States, corporate law and securities regulation obey a principle of regulatory division of powers,[161] i.e., are dominated exclusively by shareholder and investor interests, competition among various enabling state provisions may lead to beneficial results. Yet European company laws often have a broader social policy mandate to integrate concerns of creditors, workers or a broader general public. As soon as such other values come into play, a federal solution becomes practically inevitable.[162] The American experience

[158] Negligence of institutional realities and deficiencies of mere efficiency considerations are also criticized in COFFEE, *supra* note 116, at 746; FIFLIS, *supra* note 117, at 80 ff; MANNING, "State Competition: Panel Response," 8 *Cardozo L. Rev.* 782, 783 (1987).

[159] European legal scholars are as the Lugano Symposium itself has revealed much more skeptical with respect to economic theories' significance for and impact on legal doctrine. *Cf.*, e.g., TUNC, *supra* at 24; FITCHEW, *supra* at 1ff. In addition, European economists are often reluctant to promise significant guidance for legal questions, particularly in the field of harmonization. See SCHMIDT, *supra* at 59.

[160] The following qualifications confirm in many respects SCHMIDT's conclusion (see *supra* at 59) that economic theory does not provide much help regarding the question of optimal allocation of regulatory authorities.

[161] *Cf.* text accompanying notes 10-11 and 38 *supra*.

[162] This diagnosis coincides entirely with the conclusion of BUXBAUM & HOPT, *supra* note 1, at 273, that harmonization by state competition functions best in the area of enabling law without involvement of broader public policy considerations. The problems of a market model in a company law environment characterized

indicates that distributive justice goals cannot be realized by decentralized competitive systems.[163]

Other appealing hypotheses of modern economic theory have their weaknesses as well. Market mechanisms, as far as they monitor management behavior at all, suffer from many structural deficiencies and functional problems. Voluntary disclosure incentives alone cannot prevent a systematic underproduction of corporate data, and mandatory information rules have positive effects even within efficient capital markets. Finally, the much-quoted empirical evidence is not yet mature enough to support the underlying hypotheses. The results themselves are frequently inconsistent. In addition, the tests are troubled by substantial methodological problems. Finally (and perhaps most importantly), the empirical findings are often followed by overreaching normative conclusions.

by broader public policy concerns has been emphasized during the Lugano Symposium. *Cf.*, e.g., TIMMERMANS, *infra* at 29 ff.

[163] See generally ROSE-ACKERMAN, *supra* note 19, at 158, 162 ff. *Cf.* also (with reference to the fiscal federalism theory) BUXBAUM, *supra* note 11, at 287.

B. Discussion

I. Introductory Remarks

Edmund Kitch

As I understand the role that Prof. Buxbaum had in mind for me, he hoped that I might argue clearly and cleanly the position that economic models could be used to lead to the conclusion that the choice of local jurisdictional competence would always result in a superior set of legal arrangements and he could then beat me roundly about the head for such a position. I do not have that view, although I think it is important to recognize that there are values in jurisdictional competition, and both the papers on the use of economics[1] and the *Buxbaum* and *Hopt* book itself[2] are pretty much in agreement on that point.

You do not get decisive answers to these questions from economic models. There seems to be a consensus on that and I think it is correct, although perhaps unproductive of a lively argument. Economics does not have much at all to say about these questions. What it does say is that one must think of legislating jurisdictions as if they were firms competing in a "market" of legal regimes with a product ("their law"), and then analogize to the economics of firm size in industrial product markets.

Actually, although economics has clearly long been interested in the question of firm size, economists do not have a lot to say about firm size even in industrial product markets. They can point to the factors which will dictate firm size, which turn out to be cost factors. They can say that the efficient scale of a firm will vary depending upon the activities of the firm and the technology of production, but they would not be very good at predicting the optimum size for particular firms in particular industries. Indeed, they would tend to fall back on the position that the observed firm sizes would over time be the best source of information about what is the optimum firm size.

If you apply that approach in the legal context, you tend to come back to the conclusion that whatever is must be the optimum, unless change is taking place, which would be evidence that there is something about it that is not optimum. That does not provide very much normative power.

[1] See *supra* at 35 ff, 51 ff and 61 ff.

[2] R.M. BUXBAUM & K.J. HOPT, *Legal Harmonization and the Business Enterprise* e.g. at 272 ff (Berlin/New York 1988).

In my paper,[3] I tried to set the problem of harmonization in a larger context and indicate that one of the difficulties for analyses of these questions is that the magnitudes are small. In light of some of the other comments that have been made and particularly Mr. Fitchew's comments,[4] I want to clarify a bit what I mean by that. I find as the seat of the pants matter that Fitchew's suggestion[5] that this programme might produce an increase in economic activity of the order of 5% which would not otherwise have occurred, is perfectly consistent with what I think might be correct. Then the question becomes, if you were to accept that very rough and seat-of-the-pants estimate, whether 5% is large or small. From many perspectives, I think it is easy to see that it is small. Capitalist economies display a rather robust ability to produce economic growth around 1-4% a year (2% a year is not uncommon); so if your total gain is 5%, you are talking about being somewhere between 18, 24, 36 months ahead of where you otherwise would have been had you not had the programme. At least from my present position in life, 24 months seems to me a fairly short period of time.

So, in some sense, I think it is perfectly reasonable to describe it as small. On the other hand, it is also, it seems to me, very large; that is, the work of the world is accomplished by all sorts of small "things" and, in fact, the ability to capture say 5% of economic growth that would not otherwise have been available is a unique, rare and very good opportunity. However, when we turn back to the academic literature and the theoretical question, these are magnitudes that are small in the sense that they escape the measurement powers of any social science; that is, 5% shifts in social behavior are not big enough to be picked out with any type of econometric or statistical study. They are the sorts of phenomenon which, although in fact very important, will get lost in the statistical noise and just won't show up in the studies. Therefore, it is beyond hope to get any clean demonstration in an empirical sense that we are clearly better off along one road rather than the other one.

I also think it is important from a larger perspective to keep in mind that it is not necessary to commit the economic harmonization programme of an organization like the Common Market to a programme of market liberalism. Where you enlarge the economic scope of a governing body, it carries with it the possibility and the opportunities for various kinds of market interventions, which can in an economic sense be even more harmful than those that were ever within the potential power of the Member States. Although I think that the national government in the United States has, on the whole over its history, a fairly good record as being a protector of open and liberal markets, it has also engaged in some activities which have been quite abusive of that principle and it has the potential power to do far more

[3] See *supra* at 36 ff.
[4] See *supra* at 5 ff.
[5] See *supra* at 6.

damage to the American economy than the States do. So it is a matter of continuing statesmanship or political statesmanship or political management, if you will, that the power which comes with size is used constructively.

Hartmut Schmidt

I will also try to stick to the spirit of the letter you wrote to us, asking us to restrict our opening statements to 4-5 minutes. My assignment as I understood it may be expressed by two related questions. First: what guidance can economics provide as to scope, intensity, etc., of legal harmonization? Second: will the answer to the first question have a specific European touch to it if it is given by a European and not by an American?

Let me deal with the second question first. I am a pupil of Wolfgang Stützel and he used to say: "Economics is always world economics." This in principle settles the second question. Of course, an American will use different works of reference and this may lead to a specific American flavour, but the bottom line will be about the same. Economic conclusions should be quite similar. I have no reason to reject this thesis after reading Prof. Kitch's paper. He draws conclusions similar to mine. Let me state a few of these. As Prof. Kitch just mentioned, any welfare effects of legal harmonization are likely to be small. Second: economic analysis will get nowhere unless one selects a proxy for welfare. He did not say so, but he used cost-benefit analysis and this means that he excludes any distributional effects. Third: there is at work a harmonization by market which I contrasted with harmonization by bureaucracy, and this harmonization by market is based mainly on approximation pressure from abroad. In general terms, it is based on choices available to businesses and you may call it in "Fitchew language"[6] the fear-and-greed mechanism. Fourth: a regulatory system should be designed in a way that provides for competition among regulators. We touched on this and I think this conclusion also flows from the fact that we have competing models in social sciences. Since nobody is in possession of the true model in many areas, nobody can say what is the best regulatory system.

Of course I do not agree with all of Prof. Kitch's arguments. For example, he explains[7] that the major innovations in securities trading have come from the commodities exchanges. I myself would first point to the Maloney Act and to the exchange competition provided within the framework of the Securities Exchange Act of 1934. And I do not share the views of some of you, expressed in various papers, that this came about by accident or by quirk of history. I think there were all these reasonable persons around and they may not have laid down the reasons why they voted for a certain piece of legislation, but I would grant them a lot of common sense; for example,

[6] See *supra* at 17.
[7] See *supra* at 47.

when the Maloney Bill was voted on, which brought about the NASD, they realized the need for an additional power base in the securities markets field if there was to be progress. We have seen this in the United Kingdom too. There are a number of self-regulatory organizations, they will engage in some competition and move the industry up.

I also admire the ability of Prof. Kitch[8] and others to comment on the proper allocation of corporation law, securities law, antitrust law, labor law and what you have to the State or federal level. I could not do this. I believe in clause-by-clause analysis. If you go through a piece of legislation you may say: "This clause is properly allocated but the next one may not be." And the first clause may be soundly based and another clause may not be.

Anyway, in spite of these differences at the bottom line there are obvious similarities.

The question of economic guidance is the main question and is quite a bone to chew on. There is some literature, but it does not seem to be firmly based. I therefore decided to start from scratch and I tried to make it very clear that an economist may come up with a very strong and clear-cut answer to the main question if he is prepared to pass a lot of judgements as he carries his analysis forward. I did not get that far because I was not prepared to make more than three value judgements. Number one: regulators prefer welfare gains now to welfare gains later. Second: regulators are concerned with efficiency, not with distribution effects. Third: the economy is dynamic, that is, needs and technology do change. These are the three judgements and from this basis I have drawn my conclusions. My main conclusion is that the regulatory system must be conducive to prompt progress and law.

One related question that I did not dare to address and which Prof. Kitch also brought up only during this discussion,[9] is the question of the optimal size of regulators. If you equate for a moment countries and regulators, my guess would be that countries like the US, France or Italy are too large. Luxembourg, Denmark or the Netherlands may have the right size. Let me close with two reasons for my guess.

First, innovative regulation by a large country may be such a threat to major powers that it cannot be tolerated. The threat of innovative regulation by a country like Luxembourg is fairly limited because her resources are rather limited. She has got a lot of banks but she obviously cannot have all the banks within the Community. She just does not have the population to provide all the financial services of Europe. Half of the Luxembourg workforce is already employed in banking and most of the rest is probably catering to it.

Secondly, the incentive and the ability to maintain an attractive regulatory environment seem to be stronger for countries that are rather small. This

[8] See *supra* at 42 ff.
[9] See *supra* at 89 ff.

appears to be in line with the Romano hostage argument reported by Prof. Kitch.[10]

This perspective suggests that oversized regulators will tend to employ outdated regulation in many fields. But this may not be as bad as it appears at first sight. If the oversized regulators jointly (as in the Cooke Committee) and belatedly follow the lead of the innovators, this may reduce threat and fear and it may contribute to a reasonably stable and peaceful world.

Christian Meier-Schatz

Let me begin with two clarifications as to my background and assignment. I am neither a specialist in EC law nor a trained economist. I am merely a legal scholar who is interested in economic theory and its application in the legal field as well as limitations as regards the legal doctrine. Moreover, my assignment was not so much directed towards economics and EC law but was meant to provide a critical evaluation of recent American developments from a European point of view.

Accordingly, my first problem was to define what might be instructive and illuminating from a particular European perspective. Two elements are, in my view, worth emphasizing. The first relates to somewhat opposite trends regarding centralization versus decentralization in company and capital market law. In the EC, we face a very clear trend towards federal law. Mr. Fitchew has also stressed[11] that the Commission intends to go on in that direction. In the US, however, I perceive a rather opposite tendency towards defederalization. On the one hand, important Supreme Court decisions have recently been strongly stressing and protecting State authorities and State rights. On the other hand, powerful and influential academic commentators have been defending the State regime in the corporate law area or even attacking the securities law scheme at the federal level.

The second element I thought interesting to look at is the fact that the status quo of theoretical (especially economic) foundation and discourse is quite different in the EC and in the US. As far as the EC is concerned, many (including participants in this seminar) have bemoaned the relatively poor theoretical foundation of legal rules whereas in the US an immense body of literature has been created, especially in the area of corporate law and securities regulation. I am thinking, for instance, of the whole body of microeconomic theories but also of the broad fields of the theory of finance.

If I take up the first subject of my analysis under such a comparative aspect, it is important to know that the status quo of US law is, as I mentioned in my paper,[12] rather the result of very particular historical developments than of a rational conceptual outline. Here I disagree, from a

[10] See *supra* at 44.
[11] See e.g. *supra* at 18.
[12] See *supra* at 63 ff.

historical point of view, slightly with what has just been said.[13] This historical contingency relates to the allocation of regulatory authorities as well as to the content of the rules themselves. In that context, I found very interesting the remark of Prof. Kitch[14] that the historical starting point is a decisive and important factor in judging the question of whether to change a legal regime. With respect to economic theory, we saw in the US a very sophisticated academic discourse. Yet it did not have any immediate impact on the basic regulatory schemes. Some influence may be felt – Prof. Buxbaum has mentioned a couple of instances[15] – but the main elements of the regulatory structures have been maintained without an underlying sophisticated economic theory. Here again a historical comparison with EC law is interesting because at the time of the formation of the regulatory framework, the US legislators were working on a relatively weak theoretical basis as well. Accordingly, we may face a similar historical configuration in the sense that the arrival of an advanced economic theory came at a relatively late stage in the legislative development.

As to my second topic relating to the issue of whether economic theory did help solve legal questions, I have to emphasize that I am talking here, in accordance with my assignment, exclusively about the American experience. I have mentioned the extremely rich body of sophisticated economic literature in the US.[16] Although most of these writings are quite new, they make extremely far-reaching explicative and normative claims. This is again particularly true for microeconomic theories and the theory of finance. They, of course, led to an interesting tension between old historically contingent rules and new theoretical insights.

As you have already seen from my paper,[17] my main hypothesis and overall assessment is that one has to be rather skeptical with respect to the functional value of modern economics for legal doctrine. Here I agree fully with specialists in the field as to the significant limits of economic theory, both in terms of overoptimistic analytical expectations and of overinclusive normative implications.

So let me then very briefly list the most important theoretical issues and problems. Probably the most interesting topic for our purposes relates to the arguments calling for an active market for corporate charters. Four points, already outlined in my paper,[18] can be made in order to elaborate on this theoretically fascinating concept. To begin with, competition among legislators is obviously something quite different from competition among firms. The US experience teaches a clear and illuminating lesson as to the structural deficiencies of the competitive process. For instance, the tax-and-

[13] See *supra* at 91.
[14] See *supra* at 41.
[15] See *supra* at 21.
[16] See *supra* at 62.
[17] See *supra* at 74 ff.
[18] See *supra* at 74 ff.

fee motivation appears to have been significantly overestimated. In addition, there is some kind of an oligopolistic market with Delaware playing a very strong market-leader role. Secondly, we do not have – despite excellent new research particularly by Prof. Romano (mentioned already by Prof. Kitch[19]) – conclusive results as to whether indeed shareholders or management benefit from this market for corporate charters. A third factor which has been, in my opinion, neglected or at least underestimated by promoters of the market for corporate charters is the agency cost issue. There is a very severe agency cost problem in reincorporation decisions which are, in my opinion, not sufficiently controlled by markets. Finally, we have one significant problem which intellectually remains unsolved, namely the existence of restrictive State takeover laws. Even very convinced promoters of the corporate charter market admit that we probably do not have optimal results in this regulatory field. Theoretically even more important is the fact that this area of State takeover cannot convincingly be distinguished from other areas of corporate law. This problem is also quite important for the EC discussion – and we might come back to it in connection with Prof. Timmermans' paper[20] – because the Community also faces the question whether it should, as a matter of policy, try to implement more of a market for corporate charters, for instance by introducing some sort of a (mandatory) incorporation principle.

A second field in which economic theory has played a major role is corporate disclosure. I would like to touch this topic only under the aspect of federalism. I tend to believe that we have quite good theoretical arguments not only for disclosure rules in general but also for an allocation of regulatory authorities at the federal level. For there are considerable spillover effects and externalities in connection with State legislation which call very strongly for a federal regime. This can best be shown by the two regulatory approaches which historically have been followed in the US. One is a disclosure regime for companies incorporated in a particular State. Here you face clearly a tendency towards an underproduction of disclosure rules because only State corporations pay the costs, whereas all the rest of the corporate and financial community can benefit. On the other hand, disclosure rules based on securities sold in the individual State trigger an inverse incentive scheme because all State residents benefit when costs are also paid by external companies. And that then probably leads to an excessive production of disclosure rules.

Let me close with this final conclusion regarding disclosure and federalism. The foregoing remarks reveal that we have, beyond the capital market promotion and Scitovsky model of higher competition, a second theoretical argument for allocating authority for disclosure rules at the federal level, namely negative externalities in a decentralized system. And this may also

[19] See *supra* at 44.
[20] See *infra* at 153 ff.

be an important insight we can get from economics and the US debate for the ongoing EC discussion.

II. Level of Regulation and Competition Among Regulators

A. Global Supervision

Klaus Hopt

I would like to address a problem which concerns all of us. Mr. Fitchew has rightly mentioned the possible instances where only global supervision would be adequate.[21] I mean worldwide supervision. This may be a long way ahead. I wonder what should be done in the meantime. If we define something as needing global supervision, what would be the best place for it in the meantime: would it *eo ipso* be better to have the matter at least at a regional, i.e., the federal level in the EC, or rather to leave it where it is right now and to attack global regulation directly and immediately without an intermediate stopover in Brussels?

Alain Hirsch

I would like to take up the question put to all of us by Klaus Hopt. It is related to Mr. Fitchew's remark[22] in the case of an intervention being necessary on a global level. Should regional integration still be tried?

Of course I am quite interested in that question insofar as in my own paper about banking and securities regulations worldwide, I advocated[23] that regional integration probably did not make very much sense in either of these areas. Regional integration, and EC integration in particular, may be a first move towards worldwide harmonization and then the answer is quite obvious: it is a good thing. On the other hand, it may also be a move which has the so-called "petrification effect," which renders worldwide harmonization more difficult. Clearly, in the banking field the situation does not really appear, because the efforts are made in parallel in the Community and worldwide. It could well be that for securities regulations, the Commission works faster than worldwide efforts: and then, what if the regional harmonization makes it more difficult to come to a worldwide harmonization at the end? Would the Community think that possibly harmonization in Europe could weaken their competitive position worldwide?

[21] See *supra* at 3 and 9.
[22] See *supra* at 32.
[23] See *infra* at 350.

Geoffrey Fitchew

I expect it has to be answered case by case, there is no single answer to it. But the point that I would like to make is this: in the banking sector (and this will also apply in the securities market sector), our proposals for harmonization on in particular capital adequacy[24] are linked with the creation of the single licenses for banks[25] which are subject to this regulatory regime within the Community. In other words it is linked with the removal of obstacles to the exercise of the right of establishment, and the right of cross-frontier trade in services, so that there is a separate Community motive for proceeding with this harmonization quite apart from the global trends that have taken place.

The fact is that in banking there still are, despite the earlier directives, obstacles to setting up branches: eleven out of twelve Member States impose a local endowment capital requirement, earmarked capital, for any branch that is set up, as if it were an entirely separate bank. That is clearly an entry cost which discourages branching and separate authorization has to be acquired to set up any branch. In several Member States cross-frontier advertising and marketing, advertising to deposit in particular, by a bank in another Member State, cannot take place. Now one of the preconditions for moving those obstacles is agreement on a common regime for capital adequacy.

The point I am making is that even where an effort at global regulation is taking place, there may still be a valid motive within the Community for our imposing our own regional rules. I think in those circumstances, all one can say is that both the Commission and the Member States have a duty and an interest to ensure that what they are doing is compatible with the global efforts or can be adapted in line with any changes that take place at the global level.

L.C.B. Gower

What about the *cordon sanitaire* around the EC market?

Geoffrey Fitchew

We do not want to create a *cordon sanitaire* around the EC market. There is the argument going on about reciprocity, as you know, where what we say is that we simply want to have the reciprocity clause as a negotiating lever, in order to secure comparable concessions in other markets. There is a lot of humbug talked about this because actually, under the OECD Capital

[24] Directives in this field adopted in 1989: see O.J. L 124/16 (1989) and O.J. L 386/14 (1989).

[25] Directive adopted in 1989: see O.J. L 386/1 (1989).

Movements Code, virtually all the OECD countries have entered reciprocity exemptions in relation to banking or securities and insurance.

Alain Hirsch

Could I suggest that capital adequacy is less important for the protection of individual clients and for the freedom of establishment than for the general safety of the international financial system? Today, as I see it, most banks and important investment banks are just extending credits towards other banks and investment banks worldwide, without checking their financial situation very carefully. There is a great interbank market in which many non-bank institutions are also active. So that assuming for a moment (perhaps it is completely wrong, but let us assume for a minute) that European harmonization of capital adequacy would render more difficult some harmonization at the worldwide level, it might indeed mean that the individual clients of the European broker-dealers and investment banks would be safer, but it would also mean that all European banks and broker-dealers would be less safe insofar as they are lending to American, Japanese or Canadian institutions on the interbanking market. For example, the American investment banks are dependent on holding companies, which are wholly unregulated; nobody knows their financial situation. This is clearly a danger for the international financial system. I would suggest that if some regional regulation were to impede worldwide efforts to improve this situation, it would be a pity.

Another problem: even if you decide that, with the strict reciprocity rule, a foreign firm cannot advertise in Europe, it remains true that the most important clients are the institutionals. They are big enough to look at screens and to go to whichever broker-dealer they want in the world, and take their risks (for which individuals are possibly suffering at the end of the day). So I wonder if in today's technological world a real reciprocity rule or real *cordon sanitaire* is workable.

My conclusion is that in these fields I would suggest that the global harmonization of the financially developed world is really the thing to be aimed at in everybody's interest.

Geoffrey Fitchew

I agree and I think that maintaining the stability of the international financial system is in my personal view a more important motive for harmonizing capital adequacy rules than the protection of individual investors, although clearly good capital adequacy rules serve both purposes.

I think that in practice, in the banking and securities market field, the efforts of the Community and of the wider international institutions have been complementary and I hope that they will continue to be. Indeed we would say that we had started the work on capital adequacy of the banks before Basle did. It is clear there have been continual and useful exchanges between the two centres.

In relation to securities markets, the work is much less far advanced, both within the Community and internationally, and there is a much more strongly established arrangement for cooperation between banking supervisors than there is between securities market supervisors. But again I think the efforts are beginning to be developed in parallel within the Community and more widely.

So I agree, I think it is very important that the Community takes account of the wider international effort.

Hartmut Schmidt

I want to point to the differences between securities industry capital adequacy rules and commercial banking capital adequacy rules. As they stand in the United States, the capital adequacy rules for banks are of the going concern type, whereas the capital adequacy rules as promulgated in the area of the SEC measure capital adequacy by potential liquidation proceeds measures. You have to have a surplus over your liabilities even if you liquidate your assets today. This is much more stringent than the banking regulations and I think that it would be very tough on banks to be forced to take the same approach.

Alain Hirsch

The capital rules for the securities industry are not consolidated, which means that they are much less stringent.

Hartmut Schmidt

I do not know whether this is such an important point given the structure of the industry, but I wanted to say something for a different reason.

I was very puzzled by your remark, Mr. Fitchew,[26] that in exchange for obeying the capital adequacy rules of the Commission we have to give the banks some privilege. The sweet somehow has to come with the sour. On the face of it this says: "Well, these capital adequacy rules may be overdone, and in order to keep the business of banking under these regulations, we have to give the banks some incentive to do so." I think this is an approach which somehow is likely to result in action from other regulators. They may try to do it with lower capital requirements and with no incentives and this is something which the market is going to accept. If you need an incentive to the banks in order to make them willing to accept these high capital requirements, there is obviously something wrong.

[26] See *supra* at 97.

Geoffrey Fitchew

I am so sorry, I think I gave a rather misleading description of that. Two rather different exercises have been going on at the same time. One is a general move in the banking community to strengthen the capital adequacy in banks because during the 1970s the capital position of banks worldwide had become weaker and all the supervisors, including European supervisors, perceived a need to strengthen the capital position of banks, and also to bring within the supervisory framework the various off-balance sheets activities that banks were increasingly undertaking. And those two concerns lie behind the efforts on capital adequacy that were taking place in Basle and also in Brussels at the same time. And we would have been doing that anyway in both Basle and Brussels, even if we had not had the drive to the internal market.

What I was trying to say, and I described this in a misleading fashion, is that in preparing our proposal for the creation of a single banking licence in the Community,[27] the results of which would be that a bank which has been authorized in one Member State, can then without further authorization throughout the Member States set up a branch or engage in cross-frontier advertising and marketing in a way it cannot do in large parts of the Community at the moment. In making that proposal, we had to ask ourselves, and the Member States in any case raised the question: "What are the minimum conditions to be met? What is the minimum level of harmonization of the supervisory rules which have been met in order for us all to agree that there can be a single licence and mutual recognition?" And there was unanimous agreement that a harmonized capital adequacy rule[28] was essential for that purpose.

So describing it as privileges in exchange was very misleading. That is really the link that I was trying to make.

B. Sets of Regimes

Klaus Hopt

Prof. Schmidt, to your specific sets, I would like to have examples. You said:[29] "The choice among various sets of mandatory regulations provided by a single central regulator." Does this mean competition between two sets of mandatory law? Frankly I have difficulties with this concept. It would be easier to find illustrations for your second proposition, i.e., the choice between a mandatory central regime and various sets of Member State regimes. The *Societas Europaea* would be a perfect example for this, since if

[27] See *supra* note 25.
[28] See *supra* note 24.
[29] See *supra* at 59.

this idea were realized,[30] the entrepreneur could choose either to incorporate locally or under the European system. As a third possibility you mentioned the choice among the regimes and sets of regimes of two or more central regulators. Would something like the American banking regulation fit this?

Hartmut Schmidt

There are three classes that I mentioned.[31] First, various sets of mandatory regulations provided by a single regulator. Examples would be various forms of corporation (GmbH, *Aktiengesellschaft*) or various levels of listing (USM, official market). Second, mandatory central regime and various sets of Member State regimes. A close thing would be national bank charter versus State charter, or SEC primary market disclosure regime versus blue sky law disclosure, if you could have simply an intrastate issue. The third class I had in my paper was competitive central regulators, for example the Bank of England and the Securities and Investments Board; competing central sets concerning company finance would be SEC and bank regulation. This is a very nice system, this chartering by State or federal charter that you mentioned.

Klaus Hopt

But you would react positively to the American structure of banking regulation, this kind of division?

Hartmut Schmidt

The problem is that you could not do business in other States with a charter let us say from New York. If you had a New York charter or federal charter you could not do business in California, and this is a problem. But as soon as you can do business in California with such a charter this would be a very interesting approach.

Klaus Hopt

My understanding is that in American practice these layers upon layers of banking regulation do not work very satisfactorily. But maybe our American friends can elaborate on that.

[30] New proposals published in 1989: see O.J. C 263/41 (1989) and O.J. C 263/69 (1989).

[31] See *supra* at 59.

Richard Buxbaum

Well, on the question of dissatisfaction, I think we have to put that very contingently. First of all, it is the large banks trying to break the interstate barrier that are dissatisfied. From the perspective of regulators, the problem there is more in your insurance deposit situation. You have the flip-flop between State and federal charters as a way of escaping premium costs. It is very disaggregated to answer what element of dissatisfaction exists. You could not give a generic answer to the conflict of State/federal jurisdiction in the financial services sector. I think you would have to break it down by the functional issue that is on the table.

Hartmut Schmidt

If you were a State chartered bank, you did not have to maintain any minimum reserves which paid no interest. So this was clearly an advantage. And the Federal Reserve of course was in favor of very high reserve requirements because this facilitates greatly the job of managing the money stock. So it is obviously just for the convenience of the regulator. There is no other reason and it works as a special tax, and basically it drives the banking activity out of the banking system. So it was very nice to get State charters, because they forced the Federal Reserve to back down and to come to the point where they said: "Well, we can live and manage to do our job with very low minimum reserves requirements, with a very low tax."

Richard Buxbaum

Well, it is the competition of regimes on a State/federal basis. Because of the peculiar statutory system it dragged the national regime, which of course was following a stabilization policy (I mean they are monitoring supply questions), down to the level of being merely one competitor with the State regimes, at the cost, of course, of sacrificing certain stabilization goals to the (let us say, for the sake of argument) allocative efficiency support goals. But whether that is good or bad is a different issue.

Hartmut Schmidt

If you have less friction in a system, you have a better system. The Fed can do the job at low minimum reserve requirements and they can do it at high. So they can do a job with high cost and they can do it with low cost. So let them do it at low cost and let them be forced to do it at low cost.

Richard Buxbaum

While I would certainly agree that low reserves and capital adequacy are not quite the same thing, I think the present American experience with bank failures ought to suggest a certain amount of qualification on that statement. What you have given is a nice "good-times" argument on this point.

Hartmut Schmidt

All right. I think you will see a great deal of activity being squeezed out of banking by new high capital requirements. I would say that the bad experience of American banks does basically arise from bad regulation. If a bank cannot do business except in the Midwest and the Midwest goes through hard economic times, of course it will have more problems than banks in New England where the situation is rather stable. And you have very high loss ratios indeed in the Midwest. I think if we really went into detail, we would find many regulatory incentives to risk-taking and to lack of diversification and nobody should expect anything different.

Richard Buxbaum

Well, this is a factual question to a great extent. First of all, I am not competent enough in banking or banking regulatory law to want to debate it this way, but from a relatively incompetent side I have to say that current arguments about moral hazards in bank management being a major factor, rather than regional stickiness, look pretty convincing to many of us. The fact is that a lot of the Texas regional problem, for example, affected non-Texas banks which through their holding company affiliate structures were very actively and very happily taking positions there. So I do not think we have as much regional stickiness as the restrictions on interstate banking might otherwise imply. But as I say, these are heavily factual issues.

Hartmut Schmidt

American regulation has promoted taking on interest-rate risks, especially by savings banks and savings and loan associations. It is well known that the federal insurers are basically not able to carry on business any more. If they were private organizations, they would have been out of business for a long time. And now they are trying to get rid of their problems by selling these problem institutions off to others and this causes additional problems. So it is very hard, I agree. I did not bring this matter up, you brought it up. I agree it is a very tough one, but my proposition is that the source of the problem is a regulatory problem and I come back to Prof. Hopt's question.[32] If there is room for competition by regulators that does not result in competition among regulators, this "competition" does not lead anywhere, and this was the situation in the United States for a long time. It is now changing. If there is indeed competition by regulators and if the

[32] See *supra* at 100.

regulated banks, securities firms and what have you compete, then this should be a beneficial approach and promote progress in law.

Gérard Hertig

How do you deal with oligopolies in that field? Because that happens very often. If you do have competition, as you said, then you just have cartels.

Hartmut Schmidt

Who should have the oligopoly? Delaware? There are fifty States, and lots of them are at least of equal size and equal economic power. So if they wanted to compete I think they could. There are no entry barriers. But if a State is really good at something, is a specialist and continues to be one, it may look like a monopolist, but it cannot afford to behave like the monopolist that may be on your mind who just sits back and nothing is going to change. The State regulator would be sitting there and saying: "What is the next step that maintains our lead?" And this is a very different game than just being the monopolist and somehow exploiting somebody. I really agree with your statement that you cannot immediately compare competition among firms and competition among regulators. But that does not say that competition among regulators is not a useful concept.

Geoffrey Fitchew

But I would like to challenge that competition between regulators is always beneficial. The fundamental problem is that the justification for regulation of a particular sector is that the market system is defective in some respect or other; one clear example of this is the banking sector that you have just been discussing. The market process does not necessarily produce stability of the banking system. Stability of the banking system is in that sense, I would argue, a pure public good.

If in a global or a regional market you allow competition between regulators who are trying to secure the public good of stability of the banking system, there will be a very strong tendency, particularly in the circumstances of the 1980s, for competition in laxity between the regulators; because banking business will move to the most lax centre of supervision the result will be that Gresham's Law will operate in respect to supervision. I am not arguing that this is the case in respect of all types of regulation, but I think there are examples (banking, securities markets) that certainly fall under this heading.

Edmund Kitch

Why do you think that investors will deposit funds in banks that are in the laxest jurisdictions? Banks without deposits are not very large banks. If the regulation is truly lax, that will threaten the safety of the deposits and drive depositors away.

Hartmut Schmidt

That assumes that depositors are plain stupid because they do not see that they are getting higher interest because they run a higher risk. Why do many investors invest in the United States?

Gérard Hertig

Prof. Schmidt, I could give you a lot of examples of investors who are "plain stupid" and give their savings to somebody just because he is paying higher returns without looking at the risks. I have a very recent example in Switzerland.

Eddy Wymeersch

Examples of competition among regulatory systems are met frequently even among the European markets that are subject to EC harmonization measures. Clear examples to the point are the fields of investment funds, subject to a 1985 harmonization Directive.[33] Luxembourg has enacted a very broadly framed enabling legislation, facilitating the formation of investment funds for a wide variety of purposes, thus attracting all those fund managers who did not want to step into the single protective mould the Directive of 1985 has prescribed. These funds often offer investments with a higher risk factor, but also investments in new investment vehicles, in art collections, real estate, etc. This legislation creates a limited "free playing field" that acts as an effective competitor within the harmonized regulatory system.

A somewhat comparable situation is found in the field of prospectuses relating to the listing of securities to stock exchanges. The regulatory requirements relating to these prospectuses have been thoroughly harmonized by the EC Directive of 1980.[34] This directive has by now been implemented by most of the Member States. The directive imposes the minimum level of regulation, and therefore limits the race for laxity. However, some differences remain, e.g., with respect to publication of prospectus, or liability of its signatories. With respect to these points effective competition subsists. It is not clear whether this limited form of competition really creates a risk for the investors, or for the organization of a fair market. In as far as it does create merely regulatory advantages, these small differences are not detrimental to the integration of the markets and therefore can remain as minor competitive advantages.

[33] O.J. L 375/3 (1985).
[34] O.J. L 100/1 (1980).

Hartmut Schmidt

I agree that you will have problems in banking if you leave it all to the market, but I see only one reason for this. If you have depositors all over the country at various banks and they can always draw money at the same time, and this money which has to be paid to them is available only in a limited supply (in the old days it was gold), and you have a multiple of that as outstanding deposits, obviously the system must fall apart as soon as everybody tries to get the definitive money. This has been solved by putting up central banks and they can create definitive money and the depositors can get paid off. This has been done particularly in the United States. I think this is very well regulated in the Federal Reserve Act, and in due course the bank regulator has to come up with some rules on who would be able to get central bank support, who can come to the advance or discount window and who cannot. And those banks who behave as the rules require can come and get definitive money.

At first sight it does not matter whether there is minimum regulation or maximum regulation. But if there is maximum regulation, the result will be that these banking activities will go elsewhere, and I think that the whole business about securitization is a marvelous illustration of this point. The regulatory requirements have been raised and the business is done differently and it will go elsewhere. I think, for example, that it is counterproductive to have high capital requirements on loans, as the Cooke Committee has in its proposal, because if you have a perfectly diversified portfolio you do not need any capital to support it. And then what happens? Banks put these portfolios of consumer loans together and market them in the form of securities and they do not need much in the way of capital. I think they put up 1% and some guarantees.

A regulator can do whatever he wants, but the market will decide whether this is going to work or not.

L.C.B. Gower

Your argument as I understand it is that people will rush to the least regulated place, is that not it?

Hartmut Schmidt

They will rush where they can get the same quality product with the highest yield or at the least cost, which amounts to the same. Of course you may say we have all kinds of examples where people seem to behave irrationally. Well, if you give up the idea that people behave in a rational manner then we do not get anywhere. At least we have to say that if there are two offers, safe investment, same term, and one yields 4% and the other 5%, then the people will go for the one with 5%. If not, I cannot argue any more, I go home.

Gérard Hertig

We know that people are not rational. But, most importantly, they do not have or do not use all the information. They are just looking at some pieces of information.

Hartmut Schmidt

All right, that means that they have costs. I myself go and put money into the bank because I can't be bothered to sit down and get the information and figure it out in order to get the higher yielding asset. This is a convenience argument which translates into costs. But others do have the time and much more money than I do. For them it pays to say: "Well, should we invest in this way or in a different way?" But I would still claim to be rational in spite of investing at times in the lower yielding asset.

André Tunc

I may say that I fully agree with most of the content of the reports we are discussing. I found many very interesting points in them. But I think I do not need to comment on them and I would rather like to speak on the points on which I have some difficulties.

First, I would say that the Delaware experience, which has been mentioned,[35] is not easy to study and does not lead to clear conclusions. The statutory law of the State, on one hand, is very lax. But, as emphasized in one of the papers,[36] the Chancellor has great power to impose equity, and to set aside an operation which is perfectly legal, but still appears to him unacceptable to a judge of equity. And that is a great counterweight to the laxity of the statutory law of Delaware. See the famous decision of *Singer v. Magnavox*.[37] Now the relationship between a State and the federation is again difficult to observe in the case of Delaware, because one may wonder whether the *Singer v. Magnavox* decision would have been made if there had not been the threat of federal intervention. The SEC and the Congress were studying the "privatization" of corporations, the "freezing out" of shareholders, and the Chancellor may have intervened strongly to protect the shareholders in order to prevent this federal intervention.

Furthermore, we must not forget the cost of the intervention of the Chancellor, i.e., litigation. In many situations, in nearly every takeover bid, there will be litigation. Whatever the decision made by the directors, they will be sued before the courts. That may be acceptable, but that is a very serious cost. So you see that it is not easy to present Delaware law as a model.

[35] See *supra* at 42 ff, 55 and 83 ff.
[36] See *supra* at 44 and 44, note 17.
[37] 380 A.2d 969 (Del. 1977).

I am also somewhat skeptical towards the present American trend towards deregulation and "giving back the powers to the States." I have been trying to follow American politics for forty years now, I think. I am always hearing of "giving back the powers to the States." It is not easy. At present it is done to a certain extent. Will it be continued? Frankly, I doubt it. What about deregulation, which is so fashionable? Whether it will be continued for a long time I do not know. President Carter started the deregulation of air traffic. What is the result of deregulation? The fact is that everyone complains about congestion, delays and decreased security. Probably it will appear necessary to impose some regulation and we shall take again the road to more regulation and more federal regulation. Similarly, we have spoken at length about the deregulation of banking.[38] It has been followed by a great number of failures of banks and financial institutions. Is it sequence in time or is there a causal connection? I cannot say, but I suspect that the need for more regulation may appear.

Similarly Prof. Schmidt's example of South Dakota[39] does not seem to me very convincing, but that has been discussed already to a certain extent.[40] South Dakota has been able to attract banks making higher risk loans. Well, is it good to attract higher risk loans? Anyhow, what is gained by one State in terms of jobs and profits is lost by the other States. But, beyond that, high risk loans entail more failures of debtors, hence more failures of banks. Furthermore, the high rates of loans are passed on to customers. I doubt again whether South Dakota is a model. You attract people, but you create dangers; some regulation is certainly necessary.

Hartmut Schmidt

Prof. Tunc said my South Dakota example did not convince him at all. Okay, I can go along with that. If you have a ceiling let us say of 20%, then certainly you won't give any loans to people who are high risk. Let us say the regular rate of interest is 9%. Then you can make loans that require an 11% risk premium. If there was a need for a risk premium of 15 or 16 or 20%, these applicants would be cut off. And if you now say these people should not get loans even if banks were able to diversify these loans and combine them into a completely risk-free portfolio, that is your value judgement.

I can respect it but I could also say: why should somebody who is a risk but is still able to get away with a risk premium of 11% get a loan, and an even poorer chap not get a loan because his risk premium would be 16% and this would put him above the ceiling? And it complicates matters if you take into account that interest rates tend to change. If the interest rates go

[38] See *supra* at 100 ff.
[39] See *supra* at 56.
[40] See *supra* at 100 ff.

from 9 to 12% in the market for risk-free investments, then people with a risk premium above 8% do not get loans.

I think this is a terrible situation and therefore I thought that the South Dakota move was very much in the interest of people who like to take out consumer loans. Of course, you may stick to a value judgement that would restrict risk lending. You would say South Dakota is not for me. But the favorable market response indicates that obviously it has had value to others.

André Tunc

I would disagree (but I am afraid this has been discussed already at least in part[41]) with Prof. Kitch's statement[42] that there is no reason why in a federal system the constituent States cannot regulate their own exchange. To go to a less safe market will probably be slightly cheaper; therefore many people will go and one day they will be cheated (consider the Barlow Clowes affair, even on a market such as the London one). The price of a safer market is comparable to an insurance premium. Some people will always prefer not to pay insurance premiums. But when a fire or some disaster occurs, it is nice to have insurance. We have to protect people against taking unreasonable risks, and that may require federal regulation.

L.C.B. Gower

I was going to ask a question also on the statement Prof. Tunc has just referred to. What I was not clear about in Prof. Kitch's paper was that he concedes at the beginning[43] that some kind of effective federal securities swindle control agency is likely to be an aspect of any modern system of capital market regulation. But, later on,[44] he suggests as I understand it that a federal regulator of securities exchanges is likely to be less innovative than the State system.

I think Prof. Tunc disagreed with that statement and so frankly do I. In the United States the innovation has come through the NASD and not through the individual exchanges. And certainly in the British experience, it was only when the British Stock Exchange realized that if it was going to survive as an international market in the brave new world, it had to do something at last about its utterly obsolete technology etc.

But what I wanted to ask Prof. Kitch is: what exactly does he mean by "some kind of effective federal securities swindle control agency?" Does he envisage this as some means whereby you catch the swindlers after they

[41] See *supra* at 100 ff.
[42] See *supra* at 47.
[43] See *supra* at 46.
[44] See *supra* at 47.

have swindled and do something about it, which I would regard as a totally inadequate investor protection regime?

It seems to me that if you accept that you have got to do something about this, then you have got to provide a prevention rather than some form of punishment (which is not a cure) at the end of it, which does really mean that you have got to have, I would have thought, a federal regulation of the securities industry. And that certainly would be the view on which I think we have been working in the UK.

Edmund Kitch

I think that particular confusion is coming from the fact that I am splitting securities regulation in a way that is not traditionally done. I am thinking of the regulatory agenda which has to do with the organization and operation of exchanges, the privileges of floor traders, the conventions for order execution, the rules about membership access and so forth as one regulatory programme, and the area of prospectus requirements, fraud remedies, and so on as another.

L.C.B. Gower

Can you sort of cut off the exchange rules and say, well...

Edmund Kitch

I am implicitly rejecting the strategy of providing investor protection by creating an attractive position for the industry free from competition, so that they are doing so well that they are not under any pressure to abuse the public. That has been a strategy regulation which I think is misguided, and we can argue that across the board; you have similar issues in airline deregulation. I think these issues about exchange regulation can be separated from the effort to regulate the terms and conditions under which securities are sold to the public, the representations that are made, who is authorized to do the selling and so on. I am quite open to innovation and diversity in the organization of trading and reporting of prices and all those questions.

I think there is a separate problem about how securities are sold to the public which, when you get an international market, creates cross-jurisdictional problems that are very serious. My thought about an effective federal securities swindle control agency is that to effectively police cross-border fraud it is necessary to have a cross-border agency. In today's world we need an international, effective agency to protect against swindle. I do not think anybody has got one, but, when you have a national enforcement bureaucracy, like the SEC, and you have a Bernie Cornfeld Investors Overseas Services – to take a good illustration of how an operator can get himself positioned between national regulators and find a very large opening for questionable operations – the SEC (and the other national regulators) are pulled up short. I think this is an increasing problem. At the very least, the enforcement agencies in the Community will have to cooperate and exchange information or the EC will have to do something.

But that was the sort of problem I was thinking about. There have, for instance, been problems relating to the sale of American options products in Europe to Europeans by brokers who are taking advantage of the fact that the Europeans are very unfamiliar with the American arrangements and cannot evaluate what they are being told. And then the European regulators are not familiar with the American products and it creates confusion which a con artist can exploit.

These are problems that require cross-national cooperation – indeed, cooperation that extends beyond the EC. But it surely can and should start there.

Geoffrey Fitchew

Two questions to Prof. Kitch on what he has just said. First of all, in this division that he suggested between the responsibilities at the federal level and the responsibilities at the lower level, the level of the exchanges, at what level would he place solvency and margin requirements?

Secondly, I think this is perhaps picking up a point Prof. Gower was making, an effective swindle control agency may well require access to a good deal of information about transactions. But you suggested that reporting requirements would be the responsibility of the lower level. How can you reconcile that dilemma?

Edmund Kitch

I am troubled by the separation between theory and its application, and we are coming back to practice. Securities markets are one of the most interesting harmonization topics. They should be controlled at the "lower" level. I do not have a highly detailed programme of division. I would think of the margin requirements and solvency requirements for brokers as part of exchange regulation designed to protect the integrity of the trading and dealing procedures.

Hartmut Schmidt

As a strong believer in the clause-by-clause approach, I strongly share Prof. Gower's position.[45] Most of the operational rules of securities markets do have investor protection elements. You cannot separate the reduction of transaction costs function in the usual sense, the main function of these rules, and the investor protection functions. In addition, the intertwining of

[45] See *supra* at 109 f.

many of these functions would suggest that there will be one agency taking care of investor protection and general efficiency aspects, but there would be nothing wrong with having competing agencies and as a result competing securities markets or differences between the regulatory design of one agency and competing self-regulatory organizations.

And the SEC I would say has been an enlightened agency as far as this is concerned because in the '30s, '40s and '50s it made sure that the regional exchanges survived. Without the SEC they would probably not have survived and these regional exchanges promoted efficiency by coming up with innovative clearance and settlement devices and other processing devices. Then the SEC brought the NASD into play with the NASDAQ system.

But you could have got a similar effect by employing a set of different regulators. For example in Germany we have allowed *Länder* or State regulation of stock exchanges and there is also some degree of competition, though it is tempered by the fact that the membership of the various exchanges is almost identical, and the competition that we would need does not come about. We did not have an enlightened regulatory agency promoting competition. The problem may be the size of the regulators. Our institutions that can act as market regulators are too large or too complex. They think other points are more important and they do not care about securities markets.

Eddy Wymeersch

Just a reference to Prof. Schmidt's remark. Do you mean that the German stock exchanges are acting as one single cartel?

Hartmut Schmidt

Yes, they are. I can say so with great emphasis. I would recommend you to read the Charter of the *Arbeitsgemeinschaft Deutscher Wertpapierbörsen.* The regional exchanges were forced to give away their ability to compete; for example in the area of marketing, the marketing functions were centralized. But on the fringes this effort to eliminate competition has not been successful. There is a cartel in many areas, but the various exchanges still try to "cheat," as is the case in all cartels.

Christian Meier-Schatz

As a matter of principle, I do not deny either the fact that competition among the American stock exchanges takes place or the fact that the SEC was enlightened in promoting it. But I would just like to emphasize – Prof. Buxbaum could certainly tell us more about the subject[46] – that recently

[46] See *infra* at 114 f.

this competition among stock exchanges has become controversial with respect to certain results. I will mention just one example: for a long time, the stock exchanges had a mandatory one-share-one-vote rule. Heavy pressure from many managements in defensive takeover situations then induced one stock exchange, followed by others, to abandon that rule. Whether this is a positive or a negative event is quite another question. Yet it might be significant that the SEC immediately adopted a proposal mandating again the one-share-one-vote rule.

My point is not so much that you are wrong but that in recent times, especially with respect to agency problems and takeover situations, the beneficial effects of regulatory competition among stock exchanges have become more doubtful.

Hartmut Schmidt

I have not followed the American discussion on that recently, but when I did my second report for the EC on small business financing, it was an important question whether one should facilitate the equity financing of companies by allowing the issue of participation certificates or *Vorzugsaktien*, preferred shares or similar instruments. I could not find anything wrong with these. Of course, our friends in Belgium especially, the *Commission Bancaire*, strongly disagree.

But again, what is wrong, if an investor realizes that he gives up voting rights and in exchange for that he will get a higher yield? He knows this in advance. So if he prefers higher yield to voting rights, I think we are in no position to pass a value judgement that this ought not to happen.

Alain Hirsch

In this discussion about competition between regulators, it is just very difficult to abandon a value judgement. If you think that German stock exchanges are underregulated, is it not because it is not possible in Germany to regulate different stock exchanges separately? Only a central regulation of German stock exchanges is possible because in fact they are one market anyhow. Is there not a real contradiction between good regulation and competition between regulators?

Hartmut Schmidt

What I said regarding the optimal size of regulators[47] certainly applies to Germany: we have State regulators, there is one chap in each *Land* doing the securities regulation and he is doing it just one-eighth of his time or even less, this is certainly not the optimal size for a regulator. I think we should have a different set-up. But the actual situation is more complicated because

[47] See *supra* at 92.

the *Bundesbank* may be seen as the main regulator of the securities markets. Formally, it is not, but informally it may be, and the *Bundesaufsichtsamt für das Kreditwesen* can also be seen as the main regulator – which it may be.

Now Giersch and myself concluded: "Let us set up two regulators, one for securities business and one for the banking business. And then we will see how they perform: hand in glove or in competition. This is a reasonable ball game, and let us see where the customers go." I am certain that such an approach is superior to a single regulator in this field, who could impose and maintain rules that would never survive if there was a choice.

Desmond McComb

I find myself wondering if the analogy with American banking that was frequently brought up[48] was an entirely valid one, because banking throughout Europe is a very variable kind of industry, ranging from the almost pure deposit-type banking that one can find in the major banks in the United Kingdom through to the very comprehensive banks that one finds in Germany which not only engage in deposit banking but also engage in investment banking and have actual involvement in participation on boards of companies so that they are directly concerned with the administration of companies.

Much of our discussions seem to me to be linked to the idea of deposit banking rather than investment banking which is a function of some parts of the banking system in Europe, and I wondered if our ability to harmonize in that type of situation was going to result in any meaningful benefits to the European Community or to the banking industry or whether it simply meant that banking would move towards Switzerland or, as I said over lunch, towards East Germany – because there is nothing to prevent us thinking of the Eastern countries of Europe operating as financial manipulators in such a situation while the rest of Europe creates its own difficulties.

Richard Buxbaum

This has been a fascinating discussion. It is, however, going on in a sense at various levels and in a way that will be difficult to unpack. I would like to take a minute just to state a slogan or two for the different levels at which we are discussing, but I cannot resist first a joke, not my own. One of the nicest comments was in Prof. Schmidt's original contribution when he pointed out[49] that the United States, France and, I think you said, Italy are at too large a level for regulation; and then went on to point out: "But luckily that only means that they cannot regulate effectively." So what they will do is the relatively innocuous backward-looking or traditional regulation, always catching up from being behind. You have just recapitulated one

[48] See *supra* at 101 ff and 108 f.
[49] See *supra* at 92.

of Will Rogers' best lines, when he once said: "Thank God we do not get the government we pay for." It is interesting how pervasive that home truth seems to be.

I would like to just unravel two separate points. One has to do with the question of free choice among competitive regimes, and you spoke[50] of the dual-class phenomenon and why should not investors who know they are getting less return not be allowed this choice. The basic problem is that it may be that more interests are affected by that choice than are making the choice. So far, in the actual historical sense, we have assumed a certain prohibition of dual-class voting stock. We have been resting on that assumption in lieu of regulation. Now we find that the exchanges are trying to get out of that prohibition because they have to compete for listings, and therefore the Gresham's Law that was spoken of[51] applies. Now the problem is, since we were delegating by inference, but by real inference, a public function to the exchange, we cannot automatically accept the choice of investors, even if it is one that is informed and not institutionally sticky (i.e., one with agent monitoring problems and so forth). So that is simply one problem. We are sometimes in situations where the question of choice itself is the wrong question.

Secondly, I just want to emphasize again from specific historical experience Prof. Meier-Schatz's point[52] that there are significant agent-monitoring problems in some of these choice issues, so that when you have the Delaware reincorporation syndrome, and so forth, you cannot sweep from the table the question of why it is that people vote for such steps. I do not want to take up here the question whether the Romano or the Winter arguments about the share prices being a surrogate for proving their vote is rational is itself convincing, but at least that is a separate issue.

But now I want to come to one more fundamental problem. Someone struck a nerve[53] and you responded as all good economists do to the one thing that they cannot question; that is, of course, the rationality of the actors. Now in a political situation that is unfortunately an inherent problem that even economists cannot escape. And I want to phrase it just in one way: the rational investor, when defrauded, turns into the irrational voter. Put more generically, there is no obligation and no human possibility of rationality being consistent right through the experience of the particular citizen-investor; and if political reaction is irrational, that is itself a rational thing that has to be taken into account.

And I think it is not paternalism to do so. This is a tricky problem, but I do not think it is paternalism for a society to decide that certain things are not to be left to the free choice of potentially deceived persons, if that free choice when made and when soured comes back in the form of irrational

[50] See *supra* at 113.
[51] See *supra* at 104.
[52] See *supra* at 76.
[53] See *supra* at 105.

political reaction. If the Association of Retired Dentists of Southern California, disappointed that their 36% per month investments in Mexican peso bonds soured, ends up pressuring their local representatives for compensation, you cannot just go back to them and say: "Wait a minute, you have got to be consistently rational here. You first went into this thing and now you are trying to be inconsistent and tell us that we have got to have redistributive mechanisms here to pay you back." Unfortunately that is political reality, and I do not think it is paternalistic for a politically democratic society to take that into account in advance. And while that may be a rather vague comment, I do think it is an underlying comment that has to temper this issue of informed rational choice. We are doing it inside specific policies.

C. Public Goods and Regulation by the Market

Alain Hirsch

Do you not think, Prof. Schmidt, that what you are saying[54] is that the market is a better judge than the regulator, which is perfectly possible in many instances? It seems to me that you suggest that there should be no regulation at all and that the market forces should go ahead. In any regulation (banking, securities, cartels, taxes, etc.), insofar as regulation is bad, competition between regulators is good because it tends to make regulation disappear or go to the bottom. But, insofar as regulation is necessary, then the argument seems unconvincing.

Let us take the example you used.[55] If you think that the regulation to impose one-share-one-vote is a good thing, then obviously you are not in favor of competition on that; and if you think it is a bad thing you are in favor of competition. Can you tell me one example in financial regulation where you would suggest that a regulation is necessary and nevertheless you would suggest that competition (leading possibly to abandonment of such regulation!) is good?

Hartmut Schmidt

I started comparing the German stock exchanges and their regulations to the American stock exchanges and their regulations back in the '60s. My position then is the one I am still maintaining, and my position was that the German stock exchanges are underregulated. There ought to be much more regulation. I cannot accept it if you say: "No regulation would be my ideal." I think you need a lot of regulation. There is a lot of regulation out there that makes sense, that improves both the operations of the markets and of the banking system and the position of the investors. And it has been

[54] See *supra* at 59 f and 101 ff.
[55] See *supra* at 113.

expanding and improving due to pressure, due to competitive pressure from abroad, most notably in the UK. But there is also a regulation out there that simply rests on value judgements.

Christian Timmermans

My remark refers to the issue of harmonization by the market. It has been rightly said[56] that company law is more than a matter of resolving private party interests, the limited liability company is more than an axis of various contractual relationships, it also implies specific public goods. In my view it is impossible to leave this to the market and in that respect it has been rightly said in the *Buxbaum* and *Hopt* book[57] that the situation in Europe is quite different, as far as company law and perhaps also capital market law are concerned, from the situation in the United States.

I would add one other complication as far as company law is concerned, and that is the institutional approach towards the company which is more or less common to the European countries. I say more or less because there are important differences in that respect. By institutional approach I mean that the company is not seen as a mere instrument of shareholders and available to further their interests, but (and I speak now for my own country) it is seen as a specific institution that in its structure and in the exercise of the competences of the organs of that institution has to take into account a whole scale of varying and diverging interests of which the shareholders' interest is certainly a category but only one among others. That approach complicates particularly the legal regime for groups of companies, because it applies also to the subsidiary companies.

Klaus Hopt

Prof. Schmidt, you mentioned at the beginning of your paper[58] that the good old public goods theory would not be very useful for our specific purposes. Probably this theory is useful for regulation in general, but does not explain very much as far as integration is concerned. Did I get that right?

Considering the question mentioned just now, would it be possible to say that – provided we follow the public goods theory – if a public good is concerned, then it is still better to have regional harmonization even if in the long run a global one would be best? A reason for this could be that if one states such a policy it is in any case better to start by moving the center of regulation upwards. Yet in a way this leads back to the discussion we had earlier,[59] namely how to distinguish all this. What is the area to be left to

[56] See *supra* at 22.
[57] BUXBAUM & HOPT, *supra* note 2, e.g. at 22.
[58] See *supra* at 51 f.
[59] See *supra* at 100 ff.

competition between the regulators or where are the instances in which we are or should be willing to start saying: "Well, we set specific goals and as European regulators we shall go after them."

Hartmut Schmidt

I have two questions here: the public goods, and where competition does work and where it does not work. I cannot handle them together.

The public goods: I was pleased to see that you, like me, do not think that the public goods approach will lead to an answer to the question I had to deal with simply because you would have to devise some rule as to when a public good should be produced and when it should not be produced; you could go back to Wicksell and the unanimity principle, but because of distributional problems I think we would not get anywhere. If you come up with some social welfare function, you would have to make so many value judgements, that again it would be highly questionable what the outcome would be. Maybe you would comment differently on the public goods approach, I cannot.

Then let me turn to your other question. Where does competition work and where not? It is basically the question of what is a swindle and what is not, how do you separate these two areas? In the swindle area, competition does not work, this is the fly-by-night operation, very short-term oriented. You are in Germany for three weeks and sell commodity options and then you go to London and then to Spain. Competition is obviously not going to work in this area. No way. But competition is very likely to work if there is a long-term value maximizing behavior or at least a long term outlook. Exchanges for example are most likely to be institutions which have been around for hundreds of years and they will be around for many more years. You can rely on their long-term interest to behave in a way that gives everyone involved a fair deal.

The problem is how to distinguish a fly-by-night operator from somebody who will be around for a good number of years. This is obviously a problem that cannot be neatly solved. But it confronts regulators and investors all the time.

Let me give you an example. In 1975, when I did the field work for my first study for the EEC, I went to the Bank of England to find out what the markets were like in that country. I was told: "Look at the *Times*, there is a company called Nightingale and they advertise their quotes." And I was told: "Please do not go and see these people. They are bad." I think they are not bad at all. Nightingale is an excellent example of how competition works, and I certainly saw these people and had good long discussions with them. They gave me their listing agreement and I realized that their listing agreement was better than the listing agreement of the London Stock Exchange. For example, on insider trading it said that company insiders must not deal except in the two weeks after interim reports have been sent to the shareholders and during the two weeks after the annual accounts have been referred to the company shareholders. Since they were in charge of the market, they could control this.

Other over-the-counter (OTC) houses earned themselves a bad reputation but if you say the Nightingale market is the same as the others, then of course you throw out the baby with the bathwater. I would say you have to look at the things case by case, if you want to know where competition may work. Regarding that first case, I was impressed by their listing agreements, by their "legal" framework. Then I was impressed by the kind of backing they had. What impressed me most was that they said: "We are not going to take our provisions in the forms of fees. Our compensation is mainly in the form of long-term warrants." So they had warrants which they could not exercise before seven years or ten years.

L.C.B. Gower

If these were given to individuals, they could still exercise them although they had long since left the firm. However, I have no wish to criticize Nightingale.

Hartmut Schmidt

There is no problem if these individuals can exercise these options after they have left. The main thing is they cannot exercise them until the option has been in their hands for a number of years because that prevents taking advantage of private information on a short-term basis. Those who take this form of compensation must be somehow certain that this is a reasonable long-term investment. And I think you have to look at things in this way and in a very specific way to find out where competition is likely to work and where not.

Klaus Hopt

Can I quickly come into this long-term operation debate? I think that there are grave practical difficulties. Let me give you three examples.

First: you talk about institutions. They by themselves are long-term. Maybe the market can distinguish between more reputable institutions and less reputable institutions. But if you talk about individuals, how do you want us to distinguish there? Is there not the possibility, and are there not in fact many examples of people entering the market just to reap a quick profit and then going off with it?

The second set of difficulties: how do you cope with the problem of extraterritoriality? Somebody may stay in Switzerland and from there do business in the UK and endless other markets. He can do that on a very long-term basis without really being caught.

The third group is fraud by hidden operations. How can the investors find out and react until it is too late? The so-called entrepreneur may be confident enough of not being caught, this may even be the primary motivation. Then this can go on quite a long time.

Hartmut Schmidt

In the first case they would soon go out of business. This is not necessarily a problem as long as the interests of the salespeople and the investors are converging. If you take compensation and long-term options, for example, you have a linkage of interests and even if they go out of business most likely they will have sold decent investments to their clients; so it is not really a problem if somebody goes out of business in the end. But they will usually stay because once they have a good reputation they will try to capitalize on that.

Shifting from territory to territory, I think this is a more critical case because this means that you do not cater to the same group of clients, building on a certain reputation, and I would say this is really a danger signal.

And your third point was the hidden operation or the hidden payments situation, for example some relationship between the auditor of the company and the owner of the company who wants to distribute shares to the public. Well, I think this can always happen but the probability is much smaller if you have a lot of signals that point to solid establishment.

Eddy Wymeersch

I would like to dispute some of these points.

I think that the last speaker, my most honored friend, Prof. Schmidt, rather lost sight of the preventive function of the regulations. Entry rules for broker-dealers, prospectus rules, and similar prescriptions have a strong preventive function in that they limit access to those participants, or those securities that are clearly unfit for public trading. It goes without saying that it is preferable to protect investments in advance. Once the damage has been done the remedies often do not offer any effective protection to the victims of the wrongdoing and the money is gone for the economy as well. This underlines the need for administrative action and monitoring in these markets, provided of course that these are effective.

My second remark relates to the idea that one should mainly act against the fly-by-night operator. Unfortunately, there are many examples of well-established businesses that have turned sour. Even well-established institutions like the Hong Kong Stock Exchange have not proved fail-safe against abuses or even fraud. In cases of fraudulent peddling of securities to investors, one often wonders how these abuses could have gone on so long, as long as five years in a case I recently studied that resulted in a $100 million loss. And the general press mentioned recently the collapse of a major investment group with ramifications in Switzerland, Germany, France and so on. This was a well-established business, with offices e.g. in

Basle. A similar point could be made about commodity speculation where huge losses were incurred, while obviously the courts' repeated convictions or liability decisions did not induce these brokers to stop their excessive practices.

Hartmut Schmidt

Do you mean that if you have a strong regulatory system you will have no abuses? I think it is a matter of degree and all I am saying is that you have fewer abuses if investors and regulators watch out for signs of short-term interest. Thus I do not see a great deal of difference in our arguments, my honored friend.

Your first point is the preventive function. Of course, Nightingale had much better prospectus and listing requirements than required under the law because they knew that only if they adhered to what investors would consider as additional preventive measures would they be able to build up investor confidence and that would induce investors to buy their financial services.

Eddy Wymeersch

But the rules are made to catch not Nightingale, but the other ones.

III. Various Other Topics

Klaus Hopt

Mr. Fitchew, what about the use of economics within the Commission? Are there any organizational structures for this? What about the role, relationship and institutional competition between lawyers and economists within the Commission? Are there plans to do more in this area? Or is the Commission relying more on economic knowledge and advice from outside, as for example in the case of the *Cecchini* study?[60] In private enterprise this is the well-known, but difficult choice between outside advice and in-house counsel or a bit of both.

Alain Hirsch

Mr. Fitchew, is there a fundamental difference between the economic model for legal harmonization and the study leading to some general aim of regulation proposed by Eddy Wymeersch?[61]

[60] EC COMMISSION, *Research on the Cost of "Non-Europe"* (Cecchini Report, 16 vols., Brussels 1988).

[61] See *supra* at 120 f.

Today, no Member State is legislating with either clear economic models or clear general aims (if that is different). It would certainly be better to legislate at the level of the European Community than at the level of the Member States. I am just wondering whether it is fair to ask the Community not only to harmonize what has been already done by the twelve Member States, but to have a much higher standard for any harmonized legislation than for a national legislation.

Christian Timmermans

I would like to enter a remark on what Prof. Hirsch has just observed. Basically he said: "Is it fair to put the Commission, and the Council implicitly also, to such a severe test of developing general theories and principles and studying the economic impact before launching a harmonization initiative, when at the level of the Member States we might be less strict?"

I agree on that, of course, that we should not be more strict with regard to the Community, but perhaps there is indeed a risk that the Community will be less strict than the Member States. I say that because of the inherent complication of harmonization in itself. When the Community starts harmonizing it is to some extent legislating at the same time but starting from quite a different perspective. It starts harmonizing because of difficulties deriving from divergent national laws for the functioning of the Common Market. That is a different perspective which may in practice, particularly for the Commission, cause it to lose sight of the legislative aspect, that is not concentrate sufficiently on the question whether the solutions it is going to propose are intrinsically good solutions.

Prof. McComb has mentioned the example of the disclosure directives.[62] I think he is to some extent right in making the reproach that the Community has insufficiently taken into account the quality of the solutions put into these directives. I think that the important test in that case has been comparability rather than the quality of the various methods admitted by the directive.

Another example is the Commission's Green Paper on workers' participation.[63] There, I think, the Commission has really argued from a legislative point of view: what is a justified approach?

What I mean to say is that in talking about harmonization there is a risk that the Community is preparing its proposals less well than a national legislator would normally do.

[62] See *infra* at 238.
[63] *Bull. EC*, Supp. 8/1975.

Alain Hirsch

In relation to Prof. Timmermans' question, would you say that the political resistance to legislation would be more important in the Community area or in the Member States? It might mean that the danger of making wrong harmonized law is lower in the Community.

Geoffrey Fitchew

First of all, I think there is a danger that Community directives may not always be adequately researched before the proposal is put forward. I think that is primarily a problem of resources for the Commission so we could do more to make use of outside resources, commissioning preparatory surveys and so on. To some extent the danger is reduced in those cases where what we are proposing are minimum standards because Member States can remain free to propose tougher standards.

On Prof. Hirsch's question, I think on the whole there will be more resistance to legislation at Community level than at the national level and the often agonizingly slow process of reaching agreement on directives at Community level does on the whole mean that defects in the proposals are exposed and in part this substitutes perhaps for any omissions in the preparatory stage within the Commission.

Let me emphasize that we do try to prepare our proposals with great care and there is a very widespread consultation of interested parties and of national experts before we launch any proposal, very often lasting over a period of several years before we launch a proposal. But I think where the omissions tend to arise is in the lack of economic and statistical information available to us to make very detailed predictions about the likely impact of what they are proposing.

Klaus Hopt

A remark on Prof. Kitch's paper. You expressed the fear[64] that the national government would be more inclined to curb free trade than the States. That may be true within the US. Yet I wonder whether this is the case also in Europe.

My perception is that in Europe, at least up to now, the nation States have been more inclined to curb free trade. This shows clearly if one looks at most of the subsidies (maybe with the exception of agriculture, but even there the driving forces are national) or if one remembers the *de facto* closing of the frontiers for certain Japanese imports by France, for example the video affair.

[64] See *supra* at 47.

Christian Timmermans

I must say that I strongly back the remarks made by Mr. Fitchew in his paper,[65] refuting I would say in a cautious way, as also has been just said by Klaus Hopt, the thesis that States have so much interest in free trade that in many respects regulation is superfluous.

I must say that when the experience of European integration teaches us a lesson in this respect, then it is that the interest of free trade as perceived by States is certainly not sufficient to guarantee and ensure free movement of goods, persons and services in the integrated European market. I must say the extent of free movement of goods that has been achieved up to now is due to a large extent to the daring case-law of the Court of Justice to say no to Member States' interventionist and protectionist reflexes – perhaps also more frequent in the '70s than now, because then more than nowadays Member States thought that they were able to solve their economic problems by measures protecting their national markets.

I might add that on a more international scale, too, I wonder whether this thesis holds true. I just read reactions in the European press regarding the recent American Trade Act. I wonder whether in this case the interest of free trade has really been served in all respects or whether protectionist reflexes have also crept into it. I think the answer is quite simple. Many governments think to achieve short-term political gains with these reflexes, even acknowledging that perhaps in the longer run they run counter to the economic interest of us all.

Edmund Kitch

Whether the constituent States are more inclined to curb free trade. I think the answer to that has to be that there is no clear-cut answer. On the one hand, I think it is easier for special interest groups to capture smaller governmental units to serve their own purposes. On the other hand, it is harder for smaller governmental units to serve those interests effectively, and so the fact that a larger government with more economy to control has more to offer will set off incentives to capture it, and I would give EC agricultural policy as an example of the ability of a larger jurisdiction to impose more severe market distortions than a local jurisdiction.

[65] See *supra* at 5 ff.

IV. Concluding Remarks

Christian Meier-Schatz

I have two final remarks with respect to the question Prof. Schmidt addressed,[66] namely: where does competition work and, as I would like to add, in whose interest does it work?

Let me for this purpose, from the American point of view assigned to me in the Symposium, come back to the US market for corporate charters. The Delaware phenomenon is today probably both theoretically and empirically the most thoroughly investigated issue of regulatory competition. A lot of research efforts have been invested in this topic. And yet the results are still quite inconclusive. All we know is that reincorporation decisions are mainly made for three reasons, namely in connection with public offerings, mergers tactics and takeover situations. But it is absolutely unclear in whose interest those transactions occur. In particular, one cannot exclude the hypothesis that they are primarily made in order to save litigation costs for managers. On the supply side of the corporate charter market, we know that there is a political disequilibrium since the legislative process is heavily dominated by the corporate bar. But again there is no guarantee that the regulatory outcome finally favors shareholder interests and that it is dominated by efficiency considerations.

And exactly at this point I feel tempted to come back to what Prof. Hirsch stressed earlier,[67] namely that the answer to the question of whether you like competition, or which competition you like, depends mainly upon which outcome and results you like. The only thing which is fairly well established is the fact that regulatory competition probably leads to a race to the bottom. And you can clearly see in the American debate that people who prefer an outcome which minimizes shareholder protection rules, and those who subscribe to the contractual view of the corporation, prefer a competitive market. On the other hand, commentators who write on the traditional Berle/Means line are rather skeptical with respect to market mechanisms. Given the pretty inconclusive theoretical and empirical evidence, much indeed then depends upon (to use a hermeneutical term) the *Vorverständnis*, i.e., upon the basic political side of the corporate law debate on which you are standing.

My second point relates to the one that Prof. Timmermans has already raised.[68] I deem it important to emphasize that competition may work in some efficiency-oriented cases. But it certainly does not work as soon as broader public policy goals are introduced with some form of distributive implications. Given the fact that American corporation law is mainly dominated by efficiency, shareholder or investor oriented considerations, there might be indeed more room for a decentralized type of regulatory

[66] See *supra* at 118 f.
[67] See *supra* at 116 f.
[68] See *supra* at 117 f.

systems. In the EC, however, whose corporate laws also include broader public policy goals, there would be severe problems in realizing these objectives by a purely comparative model.

Edmund Kitch

I am concerned that the nature of the topic on which I undertook to write: economic models in light of the American experience, distorts the American constitutional tradition. The arrangement of competencies under the American constitutional scheme is in no way based upon an ideology of efficiency or free markets. It has quite different and I think more stable origins.

The theoreticians of the Constitution such as Hamilton and Jefferson and Madison were not focussed on questions of efficient economic organization. Their programme was human freedom, and the preservation of individual freedom under a stable government structure, and I think they were very wise and insightful on those questions. The basic idea was to try to set up a government system which had lots of competing power centers, quite self-consciously aware that this tended to make things quite messy and might even, at least in the short run, impose substantial cost.

They really held the view that it was better to be free and poor than to be rich and in chains. They did so much better than many do in understanding how the system they were creating would work. Subsequent history, I think, is largely consistent with that and you get a lot of really quite irrational movements between powers and bodies, so the resulting picture is quite helter-skelter and I do not think can really be very well explained on efficiency arguments and there is a lot after-the-fact justification in some of the rationales of competing jurisdictions, the role of Delaware and so on. And you get a lot of historical shifts. But it is clear that the power centers created in the system have survived and been stabilized and have always been available to hear claims that some other power center in this system was abusing its authority.

I must say that listening to the talk about the Single Market, I find myself a little concerned that the Single Market programme has been sold as an efficiency programme and is based on a kind of bread-and-butter notion that a system of technocratic management from Brussels can direct the economy of the Single Market through knowledge of economic efficiency, so everybody will simply have more, and is not that wonderful?

Our discussion on all the particular points quickly illustrates that the efficiency norms are highly indeterminant as to particular rules and mistakes are likely to be made. And I would predict that assuming for the moment that the "open market in 1992" programme moves ahead to completion, then the real crisis for the Single Market will come about when the second-order effects of that liberalization start to feed back to the constituent members of the Single Market and upon their internal political system which will then cause appeals to be made to the Center for additional actions and responses to those effects. I am thinking of the labor union problem which I mentioned in my paper.[69] It seems to me the labor unions are not going to be happy with the collective bargaining effects of an open European market if there is no European labor law, and I think you can see a set of cascading effects (plus presumably at some point you will have a recession), and at that point the programme will not look so obviously desirable.

Questions can always be raised about whether the wrong choices have been made, and at that point do you suddenly turn your back on it and say: "Well, we thought it was going to make us rich but it does not seem to be doing it now?" Or do you unify around the programme based on some longer-term commitment?

As an American, what seems to me to be so wonderful about the Commission is that it does create a power center which is able to raise questions about the policies of the governments of Europe and force them to justify them; it is the dialogue and the discussion which take place which is the great positive contribution. But if the programme is really just sold as a "we'll-get-richer programme," I would think in the long run it would be an unstable institution because it will not be able to deliver year in and year out. There will be bad years as well as good ones.

Hartmut Schmidt

Prof. Timmermans[70] and Prof. Buxbaum[71] indicated that the question of choice may be too narrow. Or stated differently, if one leaves it to the choice of an individual one may not get the full picture and may not take into account all the problems. Of course this is a very valid statement and I wholeheartedly agree with it. But I think you ought to show on a case-by-case basis what other interests are involved. If you do not I think this blanket statement is a discussion stopper.

Rationality and irrationality.[72] I would like to say that Georg Engler, back in the '60s, said: "We ought to have more investor protection because our rational investors will act irrationally once they have had bad luck." This was a rather convincing pitch but nobody speaks of it today any more because German investors behave differently or because there was successful regulation or what have you. At least we do not have examples like, what was it,[73] the Association of Retired Dentists of Southern California?

If I may make a final comment. Where does competition work? I have closely followed the stock exchange competition and I think the Nightin-

[69] See *supra* at 48.
[70] See *supra* at 117.
[71] See *supra* at 114 f.
[72] See *supra* at 115.
[73] See *supra* at 116.

gale market[74] is a case in point. There was one man with one idea: he came up with a set of contracts and established the first European over-the-counter market. Regulatory constraints would have been hostile to such an attempt on the Continent, British law permitted it. Nightingale's competition caused the London Stock Exchange to come up with the Unlisted Securities Market. It caused it to come up with the Third Market. It indirectly caused changes in the exchange structure all over Europe. There are other impressive examples for successful exchange competition. What has it done? Basically it has driven out anticompetitive rules which were frequently disguised as investor protection rules and by doing so it has benefitted issuers and investors.

[74] See *supra* at 118 f.

Chapter Three

Methods and Tools for Integration

A. Report: Christian Timmermans

I. Introduction

There is no reason to question the need for and merits of the comparatist approach followed by *Buxbaum* and *Hopt* in their book.[1] Their analysis of the US experience in the accommodation of state and federal authority at the legal level of enterprise within an integrated market, is most useful as a background for reevaluating the ongoing European experience. The American experience disposes the European observer to modesty about the actual results of that European experience. Although the actual results of market integration, given the short period of its evolution thus far, are in fact quite impressive, the intellectual and legal quality of concepts and standards underlying the EC harmonization efforts on company and capital market law is quite limited. Not only the political decision-making process within the EC institutions but also the contributions of academic debate lack sophistication. The EC harmonization process, particularly in the company law field, seems to be a matter of "muddling through" much more than an overall policy oriented by clear concepts of what market integration requires. The grand design of the European Commission at the end of the sixties[2] – again I refer mainly to the company law field – has faded. A clear philosophy with regard to the important category of private companies, for instance, is still lacking; instead, priority has been given to initiatives of relatively minor importance. I must concede however that the Commission, quite recently, has taken steps to reawake that dormant beauty, the European Company.[3]

[1] See R.M. BUXBAUM & K.J. HOPT, *Legal Harmonization and the Business Enterprise* 22 (Berlin/New York 1988).

[2] See *Berkhouwer* Report, European Parliament, Session Doc. No. 53/1966-1967; Memorandum of the Commission of the EEC regarding the introduction of a European Company 1966, *Bull. EC*, Supp. 9-10/1966; Memorandum of the European Commission on industrial policy, 1970.

[3] Memorandum from the Commission of 15 July 1988, Doc. COM(88)320 final. See also the new proposals of 1989: O.J. C 263/41 (1989) and O.J. C 263/69 (1989).

Confrontation between the mature American system and the just budding European experience invites a rethinking of the necessity and scope of the EC harmonization in these fields. *Buxbaum* and *Hopt* themselves have resisted this temptation. They even question the appropriateness of developing new approaches and concepts, an exercise they find to be of no more than theoretical value.[4] They can, however, hardly disqualify law professors from such an activity. Furthermore, their reluctance is objectionable for practical reasons. One should not underestimate the new potential for decision making created by the recent political thrust of the internal market 1992 movement. The political climate has changed considerably since the time *Buxbaum* and *Hopt* wrote their book, which also gives a fresh stimulus to reopen the academic debate.

I shall therefore begin this paper with a few comments, inspired by the book, on the aims and scope of harmonization (II). Some remarks follow on the methods and tools of harmonization (III).

II. The Necessity of Harmonization, in Particular of Company Law

(1) The appraisal by *Buxbaum* and *Hopt* of the stated aims of company law harmonization, of its present realization and its prospects for the foreseeable future is put in rather negative terms ("bold, if not indeed utopian," "slowdown of meaningful harmonization efforts," "prospects ... are relatively dim"[5]). The authors question the contribution by the harmonization of company law to market integration, at least they enumerate the theoretical weaknesses of this relationship, as stated by the Community institutions.[6] Their analysis of the harmonization efforts regarding capital market law (and harmonization of disclosure rules) is more positive.[7] In their economic model, priority could be given to this harmonization.[8] I agree that capital market harmonization is more obviously linked to market integration, resulting in improvement of capital allocation and, more generally, realization of a European capital market. Because of differences in aims and scope, both fields should be clearly distinguished. Indeed, the analysis of company law harmonization seems to be more delicate and difficult, but for that reason also more interesting theoretically. I shall therefore limit my comments to the domain of company law.

[4] BUXBAUM & HOPT, *supra* note 1, at 17.
[5] *Id.* at 193, 271, 19.
[6] *Id.* at 200-201.
[7] *Id.* at 202-203.
[8] *Id.* at 280-281.

(2) Any discussion about the scope of harmonization requires as a first step a clear analysis of, and consensus about, its aims. The EC institutions themselves appear to shy away from such a debate. The Commission, as the authors rightly say, is generally pushing for harmonization; the Council is counteracting. This is a highly politicized process, the final outcome of which is more often a political compromise than a solution well-founded on premises derived from the aims of market integration. The Commission itself is, at least publicly, not really arguing its proposals for the sake of market integration. Nor do the predrafts and comparative law reports prepared by its special advisers on company law take a strong stand.[9] Arguments of this nature put forward in the preamble of Commission proposals for harmonization directives are scarce, fairly vague and not always very convincing. An obvious example can be found in the preamble of the Second Company Law Directive,[10] also referred to by *Buxbaum* and *Hopt*. The First Directive[11] still included all categories of limited liability companies in its field of application; the Second Directive applies only to the category of public companies (public limited company, *société anonyme*, *Aktiengesellschaft*). This limitation of scope is justified in the following terms: "because their activities predominate in the economy of the Member States and frequently extend beyond their national boundaries."[12]

This statement in no way explains why the aims of market integration require that priority be given to the public company. At least in Member States like the United Kingdom, Germany and the Netherlands, the private company is a much more common vehicle for doing business than the public company, and is certainly not limited to the smaller businesses alone. From the point of view of cross-border trade in goods and services, but also as far as the exercise of the right of establishment is concerned, private companies are anything but a negligible factor or of minor interest only to the functioning of the Common Market. In practice the Commission, with the exception of the Green Paper on workers' participation,[13] argues its proposals mostly on technical grounds of company law, not in terms of integration policy.

This is not to say that the Commission has no philosophy on these matters, but such a philosophy must be researched in general statements and occasional memoranda submitted to the Council, e.g. the Memorandum on

[9] See SCHWARTZ, "30 Jahre EG-Rechtsangleichung," in *Eine Ordnungspolitik für Europa, Festschrift für Hans von der Groeben zu seinem 80. Geburtstag* 338-339 (Baden-Baden 1987).

[10] O.J. L 26/1 (1977).

[11] O.J. L 65/8 (1968).

[12] See Second Company Law Directive, *supra* note 10, at 1.

[13] *Bull. EC*, Supp. 8/1975.

industrial policy of 1970. The debate on the aims and scope of company law harmonization has been mostly an academic debate, no one between the EC institutions.

The somewhat hidden nature of, in particular, the Commission's views on the aims of company law harmonization might explain why *Buxbaum* and *Hopt* are not entirely thorough in their survey of the aims of harmonization. Indeed, the original aim of this harmonization, as intended by the authors of the EEC Treaty themselves, has not been mentioned in the book. *Buxbaum* and *Hopt* only mention the end-means relationship of harmonization in terms of fostering market integration. Certainly, apart from disclosure rules, an aim towards integration cannot easily be established, let alone proved. However, the Treaty authors seem not to have intended this harmonization as an additional instrument for market integration at all. As far as I know, it has been only since the seventies that the European Commission has advocated this approach.

(3) Some delegations negotiating the EEC Treaty were concerned that by granting a right of establishment to companies incorporated under the law of any Member State, national markets would open up to foreign companies, whose incorporation statute would afford much less protection than was required by the company law of the host state. The Netherlands in particular, because of its at that time fairly liberal and lenient company law system, was feared to become the Delaware of Europe. The harmonization requirement of Article 54(3)(g) was therefore included in the Chapter on the right of establishment as a counterpart to the liberal grant of this right to all companies incorporated under the law of a Member State as further defined in Article 58.[14] The idea seems thus to have been a free movement of companies from Member States throughout the common market, provided that their statutes of incorporation afforded equivalent protection to shareholders and third parties, creditors in particular. The fairly vague wording of Article 54(3)(g) reflects this concern quite well.

This approach puts the company law harmonization in an entirely different perspective. The harmonization is then not so much an instrument to facilitate market integration, as a counterpart, a *quid pro quo*, the price asked by some delegations during the EEC Treaty negotiations for their agreement to grant the right of establishment also to companies. Whether this harmonization was originally meant to precede the grant of this privilege, or was intended merely as an accompanying measure, can remain unanswered. The Court of Justice has ruled the right of establishment under Article 52 to be unconditional and directly applicable since the end of the transitional period, irrespective of the progress or completion of the harmonization process.[15]

[14] For the relevant literature, see my article on harmonization of company law, "Die europäische Rechtsangleichung im Gesellschaftsrecht," 48 *RabelsZ* 1 and 2, note 1 (1984).

[15] Case 2/74, *Reyners*, [1974] E.C.R. 631.

Were this an accepted interpretation of the aims of company law harmonization, any justification of individual harmonization proposals on account of their contribution to market integration would become superfluous. The main point would be to achieve equivalence of protection for members and third parties, which the text of Article 54(3)(g) indeed requires; in practice this aim has been the main justification given by the European Commission.

(4) It should be noted that the feared outcomes mentioned above, particularly a kind of Delaware effect within the European context, have not materialized. The harmonization of company law is far from complete, particularly with regard to private companies. Important differences remain as to levels of protection afforded by the national company law systems. Nevertheless there is no question of "statute shopping" within the European Community, at least not to an extent comparable to that in the states of Delaware and New Jersey. The reason is obvious: most Member States, those of Continental Europe in particular, continue to apply the *siège réel* approach to international company law and rules of conflict. Foreign companies having their effective seat within the territory of these states are either not recognized as a legal entity (France) or obliged to apply the rules of local company law. In fact, a freedom of incorporation, as it exists in the United States, is unknown in Europe and would be unacceptable for most Member States. In this respect, the situation in the Community nowadays is very similar to the one existing in the United States about a century ago. I refer to the Supreme Court decision of 1868 in *Paul v. Virginia*.[16]

In practice, conflicts of company laws within the Community are the exception. In exercising the right of establishment, companies prefer as a rule to organize sizeable foreign establishments in a company form under local law. When they do otherwise, however, painful situations may follow. In recent case-law of German courts, for example, English limiteds with their *Verwaltungssitz* (headquarters) within Germany were treated as *offene Handelsgesellschaft* under German law.[17] Consequently the directors were held personally liable for the debts of their company. Such accidents explain why prudent European business lawyers normally advise their clients to incorporate foreign establishments under the law of the country of establishment.

(5) Were the fears of (some of) the EEC Treaty authors regarding the import of less protective foreign company statutes and a possible Delaware

[16] 75 U.S. (8 Wall.) 168 (1868). See BUXBAUM & HOPT, *supra* note 1, at 36.

[17] See B. GROSSFELD, *Internationales Gesellschaftsrecht* (Internationales Privatrecht, vol. 1a, No. 2, Berlin 1981) at 309-310 with references to case-law, 323 ff and 400 ; see also H. WIEDEMANN, *Gesellschaftsrecht* 794 (vol. I, Grundlagen, Munich 1980). For recent cases see also: Bayrisches OLG, Beschluß vom 18.7.1985, 31 *AG* 45 (1986); see also NIESSEN, 31 *AG* 116 (1986); Landgericht Itzehoe, Beschluß vom 16.1.1985, 2. Zivilkammer (Nr. 20259/83) and Oberlandesgericht München, Urteil vom 6.5.1986, 32 *RIW* 820 (1986).

effect resulting from the liberal grant of the right of establishment then totally unwarranted? An opposite impression results from an analysis of Article 58, the provision in the Chapter on the right of establishment which grants this right to companies under the same conditions as apply to natural persons. This Article goes quite far in accepting a freedom of incorporation for the Common Market. Indeed, the right of establishment can already be invoked by companies incorporated under the law of a Member State and having only their registered office within the Community.

As for the exercise of the right of establishment by companies, distinction is to be made between primary establishment (the main business of the company) and secondary establishment (agencies, branches, subsidiaries). The right to set up a primary establishment is, within the meaning of Article 58, granted to companies without further conditions. However, the right to set up a secondary establishment can only be invoked by companies that are "established in the territory of any Member State." The Council has construed this condition for companies to ensure that they have at least an economic link with one of the Member States.[18]

Now the question arises of whether the exercise by companies of the right of establishment, which is a directly applicable right enforceable through the national courts, can be thwarted wholly or partly by application of a rule of conflict in the country of establishment requiring obeyance of (rules of) local company law. Do the Articles 52 and 58 EEC Treaty not oblige the forum state to accept the foreign statute of companies that are beneficiaries of the right of establishment under the Treaty? This tenet has occasionally been defended in academic writing.[19] It is interesting to note that recent case-law of the Court of Justice is also moving in that direction.

(6) In the *Segers* case, decided by the European Court on 10 July 1986,[20] Mr. Segers, who was the owner and director of an English private company with its sole establishment in the Netherlands, had invoked the benefit of Dutch social security legislation, as it applied (at that time) also to directors of Dutch companies. The competent social security authority, however, refused to treat the limited in question as it would Dutch companies. The argument was that the limited had no link at all with the United Kingdom, Segers' business being in all respects a purely Dutch business. In subsequent proceedings before a national court, Segers invoked Articles 52 and 58 EEC Treaty. He argued that the private company of which he was a director,

[18] See General Programme for the abolition of restrictions on freedom of establishment, O.J. 36/62 (1962).

[19] See BUXBAUM & HOPT, *supra* note 1, at 228; see also TIMMERMANS, "Erkenning van vreemde vennootschappen en rechtspersonen," in 81 *Medelingen Nederlandse Vereniging voor Internationaal Recht* 46-50 (1980) with further references.

[20] Case 79/85, [1986] E.C.R. 2375. See also the analysis of this decision by CATH, "Freedom of Establishment of Companies: A New Step Towards Completion of the Internal Market," in 7 *Yearbook of European Law* 247 (F.G. Jacobs ed., Oxford 1987).

being formed under the law of a Member State and having its registered office within a Member State (UK), was a beneficiary of the right of establishment under Article 52 and could therefore invoke the principle of equal treatment embodied in this Article in relation to national companies. According to the social security authority, however, these Articles of the Treaty do not apply in a situation where the undertaking as such is established in the Netherlands only, and the private company in question is not exercising any economic activity in the United Kingdom.

The Court of Justice, in answering preliminary questions submitted by the Dutch court, held that once a company satisfies the criteria of Article 58 EEC Treaty, the provisions regarding the right of establishment apply irrespective of whether the company in question operates only through an agency, a branch or a subsidiary in another Member State. The public order exception of Article 56 allows Member States to take, within limits, special measures against fraud if justified to protect public order, public safety or public health. The Court, however, ruled that refusing the benefit of a social security scheme cannot be considered an appropriate measure for that purpose.

The obvious conclusion seems to be that pseudo-foreign companies too, provided they have been formed in accordance with the law of a Member State and have at least their registered office within the Community, are beneficiaries of the right of establishment and consequently of the freedom to supply (and receive) services by virtue of Articles 59 ff EEC Treaty, which refer back to Article 58. Thus, within the scope of the EEC Treaty, any discrepancy between the Member State of incorporation and the Member State where the company has its effective seat, seems irrelevant. The registered office determines in principle a company's statute. This seat, so the Court states in the *Segers* decision,[21] has the function of ascertaining the connection with the legal order of a particular Member State ("*rattachement à l'ordre juridique d'un Etat Membre*"), just as nationality does for natural persons. This seems to imply that recognition cannot be denied to a foreign company that can invoke Articles 52 and 58. If so, a Member State like France which adheres to the classical form of the *siège réel* system, would not be allowed to follow this approach with regard to EC companies. As far as the choice of a legal form for doing business is concerned, this interpretation of Article 58 propagates a system of freedom of incorporation quite comparable with the actual situation in the United States.[22] The possibility to combat fraud allowed by the Court in referring to Article 56

[21] A similar interpretation was already given by the Court in Case 270/83, "*Avoir Fiscal*," Commission v. France, [1986] E.C.R. 273.

[22] See also the conclusion of Advocate-General Darmon in *Segers* (case 79/85, *supra* note 20). Darmon (*id.* at 2381) has no difficulty in accepting that a national of a Member State benefits from:

"*la souplesse du droit britannique des sociétés et d'exploiter l'effet d'attraction exercé, selon lui, sur la clientèle, par une appellation à connotation anglo-saxonne.*"

seems of limited scope only. Postponing further analysis, let me first interject a few critical comments on the *Segers* judgment.

(7) The European Court has no difficulty at all in accepting a pseudo-foreign company as beneficiary of the right of establishment. According to Article 52 EEC Treaty this right implies for nationals of a Member State who are established within the Community the possibility of setting up an agency, branch or subsidiary in the territory of another Member State. Legal persons formed in accordance with the law of a Member State and with at least their registered office within the Community are by virtue of Article 58 to be treated in the same way as nationals of Member States. Therefore, Article 52 also applies to a legal person operating, like Segers, only in the Member State where a branch has been established. In my view this syllogism is not convincing, for a number of reasons.

First, it is debatable whether a pseudo-foreign company really constitutes a cross-border establishment. Segers had apparently acquired an "empty" English limited (shelf company), and in doing so did not obtain an establishment in the United Kingdom. The limited, by becoming the owner of Segers' undertaking, acquired an establishment in the Netherlands, but this operation merely involves a change of ownership. Such a manoeuvre has nothing to do with cross-border establishment, which is in substance what Article 52 EEC Treaty is about. Before and after the operation which brings the undertaking into the limited, there is only one undertaking exclusively established in the Netherlands. The Court however does not consider this of any relevance. The Court's decision is the more astonishing because the Court has repeatedly ruled that the Treaty regime regarding the free movement of goods, persons and services does not apply to internal situations within one Member State which have no cross-border aspects. I refer to the *Debauve* case, in which Article 59 regarding the free movement of services was said not to apply to activities all the relevant aspects of which remain limited to one Member State.[23] Now, I shall not deny that in the *Segers* case there is an international aspect because of the limited; the question is only – we are dealing with a *pseudo*-foreign company – whether this aspect is relevant in the context of the right of establishment. The Court does not really answer this question.

There is more to say about this. In the case-law of the European Court one finds decisions which refuse wholly or partly to apply the principles of free movement because the parties concerned have in fact used or attempted to use the possibility of free movement in order to escape national law. The *Van Binsbergen* case[24] is a classic example. The Court did not accept the applicability of the freedom to supply services in a situation where a service

[23] Case 52/79, [1980] E.C.R. 833. See also Case 115/78, *Kroon*, [1979] E.C.R. 399; Case 175/78, *Saunders*, [1979] E.C.R. 1129; Case 35/82 and 36/82, *Morson*, [1982] E.C.R. 3723; Case 180/83, *Moser*, [1984] E.C.R. 2539 and Case 298/84, *Paolo Iorio*, [1986] E.C.R. 247.

[24] Case 33/74, [1974] E.C.R. 1299.

provider whose activity is entirely or principally directed towards the territory of a Member State, uses the freedom to supply services under Article 59 EEC Treaty "for the purpose of avoiding the professional rules of conduct which would be applicable to him if he were established within that State."[25]

A yet more pertinent precedent seems to be given by the "*French Book Case*" (*Leclerc*).[26] The Court considered the application of a regime like the "*Loi Lang*" (fixed book prices) to books imported from another Member State incompatible with the principles of the free movement of goods (Art. 30 EEC Treaty). That conclusion also applied to books published in France, exported to another Member State from which they were re-imported into France (U-turn). The Court, however, makes an exception for the case when it would be objectively established that the books in question had only been exported and re-imported in order to elude the national legislation involved.[27]

A comparison of the "*Book*" case with the *Segers* decision shows that obvious abuse in the "*Book*" case results in the utter non-applicability of the EC regime regarding the free movement of goods. In the *Segers* decision, in contrast, free movement (right of establishment) as such applies also in case of fraud which, by the way, has not been defined further by the Court. Although the *Segers* case upholds the public order exception of Article 56 EEC Treaty, this approach leaves Member States much less freedom of action.

Another objection to the *Segers* decision regards the applicability of the right of secondary establishment to this case. It has been observed already that this right can be invoked only by companies having an economic link with a Member State. That condition, however, seems not to be satisfied in the case of Segers. The limited in question was an empty company and thus had no economic link with any Member State. Furthermore, the establishment in the Netherlands was not a secondary but the primary establishment of the limited. By the way, Article 52 EEC Treaty does not require an economic link with regard to primary establishments. In my view, therefore, the Court should have qualified the situation in the *Segers* case as regarding the exercise of the right of primary establishment. To qualify the main establishment of a foreign company as a branch is not compatible with the distinction between primary and secondary establishment as implied by Article 52. A branch, not only in colloquial language but also in the system of Article 52, typically is an adjunct, not the main establishment of the company. The Court has, by the way, interpreted the notion of a branch

[25] Case 33/74, *supra* note 24, confirmed by Case 205/84, Commission v. Germany, [1986] E.C.R. 3755.
[26] Case 229/83, [1985] E.C.R. 1.
[27] *Id.* at 35.

accordingly, within the framework of the European Judgments Enforcement Treaty.[28]

(8) The *Segers* decision thus seems to warrant the conclusion that Article 58 EEC Treaty, in determining the category of companies and legal persons which are beneficiaries of the right of establishment, makes no stricter demands than that they conform to the incorporation system. In other words a discrepancy between the Member State of incorporation and the Member State of the effective seat is irrelevant within the context of Article 52. The question, however, remains unanswered as to what extent Member States remain competent to apply rules of their own company law to foreign companies. The Court itself mentions the public order exception of Article 56 as a possible legal basis for national action against fraud. Yet it is doubtful that this allows for the application of national company law or parts thereof to (pseudo-)foreign companies. The Court's case-law regarding this and similar public order exceptions shows that their use by Member States is subject to strict conditions. The Court has limited the application of this exception to cases where a sufficiently serious breach of public order can be proven. Moreover, the necessity of the national intervention is submitted to a strict test of proportionality.[29] The mere quality of being a pseudo-foreign company seems to present insufficient reasons to claim such a breach of public order. Did the Court in the *Segers* case not accept the incorporation under the law of a Member State as a perfectly normal use of the right of establishment, although no economic link whatsoever existed with that Member State? Must other elements be added to justify the use of the public order exception? The intention (to be demonstrated) to escape the company law of the host state for instance? An *animus fraudendi*? These are still open questions. It is doubtful that Article 56 would allow for the application of particular rules of a host state's company law as scope rules (*règles d'application immédiate*). Article 56 requires a substantial threat to public order. This condition differs from the international public order exception under international private law, or from a scope rule which, because of its special nature, is considered to be immune to the claims for validity of a foreign company's statute. Article 56 is an exception clause for special circumstances in which foreign companies in practice, e.g., because of their object's clause or the activities they enter into, cause a serious threat to public order. At any rate, at least in my view, Article 56 cannot be used as a backdoor to justify a general application of (parts of) national company law to companies incorporated in another Member State.

This is not to say that the privilege of the right of establishment granted to a foreign company obliges it to accept *in toto* the foreign statute, and excludes any application of national company law rules by the country of establishment. In my view, Article 52 EEC Treaty leaves some scope for such an application, provided that the exercise of the right of establishment

[28] Case 33/78, *Somafer*, [1978] E.C.R. 2193.
[29] Case 36/75, *Rutili*, [1975] E.C.R. 1232.

remains unaffected. To require the foreign company to organize according to all standards of the local company law would certainly frustrate the exercise of the right of establishment, at least as far as primary establishments and branches are concerned.[30] The company in question would in fact be forced to incorporate its establishment under the local company law, as is still normal practice at present. The Court, however, has stressed explicitly that companies must have a real choice between setting up either a branch or a subsidiary, that is incorporating the foreign establishment in a legal form under the law of the host country.[31]

Where the right of establishment however remains unaffected, Article 52 EEC Treaty cannot be invoked to oppose the application of rules of local company law as additional guarantees required by the host state next to the statute of incorporation.[32] These rules must, however, be compatible with the statute of incorporation and in effect provide for a higher standard of protection. Otherwise their application to the foreign company would not be justified objectively and thus would entail a restriction of the right of establishment incompatible with Article 52 as interpreted by the Court of Justice.[33] Moreover the rules in question must not have been subject already to EC harmonization, as for instance the rules of capital protection regarding public companies. I would think that once harmonization has been achieved, the foreign company's statute must be recognized as presenting an acceptable level of protection, provided of course that the directive in question has been correctly implemented and only for issues covered by that harmonization. This situation approaches the actual position in the United States: freedom of incorporation, with some latitude for Member States to require local standards to be satisfied also by foreign companies, provided that their free movement is not affected.

(9) My comments on the *Segers* decision of the European Court have been extensive because in my view this case-law is essential, and that for at least two reasons.

First, this case-law demonstrates that the Court of Justice may also intervene in matters of international company law. Further evolution in this field might be expected.[34] The EEC Treaty might have more important consequences than legal doctrine has been prepared to accept, and not only

[30] Examples are given by the case-law of German courts referred to in note 17 *supra*.

[31] Explicitly so the "*Avoir Fiscal*" decision referred to in note 21 *supra*.

[32] *Cf.* the "*Überlagerungstheorie*" developed by SANDROCK, "Ein Amerikanisches Lehrstück für das Kollisionsrecht der Kapitalgesellschaften," 42 *RabelsZ* 227 (1978); a similar approach has been defended in the Netherlands by P. VLAS, *Rechtspersonen in het internationaal privaatrecht* 65 ff (Leiden 1982).

[33] E.g. Case 33/74, *supra* note 24; Case 71/76, *Thieffry*, [1977] E.C.R. 765; Case 15/78, *Koestler*, [1978] E.C.R. 1971; Case 16/78, *Choquet*, [1978] E.C.R. 2293; Case 110/78 and 111/78, *Van Wesemael*, [1979] E.C.R. 35.

[34] Another important case in this respect is the still pending Case 81/87, *Daily Mail*. Case since decided: see [1988] E.C.R. 5483.

in the context of the right of establishment.[35] The free movement of services (Art. 59), and even the principle of free movement of goods, in particular Article 30, might have implications. In my view *Buxbaum* and *Hopt* somewhat underestimate the potential of the Court's case-law for this field. The European Court may not be placed in a hierarchical relationship to national courts, and therefore may lack a federal status that would make it fully comparable to the US Supreme Court.[36] Nevertheless, in the last thirty years the Court has built up quite an effective cooperation with national courts by virtue of the successful functioning of the preliminary procedure of Article 177.[37] This cooperation has increasingly ensured a uniform application of Community law in Member States, with priority over national law.

A second reason why the *Segers* (and "*Avoir Fiscal*"[38]) case-law seems to me of great interest is that it also could change the environment considerably for the harmonization efforts in the company law field. If freedom of incorporation within the European Community were to be realized further by the Court's case-law, companies incorporated under the law of any of the Member States would be free to move throughout the internal market. Their statute would have to be accepted in all Member States. No longer would there be reason, at least in the context of company law, to organize an establishment in another Member State in a company form of that state. A harmonization would not be necessary to enable or to facilitate this free movement. On the other hand this freedom of incorporation would certainly favor something like a Delaware effect in Europe. One might expect that companies will be tempted much more than today to opt for a lenient statute when the risk of confrontation with foreign company law, through the application of the effective seat approach, disappears. Could the resulting free competition between national company law systems not have a harmonizing impact on these systems as has apparently occurred in the United States?[39] At least regarding the more technical rules of company law, such a harmonization is certainly not to be excluded. Personally, I have the impression that this is already happening to some extent in actual practice. In the Netherlands, for instance, the legislator has sometimes refused to go further than the minimum level required by company law directives arguing that otherwise Dutch business would be disadvantaged in its competition with companies from other Member States. This argument has occasionally

[35] In the German literature, for instance, Art. 52 and 58 EEC Treaty are generally said to have no immediate effects in the field of international company law because of the mere programmatic nature of these provisions (*Programmsätze*); *cf.* e.g. GROSSFELD, *supra* note 17, at 328, and WIEDEMANN, *supra* note 17, at 794.

[36] BUXBAUM & HOPT, *supra* note 1, at 5-6.

[37] See TMC ASSER INSTITUTE, *Article 177 EEC; Experiences and Problems* (Amsterdam etc. 1987).

[38] See *supra* note 21.

[39] BUXBAUM & HOPT, *supra* note 1, at 128.

even motivated the Dutch legislator to abolish existing provisions, e.g. in the field of financial disclosure, that as such were allowed by the directives but went further than the imposed minimum level. Such an evolution is however much less probable with regard to highly politicized rules of company law like those on workers' participation.

(10) In light of these developments, and taking into account also the extremely cumbersome nature of the harmonization process which the subsequent accessions of new Member States have only increased, the question arises whether the time has not come to reconsider the necessity and scope of company law harmonization. Perhaps the Commission should develop a new approach, as it has done in the field of free movement of goods, with regard to the so-called technical obstacles to trade. Of course, the EEC Treaty requirement under Article 54(3)(g) remains. This harmonization, intended as a *quid pro quo*, may even become more relevant when the right of establishment is interpreted by the European Court as to imply a freedom of incorporation. But would a harmonization of more limited scope not be sufficient? Three general suggestions follow, which require further thought and research.

a. A harmonization of international company law must be considered. The efforts to bring to life the Recognition Treaty of 1968 have failed. That is certainly not a matter for regret considering the unbalanced solutions contained in this treaty; these were partly contrary even to the EEC Treaty.[40] Nevertheless, a case can be made for a harmonization of conflict (and scope) rules, not in the form of an international treaty between Member States based on Article 220 EEC Treaty, but by a directive under Article 54(3)(g) EEC Treaty. In view of the evolution of the Court's case-law, the delineation of the extent to which a foreign company's statute must be accepted appears appropriate. Furthermore, this harmonization must determine the remaining scope within which, and the conditions under which, Member States may apply rules of national company law to foreign companies. This harmonization seems necessary first to promote legal security for companies, their members and third parties, and secondly to prevent Member States from infringing upon the principles of free movement of companies within the internal market. Such a harmonization by the way of international company law would not be completely new. The Commission has indeed already taken a first step in submitting to the Council the proposed Eleventh Directive on disclosure by branches established in a Member State by companies from another state.[41]

Special attention must be given in this context to rules, embodied in company law, regarding workers' participation. Does the necessary acceptance of the foreign company's statute prohibit the application by a Member State of its own regime of workers' participation in a situation where the primary establishment of the foreign company is within the territory of that

[40] See TIMMERMANS, *supra* note 19, at 64-71 with further references.

[41] O.J. C 203/12 (1986). Directive adopted in 1989: see O.J. L 395/36 (1989).

Member State? To what extent can Article 56 EEC Treaty be invoked successfully by that Member State? Admittedly, Article 56 can be beneficial in cases of clear abuse, that is, when there exists no economic link at all with the Member State of incorporation, and the intention to elude the regime of the country of establishment is obvious. Unfortunately, proving an intention is often in practice a difficult matter. At any rate, a blockade under Community law to the application of a national regime of workers' participation will be an extremely sensitive political issue. If the foreign company were to satisfy at least one of a series of alternative models admitted by a harmonization directive, the acceptance of its statute would probably be easier.[42] This must be explored further.

b. In each particular case harmonization should remain limited as much as possible to principles, without in-depth involvement in technical details. Decision-making practice until now has shown an irresistible tendency for the opposite. Largely responsible were attempts by Member States to insert detailed exceptions into the directives, mostly in the form of options for Member States to maintain particular solutions of national law. Demanding less detail is indeed an old query and may sound rather gratuitous. There is a new argument, however, that might make it easier for Council and Commission to reverse this trend. If a real freedom of incorporation seriously limits the Member States' ability to apply their national peculiarities to foreign companies, it becomes less interesting to strive for their maintenance in the harmonization process. On the other hand, it might also become easier to restrict harmonization to principles when all partners in the decision-making process, the Commission included, accept the *quid pro quo* approach, that is, the achievement of an equivalent minimum level of protection, as the primary aim of this harmonization.

c. Separate attention must be given to the question whether special harmonization measures are required for specific cross-border operations of companies which become legally complicated because of the necessity to satisfy various national company law systems at the same time. Obvious examples are the functioning of international groups, international mergers for which the Commission already has rightly taken a special initiative (proposed Tenth Directive[43]), and the transfer of a company's seat from one Member State to another.

III. Methods and Tools of Harmonization

Buxbaum and *Hopt* distinguish between direct and indirect methods and tools for integration of company and capital market law.[44] I do not dispute

[42] See the Amended Proposal for a Fifth Company Law Directive (O.J. C 240/2 (1983)), Art. 4(2).

[43] O.J. C 23/11 (1985).

[44] BUXBAUM & HOPT, *supra* note 1, at 226.

the usefulness of this distinction, but I raise two questions with regard to the classification of two particular methods. Conflict of laws is considered by the authors as an indirect method of integration. I am inclined to range a harmonization of conflict and scope rules as suggested above with the direct methods. It follows from the preceding paragraph that in my view this method, that is a harmonization of international company law, should be given more weight. My second question relates to self-regulation "in the shadow of Community law." Whereas *Buxbaum* and *Hopt* consider this a direct method, I would consider this much more an indirect method of integration precisely because of its voluntary nature.

A few sketchy comments follow on the methods and tools as they have been analyzed by *Buxbaum* and *Hopt*,[45] though presented in a different order.

A. Directives

(1) Directives remain in practice the most important instrument for the integration of company and capital market law. In my view they are also the most adequate Community instrument for that purpose, largely superior to the other instruments, regulations included. Directives advance integration, and at the same time respect the national legal environment. They are an intrinsically *federalist* instrument, therefore preferable to regulations which are much more supranational by nature. The latter are appropriate when intended to introduce a uniform body of rules throughout the Community. That is not to say that directives cannot (or should not) seriously affect national sovereignty and limit considerably the regulating powers of the national parliaments.[46]

(2) Harmonization directives under Article 54(3)(g) EEC Treaty can be enacted by a qualified majority. The Fourth Directive on company accounts[47] is a practical example. There is no need for applying Article 100A in this context.[48] I doubt, moreover, that this provision can be applied at all for the purposes of company and capital market harmonization. Article 100A(2) explicitly excludes the use of this Article in the field of free movement of persons. Admittedly, the application of this Article would be more acceptable for capital market harmonization, due to its links with the free movement of capital and with the realization of a European capital market.

[45] *Id.* at 226-250.

[46] According to BUXBAUM & HOPT, *id.* at 233, this would, however, be contrary to the intention of the drafters of the Treaty. That might be so – the *travaux préparatoires* being destroyed, there is no real basis for discussion on this point – but the Treaty itself certainly does not impose this interpretation.

[47] O.J. L 222/11 (1978).

[48] As suggested by BUXBAUM & HOPT, *supra* note 1, at 236.

In terms of legal bases, another problem arises. Some of the (proposed) directives also include companies incorporated under the law of non-EC Member States into their scope, in so far as these companies have an establishment within the Community (proposed Eleventh Directive[49]) or have their shares listed at a Member State's stock exchange. In the past, Article 100 EEC Treaty was used as an additional legal basis to justify the inclusion of third country companies. The European Commission appears to have abandoned this approach, and now apparently considers Article 54(3)(g) as a sufficient legal basis even with regard to these companies. The argument seems to be that not including these companies would constitute a discriminatory treatment of companies incorporated within the Community (recitals proposed Eleventh Directive). This reasoning is shaky. Article 54(3)(g) is so closely linked to the right of establishment, which is exclusively granted to companies from the Community, that, so it seems to me, Council and Commission have no authority under this Article to take action with regard to third country companies. In my opinion, Article 100 remains the necessary additional legal basis for including these companies into the scope of a harmonization directive. Could Article 100A be used for that purpose? Such an application is unlikely, for the reasons already mentioned, unless this Article is applied only where divergences between national laws distort competition.

(3) The correct and timely implementation of harmonization directives by Member States remains problematic. Control by the European Commission is not sufficiently assured, particularly when the implementing national law is amended at a later stage. Direct effect, that is enforcement of the application of provisions of a directive through the national courts, continues to be by far the most adequate instrument for the maintenance of the result of harmonization within Member States. The direct effect of directives in the field of company and capital market law is, however, fairly limited since the European Court has denied the so-called horizontal direct effect of directives.[50] The Court has excluded the possibility that directives might impose duties or obligations on private parties directly, that can be enforced through national courts. What the Court did accept, however, is a duty for the national courts to interpret the national law in the light of the relevant directives.[51] To this extent the statement of *Buxbaum* and *Hopt* that[52]

> "there is a great potential for individuals, courts and authorities within the Member States to take action to implement the directives, even where the States themselves have not enacted implementing legislation"

[49] See *supra* note 41.
[50] See Case 152/84, *Marshall*, [1986] E.C.R. 737.
[51] E.g., Case 80/86, *Kolpinghuis*, [1987] *E.C.R.* 3969.
[52] BUXBAUM & HOPT, *supra* note 1, at 239.

is still correct. But this can only be true when the national law leaves sufficient latitude to be interpreted according to a Community directive. When there is a clear conflict between the two, there is no way to overrule national law by invoking the directive, at least not against private parties.

An exception can be made in a situation where a directive has been correctly implemented at first, but a subsequent amendment of the national law would be contrary to the directive. Such an amendment could in my view be regarded as *ultra vires* and be invoked as such, also against private parties. This blocking effect of directives has been accepted to some extent by the Court. On several occasions the Court has interpreted the rules laid down by a directive as complete and excluding therefore national rules of a different or more far-reaching nature. This exclusiveness of the directive can be invoked against those national rules in the national courts.[53] *Buxbaum* and *Hopt* have fundamental objections against such a blocking effect of directives.[54] I regard this preemptive effect as an essential and indispensable guarantee of maintaining the result of harmonization, especially since the Court has (rightly, in my view) refused the horizontal direct effect of directives.

Even when direct effect of harmonization directives in the fields of company and capital market law is of limited scope only, it still remains quite important that national legal practice be correctly informed on how and by which rules a directive has been implemented into national law. For that purpose an obligation could be envisaged – I repeat a suggestion I have made earlier[55] – for Member States to set up a register of implementation, publicly available, for each directive. This is only to record (not to control[56]) the implementing national measure and subsequent amendments thereof, for each provision of the directive. Thus, the link between the directive and the national implementing laws can be retraced, and followed up in the longer term.

(4) Are national legislators generally obliged to incorporate the contents of a directive verbatim into their implementing laws? *Buxbaum* and *Hopt* assume this obligation so as to avoid as far as possible conflicts between the directive and national law.[57] I would not go so far. Apart from the fact that vagueness of drafting will often render verbatim transposition undesirable, to accept such an obligation would also run counter to the inherently flexible nature of the directive, as defined in Article 189 EEC Treaty. The directive is mandatory only as to the result, not as to ways and means to

[53] E.g. Case 148/78, *Ratti*, [1979] E.C.R. 1629; Case 158/80, *Butterfahrten*, [1981] E.C.R. 1805; Case 28/84, Commission v. Germany, [1985] E.C.R. 3097; Case 278/85, Commission v. Denmark, [1987] E.C.R. 4069.

[54] BUXBAUM & HOPT, *supra* note 1, at 242.

[55] TIMMERMANS, *supra* note 14, at 32-33.

[56] The criticism by BUXBAUM & HOPT, *supra* note 1, at 265, note 377, overlooks this point.

[57] See *id.* at 240.

achieve this result. Nor does the Court of Justice require a formal and textual transposition of a directive's provisions into national law, provided full implementation of the directive is ensured.[58]

B. Regulations

As stated above, regulations seem less appropriate as instruments for harmonization. Nevertheless, regulations have been used for the European Economic Interest Grouping (EEIG)[59] and the European Company (SE).[60] In these cases regulations were used wisely because the objectives were not to harmonize national law, but to create a directly applicable, uniform statute of European law; these new legal instruments could then further cross-border concentration and cooperation within the Community. *Buxbaum* and *Hopt* doubt the need and attractiveness of a European Company Statute in view of the frequent failures of multinational mergers within the Community (Hoesch-Hoogovens, Fokker VFW).[61] However, one could present a different hypothesis. Because of the necessity to accommodate with divergent national company law systems, these multinational groups were not able to integrate into a homogenous structure that could bridge national cleavages and compartments within these groups.[62] The European company form, on the contrary, would allow to construct an integrated group structure.

C. Recommendations (and International Codes)

Recommendations have scarcely been used as an instrument to achieve company and capital market law harmonization. If the binding directive meets already with so many problems of effective implementation, the non-binding recommendation cannot be a very promising instrument of harmonization. The fate of the Commission's Recommendation of 25 July 1977 concerning a European code of conduct relating to securities transactions[63] corroborates this rather gloomy view. Recommendations issued by the Council itself might be more effective, particularly in combination with a follow-up procedure to monitor the implementation by Member States. The actual practice of the OECD Guidelines on multinational companies shows that this approach has potential. The Community, by the way, is involved in the implementation machinery of these Guidelines. The Council has even recognized the exclusive power of the Community with regard to

[58] Case 363/85, Commission v. Italy, [1987] E.C.R. 1740.
[59] O.J. L 199/1 (1985).
[60] O.J. C 240/2 (1983). See also *supra* note 3.
[61] BUXBAUM & HOPT, *supra* note 1, at 202, 245.
[62] Hoogovens mentions this as one of the reasons for the failure of its merger with Hoesch; see my article in *supra* note 14, at 19-20.
[63] O.J. L 212/37 (1977). See BUXBAUM & HOPT, *supra* note 1, at 231.

issues of financial disclosure and a harmonized development of accounting standards within the framework of the OECD. Member States have also practiced, not entirely without success, the form of a non-binding code of conduct with regard to policies of European companies through their subsidiaries in South Africa. This initiative has taken place within the framework of European political cooperation.

D. International Conventions Under Article 220 EEC Treaty

Whenever an instrument under Community law is available, the thorny path of Article 220 EEC Treaty should be avoided. The intergovernmental international treaty-making procedure is still more cumbersome than the Community decision-making process, in part because these international conventions require approval by Member States in accordance with their national ratification procedures. I refer to the sad experience of the European Community Patent Convention. Moreover, these conventions do not belong to European Community law, so they are not *eo ipso* subject to the preliminary procedure of Article 177. For each convention negotiated under Article 220, Member States must therefore achieve consensus to adopt the preliminary procedure, so as to ensure its uniform interpretation by the European Court of Justice. Member States are, however, increasingly reluctant to accept jurisdiction of the Court for such purposes.

As far as the subjects of international company law mentioned in Article 220 EEC Treaty are concerned, Article 54(3)(g) could be used as a much more appropriate legal basis for the enactment of the necessary measures. It is a welcome development that the Commission has now followed this approach in submitting to the Council a proposal for a Tenth Directive regarding international mergers.

E. Self-Regulation and Bottom-Up Harmonization

(1) *Buxbaum* and *Hopt* discuss the possibility of implementing directives by way of self-regulation. Analyzing the case-law of the European Court, they conclude that under Community law this method of implementation seems unacceptable: "A directive cannot be transformed by the mere voluntary adherence of business."[64] This is certainly true in general. Recent case-law of the European Court, however, adds a small nuance. The Court has indeed accepted the implementation of a directive by way of a collective agreement – to be seen as a form of self-regulation by the social partners – provided that the protection of interested persons (workers), as prescribed by the directive, is fully ensured by virtue of the collective agreement. To the extent that is not the case, the public authorities must step in and enact

[64] BUXBAUM & HOPT, *supra* note 1, at 248.

the necessary regulations.[65] A similar approach has been followed by the European Commission in its amended proposal for a Fifth Company Law Directive. This proposal accepts, as one of the alternative models for workers' participation, the realization of workers' participation by collective bargaining. A Member State opting for this model, however, must enact legislation, as a fall-back in case collective bargaining fails or the agreement reached does not realize fully the requisites of the model according to the provisions of the directive.[66] So it appears that self-regulation can be an acceptable method of implementing a harmonization directive, provided it fully realizes the harmonization result, and the national public authorities step in where lacunae remain or arise.

(2) On the other hand, self-regulation could be envisaged as an instrument at the Community level for the harmonization of norms, standards or practices in the field of company and capital market law. Self-regulation can be an exponent of bottom-up harmonization. This is a phenomenon of growing importance in Community practice. I refer to the activities of the European organization of accountants. Another possible example would be agreements entered into by the competent authorities of Member States' stock exchanges to structure cooperation or to coordinate procedures, for instance regarding insider trading. Community institutions should foster such initiatives, and even consider backing up the eventual results of self-regulation by Community law. Here too, Community practice already presents an example: the reference, by Community directives in the field of technical obstacles to trade, to the technical norms developed by private organizations like CEN or CENELEC.[67]

[65] Case 143/83, Commission v. Denmark, [1985] E.C.R. 432 and Case 235/84, Commission v. Italy, [1986] E.C.R. 2291.

[66] See amended proposal for a Fifth Directive, *supra* note 42, Art. 4h.

[67] See White Paper from the Commission to the European Council of 28-29 June 1985, Doc. COM(85)310 (14 June 1985).

B. Discussion

I. Introductory Remarks

Christian Timmermans

Of course, I prefer you to comment on my paper rather than doing it myself. Nevertheless, I am happy to be able to make some introductory remarks.

(1) The first introductory remark is that I have somewhat abused my invitation to write a paper by not sticking to the subject. The subject was "Methods and Tools for Integration," but more than half, I think, of the paper deals with a different question: why harmonization, to what extent, what should be the scope?

I have done that for two reasons. First of all, to my mind in the *Buxbaum* and *Hopt* book[1] the background of this discussion was perhaps not completely put into the right historical perspective. I refer to the discussion in the '60s which was particularly dynamic in the Netherlands, perhaps another justification for me to tackle the subject again. The Netherlands at that time had the most flexible company law of the six original Member States of the Community, and particularly in that country therefore fears arose once the Commission had presented its first proposals and one started to realize what the impact of this harmonization would be.

The other reason to do this was the interesting, or rather perhaps intriguing, case-law of the Court of Justice,[2] a case-law which is interesting in two respects I think.

a. I venture to suggest that the Court's case-law seems to be developing a principle of free incorporation in the Community which for a number of Member States, in fact most Continental European States, would have, I think, to some extent revolutionary effects because it would indeed prevent the application of the effective seat approach, the *siège réel* approach, to the recognition of foreign companies. I do not think that the reasoning of the Court in this particular case is very convincing insofar as we find any reasoning of the case. But I think the interpretation of the EEC Treaty can be defended in that the right of establishment implies recognition to such an extent that the *siège réel* approach is not permitted in those cases where a cross-border establishment comes within the scope of Article 52. On the

[1] R.M. BUXBAUM & K.J. HOPT, *Legal Harmonization and the Business Enterprise* (Berlin/New York 1988).

[2] See *supra* at 134 ff, and Case 79/85, *Segers*, [1986] E.C.R. 2375.

other hand, I think that the conclusion the Court seems to draw is quite compatible with the idea of an internal market because in fact it is nothing more than the "*Cassis de Dijon*"[3] doctrine implies for goods. A company which has been legally formed in a Member State must be able to circulate freely on this internal market, its statutes must be accepted everywhere in all Member States. So there is no chance of applying the whole body of stringent company law rules of the country of establishment. To some extent also that would reflect the approach to harmonization in the White Paper,[4] I think, because it would be a kind of home rule solution. In fact, it would mean that again the statute of the country of incorporation would have to be accepted by all other Member States. One could even raise the question whether for the functioning of the internal market that would not be enough. I leave aside the problems of cross-frontier mergers. Would not this free movement of companies be sufficient and make harmonization to a large extent superfluous? Personally I do not think so, but that question, at least, has to be thought over.

b. And then I come to my second point, the second possible consequence of this case-law of the Court of Justice. If indeed this free movement, this free incorporation of companies has to be accepted under the Treaty, then and only then for the first time a Delaware effect could become relevant within the Community. Until now a lot has been said about it but those fears have not materialized for the simple reason that it was not possible, or at least rather dangerous, to move primary establishments to those Member States where the *siège réel* approach is followed. Once that is not possible any more under the Treaty, then it becomes of course attractive to look for the most lenient company law system for incorporation. What would the effect be then?

Bottom up harmonization like in the United States, if I have understood correctly. I do not think so. I do not think that free competition between company law systems will emerge in such a situation and that a minimum level of protection will be accomplished more or less automatically in Member States.

Another alternative could be a race in laxity between Member States. That, I think, is no more probable. I do not see valid reasons for Member States to make existing company law more lenient in order to attract the incorporation of business out of other Member States. To attract only the legal form, of course, because the business will remain situated in other Member States, like in that *Segers* case I have discussed in my paper.[5] What could happen, I think, is that those Member States where the phenomenon of the quasi-foreign company really became more frequent because of this freedom of incorporation, would push the Community to continue its

[3] Case 120/78, Rewe-Zentral AG v. Bundesmonopolverwaltung für Branntwein, [1979] E.C.R. 649.

[4] See *supra* at 4 ff.

[5] See *supra* note 2.

harmonization effort in order to realize a minimum level of protection. If the Community will not do so, and now I am thinking particularly of private companies, then I think that the risk will be that those Member States will increase the particular rules applying to those foreign companies with of course the risk of incompatibility with the Treaty regime.

I must say that in my country the political discussion on that point has already been going on for three or four years. In my country the incorporation system has been the classic approach to the problem of recognition of foreign companies. We were, by the way, the only one of the original six Member States which did not ratify the Recognition Treaty,[6] the reason being that it made too generous an allowance for the *siège réel* approach. In the meantime, because of company law reform, the Netherlands have become more reticent about the merits of the incorporation system, precisely because of the increasing number of quasi-foreign companies. More and more businesses in the Netherlands are opting for forms of foreign corporation, not only the limited company under United Kingdom law but also corporations under the State of Delaware. We have quite a number of examples of that. In Amsterdam you can even buy foreign shelf companies, private companies; they are advertising for it.

The only thing I want to say on this is that if no harmonization occurs to make the protection level equivalent, then the risk might be that Member States increase the rules applying to foreign companies having establishments on their territory. That would be a bad development of course for the functioning of the internal market.

So far this is my first subject, which was not the subject I had to deal with.

(2) My second introductory remark is about the subject "Methods and Tools." Well, that has already been discussed to some extent. I will make a few remarks on that.

First, as far as directives are concerned, personally I think that directives remain an excellent and most attractive instrument for harmonization. It has been I think a marvelous invention of the Treaty authors – by the way you find it already in the ECSC Treaty under another heading. It is so good as an instrument because it is binding on the one hand, flexible on the other hand. And therefore I think that when we discuss harmonization, directives remain an appropriate instrument, much more appropriate than regulations which have obvious disadvantages because they are directly applicable in the Member States and cannot be adapted to the national legal environment.

A point that has been raised in some of the papers refers to the statement in the *Buxbaum* and *Hopt* book regarding the blocking effect of directives.[7] The book criticizes or at least queries that blocking effect. I would like to repeat, because I think it an important point, what I have written in my paper[8] and that is that, in my view at least, this blocking effect is really

[6] See *supra* at 141.
[7] See BUXBAUM & HOPT, *supra* note 1, at 242.
[8] See *supra* at 145.

essential to preserve the harmonization result. That is the more essential since the Court has rejected, using the technical term, the horizontal direct effect of directives, has refused the possibility – which is of course particularly relevant for these company and capital markets directives – of invoking them against private parties in a national court proceeding. This might be different for the blocking effect that as such might have direct effect. It would mean that to some extent Member States have lost competence and that any amendment which would run counter to a directive or transgress a limit traced by a directive would be *ultra vires* and could be challenged within the national court. I think that would at least be some guarantee to prevent the harmonization result being weakened by later amendments in Member States.

I have a remark here on implementation control in connection also with the risk of petrification. I think that the control really exists at the moment of implementation, the control by the Commission services of course. I think the Commission is indeed controlling what happens at the first stage of implementation, but I wonder whether this happens at later stages, when the law of implementation is again amended, which quite frequently happens in fact in the field of company law. I have seen that happening in my Member State a number of times rather soon after an implementation act. I fear that those subsequent amendments are not submitted to the Commission and that in that respect the control is nearly absent. I think that is really presenting a great risk and therefore I would plead for this possibility of a blocking effect with direct applicability.

I made a very practical suggestion earlier, and I have repeated it in the paper,[9] that Member States should be obliged to organize, to set up, a sort of register of implementation, publicly available, which simply means that for each Article of a directive they should make available the information on the actual legislation of the Member State, implementing the directive's provisions. That would make it possible for interested persons to know whether and how a directive provision has been implemented. That knowledge is not so easily available. I do not know whether you have ever had the necessity of controlling the implementation of a directive on a specific issue in national law. I had that experience and quite often it was really difficult to know where to look. Such a register could make at least the relevant information easily available and by doing so also contribute to the success of implementation and the maintenance of the harmonization result.

A final remark: on self-regulation. I must admit that I never know exactly what self-regulation means. I refer to the debate on "can directives be implemented by self-regulation?"[10]

Well, I think it is possible. Once self-regulation is really binding on the interested persons and there is a possibility of sanctioning infringements, that might be the case. Collective bargaining is, I think, an example and I

[9] See *supra* at 145 and 145, note 55.

[10] See BUXBAUM & HOPT, *supra* note 1, at 246 ff.

have referred in my paper to case-law of the Court of Justice[11] which recognizes the possibility of implementing directives by self-regulation. But if self-regulation means for instance a merger code such as it exists in the Netherlands without any possibility of effective sanctions, I do not think it would be an acceptable method of implementation. Therefore I think in each case one must decide what self-regulation implies in terms of binding effects and sanctions.

II. Freedom of Establishment and the *Segers* Case[12]

Richard Buxbaum

I was fascinated by the paper of Prof. Timmermans but I have very little from the outside to add to it or comment, so I would only like to ask a question which may reflect a very American perspective on the difference between a private law and public law norm.

I would have characterized the question of the social security demand that was made in the *Segers* case as one arising not from the *statute* or particular charter of the corporation but simply from the application of such law; and therefore I would have seen that as a public law issue in this sense. There may or may not be a contradiction to freedom of establishment, movement of juridical persons and so on in the effort of the Dutch authorities to deny application of these benefits, but that has no correlation to the pseudo-foreign structure. I personally would reserve the pseudo-foreign concept to the problems of the internal affairs of the corporation; in other words, to the question whether the State of incorporation's legal rules governing those internal affairs are to be honored by the other units in the jurisdiction.

So from that perspective the hair on the back of my neck does not rise quite to the same extent that yours does about that case, because the real issue, it seems to me, is simply whether the Court was a bit exorbitant in its finding of a violation through the Articles 52/58 EEC Treaty mix in this particular situation. That might be analyzed in American terms as a supremacy clause problem of preemption by the federal system, possibly of a commerce clause violation in the negative commerce clause sense, but I do not find implied in it the concept of the pseudo-foreign corporation.

If that is too American a view of it, I would like to stand corrected. I would really like to hear the response to that because in that case I do not quite understand the role of that concept in the European legal doctrinal setting. That is my only comment for now.

[11] See *supra* at 147 f.
[12] Case 79/85, [1986] E.C.R. 2375. See also *supra* at 134 ff.

Geoffrey Fitchew

I think, on the *Segers* case, having mentioned it, I should expand a little bit on what I said this morning.[13]

I unfortunately only read Prof. Timmermans' paper on the day before yesterday but I was very struck by his analysis of the *Segers* case, of which I was not previously aware, and I consulted my colleagues very quickly before leaving Brussels yesterday and our view would, I think, be really rather close to what Prof. Buxbaum was saying.

That is to say both the *Segers* case and parallel "*Avoir Fiscal*" case[14] were essentially concerned with concessions or benefits provided by the governments in the two countries concerned to enterprises operating on their territory and that the essential concern of the Court was to prevent any abusive use of that facility by the two governments concerned, in a way that would distort the conditions of competition between enterprises operating on the territory. So the rather extensive interpretation given to it, suggested by Prof. Timmermans, is not accepted by the Commission's lawyers.

I had the impression indeed – Prof. Timmermans can say if I have misinterpreted him[15] – that the thesis he was advancing was somewhat more limited, namely that the *Segers* case might have that potential. But we do not know yet whether it has. Indeed that is illustrated, I think, by the other example he quotes[16] in the opposite sense of the treatment by German courts of English private companies often as *Handelsgesellschaft*. And presumably one would only know if the wider interpretation of the *Segers* case is what the Court intended, if one of those private English companies in Germany managed to get a case to the Court.

L.C.B. Gower

Very briefly. I found Prof. Timmermans' discussions of the *Segers* case very interesting but was slightly surprised, as I think Prof. Buxbaum was, that he thought it so horrifying. I noticed that Mr. Fitchew said the lawyers in the Commission did not go quite so far as Prof. Timmermans seems to think the case goes. I have always understood that if a company was validly established in one Member State, it was the obligation of another Member State to allow it to establish itself or to provide services in that country and not to discriminate against it, but that in doing so it would have to observe local marketing rules and so on. And it did not seem to me that the *Segers* case had done anything to alter that.

[13] See *supra* at 18 f.
[14] Case 270/83, [1986] E.C.R. 273.
[15] See *infra* at 158.
[16] See *supra* at 133.

Alain Hirsch

A further contribution on the *Segers* case. There are two different views on the problem of corporations with a fictitious incorporation. One is to consider that the corporation is non-existent, i.e. null and void. The other is to apply to this corporation part of the substantive law of the place where its real activities are pursued. The second solution is clearly better.

In this perspective, the *Segers* case just says that the company has to be recognized as existent. It does not say anything about possibly applying Dutch law to the company (and paradoxically if you apply Dutch law, then *a fortiori* the director should have received the social security benefits!). In this perspective, there should be no race for laxity because even if you choose a fictitious seat, the law of real activities would apply, at least in most cases.

So I think that the really important point is your suggestion[17] that it would be very important to harmonize the international private law of companies within the EC. I suggest that this would be a very nice piece of useful harmonization, because it would prevent a race for laxity.

Christian Meier-Schatz

Obviously, like everybody else, I was fascinated by the paper of Prof. Timmermans. What struck me in particular was the way in which Prof. Timmermans demonstrated how the freedom of establishment clause could be used to change national conflicts of laws in the field of company law.

I would even go one step further and put that issue as a public policy topic in the following sense: should, not only can, but should a federal preemption clause be implemented as an alternative to the national *siège réel* approach? This public policy issue is particularly relevant with respect to the conclusion *Buxbaum* and *Hopt* reached in the book,[18] namely that the EC should try to implement more harmonization from below. A federal incorporation concept (based on a preemption rule) could be an instrument to create more room for such a harmonization from below. That is especially true with respect to the traditional American field of enabling rules. This may then indeed lead to a fresh perspective on where to draw the line between harmonization from below and from above.

Finally, I asked myself whether such a development could in fact take place, that is to say whether it would be feasible to implement a European market for corporate charters dictated by a preemption clause. To answer this question I took a short look at how American economists are outlining the preconditions for a functioning market for corporate charters. One of the leading writers in the field, Prof. Easterbrook, mentions three elements: high mobility of corporations, large number of jurisdictions and freedom of

[17] See *supra* at 141 f.
[18] BUXBAUM & HOPT, *supra* note 1, at 271 ff.

jurisdictions to legislate. Whereas the third component would probably be given, I am rather skeptical with respect to the other two. I doubt whether the number of realistically attractive jurisdictions would be large enough. In addition, I have some difficulty in predicting a high mobility of European or national corporations in a European market for corporate charters. I think that psychological and cultural barriers would still play a prominent role here.

This leads me in my speculations to the conclusion that probably even a federal preemption clause, however desirable it may be, could *de facto* barely establish a truly active market for corporate charters in Europe, comparable with that one in the United States.

Richard Buxbaum

In technical terms, speaking now of American technical terms, first of all the consequence of the *Segers* case is a type of negative commerce cause analysis. That is to say, it is the function of the Articles of the Treaty directly without intervention of regulation or directive by the enforcement authorities, that has generated this right of Segers and his company to make that demand against the Dutch authorities.

I have a question in that regard. First, since that is based on freedom of establishment, would you say in general that freedom of establishment is a somewhat more perfectionistic concept that is the analogous negative commerce clause concept in United States law? It would be paradoxical if that was so, but I would be interested just to have a substantive ranking, you might say, of those two concepts, brief as that might be.

Christian Timmermans

I think you have given me a lot of work and I will try to finish the work in a relatively short period of time.

The interpretation of the *Segers* case. Your first question, Prof. Buxbaum, was:[19] "What has this demand of application of the social security scheme to do with the right of establishment under the EEC Treaty?"

I think the answer to that is easy because the question whether Mr. Segers could invoke the principle of non-discrimination under the Treaty was entirely linked to the question whether in this particular situation the right of establishment was implied, whether Article 52 applied. Mr. Segers' claim for the payment of the social security benefit was a derivative of the right of establishment. So if there was no right of establishment, there was no possibility, at least not under the Treaty, that he would get what he asked.

If I have understood rightly what you meant by asking whether this right of establishment, this Article 52 of the Treaty, has an impact which is somewhat similar or comparable with what you mean by referring to the

[19] See *supra* at 153 f.

negative commerce clause, a commerce clause rationale, I think the answer is yes, at least if you follow my interpretation, because it would mean that those persons and companies which can invoke the right of establishment can to some extent also prevent the application of national legislation – and we are talking here about legislation in the field of company law – that is affecting their chance of setting up in that particular Member State. Hence the preemptive effect.

To be a bit more precise on the interpretation and the question whether the *Segers* case should really have any bearing on questions of international company law and the application of the *siège réel* approach, we have to look more closely into the reasoning of the social security agency which pleaded in this case the non-applicability of the EEC Treaty and the right of establishment for the simple reason that Mr. Segers' business was an entirely Dutch business. He had in fact economically no link at all with the United Kingdom, and for that reason there was no right of establishment involved in this particular situation.

On that point the Court was extremely explicit and had no difficulty in acknowledging the application of Article 52.

Now what does this mean? This means that the Dutch authorities were not able to qualify and treat the limited company as in fact being a purely Dutch undertaking and therefore remaining outside the scope of Article 52, because all the business or, in other words, the primary establishment of this limited company was situated on the territory of that particular Member State. Now if that possibility does not exist, at least it is plausible, if you continue that reasoning, that a Member State is not allowed any more to refuse recognition in such a case, and that is the first solution you mentioned, Prof. Hirsch,[20] in the debate on international company law: to refuse recognition of the foreign company for the reason that it has its primary establishment on the territory of another Member State.

I go a step further and come to the second solution mentioned by Prof. Hirsch, which is in fact the solution of Article 4 of the Recognition Treaty,[21] which allows a Member State to apply all stringent rules of its company law to foreign companies having their central administration on its territory. It has to recognize the company but in fact – and therefore I do not think that solution is in practical terms so much different from the first one – the company in question has to respect all stringent rules of the local company law. I can imagine no example in practice where that will be possible, where a company will be able to respect two sets of company rules at the same time. The effect will normally be that the company cannot function, that the decisions of its board will be annulled by the courts because the board structure and the division of powers will not be in conformity with the local rules.

[20] See *supra* at 155.
[21] See *supra* at 141.

So to answer that question immediately, if we accept that the right of establishment implies a necessity to recognize a company formed under the law of another Member State, I think that also has to exclude the possibility of applying all stringent rules of company law to that company. There remains the possibility of applying local rules but only insofar as in doing so the company will not be prevented from exercising the right of establishment. That is a rather abstract criterion, but I think in practical terms it might produce acceptable results.

I am trying to answer another aspect of the question of Prof. Buxbaum.[22] This necessity to accept the foreign statute must be seen, when I read the *Segers* case closely, as a derivative of the right of establishment. But I must add, that the Court expressly accepts the applicability of the public order exception (Art. 56 EEC Treaty). So there is still a possibility of acting against quasi-foreign companies. That might for instance be interesting in cases of workers' participation. Personally I would plead for access to the exception clause of Article 56 in a case where a German company transformed itself into a foreign company form in order to evade the national workers' participation rules. Of course, if this case-law of the Court – and I have written in the paper that there is a second case pending at the Court[23] – develops further, then harmonization becomes quite important on this point because Member States must know and companies must know to what extent they can still be confronted with local company rules.

So personally I would plead for a harmonization of the conflict rules with regard to company statutes. But I must admit, of course, what Mr. Fitchew has said,[24] that this is a potential of the *Segers* decision. The Court has not been explicit on the point, neither is the reasoning explicit. Personally I think that the Court has not seen the implications of its judgment with regard to international company law. There is an indication for that because it is only a Chamber of three judges which has decided the case. I think that if they had realized the implications they would have referred the case to the full Court.

III. Horizontal Direct Effect

Eddy Wymeersch

I would like to draw attention to a point in Prof. Timmermans' excellent paper and this is the well-known question of horizontal direct effect.[25] I wonder whether the Court will, from a policy point of view, be able to

[22] See *supra* at 153.
[23] See *supra* at 139 and 139, note 34.
[24] See *supra* at 154.
[25] See *supra* at 144.

uphold its present strict interpretation of the matter, as more and more questions will be submitted for review, mainly by way of a preliminary ruling, in which horizontal direct effect will appear to be the only method of giving any effect whatsoever to a directive.

It may be useful to mention here a recent case that will probably be submitted to the European Court[26] and that relates to the implementation of the 1979 Directive on listing particulars.[27] According to Schedule C, point 2(a) of this directive the issuing company must treat all its shareholders on an equal footing. The same principle of equal treatment underpins the Second Company Law Directive,[28] Article 42, but there it is restricted to the implementation of the rules expressly prescribed by the directive. In the 1979 Directive on listing particulars, it is a generally applicable principle.

The difficulty of enforcement will show up in a situation such as the one that has recently been submitted to litigation in Belgium. It should first be mentioned that Belgium has not yet implemented the 1979 Directive notwithstanding the Court condemnation several years ago now. But what seems more relevant is the fact that according to the Bill intended to implement the directives on securities matters,[29] the legislature does not plan to render the principle of equal treatment explicit, on the basis of the idea that the principle of equal treatment is a general principle of company law, and that it is therefore not necessary to render it explicit except for the specific subjects that are dealt with in the Second Company Law Directive (e.g. preferential subscription rights, repurchase of own shares).

The specific question to be submitted to the Court relates to the refusal, by the board of directors of a stock exchange listed company, to offer to all shareholders of the company the right to acquire a substantial block of shares of the company which had previously been subscribed by a State investment company. The issuing company was entitled to repurchase these shares and to that purpose had constituted substantial reserves. The issuing company, assailed by a minority group, had transferred the option it held to a friendly third party thereby reducing the voting power of this minority. The plaintiffs claimed that the Directive on listing particulars, although not implemented, directly imposes on the board the obligation to treat all shareholders equally.[30] This application would clearly involve horizontal direct effect.

Therefore I think it would be a pity if the European legal order did not directly offer adequate protection against the refusal of national legislators

[26] See *infra* note 30.

[27] O.J. L 66/21 (1979).

[28] O.J. L 26/1 (1977).

[29] See Belgian Senate, No. 535 (1986-1987), No. 1.

[30] It should be added that according to press reports the case has been settled in the meantime and that all shareholders will be entitled to acquire the shares which were the subject of the litigation *pro rata* their shareholdings (see *Echo de la Bourse*, 3 November 1988, at 1).

to implement the rules of the directive, especially when these rules are clear, unambiguous and leave no room for national options. One may hope that the Court will modify its position on a point which, especially from the point of view of legal practice, is often seen as a major restriction on the effectiveness of the European legal order.

Alain Hirsch

I would like to add a word to what Eddy Wymeersch has said. I go even a little further because I suggest that the Court has not to change its case-law, the case-law is not settled.

The *Marshall* case[31] is a pure *obiter dictum* as our English friends would say: it was a problem of equal pay involving the State and the Court said *en passant* that it would not apply against the private individual; the *Kolpinghuis* case[32] concerns criminal law which is obviously something very special. Furthermore there is much to do within what the Court has already acknowledged, i.e. that a directive may be used for interpreting national law. For instance, equality of shareholders!

Christian Timmermans

I must say I have the same approach to the problem raised by Prof. Wymeersch as you suggested, Prof. Hirsch.

The Court has denied such horizontal direct effect but it has emphasized the obligation for a national court to interpret national law within the light of the directive. Now if under national law there is a general principle of equality, it might be possible to interpret this in the light of a principle of equal treatment of shareholders laid down by a directive.

Personally I agree with the exclusion of this possibility of horizontal direct effect. This is linked with the nature of a directive. We must realize that a directive is addressed to Member States. That is, by the way, the only argument the Court has used. A directive by its very nature imposes obligations on the Member State. An essential element of a directive is this necessity of implementation, the second stage in the legislation process. If we accept that a directive without any interference from national law is able to impose obligations on individuals within the Member States, I think considerable problems of legal certainty will arise.

Now you could say regulations have the same potential. Yes, I agree, but they are expressly stated to have direct application within Member States. Directives have not. Horizontal direct effect would entail quite substantial practical problems. What would be the legal regime applying to the company, if we refer only to the company law directives? Exactly what rules apply? This will require a judgement in each particular case as to what

[31] Case 152/84, [1986] E.C.R. 737.
[32] Case 80/86, [1987] E.C.R. 3969.

extent national law still conforms to a directive and, if not, to what extent the directive can directly apply. I must say that in the literature also the majority opinion was against horizontal direct effect.

Whether this case-law is not yet fully established because it is only an *obiter dictum*, as you have said, Prof. Hirsch, I do not think so. When I read the arguments put forward by the Court in the considerations of the *Marshall* case and particularly the *Kolpinghuis* case, I think this reasoning sounds rather definite.

On the other hand, Prof. Wymeersch, I do not think that the Court will overrule this in the near future. However there might be new answers in the case-law. I have referred already[33] to the possibility of preemption, the blocking effect of the harmonization directives. We find examples in the case-law where the Court says: "Well, the set of rules laid down by the directive is of a complete nature," which means that in fact the competence of the Community has become exclusive and Member States have no possibility on a specific issue to regulate any more. That of course remains possible also with regard to the company law directives.

So in those respects I see possibilities.

Alain Hirsch

In the *Marshall* case the decision itself, apart from the reasons, says nothing about that. And in the *Kolpinghuis* case the decision says:[34]

> *"[U]ne autorité nationale ne peut pas se prévaloir, à charge d'un particulier, d'une disposition d'une directive dont la transposition nécessaire en droit national n'a pas encore eu lieu."*

So this decision does not say that an individual is not allowed to invoke a directive. Obviously, it was not there to be decided but I am just suggesting to you that the Court only decided that a Member State which has not implemented a directive should not have the power to invoke such a directive against an individual. Is the matter not more open than you seem to think?

Christian Timmermans

It is a matter for discussion, of course, but if you read the reasons of that judgement, the Court is referring explicitly to the *Marshall* case. But although a different interpretation on those lines is possible, I personally, because you raised the question, endorse this interpretation of not allowing for horizontal direct effect of directives.

[33] See *supra* at 151 f.
[34] Case 80/86, *supra* note 32, at 3986.

Richard Buxbaum

It would be rather paradoxical, would it not, if you cannot have standing as a private party to protest the failure of the national Member State government to implement a directive if there is a directive that has been enacted by the authorities, and yet you do have standing directly to protest a national statute which you claim is in contradiction to the EEC Treaty at large. I appreciate the difference doctrinally and yet there is something dissonant about that concept. It seems to me a kind of *ad majorem* question. If you already have a negative applicability of the Treaty provisions, it strikes me – and I would like to see if I am missing something – that it is a bit paradoxical then to have this big hoohah about the absence of horizontal direct applicability in the sense of a supremacy clause analysis.

IV. Various Other Topics

Klaus Hopt

I would like to make a short remark on self-regulation, taking up the German example of insider self-regulation.[35]

Right now there is a danger that, if Germany has to accept a Community Insider Trading Directive,[36] an attempt will be made to "sell," as a national transformation and enforcement of this directive, just what we are doing now – i.e. leaving the German solution more or less as it stands. The line of argument would be that there is some supervision already, namely by the States (*Länder*). Yet in practice this is often only done by the regional ministry which is not comparable to anything like the SEC, the COB or even the Belgian *Commission Bancaire*. This is probably not so well-known outside of Germany. The second problem with the German insider self-regulation is that there are absolutely no remedies with real teeth in it. Of course this is hardly surprising. It is the very essence of a club solution.

Granted, one can be of different opinion as to whether insider regulation makes sense economically and/or legally, but once one accepts that such a regulation makes sense, then mere self-regulation is not enough, as the American, English and even Swiss examples clearly show.

Alain Hirsch

Certainly there should be an adequate sanction if self-regulation is to be admitted as a proper way to implement directives. But is it right to impose effective sanctions for self-regulation and not the same for legislation? For

[35] Insider Trading Guidelines as of June 1988, reprinted and commented in A. BAUMBACH, K. DUDEN & K.J. HOPT eds., *Handelsgesetzbuch*, (16) Insiderhandels-Richtlinie (28th ed., Munich 1989).

[36] Directive adopted in 1989: see O.J. L 334/30 (1989).

instance, I admit that civil remedies are a useful thing. But it is sometimes a useless sanction in practice. Self-regulation is sometimes much more effective than civil remedies. Is it true to say that law is more effective than self-regulation?

Olivier Guillod

With respect to self-regulation, I think probably one of the reasons why there is some distrust and why we call for more stringent conditions is the risk that self-regulation serves the self-interest of those who devise it. And it is very different from the law, I think.

Prof. *Buxbaum* and *Hopt* in their book propose another method of implementing the directives,[37] which is to remove procedural impediments and they allude to allowing class actions, or making the derivative suit more largely available to shareholders. I wonder what the cost would be of implementing these procedural helps to better implement the directives, because there might be costs for the companies due to litigation, there might be other costs as well, for the claimants and for the society at large. And so in the end I wonder also whether we should ask for 100% implementation of directives because that is impossible. We should perhaps settle for less, I do not know how much, maybe 20%... Probably the figure should be higher! Every law, every regulation, every directive should be implemented, but it is a fact of life that they are not to their fullest extent. So sometimes, especially in a political body like the European Community, it might be better to settle for somewhat less than 100%.

Hartmut Schmidt

Prof. Timmermans, I am much impressed by the idea of a central file for the regulations that implement directives. But I wonder why you suggest having this file at a national level.[38] Why do you not have it at the EC level?

Christian Timmermans

Whether a register of implementation should not be set up on European level, instead of the national level? Well that might be a better solution yet but I tried to remain pragmatic.

Klaus Hopt

A remark on the petrification danger. If we judge the European situation by analogy to the national situation, then the basic fact is that the legislator just has very little time. Legislative time is a scarce resource, and it is very

[37] BUXBAUM & HOPT, *supra* note 1, at 215 ff.
[38] See *supra* at 145.

difficult really to achieve revisions except in very urgent issues. Once you have a law that is very often the end of it. Even if it proves hard to apply or shows real shortcomings, the legislator may prefer to leave things as they are for many reasons, particularly political ones. In Germany at least, we have found a way out by having the courts interfere. So German courts very often act as a kind of quasi-legislators – sometimes even as the major legislators. I wonder why all this should be so very different on the EC level. Why should it be so much easier there to get changes if they become necessary?

Christian Timmermans

I think that up to now, as has been said in some of the papers, our experience with amendments has not been too bad. And I must say when I look to my country, a small country, with a small staffed Department of Justice to prepare legislation in the company law field, there has been an amazing number of amendments over the last ten years in the company law field. Things are very quickly amended. So, at least in my country, that experience does not exist.

Alain Hirsch

Prof. Timmermans, a remark concerning your *quid pro quo* argument for explaining the reasons for harmonizing company law.[39] In principle this is absolutely convincing, with perhaps two reservations.

First the *quid pro quo* argument would only justify the harmonization of key elements, i.e. certainly less than the very detailed directives we have on company law.

Second: it is really necessary, with the *quid pro quo* theory, to harmonize the company law of all companies, even the important number of companies which do no international business whatsoever? Could one envisage harmonizing only the rules of companies which do international business? If I may make a comparison with banking law, the directive harmonizes banking law for all banks, whereas the BIS Committee harmonizes multinational banking. Obviously I see that there may be a number of borderlines and difficulties by this distinction, but it could perhaps be envisaged.

Christian Timmermans

The *quid pro quo* rationale, you say, would be an argument for harmonization on a minor scale. I fully agree with that.

Then you added a suggestion to limit the harmonization to the cross-border situation. There I disagree. My first objection would be that of

[39] See *supra* at 132.

course when this freedom of incorporation is accepted, there remains a reason to harmonize also with regard to these smaller companies, because in practice it is probably just these businesses which will opt for a foreign company form so long as there continue to be interesting differences, such as exist now as far as capital protection is concerned, between the various company forms throughout Europe. The second objection would be that such an approach would in practice cause Member States to apply two sets of rules (one for cross-border trading companies, the other for home trading ones) which they will not accept.

Gérard Hertig

Prof. Timmermans, why are you so skeptical about international conventions between States?[40] In a federal State it may very well work. I am thinking about the Swiss experience: we do have *concordats*, they work very well and sometimes even better than federal legislation.

Christian Timmermans

Well, my skepticism on international conventions is based on the experience within the Community only and on the practice of the intergovernmental negotiations and international treaty making, based on Article 220 EEC Treaty.

I refer to the Bankruptcy Convention, to the European Community Patent Convention, to the Convention regarding international private law. I should refer also to an article of Ivo Schwartz who has compared very practically the time periods involved for international decision making with regard to the Community decision-making process on the one hand and the international treaties on the other. His conclusion is without any doubt favorable to the Community decision making. One reason is of course that Community decisions do not require ratification by national parliaments.

I clearly prefer the Community way, also because in that case uniform interpretation by the Court under Article 177 EEC Treaty is automatically acquired.

[40] See *supra* at 147.

Chapter Four

Federal-State Conflicts as Seen in the Light of the Australian Experience Regarding Securities Regulation

A. Report: Robert Austin

I. Introduction

Prof. *Buxbaum* and *Hopt* have presented us with a scholarly account of the process of harmonization of company and securities market law in the United States and Europe.[1] Their analysis leads them to cautious conclusions about the likely progress of European harmonization and to some recommendations (based in part on the American experience) to improve and accelerate that process.

Prima facie, a discussion of the Australian experience in harmonization of company and securities market law might appear to have little relevance to *Buxbaum* and *Hopt*'s themes. However, one of the authors' most intriguing recommendations is that individual States be used as laboratories of the law, where planned experimentation may take place as a prelude to federal harmonization.[2] Seen through European eyes, the Australian economic and legal systems must appear to be relatively simple, isolated and uniform, lacking the diversities produced by separate languages and cultural traditions and a variety of stages of economic development. It might seem plausible, therefore, to regard Australia as a relatively pure subject for laboratory experimentation.

To this limited extent, the Australian achievement of almost uniform company and securities market law within the last decade might be of some interest in the European context. Specifically, some lessons may be learned from a study of the problems which Australia's advanced stage of harmonization has generated. Further, some brief attention to the Australian experience may enrich the debate about European harmonization by serving to emphasize (as the authors acknowledge[3]) that the development of European goals may be assisted by comparative study extending beyond the US-European focus.

[1] R.M. BUXBAUM & K.J. HOPT, *Legal Harmonization and the Business Enterprise* (Berlin/New York 1988).

[2] *Id.* at 286.

[3] *Id.* at 278.

II. A Sketch of the Australian Political and Economic Structure

Australia has a federal political system, broadly similar to that of the United States, in which the Commonwealth Parliament is vested with limited though substantial legislative powers and the residual legislative power belongs to the six States. Under the Australian Constitution the Commonwealth has power to make laws with respect to interstate trade and commerce (Section 51(i)), and with respect to foreign corporations, and trading or financial corporations formed within the limits of the Commonwealth (Section 51(xx) – the "corporations" power).[4] Those heads of power have been used by the Commonwealth to introduce uniform antitrust law. They have not yet been used for company and securities market legislation, though some current proposals will be discussed below. To date, company and securities market laws have been enacted by State legislatures.

Although our constitutional structure was influenced by the United States, our legal system is otherwise based on the English system. Australia has a unitary system of common law applied by State Supreme Courts from which appeals lie to the High Court of Australia. English reported cases are referred to and until recently were given considerable weight as precedents, though an Australian common law is now developing quite rapidly, particularly under the influence of the present High Court. There is a Federal Court which adjudicates in respect of certain Commonwealth laws, again with appeals to the High Court of Australia. The jurisdictional problems which were created by the establishment of that separate court have recently been alleviated by the introduction of a system of cross-vesting of jurisdiction for the Federal Court and State Supreme Courts.[5]

Australia is a highly urbanized country, the six State capitals containing about 60% of the population with most of those people living in Sydney and Melbourne. Despite the country's relatively small population and gross domestic product, the Australian stock market had a turnover of $US23 billion in 1986 and $US58 billion in 1987.[6] In the latest year, the turnover was higher than AMEX and was approximately 67% of the turnover on the

[4] Other Commonwealth constitutional heads of power are relevant to company and securities market law, including the powers with respect to taxation (Section 51(ii)), borrowing (Section 51(iv)), postal and like services (Section 51(v)), banking (Section 51(xiii)), insurance (Section 51(xiv)), bills of exchange (Section 51(xvi)), insolvency (Section 51(xvii)), incidental matters (Section 51(xxxix)), and Commonwealth territories (Section 122).

[5] Jurisdiction of Courts (Cross-Vesting) Act, 1987 (Cth). See MASON & CRAWFORD, "The Cross-Vesting Scheme," 62 *A.L.J.R.* 158 (1988).

[6] Compared with a population of approximately 16 million, and a G.D.P. of approximately $US230 billion. The figures are taken from WILLIAMS, "A View from Abroad: The International Roundtable," Address to the International Securities Compliance and Clearance Strategies Conference, New York, 27 July 1988. Mr. WILLIAMS is Deputy Chairman of the National Companies and Securities Commission, Australia.

Paris Exchange. The Australian Stock Exchange conducts an active stock options market covering 20 high volume stocks, and the Sydney Futures Exchange, with a turnover in 1987 of 5.6 million futures and options contracts (including the stock index futures contract and the index options contract) ranks ninth in turnover size amongst the world's futures exchanges. There has been a comparatively high level of takeover activity with respect to Australian companies: in fiscal 1987, 11% of Australian listed companies received takeover bids, while in fiscal 1988 the figure was nearly 14%.[7]

It is obvious even from this brief description that there are enormous factual differences which will make it hazardous to extrapolate from the Australian experience to the European setting. On the other hand, the Australian federal system produces political and economic competition amongst the States which is at times reminiscent of European rivalries, and the Australian economy and securities markets are sufficiently active that many of the regulatory problems which have arisen in Europe and the United States are equally pressing in Australia.

III. The Development of Uniform Company and Securities Market Law in Australia

A. Towards the Uniform Companies Act, 1961

Until the 1950s, Australian State company law statutes were similar to one another, but were seldom identical. The similarity derived from the fact that the statutes were all based on the British companies legislation, and of course the common law was uniform throughout Australia, for all practical purposes. Company law reform tended to follow initiatives adopted in the United Kingdom, frequently with substantial delays in implementation from State to State.[8] There was no need for a Model Business Corporations Act, because the British legislation was an obvious and inevitable model.

By the late 1950s the desirability of uniform company law had come to be recognized politically.[9] One reason for its arrival on the political agenda may have been the dramatic growth of some Australian companies, which came to operate on a national basis during that period and had an interest in promoting a single regulatory regime. However, given the substantial similarity of State laws on most matters of company and securities law, it is probable that the business community's demand for uniformity was pitched

[7] WILLIAMS, *supra* note 6.

[8] See H.A.J. FORD, *Principles of Company Law* 14 (4th ed., 1986), who notes nevertheless that there were some innovations in the State of Victoria, including the introduction of the no-liability company.

[9] *Id.* at 15.

at a practical and prosaic level, with matters such as the reservation of business names and disuniform requirements for group accounts producing the greatest angst.[10]

While there is evidence of the law responding to business needs,[11] the present writer can discern no evidence of a "race to the bottom" or a "race to the top" by State legislatures in respect of company and securities laws. It could be, of course, that competitive forces were in equilibrium. It is more likely, however, that there was in fact no interstate competition, and it is interesting to speculate on the reasons for lack of competition.

It might be said that interstate competition in company and securities market law can work only when there is a sufficient number of States to prevent the formation of an anticompetitive arrangement, and accordingly that the reason for the absence of competition amongst the Australian States is that the six States had formed a cartel. One problem with this theory is that the Australian States have been fierce competitors in other economic areas where more revenue is at stake, and it is hard to see why cartel formation should be confined to an area which is relatively marginal in State budgetary terms. More generally, competition can occur even where the number of competitors is very small.

The true explanation is probably more complex. One reason for the absence of interstate competition may have been that the potential revenue gain for an aggressively competing State would be relatively small as a proportion of the State budget, especially after deducting the costs of an interstate campaign. There may also have been an intuition that the inducements which might be offered to persuade businessmen to incorporate non-locally would always be outweighed by other considerations, particularly in view of the proximity of the local Registrar of Companies to the local business center and the great distance to the nearest non-local Registrar.[12]

[10] *Id.* at 17.

[11] The most notable example is the introduction of the no-liability company to cater for the perceived needs of the Victorian mining industry.

[12] Contrast Delaware's proximity to other Eastern States. However, there has been something of a "race to the bottom" in one context relevant to company law. Share transfers are subject to *ad valorem* stamp duty in the Australian States, but at various stages in our legislative history it has been possible to avoid or minimize stamp duty by dealing in shares registered on an Australian Capital Territory or Northern Territory Register, because of the different stamp duty regime in Commonwealth territories.

B. The First Securities Industry Legislation and the Interstate Corporate Affairs Commission

Even in 1961, statutory securities market law was almost non-existent in Australia. The State Companies Acts regulated the offer of securities to the public by prescribing the registration of a prospectus, supplemented the common law duties of directors, and required the filing of annual reports by most companies. But there were no comprehensive statutory structures for the licensing of exchanges, dealers and advisers, no substantial laws for the regulation of takeovers, no special provisions for the transfer of marketable securities, and no special treatment of insider trading and market offenses.

This rudimentary state of affairs was changed forever as a result of the mineral boom of the late 1960s, which saw the shares of Australian mining companies such as Poseidon N.L.[13] escalate to extraordinary prices and collapse just as dramatically. In 1970, in response to widespread allegations of malpractice, the Australian Senate established the Select Committee on Securities and Exchange to inquire into and report on the securities industry. The Committee's investigations confirmed that improper conduct had occurred, and all governments were under considerable public pressure to act.

Some State legislatures enacted Securities Industry Acts in the period 1970-71, and revised them after the Senate Committee produced its Report in 1974.[14] The Senate Committee produced an interim Report in December 1971, adopting the view that a single Commonwealth regulatory body was needed to oversee the whole of the Australian securities industry and rejecting by implication the recent efforts of the States.[15]

The Whitlam Labor Government was elected to Commonwealth Government in 1972. Labor had been out of Commonwealth office for over twenty years, and embarked on a huge programme of change. The proposal to establish Commonwealth regulation of the securities industry was high on the agenda. Relying in part on advice from Prof. *Louis Loss* of Harvard Law School,[16] the Government produced the Corporations and Securities Industry Bill, which was exposed for public comment in 1974. Though it was prepared before the Senate Committee's Report was released, the Bill embodied the Committee's principal recommendation for the establishment of a National Commission to regulate public corporations and the securities

[13] For example, the price of fully-paid shares of Poseidon N.L. rose from $A1.05 in mid-September 1969 to $A280 in February 1970. For a graphic account of this period, see T. SYKES, *The Money Miners: The Great Australian Mining Boom* (1978). The figures given here are at 94, 204.

[14] Report of the SENATE SELECT COMMITTEE ON SECURITIES AND EXCHANGE, *Australian Securities Markets and Their Regulation*, Parliamentary Paper No. 98/1974.

[15] Senate Hansard, 9 December 1971, at 2616.

[16] See LOSS, "Comments from the American Experience on Proposed Australian Companies and Securities Legislation," Parliamentary Paper No. 190/1973.

industry. It contained increased regulation of public offerings, takeovers, financial statements and disclosure of substantial shareholdings.

The Bill did not deal with the formation, management, general financing and liquidation of companies, matters over which the Commonwealth's constitutional power was more doubtful. The Government planned to introduce a separate National Companies Bill dealing with these matters, but it was dismissed by Governor-General Kerr on 11 November 1975, the day before this Bill was due to be introduced into Parliament.

The Corporations and Securities Industry Bill was very controversial both in its structure and concept, and in matters of substantive law. It was opposed by the non-Labor governments of the States of New South Wales, Victoria and Queensland. They concluded an Interstate Corporate Affairs Agreement in 1974, to introduce uniformity of administration of company law and to eliminate duplication of registration procedures by the establishment of reciprocal arrangements, thereby (no doubt) to reduce the pressure for Commonwealth legislation.[17] In accordance with the Agreement, each of these States altered its Companies Act to produce substantial uniformity, and each enacted a uniform Securities Industry Act which came into force in the member States on 1 March 1976.

The Interstate Corporate Affairs Agreement, and the legislation which resulted from it, undoubtedly improved company and securities market law and its administration. However, the Agreement suffered from three deficiencies: it did not bind all of the States; any amendments to the temporarily uniform laws would have to be made by each State legislature separately; and the administration of the laws by separate State Corporate Affairs Offices led to the adoption of different interpretations and practices from State to State.

C. The National Co-operative Companies and Securities Scheme

The Fraser Liberal-National Party was elected to Commonwealth Government in December 1975 on a policy of "co-operative federalism." Pursuant to that philosophy the new government and the States entered into negotiations to improve the Interstate Corporate Affairs Agreement. While the negotiations were proceeding, the process of substantive law reform was effectively suspended. The situation was very difficult because the period 1976-78 ushered in the takeover boom. Under the very limited takeover laws of that time, it was possible for an offeror to obtain control of a listed target by intensive buying on the stock market, with no disclosure and no obligation to give all target shareholders an equal opportunity to participate in the bid. Some dramatic overnight changes of control, in circumstances which appeared to be unfair to minority shareholders, led to demands for urgent law reform, and the stock exchanges found it necessary to anticipate

[17] Western Australia entered into the Agreement in 1975, after a change of government in that State.

legislative regulation of on-market takeovers by introducing new listing rules as an interim measure.

The eventual product of the Commonwealth-States negotiations was a Formal Agreement between the Commonwealth and all States, dated 22 December 1978. The Agreement, which is still in force, provides for the establishment of a Ministerial Council comprising (in effect) the Commonwealth and State Attorneys-General, to exercise general oversight of the new companies and securities scheme. It also provides for the establishment of the National Companies and Securities Commission, which is funded half by the Commonwealth and half by the States on a *per capita* basis, and is responsible (subject to directions from the Ministerial Council) for the entire area of policy and administration of company law and the regulation of the securities industry. Thus the Agreement achieves the major recommendation of the Senate Committee, but it does so through Commonwealth-State co-operation rather than by imposition by the Commonwealth on unwilling States. However, the State Corporate Affairs Offices remain in existence – they are delegates of the National Commission, which has a loose obligation to delegate to them.

Additionally, the Formal Agreement provides for the creation of a Companies and Securities Law Review Committee to advise the Ministerial Council on law reform, and under the scheme legislation an Accounting Standards Review Board has been established to promulgate uniform accounting standards.

The central component of the Formal Agreement relates to the making and amendment of legislation. The Agreement provides that legislation on companies and securities matters will not be enacted by a State unless it has been approved by the Ministerial Council; and that the Commonwealth will enact such amendments to the scheme legislation as are approved by the Ministerial Council, as laws for the Australian Capital Territory (a Commonwealth territory over which the Commonwealth Parliament has plenary legislative power).

Pursuant to the Agreement, each State has enacted "application of laws" legislation, which provides that the company and securities market law in force for the time being in the Australian Capital Territory applies in the State as a law of the State. This device has two advantages: first, the scheme legislation is an exercise of State constitutional power (coupled with the Commonwealth's power over territories), with the result that the limitations of the Commonwealth's constitutional power over corporations and securities markets are irrelevant and the legislation is undoubtedly beyond constitutional challenge; secondly, amendments become operative nationally upon their enactment by the Commonwealth Parliament, and there is no need for State Parliaments to legislate.

There are, however, some disadvantages to the co-operative scheme. First, each of the major pieces of legislation which constitute the co-operative scheme[18] has been accompanied by application of laws legislation for each State and the Northern Territory (which joined the scheme after its commencement). The result is that the scheme legislation comprises more than 100 Acts of Parliament. Although most of them need not as a practical matter be consulted, there is a daunting bulk of paper and complexity.

Secondly, the scheme is merely a political agreement and will not affect the constitutional sovereignty of the member States. Hence any subsequent State Act which is inconsistent with the Commonwealth legislation applying by virtue of that State's application of laws legislation will prevail as a matter of law. Direct contradiction of the scheme legislation is perhaps unlikely, but it may happen that State legislation essentially directed to other issues may intersect with scheme legislation, and disuniformity will be the result.

Thirdly, while the scheme legislation is itself uniform, there is obviously no uniformity in the legal regimes of the States into which the scheme legislation must fit. In particular, each State's system of administrative law is distinct, and generally less advanced than the Commonwealth's. In 1982 the Ministerial Council considered the question of review of decisions taken under the scheme legislation, and was not able to produce uniformity in this area. The Administrative Remedies Agreement of 21 April 1982 has the effect that the applicable administrative law will be the law of the State whose scheme law is applicable to the decision in question. Thus, if the Commission exercises a discretion under the Companies (Acquisition of Shares) Code in respect of a takeover of a company incorporated in Victoria, it will be acting under the Victorian Code and will be subject to the Administrative Law Act, 1978 (Vic.), under which it will have an obligation to supply reasons for its decision and will be subject to an appeal on standard administrative law grounds. Had the target been incorporated in New South Wales, where there is no comparable administrative legislation, these rights would not exist.

Fourthly, there have been some jurisdictional problems. Disputes under the scheme legislation are dealt with by the Supreme Court of the relevant State. Thus, for example, a reduction of capital or scheme of arrangement must be approved by the Supreme Court of the State in which the company was incorporated, whatever the place of business of the company may be. On a few occasions, embarrassed counsel have been told by judges that they are in the court of the wrong State.[19]

[18] National Companies and Securities Commission Act (to which the Formal Agreement is a Schedule), 1979; Companies Act, 1982; Companies (Acquisition of Shares) Act, 1979; Securities Industry Act, 1980; Futures Industry Act, 1986; Companies and Securities (Interpretation and Miscellaneous Provisions) Act, 1980. In addition there are transitional provisions and separate legislation dealing with fees and other matters. The substantive, uniform part of each Act is called a "Code."

[19] Kelvin Press Pty. Ltd. v. Koala Pack (Aust.) Pty. Ltd., 1 A.C.L.C. 872 (1983); Starr v. Trafalgar Financial Corporation Ltd., 1 A.C.L.C. 872 (1983); Re Buildmat

These four disadvantages of the co-operative scheme are "lawyers' problems" which do not affect the operation of the scheme in a substantial way. Other defects, arguably more substantial, have impressed the present Commonwealth Government and have led to a current move to replace the co-operative scheme with comprehensive Commonwealth legislation.

IV. The Proposed Commonwealth Legislation

In April 1986, in response to a submission from the Confederation of Australian Industry and expressions of disquiet from Parliamentarians, the Australian Senate resolved that its Standing Committee on Constitutional and Legal Affairs should examine the role of the Commonwealth Parliament in relation to the operation and effectiveness of the companies and securities legislation. The Committee reported in April 1987, recommending that the Commonwealth Parliament should enact comprehensive legislation covering the field currently regulated by the co-operative scheme. It rejected a proposal to leave company law to the States, and to federalize securities market law, on the basis of submissions which forcefully contended that a "split scheme" would be unworkable because of the overlapping of company and securities market questions, especially in the takeover field.[20] The Committee was aided by opinions on the constitutional issues prepared by Sir *Maurice Byers*, Q.C., formerly Commonwealth Solicitor-General. Sir *Maurice* took a very broad view of the scope of the Commonwealth's powers.[21]

The Committee based its recommendation on three grounds. First, the co-operative scheme was said to be incompatible with the system of ministerial responsibility, in that the Commission is not accountable to any one Minister but to the Ministerial Council as a whole, and no one Minister takes political responsibility for the Commission's actions. Further, the Commonwealth Minister is obliged by the terms of the Agreement to introduce into Parliament an amending Bill approved by majority vote of the Ministerial Council even if he does not personally support the proposal; and Parliament itself is inhibited from amending the Bill because amendments would have to be approved by the Ministerial Council.[22]

(Australia) Ltd., 1 N.S.W.L.R. 291 (1983); Orel v. Trafalgar Holdings Pty. Ltd., 8 A.C.L.R. 382 (1983); Re Buka Minerals N.L., 2 A.C.L.C. 3 (1983).

[20] Report of the SENATE STANDING COMMITTEE ON CONSTITUTIONAL AND LEGAL AFFAIRS, *The Role of Parliament in Relation to the National Companies Scheme* 60-62 (April 1987).

[21] The main opinion, dated 22 December 1986, is annexed to the COMMITTEE's Report, *supra* note 20.

[22] The COMMITTEE's Report, *supra* note 20, para. 3.16 ff, notes some disagreement as to the effect of a unilateral amendment by the Commonwealth Parliament of a Bill approved by the Ministerial Council. One view is that the amendment would be

Secondly, the separate existence of the National and State Commissions has produced a lack of uniformity of administration. The Committee noted evidence that detailed requirements for prospectuses and takeover documents differed from State to State and between some State Commissions and the National Commission. There was, according to evidence before the Committee, a difference between the New South Wales and Victorian Commissions as to the degree of training needed for licensed representatives of securities dealers. Other evidence indicated that the structure of the scheme seemed to stand in the way of the goal of uniformity of administration. The National Commission has no control over the amount and deployment of resources by the State Commissions. While it is obliged to delegate to State Commissions, it has no effective say in the manner of execution of tasks by the delegates. The National Commission is therefore in no position to enforce a uniform administrative viewpoint.

The third ground, which the Committee did not elaborate, is that the co-operative scheme produces "lowest common denominator" legislation. There was some evidence that members of the Ministerial Council had insufficient time to assess law reform proposals, but it is not convincing. All reform proposals for the co-operative scheme since its inception have been exposed for public comment prior to enactment, and in most cases prior to consideration by the Ministerial Council. Most of the changes have been on technical legal matters, frequently after recommendation by the Companies and Securities Law Review Committee.

The first and second grounds put forward by the Committee are of more substance. The first ground could be removed, however, by some fairly simple amendments to the co-operative scheme, some of which were adverted to in the Committee's Report. If the Commonwealth Minister were made permanent Chairman of the Ministerial Council, he would become politically responsible for the actions of the Commission. He could accept this level of responsibility if the Commonwealth were given a right of veto over proposals in the Ministerial Council. The difficulty in Parliament could be overcome by making it clear that Commonwealth Parliament could amend Bills approved by the Ministerial Council, subject perhaps to a right of veto in the Ministerial Council.

The second ground for the Committee's recommendation is more serious, in the writer's view, and identifies a systematic problem with any "federal" scheme for company and securities market law. The Australian experience demonstrates that uniform legislation is a limited achievement without harmonized administration. The lack of uniformity in administration in

effective but in breach of the spirit if not the letter of the Formal Agreement, and the States would be entitled to withdraw from the co-operative scheme. An alternative view is that the State application of laws legislation applies only to laws approved by the Ministerial Council, and the State legislation would impliedly exclude from application in the State an amendment which was not part of the Bill approved by the Ministerial Council.

Australia can be overcome only by increasing the National Commission's say in the manner of operation of State Commissions. It may be that there is no satisfactory way of achieving this short of full integration of the National and State Commissions into a single administrative unit.

Full administrative integration does not entail abandonment of the co-operative scheme. There is no legal obstacle to an arrangement in which the State Commissions would become branches of the National Commission, while the National Commission would retain its present status as the product of the co-operative exercise of State and Commonwealth constitutional powers. In an integrated system the entire administration of company and securities market law could be accounted for by pooling all revenue from filing fees and deducting all salaries and other expenses of administration, in accordance with budgets approved by the Ministerial Council, with the revenue surplus being distributed to the States on a *per capita* basis. The Ministerial Council would be able to set salaries at a level which took into account alternative levels of remuneration in the securities industry, because under this system staff would be neither Commonwealth nor State employees and would not therefore be subject to Commonwealth and State civil service pay scales.

Administrative arrangements of this kind have yet to be explored in Australia. Current developments are following a different path. On 25 May 1988, acting on the Senate Standing Committee's recommendation, the Commonwealth Attorney-General introduced into Parliament a package of Bills for comprehensive Commonwealth regulation of companies and the securities industry. Currently the Bills are the subject of strenuous public debate. In addition to the issues of the desirability and constitutionality of the Commonwealth taking exclusive control of this area, there is controversy over the contents of the Bills, which propose to reduce the role of the regulatory authorities in pre-vetting documents while increasing the civil liability of those involved in their preparation and issue. There will be a Parliamentary investigation into the contents of the Bills, and amendments are likely, but it is probable that Parliament will enact the Bills in some form, and the States will then mount a constitutional challenge before the High Court of Australia.

It will be interesting to see whether the Court will be able to resolve all of the constitutional issues in a single case. Even if that is achieved, the price of obtaining constitutionally valid Commonwealth law will be an added dose of complexity to company and securities market legislation. In their attempts to attract all conceivable heads of constitutional power, the draftsmen of the Bills have replaced single provisions of the existing law with strings of overlapping provisions, each of which reaches out to a different constitutional heading.

The most serious defect of the Bills is that they do not fully address the problem of administrative disuniformity. The Attorney-General proposes to negotiate with the States with a view to retaining the State Commissions while giving the National Commission greater controlling power. If the

States do not co-operate, the Commonwealth will exercise a power under the Bills to appropriate State companies and securities records. As the States and their Commissions are at present intransigent, the prospects for effective administration of the new scheme are dim.

V. European Harmonization: Lessons from the Australian Experience?

In his paper for this Symposium, Prof. *Gower* expresses doubt as to whether the American experience in the resolution of constitutional problems and the development of criteria, methods and tools for harmonization will be helpful in the process of harmonization in Europe.[23] Even if this view is a little too gloomy, it stands as a warning against overly enthusiastic transcription of the solutions of one legal, political and economic culture to a notably different environment. In particular, the central device of the co-operative scheme, that agreed amendments become operative in member States automatically through State application of laws legislation, will probably not be politically feasible in Europe in the foreseeable future, though it may become relevant when harmonization has reached a more advanced stage.[24]

However, the Australian experience appears relevant to some of *Buxbaum* and *Hopt*'s specific recommendations for advancing the process of European harmonization.

First, Australia has always had a unitary judicial system, the temporary aberration of a jurisdictionally separate Federal Court being largely irrelevant to company and securities market law. Nonetheless, the establishment of uniformity of statutory law and administration has been a prodigious struggle. This suggests that while judicial harmonization may be a condition precedent to harmonization of laws, the achievement of judicial harmonization will not itself advance the objectives of statutory and administrative harmonization.[25]

Secondly, nothing in the Australian experience supports the view that statutory harmonization is most likely to occur in areas where business

[23] See *infra* at 308. He acknowledges that the US experience may be useful in developing substantive law. Australia probably has less to offer than the US with respect to the development of substantive law, though the Australian blend of black letter regulation and administrative discretion in takeover regulation (Companies (Acquisition of Shares) Code) and the system of enforceability of self-regulatory rules through compliance orders but not awards of damages (Securities Industry Code, Section 42), may be of some interest.

[24] Although the constitutional problems in transposing a system used within a true federal State to a structure in which there is a "federation" of essentially sovereign States should not be underestimated.

[25] See BUXBAUM & HOPT, *supra* note 1, at 272-273.

press for less cumbersome, more "enabling" rules. The current Commonwealth legislative proposals contain much "de-regulatory" material, but this has simply added to the controversy surrounding them.[26]

Thirdly, there is evidence in the Australian experience for the view that certain securities regulation aspects of harmonization, and especially the regulation of takeovers, are given high economic priority, and to this extent our experience accords with the *Scitovsky* and *Kitch* models.[27]

Fourthly, *Buxbaum* and *Hopt* commend harmonization within the legal profession and the activities of such bodies as the Business Law Section of the American Law Institute.[28] The Australian experience is that a public law reform body is more likely to achieve results that a professional body as such, although the law reform body's effectiveness will depend upon whether it is perceived to understand the subject of its recommendations, and the presence of members with professional and business expertise will be of significance in that respect. The Companies and Securities Law Review Committee, constituted under the co-operative scheme with representatives from law, accounting and business, has had quite a successful record of implementation of its recommendations, as has the Accounting Standards Review Board. In recognition of these successes, the Commonwealth Bills propose the preservation of the Accounting Standards Review Board and the replacement of the Companies and Securities Law Review Committee with a similar body, which will have an improved budget and the power to publish its reports independently.[29]

However, were a single lesson to be drawn from the Australian experience, it would be that harmonization of statutory and judge-made law is of limited use without an administrative system which will ensure harmonized application of law. The absence of such a system has severely discounted the Australian achievement. The writer would suggest that the problem of harmony in administration be addressed earlier rather than later in the European process, and that effective channels of communication amongst company and securities market administrators be nurtured.

[26] *Id.* at 273.

[27] *Id.* at 281. But other aspects of securities regulation, such as the regulation of insider trading, are treated as having more marginal economic significance. Prof. ANISMAN's paper, *Insider Trading Legislation for Australia: An Outline of the Issues and Alternatives* (1986), recommended wide ranging reforms in a context of widespread public concern, but has not been acted upon. In this area, a more incremental approach is likely to be more effective.

[28] BUXBAUM & HOPT, *supra* note 1, at 282-283, 285.

[29] Australian Securities Commission Bill, 1988 (Cth), cl. 155.

B. Discussion

I. Introductory Remarks

Robert Austin

I can say that having studied the *Buxbaum* and *Hopt* book[1] carefully I was not sure just what aspects of the Australian experience (which I clearly was intended to deal with) would be most interesting to you. In the end I chose to speak about structure rather than substantive law. There are some interesting things about Australian substantive law on takeovers, for example, which there may be occasion to refer to later.[2] This is a paper on the way we moved towards uniformity of company and securities law. While there are probably few lessons for the European development, one thing that strikes me as particularly important in Australia is our current lack of administrative uniformity.

At the present time, as the paper describes,[3] we have a uniform system of law, both for companies and securities markets. Uniformity is achieved by virtue of the cooperation of all of the States who have plenary legislative power, under a system in which the States and the Commonwealth are represented on a Ministerial Council which approves changes to the law from time to time. And under that system, once the Ministerial Council approves a change of law, it is enacted by the Commonwealth for a Commonwealth territory, the Australian Capital Territory, and automatically applies in the States because the States have already passed laws which say that the law of the Australian Capital Territory from time to time is the law of the State. So we have achieved uniformity by virtue of State cooperation, but that is uniformity of company and securities market law only. It is not uniformity of the administration of the law.

Our law, more perhaps than most other systems, has a great number of discretions vested in administrators – some very wide discretions and many very specific ones. The administrative system is that we have a National Commission but it is required to delegate to State Commissions. And as a matter of practice, the National Commission's writ runs only to the front doorsteps of the State Commissions. In other words, once they delegate a power to a State Commission, they have no control over the allocation of

[1] R.M. BUXBAUM & K.J. HOPT, *Legal Harmonization and the Business Enterprise* (Berlin/New York 1988).
[2] See *infra* at 375 ff, 384 f, 388 f.
[3] See *supra* at 169 ff.

resources by the State Commission to the exercise of that power nor do they have any effective control as to how the power is exercised. That is a very great defect of our current system. If there is a general lesson to be learned about the Australian experience, it is that even uniformity, not merely harmonization of law, will be of limited significance unless one can achieve some harmonization (if not uniformity) of administration.

Alain Hirsch

Before the discussion begins, could you say a few words about the importance of the administration in Australian company law? In most of our countries, administration may be important in securities regulation but normally not in company law, where the private law system with private claims and judges applies in most cases.

Robert Austin

It is true that the major discretions and the administration are in securities market law, particularly in respect of prospectus registration and takeovers. One of the problems we have had with prospectuses is that in the larger States, and particularly New South Wales, there is considerable delay in registering prospectuses and the State Commission staff spend a great deal of time in carefully analyzing the claims in the prospectus before registration and will frequently issue many requisitions. To take the other extreme, in Tasmania which is our smallest State, the registration of the prospectus is almost a matter of the State Commissioner taking it home overnight and letting you know the next day how he feels about it. Because most jurisdictional matters are determined by the place of incorporation of the relevant company, there is a quite arbitrary discrepancy between the kind of administration you get in some States and what you get in others.

So far as pure company law is concerned, probably the area which produces the most difficulty in practice is the rather uninteresting and prosaic matter of registration of company names. The current system is that you cannot register a company name unless the Commission agrees that it is not misleadingly similar to an existing registered name. If a new company wishes to establish itself nationally, it has to obtain a name which can be registered in each State and there are certainly differences of judgement brought to bear by the State Commissions as to what is misleadingly similar to an existing name.

But having identified those particularly important matters of administration, I have to say that scattered throughout our legislation are an enormous number of discretions and there is simply no uniformity of practice in exercising them. The National Commission issues guidelines but no guideline, however specific, can really control what goes on at the State level, particularly in relation to the allocation of resources to the pursuit of various tasks.

II. The Drive Towards Uniformity

Richard Buxbaum

Of course there is a new initiative at work now in Australia, and I wonder whether Prof. Austin could say something about the reason why this new pressure for further uniformity, including of course uniformity of administration, has developed. I am speaking of your decision to federalize company law apart from capital market law. What are the underlying business pressures? Because I think in that there may be a lesson to be derived as to common company law. I thought this would relate to a point I want to make about the relevance of the American experience.

Robert Austin

As you will see from my paper,[4] what is happening is that the co-operative system that I have described is likely to be replaced over the next couple of years with a system in which the Commonwealth exercises its constitutional power to legislate with respect to companies and securities matters. There are said to be three reasons for this move for the Commonwealth to replace the States.

The first is that there is a problem of parliamentary sovereignty in the current system. The political decision makers are a Ministerial Council of State and Commonwealth ministers and there is not one minister who is politically accountable for what goes on. And that lack of accountability is one of the reasons the Commonwealth has given for making changes. Secondly, the problems of administration that I described earlier are relied upon by the Commonwealth to justify change. Thirdly, the Commonwealth says that the standard of law reform is not high enough.

I think lying behind that ostensible accounting for the proposals there is something more going on. There is no doubt that the Commonwealth wants to flex its constitutional muscles in this area. We have a corporations power in our Constitution which has steadily been growing in scope under the influence of High Court decisions. What is likely to happen is that there will be the biggest constitutional case in the history of the Australian Federation in 1989, in which the constitutional validity of the Commonwealth proposals will be tested and the High Court will give a very broad judgement in which it endorses most of what the Commonwealth wants to do. That will give the Commonwealth a base of power which it has not yet had to regulate in the entire commercial area. I think if there is a hidden agenda it is the Commonwealth's wish to get that constitutional basis of power established.

Another issue that might be interesting for this Symposium is this. One of the claims made in support of the Commonwealth is that Australia is now a

[4] See *supra* at 172 ff and 175 ff.

single securities market. We have a single stock exchange as a result of decisions a couple of years ago and it is said that it is simply irrational to have a single securities market regulated by a group of State ministers.

That does not fully explain why we are moving towards Commonwealth company law as well. The explanation for that is the feeling that you cannot sharply draw a line between company and securities market law. It is simply not sensible to regulate, for example, the offerors' conduct in a takeover by national legislation while retaining State legislation to deal with the duties of the target directors. If you are going to have a single system for securities market law, you cannot draw the line effectively short as a single system of company law.

Richard Buxbaum

Well, that is the theme I had hoped would be stated, because I think it bears directly on the question of the relevance of the American experience. That is why I wanted to get it on the table. There are two or three congruent themes in the comments that Prof. Austin has just made.

One of them, which will come back[5] is the fact that takeover law or the takeover problem is testing as never before the presumed historical separation between capital market public law concepts and private company law concepts. I think that theme has already been sounded a couple of times in this meeting[6] and it has certainly been strongly confirmed again now by this comment of Prof. Austin. That in turn makes the problems of federalism come to the fore.

Secondly, this point is congruent with a natural and not at all in my opinion objectionable arrogation of power at a central level, that is to say whatever the original organic act, whatever the original constitutional division of power structure might have been, this flexing of constitutional muscle, as Prof. Austin put it, the effort to generate this federal company law, has an autonomy or a drive of its own. I think it is not just objectively driven by the needs of the legal system, but it is a dynamic that has to be recognized. Again I think the American experience, simply as a historical experience, is relevant to that concept.

Third, again as Prof. Austin pointed out – it sounds, incidentally, as if we harmonized the discussion but that is not the case, I think the themes in fact are on the table and I was willing to trust that that was what his experience would show – the third point is that in this setting there is of course a necessary increasing role for courts to play, not only in the testing of the constitutional parameters or limits of this exercise but also in the actual development of an implementation and enforcement potential in this legislation. I refer here to a comment of a recent historian of American constitutional legal and political history, that the United States may not

[5] See *infra* at 375 ff.
[6] See e.g. *supra* at 22 f.

have been a State in the Hegelian sense – no higher civil service, no church, no monarchy, and so forth – but it was nonetheless a State of courts and parties. Interestingly, these are the very two items which were not provided for in the original Constitution except in the limited sense that an Article III jurisdiction for courts was provided but not for the actual structure that developed.

Now to tie that just for a moment to the commerce clause. I am trying to stay away from substantive law, I just want to try to stay on the process and the federal issue. From the perspective of the commerce clause as a grant of power to the central government in a federation, the American experience is not terribly relevant. The European structure for that is in place, the free movement clause is in that sense perhaps even more powerful as an affirmative grant than the commerce clause was.

What is, however, relevant is what was mentioned briefly in the exchange with Prof. Timmermans:[7] the so-called negative commerce clause; that is to say, the ability of the judicial system to legislate officially by declaring that certain constitutional provisions have direct effect in terms of private rights and private duties, and thus in terms of public duties of the Member States or public constraints and so forth. That I do not think should be underestimated. The use of the negative commerce clause as a legislative device is still a matter that the European academic community could study with profit as a doctrinal question, not as an historical analogy, not as a contextual analogy, but as a doctrinal analogy. There is a lot of refined, nuanced work on this concept of the negative commerce clause which I do not think European constitutional scholarship has yet fully adapted to.

There are of course early and excellent studies. *Ehmke*'s study of 25 years or so ago, *The Economy and the Constitution* (in the German text *Wirtschaft und Verfassung*) has a very substantial section on the negative commerce clause. There was no particular effort or ability at that time to relate it to the Treaty of Rome. So in that setting I think there are certain relevant points, although as I say, I would not overdo the contextual or the historical analogy. Obviously those are different. But I would emphasize the fruitfulness of a doctrinal analogy there. That ties to one or two points that may come up later in the substantive law discussions, such as the takeover point.[8]

Another fact which we did not emphasize in the book is that the American Constitution federalizes bankruptcy. They say that uniform bankruptcy legislation was early deemed a very important element. To put anachronistic modern terms on it, a kind of equal starting point, equal conditions for creditors and their protection, could be hypothesized in that bankruptcy clause although I think it had other motivations as well at the time.

[7] See *supra* at 156 ff.
[8] See *infra* at 375 ff.

Now when we get to the question of groups of companies, then of course almost automatically we come to the question of creditor protection. Here too there may be some relevance to the American experience with the necessary uniformity of creditors' remedies in the context of bankruptcy structures. That ties to the point that bankruptcy law more and more ought to be seen as an element of company law. In some ways you cannot really separate the doctrinal aspects of protection of creditors from the recapture by creditors of distributions made by management to its shareholders and so forth. Otherwise you have the bizarre situation of having two parallel doctrinal tracks, a company law doctrinal track that bears on questions like distributions, and yet a totally different bankruptcy track that bears on the recapture of distributions. That cannot work, and therefore I think the American experience with both centralizing bankruptcy law and slowly, in that bankruptcy law, beginning to capture company law concepts is also a doctrinal point worth pondering.

So to recapitulate, and before even speaking about the pressure for uniformity from the business community and so on, there is a whole different issue of uniformity in which the American experience has some limited relevance, limited, obviously because of the interest group structure, the language structure, the national separation of professional groups and so on, all our critical differences. But putting those aside, and in fact putting aside the whole question of pressure from below, let me recapitulate: the autonomous dynamics of arrogation of power, legitimately, I would argue, by the courts, the role of the negative commerce clause as a doctrinal tool, and then this whole problem of the breakdown of the separation of capital market law from company law, are all matters as to which the American experience provides some lessons.

They are not all constitutional lessons. Some of them are legislative lessons, some of them are administrative lessons. They are not models. I do not mean that in any sense. Most of the lessons are negative although I am deformed enough by the American experience to recommend litigation to you all. That is a different matter. The less homogeneity of legal and political culture you have within a given legal setting, the more I think the litigation function has its own legitimating role and never mind about nasty attorneys who get contingency fees and so forth. There is a larger game at work in that role of litigation. But that is my personal deformation. I will leave that to one side.

Well, that is the recapitulation I wanted to make, not in direct response, but in the sense of reaction to the question of the relevance of the experience.

Christian Timmermans

I had exactly the same question. I was struck by this drive for not only similarity but now also uniformity in legislation on the federal level, particularly in the company law field. And that in a situation where, as stated in Prof. Austin's paper,[9] the existing company laws were already similar, and also in a situation I presume where there is freedom of incorporation, where there is no problem of recognition of the statute of a company formed in another State.

If I now understand correctly, apart from the drive as such for legislation at the federal level, the explanation seems to be that the obvious need for uniformity in the field of securities legislation leads in itself to the necessity of a uniform company law. Perhaps a small question there. Is that a feeling of academics, of politicians or is it also the feeling of the business community? I could imagine that, but perhaps you could be a bit more explicit on that point.

I must say, when we look to the United States there has apparently been no similar development because securities legislation has been federalized to a large extent, but there is no uniform federal company law. In most Member States of the European Community the situation is similar insofar as we find a separate evolution of company law on the one hand and securities legislation on the other hand. On Community level the approach has been more or less similar. In the Commission the harmonization in both fields has been a matter for successive directorate-generals for a long time. When we look to the capital market directives on prospectuses, for instance, they sometimes refer to the company law directives, particularly in the accounting field. But the work as such has not been integrated until now. I quite agree that the takeover issue is interesting in this respect because there it is impossible to separate both approaches and to do one, harmonize in the securities field and leave the company law aspects aside. In my country at present we face exactly the same question with regard to the protection devices against unfriendly takeovers where the Stock Exchange has now made quite a clear statement but is really not competent to regulate in the matter because it is a company law issue and therefore a matter for the legislator.

Robert Austin

Prof. Timmermans asked whether the drive for uniformity in company law as opposed to securities market law in Australia was really generated by academics, politicians or the business community, and what the explanation for it really is. I have three points to make and no full answer.

First, there never was a clear line between securities market law and company law in Australia, nor I believe in England and therefore the question was never seen in those terms. It is true that the pressure for uniformity has largely been in matters which we would call securities market law, particularly prospectus law reform, takeovers and market offenses such as insider trading and similar matters. But the pressure for

[9] See *supra* at 169.

uniformity in these matters was not seen as focusing on an area separate from company law.

My second point is that we have always had a system in which securities market law and company law were administered by the same bureaucracy, the same administrator, although it was the States until 1982. And so again there was no reason to discriminate between the two.

Thirdly, there are some matters of strictly company law in which there has been a particular demand for uniformity from our business community. I mentioned business names before.[10] I should add that companies operating in more than one State want uniformity with respect to accounting and disclosure procedures. In those matters there has been some pressure.

What happened in recent times is that the Commonwealth put forward some proposals for uniform Commonwealth securities market law and the States responded by saying: "You cannot draw a line between securities market law and company law." And it is true that some academic commentators, including me, fed some of the States their lines. So there has been an academic influence at the point of saying that you cannot conceptually draw a line between company law and securities market law. Interestingly that point has been taken up politically by the States.

Olivier Guillod

Listening to Prof. Buxbaum[11] I started wondering whether the Swiss experience might teach something on the issue.

Now I am very reluctant to speak of that because there are other scholars around this table who are very much better qualified than I am. But nevertheless, if I remember well, company law was made a federal competence in 1874 as the Constitution was amended. Before that, there had been a proposal to have a kind of national law on the issue not by way of a federal law but by way of an interstate treaty, what we call *concordat* in Switzerland. One of the provisions of this *concordat* provided for the creation of a federal court because it was thought at that time that it was necessary to have a federal court to harmonize the implementation of this new law on companies. However, it was deemed that such a provision could not result from a *concordat* and so the idea of a federal law on the matter came back. To materialize, it had to pass the additional hurdle of amending the Constitution. It was tried twice, and twice the people rejected it, and then eventually it was accepted at the third attempt in 1874, when bankruptcy law was also made a federal matter.

So things have happened in Switzerland the other way around: company law was harmonized first. But, more importantly, the experience of the *concordat* shows that the implementation is very important, as Prof. Austin

[10] See *supra* at 181.
[11] See *supra* at 183 ff.

said before,[12] and cannot be separated from the substantive content of the law.

Gérard Hertig

Prof. Austin, when you are saying[13] that administration should be the task of one administrative body, what do you mean by that? Do you mean that the law should be interpreted the same way everywhere or that it should also be enforced the same way everywhere? And if you say that, then I do not see the interest of having a federal State or of having several different States linked together: you have a centralized State. That is the French experience, but that should be very different from what we see now in the EC. And you only have to speak with French people living in Marseille or Bordeaux and to hear what they think about Paris to immediately realize that there is no way Brussels could play the role of Paris.

My second remark is about the *concordat* experience and the brief discussion we have already had with Prof. Timmermans.[14] The great advantage of a *concordat* is that by this means you could legalize "*Europe à deux vitesses.*" You do not need to have every State to be party to the *concordat*. You could have just some of them. You could have, for example, very broad rules at the Community level (that is the new approach or the mutual recognition approach) and some States saying: "We are signing a *concordat* because we have specific requirements which are different from the other States." Then you have something which is not uniform, not perfect, but probably workable.

Robert Austin

You asked what I meant by uniformity, and if I was referring to interpretation or to enforcement. It seems to me that listening to the discussion there are quite a few ambiguities in the term uniformity. There is a question about uniformity of interpretation. There is a question about uniformity of policing or enforcement. What I had in mind was rather different from both of those. I had in mind uniformity of the exercise of discretion to determine what particular standard would be set for meeting administrative requirements in a particular case. For example what kind of statements will be allowed in a prospectus or takeover document in this particular case. That is not so much interpretation of the law as the exercise of an open discretion within the framework of the law.

There is another kind of ambiguity and this relates to some points made by some of the other speakers. It seems to me that we might usefully distinguish negative and positive uniformity. What I mean is this: while

[12] See *supra* at 180 f.
[13] See *supra* at 180.
[14] See *supra* at 165.

Europe may not want uniformity in a positive sense, it seems to me that to the extent that you have European standards administered by national or local administrative bodies, it will be a source of perpetual grievances if like cases are treated differently from place to place. You might find it necessary to achieve negative uniformity in the sense of trying to remove those kinds of discrimination. You may not want positive uniformity because all of us want to have administrators who are sympathetic to local conditions, and it seems to me that absolute or positive uniformity is inconsistent with that kind of sympathy. My concern is with removing what I have called negative uniformity, that is to say with trying to avoid a situation in which exactly like cases are treated differently because of the accident of the geographical location of the parties. That really covers my main points.

Klaus Hopt

I very much agree with Prof. Austin's conclusion, his emphasis on the need of some uniformity in administration. Now how this is to be achieved in practice is another question. But as a topic and maybe as a goal this seems important.

Hartmut Schmidt

Of course I see the great clarity of uniformity and the advantages it has, but I think the discussion has brought out that uniformity may have enormous cost. Differences in administration may just mean that different persons in the administration respond more or less well to the needs of those whom they regulate. Therefore uniform administration may simply mean that everybody gets the same bad deal and I think there should be room for excellence in public service and this may require a lot of leeway in administration.

Of course I was delighted about what you said, Prof. Buxbaum,[15] about your greedy lawyers, that you recommended litigation. Bad motives, even non-idealistic competitors, may serve a useful function and I think this point is very important.

Eddy Wymeersch

With respect to the matter of uniformity, it is useful to emphasize that the tradition and thinking within the European Community do not favor uniformity. One can but refer to the decisions of the European Court of Justice, rendered *inter alia* during the 1970s to illustrate that the European Community is based not on a concept of uniformity, but on one of harmony in diversity.

[15] See *supra* at 185.

One should moreover be afraid of having plain uniformity dictated from Brussels. This would raise the already controversial issue of the political legitimacy of the rule-making process within the Community. This issue has been raised by many people before, and today's greater involvement of the European Parliament may somewhat alleviate the hesitation one may feel. But the issue remains. On several occasions rules have been introduced in the directives that were the result of strong and effective lobbying rather than of enlightened harmonized rule making. This procedure is especially detrimental if at the same time it has anticompetitive effects. As the rules have not been discussed, analyzed and scrutinized in public, it will be extremely difficult to avoid this form of influencing of the legislative process.

Christian Meier-Schatz

A question related to the problems of civil liability and private remedies. Prof. Austin, in your paper you emphasized the difficulties of your administrative system. Now obviously the new Commonwealth Bill reduces such an administrative enforcement in favor of civil liability.[16] Given the well-known problems of private enforcement techniques, I would be interested to hear why this is so and what are the policy reasons behind it.

Robert Austin

On the question of civil liability. You asked me to comment on why it is that our new Commonwealth proposals reduce administrative pre-vetting of prospectuses and other documents while raising the level of civil liability for contravention.[17]

This is allegedly a form of deregulation of prospectuses and other documents. The reality is that it is not deregulation, it is reregulation. What you are doing is removing pre-vetting of the documents by an administrator, but you are regulating by providing a wide cause of action for civil liability for those who make misleading statements in the documents. So it is not what I would understand to be deregulation. The pressure for it has come from large issuers of prospectuses, those who frequently issue prospectuses and wish to avoid the rigidities of the current system. My own view is that there is no justification for the Commonwealth's current proposals. What is needed is a system in which new issuers, particularly our Western mining companies which tend to be highly speculative, are still subject to pre-vetting by a public authority. But at the same time I think that where a company is stock exchange listed and has a track record of

[16] See *supra* at 177.
[17] See *supra* at 177.

substantial profits over time, there is a good case for allowing it simply to lodge a prospectus and not have it prechecked.

Geoffrey Fitchew

I would like to ask a variant to the last question. Is the drive for uniformity of administration related, is it simply a matter of tidiness or is it the result of abuses of various kinds which have led to the pressure? I would like to say in passing that I agree very strongly with Prof. Wymeersch that Europe is unlikely to be a place of uniformity, although I venture the next comment with considerable diffidence: I have always had the impression, and partly from a study that I did of federal revenue sharing arrangements some years ago, that Australia is the federation which is closest to a unitary State in many respects and therefore I suspect that there are probably not many lessons to be derived from the Australian experience for the Community. But I advance that with considerable diffidence.

L.C.B. Gower

"Where does the drive for uniformity in company legislation come from? And why is it greater in Australia than in the USA?" I would not have thought that there was a great deal of a difference. Australia – Prof. Austin will correct me if I am wrong – has purported to have a uniform company legislation for the last thirty years.

Robert Austin

The Uniform Companies Act was adopted in 1961.

L.C.B. Gower

Well 25 years. The trouble was that they started off being uniform but increasingly each State passed amendments so that after ten or even five years they ceased to be uniform and this was a nonsense. And it seems to me that the proposals now to have a federal act which cannot be subjected to such modification makes very good sense.

The drive for this, I suspect, comes not so much from businessmen, that was one suggestion,[18] but more from corporate lawyers who are the main sufferers in the lack of uniformity, and I would have thought the same applies to the drive for uniformity of company legislation in the USA. There two influences, as I understand it, have produced a measure of uniformity of law of corporations. One is the influence of Delaware, and the other is the influence of the ABA's (American Bar Association) Model Business Corporations Law. Similarly on the securities side the SEC has

[18] See *supra* at 186.

intervened on the federal side and in addition to that you have had for some years a uniform blue sky law which has been adopted by a large majority of States so that you get uniformity here, admittedly with options.

Insofar as there is pressure for more uniformity in corporate law, my experience is it generally does start with the lawyers, the corporation lawyers, rather than anyone else. That of course is dangerous because they will try to get it so that there is the least regulation possible and this may have adverse consequences so that we have got to have somebody intervening to make sure they do not just get their way every time.

Edmund Kitch

I would like to pick up one subtheme that was briefly mentioned which is the role in the United States of the law schools in the harmonization of private law. You had the emergence in the nineteenth century of the Harvard Law School model of a national law school. It was able to attract very able students and train them for practice in all of the States. The mission required that the faculty undertake to teach the American private law as a national law. I think that if you ask a law professor to teach the law of a diverse body of jurisdictions – and you see this over and over again in the American teaching materials – there is going to be a majority rule and then there is going to be a minority rule. Any other rules that cannot fit in those two categories drop out. To try and handle with the students a third or fourth or fifth and a sixth variant is just too much. So that gets dropped to the footnote or out of the materials completely as simply being too unimportant to get attention, and then the students of course go out into the jurisdictions and when they encounter rules that are so foreign that they were not even mentioned in law school, they think that they are very odd and it sets off a movement in the Bar towards harmonization. At least their State ought to be a minority and not just a complete oddity.

One thing that is interesting about the Harvard model which came to dominate American legal education was that it was achieved in an environment where you did not have free movement of credentials – that is all of the students had to go out and separately qualify in the States. Their Harvard degree did not automatically enable them to practice. But still, Harvard and other national schools like it were able to attract the best lawyers and came to dominate the Bar. Of course the enterprise of European harmonization must be a long-term enterprise which goes well beyond 1992. Is it possible that in the post-1992 environment with a principle of free movement of persons and credentials, some educational innovator in Europe would make the move to create a European law school on this model?

If such an initiative were successful and if it attracted the best of the European students who wish to be lawyers, and succeeded in establishing them in practice back in their jurisdictions, it would seem to me that over several generations, a lot of the processes that you see in the United States, such as the ALI and the American Bar Association, would slowly come about and the decentralizing tendencies would be countered in much the same way. Is that something that can happen in Europe? Or will something like this be one of the invisible hand phenomena as the free movement of persons and credentials comes about? Will law schools slowly realize that their graduates are going to be subject to competition from graduates from other jurisdictions, and this will force the change back on to the curriculum?

III. Competition Among Regulators

Hartmut Schmidt

From reading Prof. Austin's paper I have a few questions which also relate to the *Buxbaum* and *Hopt* book and to other statements which have been made.

Prof. Austin, you have been relying[19] on this notion of enabling legislation and the notion of race to the bottom, and I am wondering whether you could provide me with a clear-cut dividing line or whether you would say: "Well, the dividing line depends on the person who uses these notions." I really could not find a clear-cut dividing line between race to the bottom and enabling legislation, even though these two notions seem to be really different.

You look as if you found this an odd question... Let me give you an example. Imagine that US commercial banks, by way of legislation, get the power to do investment banking in the area of shares. One may say, this is a race to the bottom if one believes the Glass-Steagall Act is a perfect act. One may also say: "Well, the bankers wanted it," so the new power results from enabling legislation, not from a race to the bottom. Where is the dividing line between the two?

And then you made a statement[20] which I have heard before, that it takes a large number of States to bring about competition. I wonder whether you have a very special notion of competition. Some economists tend to think that competition between a small number of companies is much more intensive than between a large number. So if you have two States, I think one State can say: "We will do something which will serve the needs of the investors or the issuers or the public much better than what the other State has to offer," and I would consider this to be competition. But maybe you would say this is not competition, this is just enlightened government.

[19] See *supra* at 169 ff, 178 f.
[20] See *supra* at 170.

Robert Austin

You wanted to know if I saw where the dividing line was between the race to the bottom and the concept of enabling legislation. The answer is that the distinction is subjective.

You questioned my concept of competition. Where I referred to competition, I was really putting up an argument to knock it down and I agree with everything you said.

Christian Meier-Schatz

Prof. Austin, my point relates closely to what Prof. Schmidt has already emphasized: while speaking about State law competition in the Australian company law field you stressed that there was effectively no race to the bottom, or towards less regulation. Yesterday something like a consensus emerged[21] that normally State law competition or competition among stock exchanges leads to less stringent regulatory regimes.

Hartmut Schmidt

I said the opposite,[22] there was no consensus.

Christian Meier-Schatz

Then it would be even more important to hear why such a race did not take place in Australia despite its inviting structural framework.

Robert Austin

Why was there no race to the bottom in Australia, Prof. Meier-Schatz asked me. Well, I have done the best to answer that.[23] If he is suggesting that my answer is inconclusive, I agree. It seems to me that we had a historical tradition of following the English experience and we tended therefore not to go in for State competition in company law. Partly, I think, it was because of the tyranny of distance, the difficulty of persuading a business to incorporate outside its place of operation because of the sheer distances involved.

Christian Meier-Schatz

That is the case in America too.

[21] See *supra* at 100 ff.
[22] See *supra* at 104, 114 and 118.
[23] See *supra* at 170 f.

Robert Austin

Yes, I think that the state of communications in the United States was always better than ours and you must remember that in Australia most businesses operate in single town centres. The larger Australian businesses are either in Sydney or Melbourne and interstate regulatory bodies wanting to compete for Sydney business would have to persuade Sydney businessmen that there was sufficient advantage for them to outweigh the convenience of being able to talk personally to the regulator in their home town. I think a lot of our business people do value a personal contact with regulators. That is the best I can make of it.

It is odd and I may ultimately discover that there has been a race to the bottom or top in this area, but so far I found no evidence of competition. And what makes it particularly odd is that in other parts of regulation, such as in the area of stamp duty, in Australia there has been enormous competition between the States, yet curiously I can find no evidence of it here.

Alain Hirsch

Can I just ask something? I understand that there is no complete consensus about the question asked by Prof. Meier-Schatz about the difference between enabling legislation and race to the bottom and whether there was any objective difference or whether there was a value judgement. I wonder whether enabling legislation may be objectively defined.

Hartmut Schmidt

If you asked a Delaware economist, he would probably tell you: "We eliminated all the provisions that did not make sense and we only left what makes sense, and therefore all we have is enabling regulations." Well, other people will say: "Delaware, that is a race to the bottom."

Alain Hirsch

The concept of race to the bottom can never be objectively defined, because the bottom is a subjective thing.

Hartmut Schmidt

I think because of that you also cannot objectively define enabling legislation. This was the message I got from Prof. Austin and I think he was clear enough on that.

Klaus Hopt

But this raises once again[24] the whole discussion: where do we draw the line between areas to be left for competitive effects and others in the public domain under a public good theory and who has to make this value judgment? For a moment it seemed that we had some solution to this problem. But this turns out not to be the case.

Hartmut Schmidt

Everybody will try and should try to implement what makes sense. But it seems to me that whether he is right or not depends on the model he has and he may have good luck and have the right model, but somebody may come out with a better model, or he may make mistakes. This is the fundamental question on which the competitive approach rests. The best way to find out what really makes sense is to let regulatory alternatives compete and to watch how the market responds.

Richard Buxbaum

In a way there is some dissonance. We heard Prof. Timmermans' reading of the recent jurisprudence;[25] and while there is disagreement about its scope, nonetheless it very clearly emerged[26] that a Delawarization effect is not out of the question for the European Community's company laws in the near future as a result of the use of Articles 52 and 58 EEC Treaty criteria (if you apply them to company law internal affairs). If that is so, then why would not the nation States Prof. Wymeersch was mentioning,[27] which do not see themselves as uniform, push for central uniformity from above as an avoidance of the Delawarization effect?

Is that not really something that we have to pick up from the previous discussion and add to this question of the developing uniformity of company law?

Geoffrey Fitchew

Just on the *Segers* case.[28] Although I would agree that Prof. Timmermans' interpretation of it[29] may find acceptance in the future, I suspect and I guess that the legal experts in Brussels would hold this view that it is not a probability. I suspect that if the proposition were put to the European Court directly they would be pretty reluctant to adopt the extensive

[24] See *supra* at 100 ff.
[25] See *supra* at 132 ff and 149 ff.
[26] See *supra* at 153 ff.
[27] See *supra* at 189.
[28] Case 79/85, [1986] E.C.R. 2375.
[29] See *supra* at 134 ff.

interpretation of *Segers*. It is not excluded but it is not probable, and that is part of the explanation why there is not the pressure for uniformity from the Member States.

Christian Timmermans

We have to wait for the outcome particularly of the *Daily Mail* case,[30] but I quite agree with you that there are some conservative trends in the case-law of the Court over the last two years. But not so much in the internal market field as in the external field, the commercial policy.

[30] Case 81/87, since decided: see [1988] E.C.R. 5483.

Chapter Five

Corporate Law

A. Report: André Tunc

I. Introduction

What follows is a commentary on the corporate law side of *Buxbaum* and *Hopt*'s book,[1] which I found most interesting and instructive. What struck me in reading it, above all else, was the authors' will to achieve an objective and sober appreciation of the phenomenon of European legal harmonization.

Enthusiasm is a virtue, but it has its pitfalls. Enthusiasm is quite natural as regards European legal harmonization, especially on the part of organs of the Community. "Building Europe" is the policy to which the Member States of the EC have subscribed; such a policy is certainly most desirable for economic and political purposes. Legal harmonization, furthermore, should not only facilitate business and finance activities on a European scale – its main purpose – but contribute, by the comparative research it necessitates, to an improvement in national laws.[2] Community organs may well have the feeling that legal harmonization not only destroys barriers and distortions, but also permits the building of a new law composed of the best features of the various national laws.

Buxbaum and *Hopt* agree that legal harmonization may be beneficial to Europe and its Member States.[3] However, they carefully avoid the danger of wishful thinking. They want to make a contribution, but in strict intellectual honesty. If a new "building" is to arise, it should be built on solid foundations, not on illusions.

[1] R.M. BUXBAUM & K.J. HOPT, *Legal Harmonization and the Business Enterprise* (Berlin/New York 1988).
[2] *Id.* at 208-209.
[3] *Id.* at 193-204.

A. Petrification

A particularly striking feature of the book is its denunciation of the danger of "petrification" of Community law as a result of the adoption of directives.[4] At present, directives are, in practice, the only means of harmonization.[5] As observed by the General Editors in their foreword:[6]

> "[O]nce a measure is 'Communitarized,' the tortuous EC decision-making structure might consign it to almost automatic obsolescence given the difficulties in passing new amending legislation."

It is quite natural that a State which has adjusted its legislation to the demands of a directive should not later on depart from them. However, the delays and uncertainties of an amendment to a directive may regrettably freeze the law, unless corrective measures are taken.[7] This appears to be a very serious defect if one considers, for example, the number of amendments which were made to the French *Loi No. 66-537 du 24 juillet 1966 sur les sociétés commerciales* or to the Companies Act 1985 almost immediately after their enactment. Legislation today needs to be capable of swift adjustment to changing circumstances.

The danger of "petrification" of law was nearly realized in the shareholders' preemptive right asserted by the Second Directive[8] in case of allotment of new shares. This right did not exist in English law. Only the Stock Exchange made it a condition of admission to quotation. In consequence of the Second Directive, the Companies Act 1980, by provisions carried over into the Companies Act 1985, provided that: (a) the board of directors should not issue new shares without authorization of a general meeting of the company or the company's articles (Section 80) and (b) existing shareholders should be offered the new shares on a preemptive basis (Sections 89-96). No sooner was the new legislation enacted, however, than circumstances changed. The creation of new financial instruments, the development of private placing and the desirability of international placing called for prompt decisions to increase the financial means of a company and for disregard of the shareholders' preemptive rights. The Stock Exchange, therefore, began to encourage quoted companies to make use of Section 95 to delegate to the board, for a period of five years (Section 80(4) and (5)), the power to increase the capital without regard to shareholders' preemptive rights. The Chancellor of the Exchequer himself, in an interview published in the *Financial Times* of 5 January 1987, supported this practice.

[4] *Id.* at 243.

[5] *Id.* at 230-233, 243-246. See also CAPOTORTI, "The Law-Making Process in the European Communities," in *Law in the Making* 275 (Pizzorusso ed., Berlin 1988).

[6] CAPPELLETTI, SECCOMBE & WEILER (Gen. Eds.), in *supra* note 1, Foreword at VI.

[7] BUXBAUM & HOPT, *supra* note 1, at 243.

[8] O.J. L 26/1 (1977).

However, opposition came from the Investment Protection Committees of the Association of British Insurers and the National Association of Pension Funds. In order to reconcile the various interests involved, a working party was convened by the Stock Exchange, including representatives of UK industrial companies, which are users of the capital market, and representatives of insurance companies and pension funds, which are substantial investors in the market. On 20 October 1987, the working party issued guidelines providing for some flexibility in the raising of capital, but limiting the amount of share capital or deferred share capital that could be issued for cash on a non-preemptive basis, and providing restrictions on the possible discount and the cost of issues. These guidelines do not prohibit companies, in exceptional circumstances, from going beyond the limits outlined, but they "encourage" them in such an event "to have early consultation with the IPCs." The working group remains in existence "with the objective of refining or changing the guidelines in the light of experience."

What lessons can be derived from this experience? First, it must be acknowledged that the directive did not prevent the adjustment of the practice to new needs. The directive was drafted in such a way as to provide the necessary flexibility. But, if its effects have not been negative, they have not been positive either. For quoted companies, the preemptive right was already imposed by the Yellow Book. Its admission or rejection in non-quoted companies was not a matter of European concern: if a non-UK company wanted to invest in a non-quoted company and to be protected by a preemptive right, it could make the insertion of the latter into the articles of association a condition of its investment. Finally, the adaptation of the preemptive right to new circumstances in quoted companies was the result, not of the demands of the directive or the Community authorities, nor exactly of market forces, but rather of a compromise between opposing interests, a compromise reached under the authority of the Stock Exchange and in a reasonable way.

Comparable developments occurred in France under the influence of needs identical with those felt in England. Under present French law, an increase of capital can be decided upon only by the shareholders in a meeting with special quorum and majority. In practice, all important companies prefer to transfer the decision to the board: the board obtains from the general meeting the authorization (for a maximum period of five years) to issue shares up to a certain amount. When the authorization expires, it is renewed by another meeting. The shareholders' preemptive right is inscribed in the law. Increasingly, however, the board submits to the general meeting and obtains from it joint authorization to increase the capital and, if desirable in the company's interest, dispense with the preemptive right.[9] This right is currently set aside in issues of securities with

[9] The authorization is then valid for three years only: Art. 181-1 of the 1966 Statute, added to the Statute by *Loi No. 85-132 du 14 décembre 1985.*

a share warrant (70% of issues of bonds with a share warrant, 61% of issues of shares with a warrant, 52% of issues of pure warrants). The practice has not met with any explicit objections on the part of the institutional investors: IPCs are unknown in France. On the other hand, the *Commission des Opérations de Bourse* (COB), a public authority, has considered that the practice is dangerous and has submitted it to a working party. Again, a compromise is being sought between conflicting interests. The directive has been neither helpful nor significantly harmful, although it has prohibited some of the possible solutions which had been considered previously.

Thus, the law did not succumb to the danger of "petrification" in the case of preemptive rights. But it threatened to do so. More broadly speaking, European harmonization legislation weighs on national legislations and sometimes prevents useful reforms. In his treatise on French company law, *Pierre Bézard*, formerly head of the legal department of the COB, subsequently *Conseiller à la Cour de Cassation* as well as member of the Directorate of the COB and *Procureur de la République au Tribunal de Grande Instance de Paris*, emphasizes the wish of the *Ministère de la Justice* and the *Ministère des Finances* to simplify and reduce the French legislation, but adds, on the basis of personal experience (he was a member of the Badinter Commission on the revision of the legislation):[10]

> *"Il faut cependant noter que cet allègement a des limites ... les directives de Bruxelles établissent des normes qu'il n'est pas possible de transgresser."*

B. Enforcement

Another danger of harmonization by directives which should be kept in mind is the one pointed out by *Buxbaum* and *Hopt*:[11]

> "[T]he traditional neat division between the EC competence for enacting directly or indirectly substantive law and the Member States competence for sanctions and enforcement is a dated model. Thought should be given to the problem of how to overcome this division politically and, as far as possible, already legally. Europe too needs less law in the books and more law in action."

This remark seems to be borne out by the French experience. While insider trading has been a criminal offence since 1970 and the COB has actively sought the detection and prosecution of offenders and sufficiently deterrent punishments, it is widely feared that only small offenders have been caught and that the courts have been showing great leniency towards them. As was to be expected, the remedy has been sought in more legislation.[12] New hope may be justified.

The danger of "petrification" would be eliminated and the danger of ineffectiveness might be lessened if a "harmonization from below" were

[10] P. BÉZARD, *La société anonyme* No. 59 (Paris 1986).
[11] BUXBAUM & HOPT, *supra* note 1, at 250.
[12] *Loi No. 88-70 du 22 janvier 1988.*

feasible, as in the United States,[13] i.e. if the national experiences of the various European countries were receiving enough attention in the other European countries to create a general attraction towards the best solutions.[14] Unfortunately, this is not the case. Language barriers are as effective (if not more so) as "Chinese walls." So is the usual lack of interest in what is done elsewhere; the law is now so bulky and changing so fast that one can be excused for concentrating his energy on keeping abreast of national developments. There is no supranational administrative agency and little coordinating effort between the national ones.[15] "So far, the European Court's role in company law ... has been minimal"[16] and the prospects for a significantly increased role, even within the field covered by the directives, do not authorize optimism for the foreseeable future.[17]

With respect, the decision of the Court of Appeal of Brussels in the case *Société Générale de Belgique (SGB) and SODECOM v. CERUS and De Jode*[18] seems to provide a good example of the ignorance in one country of ideas considered as self-evident in another, even in a field where *Buxbaum* and *Hopt* consider that harmonization is desirable and "might well be left to [the] jurisprudential process."[19]

It will be recalled that, one Sunday evening, 17 January 1988, the chairman of the board of CERUS (Carlo de Benedetti) had dinner with the chairman of the board of SGB (René Lamy) and gave him notice that the next day he intended to announce a takeover bid on the shares of his company. Immediately after the dinner, the chairman of SGB held (probably by telephone) a meeting of the board; on the basis of a former authorization by the general shareholders' meeting, the board decided to issue new shares without preemptive rights for the former shareholders, in order to entrust the new shares to friendly hands. The increase of capital was realized and the memorandum of association of the SGB amended on the following morning.

The decision of the board was challenged by CERUS on the same day. The President of the Brussels Commercial Court heard the case between 9 p.m. and 10.30 p.m. He was sitting as *juge des référés*; as such, he could not pronounce on the substance of the case and could only take interim measures. On the 19th, however, at 7.15 a.m., he delivered an order declaring the board's decision invalid and ordering certain practical steps.[20] After new procedures, another order was delivered on February 9. The

[13] BUXBAUM & HOPT, *supra* note 1, at 111-163.

[14] *Cf. id.* at 286-287.

[15] *Id.* at 266-267.

[16] *Id.* at 268.

[17] *Id.* at 268-269.

[18] Decision of March 1, 1988, 107 *J.T.* 232 (26 March 1988). The whole procedure is recorded in this issue of the *J.T.*

[19] BUXBAUM & HOPT, *supra* note 1, at 272.

[20] *J.T.*, *supra* note 18, at 217.

President referred to a report of the Belgian *Commission Bancaire* (which monitors takeover bids), itself referring to Rule 21 of the City Code, prohibiting the issue of authorized but unissued shares without approval of the shareholders in a general meeting during the course of an offer, "or even before the date of the offer if the board of the offeree company has reason to believe that a *bona fide* offer might be imminent." Consequently, he again considered the decision of the board to be invalid.[21]

An opposite view, however, was taken by the Court of Appeal on 1 March 1988.[22] Sitting on an appeal of a *référé*, the court, as the judge of first instance, has jurisdiction only over interim measures. However, to fulfill his duties, a *juge des référés* is often bound to consider the substance of the case. This was particularly true in the present case. One often has the feeling that the court is forgetting the limits of its jurisdiction and making pronouncements on the substance.

The decision is a long one and cannot be easily summarized. However, it completely disregards Rule 21 of the City Code which the *Commission Bancaire* seems to have "adopted."[23] It starts (points 4, 4*a*) from the "business judgment rule" (it is the board of directors, not the judge, who decides which course of action is desirable) and does not qualify it immediately by the basic principle that the decision should be made in the interests of the shareholders and employees.[24] The idea appears in the subsequent development (point 4*b*), but takes a view of the business judgment rule which leads the court to justify the board's action by the

[21] *Id.* at 220.

[22] *Id.* at 232.

[23] See also, among the Principles of the City Code (COUNCIL FOR THE SECURITIES INDUSTRY, The City Code on Take-Overs and Mergers and the Rules Governing Substantial Acquisitions of Shares, London 1985):
"7. At no time after a bona fide offer has been communicated to the board of the offeree company, or after the board of the offeree company has reason to believe that a bona fide offer might be imminent, may any action be taken by the board of the offeree company in relation to the affairs of the company without the approval of the shareholders in general meeting, which could effectively result in any bona fide offer being frustrated or in the shareholders being denied an opportunity to decide on its merits.
8. Rights of control must be exercised in good faith and the oppression of a minority is wholly unacceptable.
9. Directors of an offeror and the offeree company must always, in advising their shareholders, act only in their capacity as directors and not have regard to their personal or family shareholdings or to their personal relationships with the companies. It is the shareholders' interests taken as a whole, together with those of employees and creditors, which should be considered when the directors are giving advice to shareholders."

[24] In the United States, furthermore, the ALI *Principles of Corporate Governance* subject the business judgment protection to the condition that the director "is not interested in the subject of his judgment," Tentative Draft No. 4, 12 April 1985, Section 4.01(c)(1).

consideration that the shareholders *might* have approved of it, in order to maintain the company as it was, without a dominant shareholder. The court considers that, notwithstanding the EEC Treaty, the board could take the national interest into account. On those points, the court concludes that CERUS has not given sufficient evidence[25] of the improper purpose of the board, and that "unfortunate statements" made by the president were only expressions of personal feeling and did not reflect the purpose of the decision. Even assuming that, in normal conditions, when the board takes a measure in order to maintain the situation as it is, the burden of proof is on the other party to establish the violation of the fiduciary duty,[26] the suddenness of the board's decision in the present case certainly raised a presumption of improper purpose which was confirmed by "unfortunate statements."

The court has also to consider the cancellation of the shareholders' preemptive rights (point 4*c*). Strangely enough, the court does not see in the measure a dilution of the company's capital, nor a breach of the shareholders' equality, nor evidence of the president's desire to stay in power (again notwithstanding unfortunate statements made "in a personal capacity"). Furthermore, the court considers that the shareholders, with the exception of CERUS, might have approved the measure.

The following parts of the decision are of lesser interest for us, even if they reveal substantial breaches of the law which are all excused by the court. What is of interest to us is that, while the whole philosophy of the City Code is to protect the shareholders of an offeree company by giving them the opportunity to make an informed and considered decision, and therefore impinging "on the freedom of action of boards and persons involved in offers," and while this philosophy was accepted by the *Commission Bancaire*, the court upholds an extraordinarily hurried decision, made by the board for the confessed purpose of remaining in power.

It is true that "hard cases make bad law" and that it was particularly hard in this case to forget what was considered as the national interest. The

25 "... *il n'est pas établi avec une certitude suffisante* ... ."

26 There is some uncertainty as regards the burden of proof. The issue does not seem squarely faced in English decisions. In the United States, the burden has often been placed on the directors: Bennett v. Propp, 41 Del. Ch. 14, 187 A.2d 405 (Del. 1962); Cheff v. Mathes, 41 Del. Ch. 494, 199 A.2d 548 (Del. Ct. 1964); *cf.* Sinclair Oil Corporation v. Lenien, 280 A.2d 717 (Del. 1971); and the recent cases discussed in TUNC, "The Judge and the Businessman," 102 L.Q.R. 549, 563-567 (1986). See also R. JENNINGS & R. BUXBAUM, *Corporations – Cases and Materials* 484-497 (5th ed., St. Paul 1979); W.L. CARY & M.A. EISENBERG, *Cases and Materials on Corporations* 668-683 (5th ed., Mineola 1980); D. VAGTS, *Basic Corporation Law – Materials, Cases, Text* 706-713 (2d ed., Mineola 1979). There are opposite cases: see R. JENNINGS & H. MARSH, *Securities Regulation – Cases and Materials* 785 (6th ed., Mineola 1987). But the modern tendency is certainly to take into consideration "the omnipresent specter that a board may be acting primarily in its own interests." Unocal Corp. v. Mesa Petroleum Co. 493 A.3rd 946 (Supr. Del. 1985).

temporary conclusion from this preliminary investigation, however, seems to be that "harmonization from below" remains for the time being a delusion,[27] and that "harmonization from above" – which, basically, can at present be achieved only by way of directives – may be useful, but also dangerous.[28] If this is the case, the benefits of harmonization must be weighed against the dangers of directives. The purpose of this paper might be to survey – pragmatically, but without forgetting the economic models which have been offered nor the lessons that American experience may teach – the various aspects of corporate law and to try to assess the balance in each of them. This paper seems to bear out what the authors have written about the prospects for integration as far as its extent is concerned;[29] it seems to conform to their wishes:[30]

> "In conclusion, it should be stressed that there has been no intention here to denigrate European harmonization in general and company and capital market law harmonization in particular. Rather, the point of this discussion was to show the ambiguities and theoretical shortcomings of European integration, especially in its relationship with company and capital market law harmonization. If these shortcomings are overlooked, there is a danger of overestimating the consequences of this harmonization for European integration, and of neglecting the more difficult pursuit of the goal of direct integration. Legal harmonization can be a palliative for the failure of progress in truly European market integration, particularly if relatively minor side issues are taken up as second best candidates for harmonization and if the dissent over the key issues is camouflaged by harmonization of details and technicalities."

At the outset, it would appear that, for the private investor (whether individual or institutional), harmonization of corporate law is of small interest. Much more important for them are securities regulation and accounting – the latter being the basis for a safe reading of corporate information. Our research, therefore, concerns mainly the entrepreneur considering the creation of a foreign subsidiary or a substantial investment in a foreign company. Obviously, we shall have to consider not only where harmonization could profitably take place, but where it has already been carried out and what results it has generated. The scope of our research, unfortunately, will be limited to French and English law, the only ones about which, in Europe, we have some knowledge.

[27] The situation may change when an increasing number of European lawyers are practicing in a European foreign country. They may, with time, influence the current legal thinking. *Cf.* BUXBAUM & HOPT, *supra* note 1, at 282-283, 285-286; TIMMERMANS, *infra* at 220. But it will certainly be a slow process: "*Ce n'est pas demain la veille!*"

[28] And may also be disappointing: BUXBAUM & HOPT, *supra* note 1, at 212-218.

[29] *Id.* at 263; see also at 271-272.

[30] *Id.* at 203-204.

II. Promotion and Formation of a Company

The fact that classification of companies in the various countries (e.g. *SARL/société anonyme, private company/public company*) is not uniform does not seem to worry entrepreneurs.[31] It is indeed a problem for the Community authorities, which have encountered difficulties in trying to pinpoint which type of corporate entities should be submitted to certain rules. Entrepreneurs, on the other hand, can easily ascertain which type of corporate entity fits their need and adjust to the regulation which results from their choice.

Similarly, the forms of their company charter and procedures of incorporation do not seem of real concern to foreign entrepreneurs.

On the other hand, they need to be clear on the validity and effectiveness of pre-incorporation contracts and on the possible liability of promoters. The First Directive[32] greatly clarified the problem of the personal liability of someone who purports to make a contract for a company at a time when this company has not been formed: it makes him personally liable. However, a comparison of the French *Loi No. 66-537 du 24 juillet 1966*, Article 5, and of the British Companies Act 1985, Section 36(4), reveals two differences: (a) the British text subjects the personal liability to "any agreement to the contrary," while the French text is silent on the matter; and (b) the French text provides that the company, when formed, may make the contract its own, in which case it is deemed to be bound by it, to the exclusion of the signatory, from the time of the contract's conclusion. British law does not seem to accept this possibility, unless it is considered covered by the qualification "subject to any agreement to the contrary," which is most doubtful.[33] On this point, which is of some importance, harmonization thus appears to have been only partial.

No harmonization has been attempted on the possible liability of promoters. On the other hand, the matter does not seem of practical importance in the contemporary world.[34]

Nullity of companies has been included in the First Directive. However, substantial differences may be found between the provisions of French law and those of the directive,[35] and English law, similarly, but for other

[31] For background, see *id.* at 185-187.

[32] O.J. L 65/8 (1968).

[33] See L.C.B. GOWER *et al.*, *Gower's Principles of Modern Company Law* 336-337 (4th ed., London 1979 and *Second Cumulative Supplement* by Pettet, 1988); C. SCHMITTHOFF *et al.*, *Palmer's Company Law* § 20-03 (24th ed., London 1987); R. PENNINGTON, *Pennington's Company Law* 104-105 (5th ed., London 1985); J.H. FARRAR, *Company Law* 44-45 (London 1985).

[34] Disagreements have been expressed on that point by HOPT, *infra* at 222.

[35] See R. ROBLOT, *Traité élémentaire de droit commercial de Georges Ripert* n. 941, 1132 (vol. 1, 12th ed., Paris 1986):
"*La liste des causes de nullité reste sensiblement différente dans la loi française et dans l'art. 11 de la directive.*"

reasons, "is at the present time in breach of the provisions of the First Directive."[36] How disappointing!

III. Issue, Maintenance, Increase and Reduction of Capital

The capital of a company has been a subject of major concern to the Commission. Capital is covered by the Second Directive, of 13 December 1976. The implementation of this directive did not require any significant legislation in France. The situation was quite different in England. The Companies Act 1980 introduced new concepts such as a minimal share capital for public companies, a minimal payment before allotment of a share of a quarter of its par-value and its whole premium, independent valuation of any non-cash consideration, and detailed legislative regulation of matters previously left to the common law or to Stock Exchange regulation.

A basic question is obviously whether the philosophy of the Second Directive was a wise one. In England, the concept of capital was much more flexible than in Continental Europe, and yet it was on the defensive, being attacked by such authorities as Prof. *Gower*.[37] In the United States, it had withered away. The 1984 Revised Model Business Corporation Act does not mention capital and makes only a single provision[38] for those operations which the Companies Act 1985 covers with roughly fifty Sections.

It is of course difficult to say which system is best. The American one implies reliable valuation of the company's assets, clarification on the methods of valuation chosen, and prudent foresight on the part of officers and directors. This is certainly not a defect in the system. On the other hand, a corollary of the wide discretionary powers given to the directors is a certain insecurity on the American scene. Is it possible to import the flexible and realistic American approach without importing at the same time an unhealthily increased litigation? Or is it possible to couple a flexible approach with a minimal amount of rules or regulation? It is difficult to answer those questions. One point is certain: contrary to what may seem desirable,[39] the directive placed the national legislations in a straitjacket and prevented any kind of experimentation.

The financing of companies is assured, not only by issue of shares, but by issue of debentures and other financial instruments. In the last years, a great number of complex financial instruments has been issued. Some have created surprises, sometimes unpleasant ones, for the individual investor.

[36] DRURY, "Nullity of Companies in English Law," 48 *M.L.R.* 644, 656 (1985). *Cf.* BUXBAUM & HOPT, *supra* note 1, at 264-266.

[37] See GOWER, *supra* note 33, at 238; see also FARRAR, *supra* note 33, at 136.

[38] Section 6.40: Distribution to Shareholders. Amended on 1 April 1987 (42 *Bus. Law.* 1207).

[39] BUXBAUM & HOPT, *supra* note 1, at 273.

Assuming the matter is within the province of our research (and not that of capital market), we would conclude that problems should be solved by the issuing houses and not by legislation. The desirable balance between the need for clarity of a financial instrument and the need to reconcile the wishes of credit seekers and credit providers should be the fruit of imagination and experience rather than being frozen by national or European regulation.

Protection should be assured to holders of debentures or special class shares against insolvency of the company or a variation of their rights. Does this protection merit an effort of harmonization? One may doubt it as regards protection in case of insolvency. Furthermore, the matter could not be dealt with on a European level without making perilous intrusions on the laws of charges and bankruptcy.

Skepticism is perhaps less justified as regards the protection of creditors or shareholders against variation of rights in case of merger. Reorganizations and mergers often entail changes of rights which probably deserve protection at the European level. It is fortunate that the Third Directive on mergers of public limited liability companies has taken them into consideration.[40] The Transnational Merger Directive proposed in January 1985,[41] if and when approved, may broaden their protection.

IV. Structure of the Corporation

Although a Fifth Directive was proposed by the Commission on the subject on 9 October 1972, and although the proposed text was amended on 19 August 1983,[42] the Council has not adopted the proposal. It is submitted that a directive on the subject might be dangerous rather than beneficial.[43]

A preliminary, but basic, problem "lies in the labor codetermination question."[44] Great respect is due to those who, in their country or on the European level, strive for a better integration of employees in a firm and for their participation in the management of the company. One may question, on the other hand, the wisdom of imposing codetermination on an international scale. The diversity of traditions among the various European nations, the diversity of unions, the difficulty of finding satisfactory mechanisms of codetermination, the fluctuations of economic and social circumstances seem to call for discretion on the part of an international legislator. In this case, persuasion may be wiser than compulsion.

40 O.J. L 295/36 (1978): see Art. 7.2 and Art. 13, 14 and 15.
41 O.J. C 23/11 (1985).
42 O.J. C 240/2 (1983).
43 As background, see BUXBAUM & HOPT, *supra* note 1, at 177-181, 182-183.
44 *Id.* at 252.

Apart from the codetermination problem, it is hard to see the benefits to be derived from a uniform or even harmonized structure.[45] What harm for the investor or the entrepreneur results from the fact that one country imposes a dual-board structure, another a unitary structure, and a third leaves the choice of the number of boards to those responsible for the company's future? Furthermore, significant progress in corporate governance has been made in the United States in recent years under pressure from the SEC; and England has progressed somewhat, under pressure from the Bank of England and the Stock Exchange.[46] A directive might be a block to further progress. We may hope that emulation, as well as persuasion by public authorities, by institutional investors and by the press, will lead the organs of the company to decide on the best organization for the company (number of directors, proportion of management and non-management directors, functions of non-management directors, number and functions of committees, number and functions of company officers, etc.), and to adjust this organization to new needs as soon as is desirable.

On the other hand, the power of the company's directors to bind the corporation is certainly a matter on which harmonization of the law is desirable.[47] It was rightly covered by the First Directive. The wording of Section 35 of the Companies Act 1985 is far from satisfactory.[48] We may hope, however, that it will be amended in the not too distant future, in conformity with a report submitted by Dr. *D.D. Prentice*.[49]

[45] *Cf.* however *id.* at 284-285:
"Harmonizing and perhaps liberalizing the rules that divide the power of corporate governance between shareholders and management ... would fit this aspect of an agenda."

[46] On PRONED, see JACOBS, "Non-Executive Directors," *J.B.L.* 269 (1987). This organization, established in 1982 and sponsored by, among others, the Bank of England, the CBI, the Institutional Shareholders' Committee and the Stock Exchange, seeks: (a) to promote the wider use of non-executive directors; (b) to maintain a register of those who are non-executive directors or are suitable to be so; and (c) to provide companies who seek advice with the name of suitable candidates to fill non-executive directorships.

[47] For background, see BUXBAUM & HOPT, *supra* note 1, at 183.

[48] See GOWER, *supra* note 33, at 184-190; SCHMITTHOFF, *supra* note 33, at ch. 21; PENNINGTON, *supra* note 33, at 128-141; FARRAR, *supra* note 33, at 300-303; L.H. LEIGH, V.H. JOFFE & D. GOLDBERG, *Northey and Leigh's Introduction to Company Law* 156-158 (4th ed., London 1987); A.J. BOYLE, J. BIRDS & G. PENN, *Boyle and Birds' Company Law* 97-110 (2d ed., Bristol 1987).

[49] SCHMITTHOFF, "Editorial - New Business Legislation," *J.B.L.* 345 f, 346 (1986); BIRDS, "The Demise of Ultra Vires," 7 *Co. Law* 203 (1986); FROMEL, "Reform of the Ultra Vires Rule: A Personal View," 8 *Co. Law* 11 (1987); HANNIGAN, "The Reform of the Ultra Vires Rule," *J.B.L.* 173 (1987).

V. Duties of Directors and Officers

What would be the value of harmonization in this matter? The question certainly deserves serious consideration.[50] The directors' duties of care and loyalty are a cornerstone of English law. They entail a great number of consequences, sometimes unexpected and severe,[51] extended by Part X, *Enforcement of Fair Dealing by Directors*, of the Companies Act 1985 (Sections 311-347).

American law is even more demanding on the subject. As a result, directors, whatever they do or do not do, are threatened by law suits based on a breach of their fiduciary duties. As found by the Delaware Supreme Court a few years ago:[52]

> "It is, of course, a fact of corporate life that today, when faced with difficult or sensitive issues, directors often are subject to suit, irrespective of the decisions they make."

In the hope of clarifying the matter, the ALI *Principles of Corporate Governance – Analysis and Recommendations*[53] devote two long Parts, Parts IV and V, to a detailed statement of the principles and consequences of these duties.

In contrast, the basic idea that decisions ought to be taken in the sole interest of the shareholders and employees after due consideration of the circumstances did not seem to inspire the decision of the Brussels Court of Appeal previously considered.[54]

In French law, the idea is purely implicit, even though it entails a detailed regulation of the contracts in which a director is interested, of the monies a director may receive from the company, or of the possibility of someone being at the same time a director and an employee of the company. Strangely enough, while the conventional idea is that French and continental legislators put their faith in principles while English law (legislative law and judge-made law) aims at precise solutions to concrete problems, it is the reverse which we see here (even though English law at present combines principles and regulation).

It is submitted that this situation is not without danger.[55] If the fundamental affirmation of the directors' fiduciary position may, as already mentioned, create unpleasant surprises for an English businessperson and even for an English solicitor, it is certainly more dangerous for the foreigner

[50] For background, see K.J. HOPT & G. TEUBNER eds., *Corporate Governance and Directors' Liabilities* (Berlin/New York 1985); BUXBAUM & HOPT, *supra* note 1, at 183-184.

[51] E.g., Regal Hastings Ltd. v. Gulliver, [1942] 1 All E.R. 378.

[52] Smith v. Van Gorkom, 488 A.2d 858, 873 (Supr. Del. 1985).

[53] See *supra* note 24.

[54] See *supra* note 18.

[55] *Cf.* BUXBAUM & HOPT, *supra* note 1, at 272-273. The authors, however, as already mentioned, place their faith in judicial harmonization.

who might be in charge of an English subsidiary, or, for some other reason, make decisions subject to English law. Even apart from the progress it would inspire in some countries (France, for instance, takes no account of the doctrine of corporate opportunity), harmonization thus seems desirable.

Harmonization should certainly be extended to the duties of a dominating shareholder, a question of great importance which may not have received sufficient attention outside of the United States, and which may be the key to a fundamental aspect of the group problem.[56]

It would certainly be desirable also to extend harmonization to the liabilities of directors, officers and dominating shareholders, whether during the company's normal life or after proceedings for insolvency.

VI. Shareholders' General Meetings[57]

Why shareholders' meetings are held is not entirely clear. They seem necessary, of course, for choosing the company's directors, even if, in practice, directors are recruited by co-optation. They approve the accounts, but this is a mere formality which could be dispensed with. They are a chance to pass on information, but information could be disseminated even if general meetings were not held. They may be an occasion for exchange of views or even confrontation of views. However, in the normal life of a large company, they are expensive and of little use. They are mainly the supreme body which has to make decisions in exceptional circumstances: competition for the control of the company, for instance, or merger of the company.

Considering this assessment of the role of the general meeting, we submitted, in our original contribution to this Symposium, that matters of voting rights, quorum, majority, procedure, types of meetings and resolutions (and perhaps even proxy regulations, although the matter is not in the province of this research) could be left, without significant harm, to the diversity of national laws. We also emphasized the danger of "freezing" law by harmonization. While the New York Exchange, for instance, has for decades required from listed companies that they grant voting rights to every holder of ordinary shares, the application of the rule has been suspended, in a framework of takeover bids and defenses against takeover bids, and the matter is under consideration by the various national exchanges, the SEC and Congress.

On reflection, however, we completely reverse our position. Considering the importance of the general meeting in cases of struggles for the control of a company, we consider that harmonization is highly desirable on all aspects of the general meeting: voting rights, proxy regulation, quorum,

[56] See TUNC, "The Fiduciary Duties of a Dominant Shareholder," in *Groups of Companies – Reality and the Law* (Schmitthoff & Goode eds., London 1991). *Cf.* BUXBAUM & HOPT, *supra* note 1, at 187-189, 222-224.

[57] As background, see BUXBAUM & HOPT, *supra* note 1, at 181-182.

procedure, majority. Perhaps Community rules could be restricted to cases of struggles for the control of the company, but the demarcation line between such cases and the company's normal life is not easy to draw.

VII. Protection of Shareholders

To the extent to which the "protection" of shareholders is a matter of corporate law rather than securities regulation, it does seem to call for harmonization on some points – even once the duties of directors, officers and dominating shareholders have been harmonized.

What are the main aspects of shareholder "protection?"

First, one should know whether it is desirable to become a shareholder in such and such a company, i.e. to invest in the company. This is a question of information, which is largely a question of accounting, audit and securities regulation – and thus outside the field of our research.

Shareholder protection also involves the power to vote at general meetings, to submit (perhaps if holding a certain percentage of the capital) resolutions, to call (subject to the same qualification) a general meeting. The matter has already been considered and, on second thoughts, we concluded in favor of harmonization. However, one example of the danger of "petrification" inherent in harmonization was given above, and another comes to mind. In the United States, while for decades, under SEC Rule 14a-8, any single shareholder was able to submit a proposal to the general meeting, in 1983 the power was restricted to "a record or beneficial owner of at least 1% or $1,000 in market value of securities entitled to be voted at the meeting," provided, furthermore, that such proponent "has held such securities for at least one year, and ... shall continue to own such securities through the date on which the meeting is held." The Rule was amended in other respects as well. In particular, the list of circumstances under which the issuer may omit a proposal from the proxy form and the proxy statement was greatly expanded. These amendments were made in response to changes in shareholders' behavior at a time of social upheaval, and even to the use of the Rule as an instrument of social pressure by persons or groups who would not otherwise have become shareholders.

The protection of shareholders may involve, thirdly, control by public authorities of investment business and actions of corporate executives. This, however, is certainly not a proper area for harmonization by way of directives.[58] It may be desirable for the SIB and the COB, for instance, to organize consultation among themselves and with other public or stock market authorities. But the SIB and the COB must adjust to their respective national environments. Aside from the public authorities, forces are at work

[58] We consider as totally outside the field of our research the question whether a European regulatory commission (comparable to the SIB, the COB or the SEC) should or could be established.

which may be powerful safeguards for the investor: the press, shareholder protection committees created by institutional investors, habits and traditions of the financial community. Every nation should do its best; if it does not, market forces may exercise some pressures on it. But the task of adjusting the regulation of the British financial services industry, for instance, to changes imposed by economic pressures was itself so formidable[59] that its promoters might well balk at the mere idea of Brussels interfering.

Shareholder protection involves, lastly, protection by the courts.[60] This raises a host of questions: should every single shareholder have the power to bring an action, in theory or in practice? On what grounds? Should this power be reserved to the holders of a percentage of the capital of a certain amount of investment, or should the exercise of this power at least be facilitated for such holders? Should it be reserved to associations of shareholders or to recognized associations of shareholders? Should "class actions" be admitted? Should a single shareholder be able to apply for help from the Secretary of State or *Ministre des Finances*, the SIB, the SROs and PRBs, the COB, the French *Ministère public*, and should these authorities have the power to bring an action against company directors and officers, for the sake of the shareholders of a company or of some of them? What should be the powers of the court? Should the procedure provide for a swift decision? Those are very important questions. In the United Kingdom, the success of Section 459 of the Companies Act 1985 reveals the extent to which shareholders feel victims of unfairness and long for judicial intervention. As rightly underlined by the General Editors in their foreword:[61]

> "[I]n legal study an analysis of the normative content of legal rules and policies – while still central – can give only a partial picture of the function and shortcomings of the law in its societal context. Normative analysis is but one layer of analysis: the effective (or otherwise) reach of the law, its implementation and enforcement, its accessibility to subjects to whom it is addressed as a source of rights and duties, is a second no less important layer."

On balance, therefore, we finally conclude that the harmonization of the shareholder's access to justice would be desirable. A directive, of course, should stop short of requiring changes in judicial organization, in rules of standing and procedure, in powers of public authorities. But an articulation of basic principles of access to courts and perhaps of support of public authorities might be useful.[62]

[59] See GOWER, "Big Bang and City Regulation," 51 *M.L.R.* 1 (1988).

[60] For background, see HOPT & TEUBNER, *supra* note 50; BUXBAUM & HOPT, *supra* note 1, at 213-218.

[61] CAPPELLETTI *et al.*, *supra* note 6, at VII.

[62] *Cf.* BUXBAUM & HOPT, *supra* note 1, at 285, who hope for harmonization by consensus as regards

"the rules that concern availability of access to courts by individual shareholders who wish to challenge dubious exercise of managerial power."

VIII. Fundamental Changes

Mergers, transfers of assets, divisions, takeovers, winding up, are all operations which are clearly dangerous for the shareholders, even if they may also in some occasions be necessary or highly profitable. Currently, they can involve shareholders of different nationalities.

As already observed, a directive on winding up will probably encounter great difficulties, since the matter is closely linked to national insolvency laws. Such a directive is, however, in preparation.[63]

On the other hand, one may understand why directives have been approved on mergers (the Third Directive),[64] corporate split-up (the Sixth Directive[65]), and why one is proposed on transnational mergers (a Tenth Directive). The latter might cover matters which are of special importance in takeover bids, such as share transfer restrictions, non-voting shares or multiple-voting shares, limits as to the voting power of any shareholder, etc. However, the proposed directive seems to face some opposition.

Takeover bids appear as a proper subject for harmonization,[66] but the matter seems outside the field of this research.

IX. Conclusion

The authors of the book which inspired our Symposium sum up their conclusion in the following terms:[67]

> "[P]rospects for the efficient implementation of appropriate harmonization policies in the company law ... field(s) are relatively dim."

We agree with this conclusion. Not only are the prospects dim, but the fields in which harmonization is justified are narrow. Leaving aside groups of companies, accounting, capital market law and securities regulation, which were all outside our domain, the only fields where harmonization would seem desirable appear, at the end of our research, to be the following: (a) protection of shareholders and creditors against variation of rights; (b) the fiduciary duties of directors, officers and dominant shareholders (and their liability towards shareholders and creditors, whether during the company's normal life or after proceedings of insolvency); (c) all aspects of the shareholders' general meetings; and (d) shareholders' access to justice.[68]

[63] *Id.* at 253.
[64] See, however, *id.* at 202.
[65] O.J. L 378/47 (1982).
[66] Proposal for a directive published in 1989: see O.J. C 64/8 (1989).
[67] BUXBAUM & HOPT, *supra* note 1, at 19.
[68] As mentioned earlier, the list is, on reconsideration of the matter, longer in this final contribution than in the original paper submitted to the Symposium, in which only the fiduciary duties of directors, officers and dominant shareholders were singled out for harmonization.

B. Discussion

I. Introductory Remarks

André Tunc

A few points before the discussion: I have already expressed in my paper my small hope for integration from the bottom, at least in the near future.[1] I devoted a number of pages to the *Société Générale de Belgique* case,[2] as an example of cleavage between the various European legal cultures and, notwithstanding the "adoption" of the Takeover Code by the *Commission Bancaire*, the acceptance of a practice which was in my opinion in complete violation of the City Code.

A second point: for a number of years, I have considered that company law as such is of secondary importance compared with securities regulation and accounting. When I say "company law as such" I mainly think of French company law. We have many detailed rules which are in my opinion of small importance. For instance, the board should be composed of at least three persons and 12 at a maximum. However, in some circumstances, the number 12 may replaced by 15, 24, 27 or 30. But then, the volume of the board decreases progressively to 12. Other exceptions are provided for directors representing the employees and for the case when the firm is taken over by its employees. Furthermore, a director should not become an employee; but a prescribed number of employees may become directors subject to certain conditions. When I compare those prescriptions and many others of the same vein to English or American law, I become extremely skeptical towards company law as such. I assume that the shareholder, whether the little guy or the institutional investor, is much more interested in securities regulation (and therefore accounting which gives a meaning to securities regulation) than in this organization of the board and all the detailed provisions that we have in France. The same is true, as far as I can see, for the businessman who wants to invest in a company or take it over.

Third observation: I have already expressed my relative distrust of theories.[3] Theories are quite interesting and I like them, but I have normally the feeling that they reveal only one aspect of the truth and that life is more complex than theories. So I have taken a very pragmatic approach. I have

[1] See *supra* at 202 f.
[2] See *supra* at 203 ff.
[3] See *supra* at 24.

tried to consider every segment of corporate law in order to see whether in my opinion, it was worth trying some harmonization by directives or whether it could be left with a certain diversity. Perhaps I have been too pessimistic. Perhaps I would today be more inclined to accept a directive on a workers' participation on some points. I am also impressed by Jim Gower's suggestion[4] that something could be done at the Community level for the control of segregation by investment businesses of clients' money. Perhaps also judicial intervention in case of mismanagement of the company or unfair prejudice to the shareholders or some of them could be governed by a directive.

Well, I cannot enter into details. I assume that you have read my paper. There are probably many points on which you wish to disagree. I will take note and try to see whether I was wrong or not.

II. The Need to Harmonize

Christian Meier-Schatz

I was impressed by Prof. Tunc's attempt to split up the various topics and fields of corporation law in order to check their suitability for a European harmonization. I would like to start with some comments on the different subjects.

I tentatively agree as far as the capital protection directives are concerned.[5] This may well be a topic in which the EC did not choose the best regime. It then seems to me that we could construct here a model case for examining the petrification problem so clearly emphasized by Prof. *Hopt*.[6] As Prof. Tunc said, one could indeed argue that the English and American systems of capital rules are finally preferable. Under these circumstances, it would be most interesting to ask whether there are not some possibilities to rewrite this Second Directive[7] in one way or another.

Substantively, I have some problems with your corporate governance comments and your reluctance as to the harmonization of this field.[8] You are founding your skepticism on an alleged progress in the corporate governance area in the US. I cannot entirely share this optimistic assessment since I do not see such a significant improvement of the American situation. Admittedly, there have been some institutional changes by introducing independent directors, various types of committees etc. But *de facto* I think it is fair to state that, as far as the effectiveness of these new

[4] See *infra* at 318.

[5] See *supra* at 208 ff.

[6] R.M. BUXBAUM & K.J. HOPT, *Legal Harmonization and the Business Enterprise* 235 f, 242 f, 265 (Berlin/New York 1988).

[7] Directive adopted in 1989: see O.J. L 386/1 (1989).

[8] See *supra* at 209 f.

control techniques is concerned, scholars are rather reluctant to see a significant institutional improvement. It may, however, be interesting to add in this context that the American ALI has submitted a reform project which – as I just learned from Prof. Buxbaum – now appears to be quite successful on the political stage. The propositions made by the ALI are typologically pretty close to those you suggested in your paper.

I have similar problems with respect to the issue of shareholder protection.[9] I agree, of course, with your diagnosis as far as real world and effectiveness of shareholder meetings are concerned. However, the argument itself seems to be overinclusive; if you really intend to eliminate systematically the shareholder element of corporate governance, the overall structure of the private corporation has to be newly thought about. Moreover, we had lately some events, especially in the takeover area, in which some sort of revitalization of the traditional shareholder governance scheme emerged. We may discuss these developments tomorrow.[10] But I would like to emphasize already today that the shareholder and the shareholder protection element may gain new perspectives in the takeover context.

Edmund Kitch

I find it very easy to be sympathetic to Prof. Tunc's general view[11] that corporation law is not a high priority area for harmonization.

Robert Austin

As to problems of corporate governance, harmonization perhaps can achieve no more than drawing boundaries around a whole range of options with respect to corporate organization and internal relationships. But still it may be useful to seek to draw those boundaries or set those limits. In other areas – and this is where I wonder whether I really am too naive – the choice seems to me to be a question of black or white. Either you have a corporate opportunity doctrine or you do not. And is there any point in using the language of harmonization where the choice is simply yes or no?

André Tunc

I must say that no doctrine of corporate opportunity of exists in France, even though we have the larger doctrines of *abus de droit* or *abus de fonction*. One of my students wrote a thesis on corporate opportunity in English and American law and then made researches in French law. He found only one decision of first instance relating to the question. In that

[9] See *supra* at 212 f.
[10] See *infra* at 375 ff.
[11] See *supra* at 215.

case, the court found nothing improper in what was, in effect, appropriation of a corporate opportunity.

L.C.B. Gower

My own view on this general problem is that harmonization of corporate law is almost totally irrelevant to the completion of the single European market. I do not believe that any of the outstanding proposals of the Commission, though many of them seem desirable, are necessary with one exception, and the one exception is some action on groups.

Richard Buxbaum

I think we are all on common ground, and certainly our book, for whatever it was worth also is clear on the point,[12] that on the scale of things traditional company law is not a priority item. From a harmonization perspective company law has a very attenuated and indirect relationship to the equal starting point issues concerning the Common Market. There are a couple of subsidiary issues, however, that might be worth looking at.

One of them relates to the perennial debate, the one held earlier too,[13] of whether or not as facilitative law, as private law, company law should just do whatever the shareholders want to have done, because we have significant problems of agent monitoring. We have an unresolved debate as to whether the law should step in to provide standard contracts with very limited rights of avoidance, in order to safeguard investors not so much from their stupidity as from the institutional limits to their achievement of their own goals. That is an area where federal standards might well be an interesting concept; that is to say, even though it is private law, nonetheless the degree to which these standard contract controls could be adopted at a federal rather than a single State level might be worth considering.

Let me take the example, and it is an example broader than the takeover field, of dual class common stock that we were briefly discussing before.[14] Of course in one sense one can say shareholders know what they are getting when they buy a non-voting common stock. Certainly if there is a new regime, and they are entering a new company, that is a totally voluntary open act. But most common stock has been emplaced under conditions that leave me less than comfortable about the degree of shareholder participation in that exercise. This kind of common stock creates a kind of internal holding company. You have a new incongruence between management and ownership that is quite similar to the old problem of pyramided levered control through very small investment. That is what the classical holding company structure was. Dual class common is to me an internal version of

[12] BUXBAUM & HOPT, *supra* note 6, e.g. at 263 ff.
[13] See *supra* at 100 ff, 115.
[14] See *supra* at 113, 115 f.

the old holding company pyramid. Now that is an area that, while it is standard-contract private law, has public implications and therefore becomes a candidate, from my perspective, for a federalizing rule. That is one example, and since I do not want to reopen every debate about shareholder autonomy and the corporation as a contractual relationship, let me just leave it at that.

Secondly, and in reverse, I think it is conceivable to think of the federalization of certain facilitative standards that for one reason or another individual national legislation adamantly or for other reasons has refused to permit. It is conceivable, for example, that a federal standard authorizing the repurchase of their shares by corporations would make some sense for a larger community and would bypass the problems of the single Member State that somehow does not see fit to adopt that facilitative regime. Why? Because certain of those facilitations do have a close correlation to the Common Market problems of equal starting positions, a sort of equal investment or lending conditions.

So while I am in full sympathy with Prof. Tunc's paper, to the degree that an outsider really has any reason to debate those issues, I do ask myself whether there may not be some areas for federal standards both on the constraint and on the facilitation side that could be tried out.

Christian Timmermans

I have just one remark because on quite a number of other subjects which Prof. Tunc analyzes as possible potential subjects for harmonization,[15] there is a link with the paper of Eddy Wymeersch,[16] for to some extent the group issues are implicitly covered.

My remark on your paper, Prof. Tunc, concerns your rather pessimistic view on harmonization from below. You say it is a delusion for the Community,[17] if I remember well. I would be a bit more optimistic and I would like to refer to two phenomena.

First, the ongoing experience of national experts (this is a very old argument) meeting in Brussels, getting acquainted in these continuous discussions on the Commission's drafts or predrafts with the legislation of other Member States. That must have some impact on the national know-how that is building up and also I think, but it is very difficult to trace (it requires a psychological research) on the decision making, on the legislating at home. I have seen that at least in my country.

Another phenomenon of bottom up harmonization, is that we look increasingly to the standards in other Member States. Business particularly starts immediately to protest where our solutions go a bit further than what

[15] See *supra* at 212, 214. See also *infra* at 244 f.
[16] See *infra* at 227 ff.
[17] See *supra* at 206.

is required in other Member States, and we have see existing solutions being deleted because they went further.

Finally, there is also some integration of law firms happening through the European law expertise that is required in law practice and I think we should not underestimate that. That is not only happening in the antitrust field, in the antidumping cases. As European law, as Lord Denning put it, works as an incoming tide, more and more fields of law are covered, and I think that also requires law practice to take into account the European dimension and that will have also some impact on the integration of practice as such. So there could be a drastic evolution in that respect, I hope. I see it happening in Brussels to some extent with the multinational law firms.

André Tunc

I am pleased to see that Prof. Timmermans is more optimistic than I am on harmonization from below. Everything he said is true, of course. Personally, however, considering the French scene, I remain skeptical. Most practicing lawyers are still very far from the legal cultures of Germany, England, Italy or the Netherlands. Some, of course, are excellent international lawyers, but most of the others are very parochial and completely ignore what is going on outside the Hexagon. Nevertheless, progress has already been made and other progress will develop in time.

Alain Hirsch

In his conclusion,[18] Prof. Tunc says that one of the most important fields in which company law should be harmonized is the fiduciary duties of directors. And probably the bulk of the law on group of companies goes also around fiduciary duties of directors. So these two conclusions are very similar.

André Tunc

Difficulty in harmonizing fiduciary duties. Yes, it will be difficult.

I assume that it would be necessary because in France, strange as it is, we do not have at all the idea of fiduciary duties. We have quite a set of regulations in order to try to avoid abuse of powers by the directors and to impose on them fair dealings with the company. For instance, I mentioned earlier[19] that they should not gain too stable a position by pretending to be employees. We have many rules of this kind. But we do not have at all the general idea, the general principle of fiduciary duties. So I assume that it would be useful to articulate those duties. You could not go into great detail but, still, you would give real guidelines to the various countries.

[18] See *supra* at 215.
[19] See *supra* at 216.

And then the courts would certainly have an important task in applying these guidelines in deffering circumstances. But still, they would not be in a vacuum. It would be a general guidance. I think that it might be useful.

Klaus Hopt

Let me start off with liability of promoters. Prof. Tunc, you mentioned this point only casually,[20] and probably you are right on the basis of the French experience and also right for other countries on the basis that it really is a corporate law rule. But I would submit that while by tradition it is placed in the corporation law, as to its nature and function it is not really a corporate law rule, but relates rather to capital markets. If one accepts that, the topic becomes much more important, and especially for our common discussion. Liability of promoters then becomes a good candidate for harmonization.

I could back this easily by the German experience. The traditional prospectus liability which concerns the stock exchange and is embodied in stock exchange law was of very limited importance. This is partly due to legal drafting, partly because it was confined to the formal stock exchange market. Yet in the '70s when the off-exchange capital markets boomed, it turned out that there was need for a promoter's and prospectus liability in the general capital markets, and since the legislator failed to act, the courts stepped in instead and developed a whole theory and practice of civil prospectus liability.

I do not want to go more deeply into this as this belongs to general civil law. But as far as our discussion is concerned, it raises two interesting points.

One is that we have to be careful not to make an artificial distinction between large companies, i.e., most of the stock corporations, and small companies, i.e., limited liability companies and general public limited partnerships (GmbH & Co.). This is the point Prof. Tunc mentioned in his contribution very convincingly.[21] In a sense the prospectus liability developed by courts in Germany is also part of the GmbH & Co. phenomenon. It shows the functional interchangeability between the different company law forms and that one has to be very careful not just to regulate one and to leave out the other. So much for the liability of promoters.

The second thing which struck me and came out is the interrelation between different fields of law which we are trained to distinguish. As to company and capital market law, we have made that very clear today.[22] As to capital market law and banking law, it was on the floor yesterday.[23] Today again[24] it was company law and bankruptcy law. Seen in a functional

[20] See *supra* at 207 f.
[21] See *supra* at 207 f.
[22] See *supra* at 216 ff.
[23] See *supra* at 96 ff.
[24] See *supra* at 184 f.

way all these fields cannot be separated nicely for the purposes of a rational harmonization. This makes the task of meaningful harmonization very difficult. The question is whether one can just say (but maybe I misunderstood you, Prof. Tunc[25]): "This is a part of insolvency law and therefore does not belong here." Maybe at the end this is the practical outcome, because it turns out to be too difficult to tackle all interrelated fields, and harmonization must start somehow. But the question how to act in meaningful combination remains both practically and theoretically difficult. Maybe there is even a certain chance to start that just on the EC level because there all these traditional cleavages and dogmatic intersections are not so entrenched. If one could have a new start there, this could induce a new way of thinking within the Member States.

André Tunc

Liability of promoters. I was surprised to learn that it is a problem in Germany. I think it is no longer a problem in France, nor in England, or in the United States.

You mentioned the danger of making an abrupt distinction between company law and bankruptcy. I fully agree with you. What I said, but perhaps I was wrong, was that I was afraid that directives on bankruptcy law would be very difficult to achieve because the problems so much involve the national systems of charges, priorities, etc. Perhaps I am too pessimistic, but that was the reason why I was skeptical about the possibility of a European bankruptcy component of company law.

Hartmut Schmidt

I am not a company lawyer at all and I am trying to come to grips with all that has been said and of course I cannot. To me it is truly puzzling for various reasons.

I am a proponent of the trading of GmbH shares and KG shares and the company lawyers in Germany always said: "This is complete nonsense because for the AG public company we have uniform governance rules and therefore their shares can be traded whereas for the GmbH and for the KG we do not have them, so their shares cannot be traded and must not be traded." And now I am here and we are talking about the EC and obviously some of you have no reservations about shares being traded from various Member States which are subject to very different governance rules. This is, from my point of view at least, a contradiction. The German company lawyers require uniform corporate governance if you want to trade the shares in a public market. Now you would trade in the European stock exchanges shares from a dozen Member States and they all would be subject

[25] See *supra* at 215.

to different governance regulations. This is one point I am a bit surprised about.

If I look at regulation of securities trading, regulation of accounting and regulation of corporate governance, then I could say, if everything is perfect in these three areas then a share of a company would sell at let us say 100 ECUS. And if there is less than perfection, if there is cheating, if there are all kinds of problems, then I would tackle that as follows: for bad accounting the investor will only pay a price of 100 minus amount A because of bad trading rules, 100 minus amount B, and because of bad corporate law the price that the company can get in the market drops by amount C. I think that this amount C may well exceed the amounts A and B, and again I would say it is very important to come to good solutions in the area of company law because there is a great chance to improve the allocation of funds to industry.

Another way to look at the company law discussion from my point of view is to take up what Prof. Tunc said:[26] "We find out what makes sense and then we try to put this into law." What makes sense in regulating securities trading can be relatively easily agreed upon. So this area is a candidate for harmonization. It is much more difficult to say what makes sense in accounting, and I think it is even more difficult to say what makes sense in corporate governance. Therefore, I basically agree with those saying: "Leave it at the State level." Maybe we need some European approach to this, but I am doubtful whether this approach should be an approach by mandatory law.

Geoffrey Fitchew

I would just remark that I agree with a very great deal that is in Prof. Tunc's paper about the priorities for company law harmonization, leaving aside the special issue of workers' participation where, as I said in my own paper,[27] the Commission's proposals are aimed at a social goal as much as at facilitating economic integration.

III. Various Other Topics

Gérard Hertig

I think that sometimes it could be easier to protect investors through corporate law rather than through capital market law: at least in my Swiss experience, it is much easier for a lawyer to disrupt the life of a corporation through corporate law (e.g. by using provisions regarding general meetings). Then it is not only a question of how much you have to pay because

[26] See *supra* at 217.
[27] See *supra* at 12.

you did this or that: the shareholder just blocks everything and that gives him a very high nuisance value. That means better enforcement, and better enforcement means better deterrence, and better deterrence means better law. And so it might be possible to put the emphasis on investor protection, through corporate law rather than through capital market law.

Eddy Wymeersch

I will limit myself to two remarks, one on petrification, and one on the *Société Générale de Belgique* affair.

With respect to petrification, I am much impressed by the argument,[28] but do not fear it so much as Prof. Tunc. There are some good examples in point, even in the field of regulation of the securities markets. The 1980 Directive[29] appeared in 1986 in need of adaptation, and this has been achieved in a very short period.[30] One could say that if Member States were as efficient in adapting their laws, the risks of petrification would be much less.

With respect to the *Société Générale de Belgique* affair,[31] it is important to recall, first, that the Brussels Court of Appeals decision of March 1st, 1988, which Prof. Tunc has referred to,[32] only had to deal with interim measures, and not with the substantive issues. Therefore with respect to the matter of proof, the plaintiffs should have made it clear that there were evident violations of the law and that by not intervening the tribunal would have put substantive interests at risk. In essence the Court decided that it had not been proved that the conditions for interim measures were satisfied, as the allegations submitted were not so evident violations of the Belgian law, also taking into account the business judgment rule. It may also have been somewhat understated that according to the Belgian law, irregularities with respect to the issue of shares cannot lead to having the decision declared null and void except for the future.

The entire matter has however raised many other more delicate and more devastating questions.

What is the legal value of a decision of the *Commission Bancaire*? In the absence of a clear basis in the law itself, it has no direct legal effect on the position of the parties. Suppose that, as was the case, the *Commission Bancaire* had given its "opinion" that, inspired by Rule 21 of the City Code, the target company may not issue additional shares to protect itself against the offeror. This order would be regarded as a polite request, not a really enforceable order as the Commission's jurisdiction extends only to the

[28] See *supra* at 200 ff.

[29] O.J. L 100/1 (1980).

[30] See O.J. L 185/81 (1987).

[31] For statement and all other decisions relating to the *Société Générale* affair, see *J.T.* 217-240 (1988).

[32] See *supra* at 204 ff.

offeror. Moreover the violation of the Commission's ruling would not affect the validity of the issue of the shares. All this is still very controversial. One could easily imagine another line reasoning, arguing that the Commission's decisions are binding as a general rule of conduct, applicable to regular dealings in the Belgian securities markets.

Also, the subscription of shares of the parent by a subsidiary is a practice which I would disapprove of, but which is not expressly forbidden by the statute: who is right?

These are clearly matters not to be dealt with by way of an interim measure, and this the Court of Appeals rightly decided. One can assume that the decision of the board to issue the additional shares was mainly taken to protect its own position. However, at the September 1987 general meeting of shareholders, the shareholders, voting unanimously, had accepted that the authorized capital – which was then introduced – could be utilized to protect the existing "shareholders structure," and thus to defend the company's autonomy.

Should one pay attention or not to the will of the shareholders? Can this expression of the will of the shareholders be set aside by a government agency? I would rather be inclined to give precedence to the shareholders. But has their will to be clearly expressed, or should it be restated during the offer, as is prescribed in the Takeover Code?

The *Commission Bancaire* has, although indirectly, been criticized for not favoring the bid of De Benedetti and for taking the side of the incumbent management of the *Société Générale*. It is not clear that this allegation can be backed by real facts, but as often happens, it is the unfavorable psychological impression that wins the day rather than the real facts. In this specific case one could mention that, probably in order to gain time, the *Commission Bancaire* issued a statement according to which no shares could be issued once the bid had been formally launched. This interpretation seemed quite improbable as the prohibition ran, not from the moment the target, although informally, had been informed about the forthcoming bid, but from the much later day the *Commission Bancaire* had formally informed the target about the bid. The improbable nature of its interpretation raised doubts as to the real purpose of the Commission's stand, and has done quite a lot of harm.

André Tunc

Thank you, Prof. Wymeersch, for your comments on the *Société Générale de Belgique* affair. It is quite true that the case was only on interim measures, but I think the courts went far beyond that in their motives.

I am grateful to all the colleagues who have taken the floor and expressed less pessimistic views. I am grateful also to the colleagues who supported the pessimistic view, so I am grateful to everyone.

Chapter Six

Groups of Companies

A. Report: Eddy Wymeersch

I. Introduction

The *Buxbaum* and *Hopt* book[1] gives a fascinating overview of what can be seen as two different but clearly interrelated subjects. Among the many striking aspects of the book is – to come to the subject presently assigned – the almost total absence of consideration given to groups of companies in the *Buxbaum* part, which is not a shortcoming of the author, of course, but the expression of the American state of mind towards groups of companies. (Many of the rules mentioned are indirectly applicable to groups.) Equally striking is *Hopt*'s recurrent mention of the importance of the group, not only in the national legal systems, but also in the harmonization process.[2] *Hopt* suggests that group law offers one of the best, but also most challenging, prospects for harmonization in the entire field of business law. His hopes are high, perhaps too high, but one should bear in mind that the harmonization process attempts the best in order to achieve the possible. In the accounting field also, when the harmonization drive started in the mid-sixties, many hoped to reach a full harmonization. Why this has failed to materialize is one focus of our discussions.

II. The Importance of Group of Companies Law

(1) The study of group law is sometimes said to be a passing fashion. Is it worthwhile to invest our efforts in a fashion exercise? Will the question not wither away with the next economic downturn?

The discovery period (not the pioneer period, at least in Western Europe) in the early seventies, was followed by a decline in academic interest, but not in real developments. Now, in the late eighties, one sees both academic and legislative interest renewed, and more important, extensive practice, in both legal constructions and case-law.

[1] R.M. BUXBAUM & K.J. HOPT, *Legal Harmonization and the Business Enterprise* (Berlin/New York 1988).

[2] See, e.g., *id.* at 187.

It is a fair guess that the law of groups will stay with us for a very long time. Comparative analysis in several EC countries indicates that the phenomenon has touched all sectors of the legal system: apart from traditional fields like company law, accounting, and even bankruptcy, more and more issues pop up in the criminal law field, or in taxation. Tax constructions are often based on the absence of group law. Individual and collective labor law (the *Vredeling Initiative*[3]), contract law, competition, banking supervision, intellectual property: no field will be spared the influence of the group phenomenon.

(2) The law only reflects the real trends of life. In several jurisdictions the "legal personality" is one of the best sold products in our legal boutique: lawyers incorporate themselves, real estate of any importance is seldom bought under a personal name, and each song of the modern rock heroes is incorporated in a different legal person, off shore preferably. I wonder whether I am myself still a natural person!

This tremendous growth of the use of the corporate form has been under way for quite some time. The American figures, cited by *Buxbaum* and *Hopt*,[4] illustrate this trend. I happen to have the Belgian figures, that, moreover, also illustrate the recent flight from the more heavily regulated company forms.[5] There undoubtedly exists a form of competition between the different corporate forms made available to the incorporators.[6] The race for laxity is not only an American phenomenon.

On the other hand, one should be very careful before attempting the slippery path of modifying the central concept of incorporation which has proved to be useful for more than a century.

[3] See O.J. C 297/3 (1980) and O.J. C 217/3 (1983).

[4] BUXBAUM & HOPT, *supra* note 1, at 26-27.

[5] The evolution of the number of companies, divided according to the different types, can be traced as follows:

	6 Feb. 1980	28 Jan. 1985	15 Nov. 1987
SA	27422	32785	42347
SPRL	58985	81594	92775
One man company			191
S. Coop.	3928	5246	147736
S. Nom Collectif	744	928	1165
S. Commandite	221	352	725
S. Command. Actions	2	4	6
Total	91302	121109	151969

SA and SPRL stood for 89% of incorporated businesses. Of these, 107 were stock exchange listed companies.

[6] Since 1985 there has been a significant difference in the regulatory weight imposed on SA and SPRL as compared to the cooperative company.

(3) More recent but not less significant is the formation, or at least the awareness, of different kinds of groups.

The group structure is not the monopoly of the larger businesses any more, but is used by everyone, small and large. Tax reasons are often the basis for group formation in smaller businesses, but many other considerations come into play. Also, more and more groups are becoming transnational, pan-European. The *de facto societas europaea* exists, as a conglomerate of subsidiaries located in several Member States and quite clearly functioning to the satisfaction of the businessmen involved. Less known, but no less important, are the groups of non-profit organizations, extremely active in health care, education, and other so-called "soft sectors." And here and there, groups of public enterprises exist and function, although often in a disparate way.

(4) From the policy point of view, whether national or supranational, it seems more or at least as important to deal with the group, as with the single legal entity.

The importance and widespread coverage of the group phenomenon is not paralleled in legislation. Except for Germany[7] and Brazil – to which the recent codification in Senegal should be added – most States have no statutory group law. Also, at the EC level, harmonization efforts have been very difficult, if not hopeless. The draft Ninth Directive on groups, submitted in 1985,[8] was widely criticized, and it would seem that the Commission might not pursue its efforts, at least not in the direction originally chosen.

III. The Need for EC Rules

(1) Is there a need for group law rules at the EC level? Several answers could be formulated.

Some will point to the complementary character of group law rules vis-à-vis the already achieved degree of harmonization: without group law, company law harmonization will show a very imbalanced picture, and leave uncovered one of the essential developments in recent company law. Within this overall approach, the EC Commission drafted the Ninth Directive as part of the series of measures in which it has sliced the subject, somewhat losing sight of a directly related phenomenon, i.e. that group law touches many of the specific rules previously harmonized.

The acquisition of its own shares by a company is a clear example: one cannot sensibly deal with this subject if at the same time shares purchased

[7] For a general survey, see WIEDEMANN, "The German Experience with the Law of Affiliated Enterprises," in *Legal and Economic Analyses on Multinational Enterprises*, vol. 2, *Groups of Companies in European Law* 21 ff (K.J. Hopt ed., Berlin/New York 1982).

[8] Doc. No. III/1639/84, reprinted in 14 *ZGR* 444 (1985).

(or subscribed) by a subsidiary are not considered.[9] The question can also be extended to cross shareholdings between companies, which some regulations have subjected to a 10% ceiling. But this rule is purposeless if it cannot be extended to indirect cross shareholdings, especially through foreign subsidiaries. Therefore, from the technical point of view, there are good reasons to complement many of the rules of "harmonized" company law with rules of group law. However, this is not what the Commission has proposed.

The technical answer can be elaborated further through the existing competition between regulatory systems and the fear of a certain race for laxity which has already shown up at the moment of adoption of the Seventh Directive on group accounts.[10] States without equally stringent rules of group law may be too attractive to business combinations.

Behind this reasoning one finds the more fundamental question of allocation of means of production. Decisions to establish subsidiaries should not (or the least) be influenced by differences in legislation, such as the potential risk of liability towards third parties, or additional, sometimes unforeseeable, obligations to local co-financiers. If any rules of group law have to exist, these are applicable preferably in the entire Community. Decisions on business location should be as free as possible from the potential liabilities, while by influencing the production costs they may distort the flows of goods and services. In this sense, harmonization of the rules on groups of companies belongs to the subjects that have a clear impact on the functioning of the common market.

(2) If one agrees that groups of companies should be made the subject of a specific regulation at the EC level, the question then arises as to how to proceed. The harmonization effort cannot draw on the large legislative experience of the Member States, as in practice only Germany has tackled the question in a systematic way.[11] German group law is first and foremost the law of contractual groups, a phenomenon to which extensive tax advantages are attached. In the field of the *de facto* groups, the correction mechanism for group influence exists but is admittedly not very effective. The major issues of group law, as seen in the other States, appear to have been left beyond the reach of the statutory correction mechanism.

In the absence of any leading model, the Community was at a loss for an approach to group law: it is not astonishing, therefore, that it relied heavily

[9] For an application, see the case of the *Société Générale de Belgique*, where a 100% subsidiary subscribed to the parent's shares in order to dilute the bidder's shareholding. Although one could have argued that the subscription was contrary to the prohibition against a company subscribing its own shares (Second Directive), the absence of an explicit prohibition could warrant the parent's opinion to proceed with the issue. The whole procedure is recorded in 107 *J.T.* (26 March 1988).

[10] O.J. L 193/1 (1983).

[11] For the German approach, see WIEDEMANN, *supra* note 7.

on the German concept of contractual groups, with a balancing mechanism for abusive action in the *de facto* groups.

This approach has been strongly criticized and has received, with the exception of Germany, rather lukewarm support from the Member States.[12] The main complaint is that the contractual group phenomenon is alien to the legal tradition in most of the EC States, while the general concept of balancing the interests and indemnifying imbalances appears too general and too vague. In other States, the prevailing business opinion sees no need nor purpose for changing the existing situation.

(3) It is striking – and was very appropriately underlined by the authors[13] – that the Commission has never launched any fundamental investigation into the sociological phenomenon of group formation and existence. So one does not have even rough figures about, for example, the number of companies that are managed group-wise, the importance of the phenomenon, its structure, the way intragroup dealings are looked at in 100% subsidiaries or in minority-dominated subsidiaries, what countervailing measures have been taken to avoid liability or criticism, and so on. Also, in the Commission's view, the specific questions are perceived very much through the lawyers' spectacles, without regard to management questions, to public policy implications, effect on allocation of funds, or other considerations. Looking at myself, I know that lawyers very often see only the pathology of the law, the dysfunction of the mechanisms, and therefore overstress the risk of abuse.[14]

Among these questions some attention has been paid to the competitive aspects, and the Community finally brought out a modified proposal for supervision of the concentration of enterprises.[15] But beyond that, the effects of group formation, whether positive or negative, are largely unknown. Are there, for example, real synergy benefits from conglomerates? Many doubt it, and recent events would rather indicate the opposite. Is growth through subsidiaries to be preferred to direct growth within the same entity?

IV. Existing National Regulations

(1) Taking all this into account, the Commission is currently attempting to obtain a better view of the evolution of group law, and this has taken place since its early activities in this field, starting with the still impressive report

[12] So BUXBAUM & HOPT, *supra* note 1, at 188 and 217 f.

[13] *Id.* at 169.

[14] The parent's liability is an appropriate example: except upon the bankruptcy of the parent, how often does it happen that a parent does not stand behind its subsidiary? And in the cases that are reported in law court reports, does one not have to do with clearly irresponsible parents?

[15] O.J. C 130/4 (1988). Directive adopted in 1989: see O.J. L 395/1 (1989).

of *Pierre Van Ommeslaghe* in 1964.[16] A working party has been brought together with the specific purpose of taking an inventory of the many fields in which group law has been developed, and of the solutions given to the conflicts as these have come up. As these reports are being made available, it appears that, like Molière's Monsieur Jourdain, we have been speaking prose without knowing it.

(2) Why is it so difficult to obtain a consensus on a subject which in all Member States is considered fit for regulation not only by law professors but also by businessmen, at least those belonging to the larger enterprises?

Many factors may explain this hesitation, several of which have been adequately highlighted in the *Buxbaum* and *Hopt* book.

So it seems clear, at least to me, that the subject was not ripe for regulation in most of the States during the seventies and early eighties. Germany is the historical exception, as it already introduced group law in the 1937 revision of the Companies Act, but the fundamental ideas such as the *Organschaft* had been developed much earlier, in tax case-law, starting from the beginning of the century. In other States, no tax nor other incentives were given to the formation of groups.

The approaches proposed in some of the Member States were too far-going for some, too fractional for others. In the meantime, substantial progress has been made in several jurisdictions, clarifying some of the fundamental issues that come into play. Also people are less prejudiced against groups than before. So, e.g., would one have found a rather negative attitude towards the group phenomenon in the sixties and seventies, probably as a by-product of the fear of the multinational enterprise. This negative attitude led, among the public and in legal writing, to the opinion that the group should be dealt with as one single entity, an idea clearly contrary to the business efficiency sought. On the other hand, the prevailing legal opinion in those days refused or at least hesitated to take into account the interest of the group, as opposed to the interest of the single company. All subsidiary decisions had to be weighed against the subsidiary's own interest, thus severely hampering group management. This trend with its unrealistic undertone has been reversed, and today it is widely recognized that while a group company may benefit from group influence, this benefit may be offset by the sacrifices group management may impose on the subsidiary. Therefore the idea of having the several group members functioning without joint liability has again become acceptable.[17]

Harmonization therefore remained impossible because the critical mass had not been reached in the seventies. In the eighties, the importance of cross-frontier establishments has greatly increased with the intensification of business relationships. Regulators have become more conscious of the

[16] See VAN OMMESLAGHE, "Les groupes de sociétés," *Rev. Prat. Soc.*, No. 5280, 153 (1965).

[17] This idea also was reflected in the first proposal for a Ninth Directive but was later abandoned.

competition between regulatory systems. In the nineties, it will become apparent that the present absence of group law – which is of course itself a system – will cause distortions in the business strategies of European enterprises, while one single State may be hesitant to put itself at a disadvantage by introducing rules that will be seen as stricter than those applicable under the present legal vacuum.

V. The Interests of Creditors and Minority Shareholders

(1) The work of lawyers and of accountants is far from over, as they will have to trace the lines of permissible group domination. It is clear that group influence may not go so far as to sacrifice all other interests to the group: the creditors and the minority shareholders are the main interests to consider. Here one lands again in the drifting sands of case-law. Should the balance struck be that of fairness, even of utmost fairness, or will it suffice that creditors and minority shareholders retain a reasonable hope of obtaining fair treatment, provided the subsidiary is managed in a diligent way? French-Belgian group law, for example, seems to be evolving towards the latter option, as illustrated in the *Rosenblum* decision of the French *Cour de Cassation*,[18] where it was held that:

> *"Pour échapper aux prévisions des articles 425 et 437 de la loi du 24 juillet 1966, le concours financier apporté par les dirigeants de fait ou de droit d'une société, à une autre entreprise d'un même groupe dans laquelle ils sont intéressés directement ou indirectement, doit être dicté par l'intérêt économique, social ou financier commun, apprécié au regard d'une politique élaborée pour l'ensemble de ce groupe, il ne doit ni être démuni de contreparties ou rompre l'équilibre entre les engagements respectifs des diverses sociétés concernées, ni excéder les possibilités financières de celles qui en supportent la charge."*

This standard is, it seems to me, not very satisfactory and affords too little protection to creditors and minority shareholders. But this conclusion may be a political, or even sentimental feeling for which there is little support in economic theory. That this loose standard has come about seems the unavoidable consequence of dealing with these matters on a case-by-case basis, where only specific decisions are subject to scrutiny while the policy implications and the long-term approach very often remain outside the judge's balance. More subtle (but not less significant) shifts of financial substance between group companies, as a consequence, e.g., of inter-company pricing, will but rarely become the subject of judicial scrutiny.

(2) In order to offer this better protection, I would suggest that future group law be developed more along the lines of procedural techniques.[19]

Among these procedures, the following deserve specific attention:

[18] Cass. crim., Judgment of 4 February 1985, J.C.P. 1986, II, No. 20585.
[19] BUXBAUM & HOPT, *supra* note 1, at 124 ff.

(a) Minority derivative suits, giving minority shareholders the right to sue the directors, in the name of the company, whether for liability or for any other remedy.
(b) The "minority expert" (*expert de minorité*), who can be appointed by the tribunal to investigate alleged abuses.
(c) For the most blatant abuses, a remedy as provided in the French law, i.e. on *abus de biens sociaux*, may constitute a certain deterrent, although the yardstick used seems too rough for private law purposes.
(d) Minority shareholders should be given the privilege to withdraw from the company, at a fair price, once it appears that group management will not take due account of their interests.

On the other hand, some form of deregulation might be envisaged with respect to matters that are related to the group's existence. If consolidated accounts are published, could one not dispense with the publication of the accounts of the single subsidiary? Could restrictions imposed by the present requirements on conflict of interests not be simplified for intragroup transactions?

(3) Pursuing this idea of conceiving new and more refined procedures, one could try to devise more preventive instruments rather than working out rules of substantive law.

So it is striking that the balancing of interests within a group context is not only a matter of reviewing one single decision or even a series of decisions. It rather seems the result of an overall and continuous action, whereby short and long-term interests should be matched, and due account taken of the (variable) importance of the interest of minority shareholders.

This more refined balancing action has been attempted in Belgium by the *Commission Bancaire*. However, the Commission has not been able fully to achieve this balancing of interests, essentially as a consequence of the business judgment rule. The Commission therefore will ascertain that the balancing by the board, or by the shareholders, takes place with all parties fully informed, possibly in the light of a third independent appraiser. But at the end of the day the Commission will not step in to appraise the ultimate fairness of the transaction.

Another approach may consist of having certain independent directors[20] within the subsidiary – but also within the parent – systematically and continuously review the intragroup matters and establish whether a sufficient balance has been kept. This approach has the advantage of internalizing the matter, and the associated remedies, by putting the review procedure right at the level where the business judgment is exercised, posing the questions in business, and not merely legal terms.

As in many other fields, no single panacea exists and the preventive function to be assumed by the independent director should be backed by

[20] See *id.* at 126.

the traditional instruments, such as restrictions on cross shareholdings, appraisal remedies for dissenters, specific disclosures, and so on.

(4) A more theoretical question may be mentioned briefly.

Is there a need for a definition of the group? In EC matters it is often admitted that a definition along the lines of the one used in the Seventh Directive will be considered the standard guideline for future regulations.[21]

From present comparative law, it appears that most definitions are instrumental to the objectives pursued by the law of which they are a part. Therefore, the definition question should be dealt with only with great caution, and be left sufficiently flexible. A definition "*à géométrie variable.*"

As long as group law rules only concerned disclosure and related obligations, the definition could be framed rather widely. This is the approach of the group definition found in the Seventh Directive on consolidation of annual accounts. The situation is comparable as far as banking supervision is concerned. The definition matter becomes much more crucial if it leads to direct obligations or liabilities, e.g. if it creates liabilities that are imposed on the parent as a consequence of its group dominance or would allow profit distribution on a consolidated basis. For these purposes the subsidiary can be taken into account only if the parent has real legal mastership over the subsidiary. Here I regret the diluted approach followed by the European directive; I prefer the American, which limits the group to the majority owned, i.e. the legally dominated subsidiaries.

Directly related is the question whether a group definition should be based on a proprietary criterion – majority of the shares – or on an influence or dominance criterion. Under German law, the group is defined as the enterprises that are submitted to "uniform management" (*einheitliche Leitung*). Under German influence a comparable definition is used in other regulations, e.g. a Belgian tax statute.

The choice between the two approaches is very much a matter of policy. From the investor's point of view, the proprietary approach looks more attractive because closer to his interest. From a management's point of view, it is important what means are under management's command, disregarding to whom these belong.

For these reasons, single definitions will limit the effectiveness of future group law. But intermediate techniques may be thought of, distinguishing within the group successive layers of group influence.

[21] E.g., the proposals for a Directive on takeovers (O.J. C 64/8 (1989) and O.J. C 240/7 (1990)) refer expressly to the Seventh Directive.

VI. The Harmonization Process

(1) A few words must be added about the harmonization process. I would be less critical than *Buxbaum* and *Hopt* about its effectiveness. It is true that uniformity cannot be achieved and that the options left to the States do not avoid wide differences of regulation. But at least we will have avoided the "race for laxity," and made the location of the enterprise more independent of the law to which it is subject (provided other segments of the law, especially taxation, are harmonized). The competition for business between regulatory systems and between States appears to me an essential ingredient of the process of formation of a common economic space. This may also explain why the directives have been so detailed, and why they have diverged from the EEC Treaty instruction to state only ends and leave the means to the States. In the meantime, protection along comparable, if not identical standards will be offered to all individuals throughout the Community: in the field of securities disclosure, Italy has first introduced the prospectus after the Directive of 1980 was adopted.[22] And we may see the same with respect to insider trading.[23]

Therefore an essential role of the harmonization directive is to foster the creation of an integrated market by reducing differences in regulatory pressure. It is not only to avoid the exclusion of foreigners, but also to prevent a single State from reaping all the benefits.

(2) Petrification is a great danger and was very correctly stressed in the book.[24] The danger must not be overrated: some directives have moved very rapidly through the Community mechanism, especially with the new procedures under the Single Act.[25]

A case in point is the 1987 Directive[26] amending the 1980 Prospectus Directive. The original directive was modified on its essential point, i.e. the automatic recognition of prospectuses approved in other States. This application of the "home country rule" could not be achieved in the late seventies, as the necessary momentum had not been reached, and as confidence in disclosure and surveillance mechanisms had not reached a sufficiently high level.[27] The amendment took only a couple of years to be enacted.

(3) An aspect that worries me more is the purely technocratic and therefore not sufficiently democratic way that Community measures are elaborated. The Single Act has certainly improved on this point, but harmonization remains very much a technocratic business. When a decision

[22] O.J. L 100/1 (1980). Directive amended in 1987 (O.J. L 185/81 (1987)) and in 1990 (O.J. L 112/24 (1990)).

[23] Directive adopted in 1989: see O.J. L 334/30 (1989).

[24] BUXBAUM & HOPT, *supra* note 1, at 235 f, 242 f, 265.

[25] *Bull. EC*, Supp. 2/1986.

[26] See *supra* note 22.

[27] This was achieved in the meantime, possibly also as a consequence of the harmonization directive.

is taken on a national level inspired by one political philosophy, it can be undone by the next government; when, on the EC level, a decision has been initiated, no change of the Commission, nor in any Member State, may have any influence. Once an agreement has been reached, it seems almost futile, at least from the point of view of anyone Member State, to attempt to have it brought up again for discussion. Here looms the danger of petrification.

VII. Conclusion

The conclusion of my reading of the *Buxbaum* and *Hopt* book is clearly that it will launch a welcome debate on the fundamental issues of the economic integration process in the field of business enterprises. By so doing it will contribute considerably to the progress of legal harmonization and, one may hope, to the harmonious functioning of our legal systems.

B. Discussion

I. Introductory Remarks

Eddy Wymeersch

The subject assigned to me relates to "groups of companies" and comes under a general heading of "substantive law." Therefore, I will enter somewhat into substantive law issues, shifting the attention from the harmonization point.

One of the striking features of the *Buxbaum* and *Hopt* book is the large and recurring attention given to questions of group law in the European part of the study,[1] and the almost total silence on issues of group law in the American analysis. This difference is due to many factors, especially to the obviously rather recent position in American legal writing of the distorting effects emanating from the group phenomenon. It would seem worthwhile to investigate further the underlying reasons for this difference of perception.

The Western Europe questions of group law have been so pervasive that hardly any section of the law has not been confronted by issues of groups of companies. Apart from the obvious fields such as company law, taxation, bankruptcy, or accounting, it appears that group questions are often encountered in labor law, in banking, in competition law, in intellectual property law, but also in contract law, or agency, not to mention the law of the European Coal and Steel Community, with respect to the division of production quota among companies that belong to one single group.

Within one same legal system this diversity of application results in a multiplicity of rules of group law. It seems that one is going to be confronted more and more, as Prof. Hopt mentioned,[2] with questions of coherence of the legal system, and that not only between the States – or even between the different Community measures – but also within one single legal system.

The definition of the group is a clear example. The group is defined differently according to the field of law in which it is used. Talking about a group for the application of tax measures will often require strong if not full control, somewhere between 75% and 100%. For the purpose of consolidation of annual accounts, more loose criteria will be used, allowing

[1] R.M. BUXBAUM & K.J. HOPT, *Legal Harmonization and the Business Enterprise* e.g. at 187 ff, 222 ff (Berlin/New York 1988).

[2] See *supra* at 222 f.

consolidation even if the shareholding is limited to a minority shareholding, or, as the Seventh Directive[3] allows Member States to opt for, if the companies act on a coordinated basis.

Does one have to worry about this lack of coherence? Within a single legal system, and until we have further insights on how questions of group law could better be dealt with, it seems preferable to proceed on a case-by-case basis, rather than by way of reasoning from a broad conceptual framework. This conceptual approach is the one followed by the German legislature, and by the proposal for a Ninth Directive,[4] but it seems that the time is not ripe for it. Also the States have not been very willing to follow that general approach.

One could look at the same issue from the angle of harmonization: should one leave harmonization to developments in the national legal systems, or should one attempt a uniform approach, imposed from above?

Harmonization of rules of group law may be based on several of the traditional arguments proposed in support of harmonization in general: free establishment, cross-frontier inter-penetration of businesses, equal treatment of businesses in all States, and so on. None of the States, except Germany, has developed any regulatory system of group law. Reportedly Portugal has recently introduced rules on groups of companies, but these would not seem to have a direct impact on the development of rules and practices in the other States.

Therefore, today we have a zero level harmonization in terms of legislation, not however in terms of practices. From the recent survey the EC Commission has ordered, it appears that in most of the States rules of substantive group law abound. Most of these are rather lax and the risk exists that a race to the bottom may be undertaken by way of judicial case-law.

Rather than leaving these developments to take place, one should attempt to canalize them and safeguard a level playing field in all European States, ensuring that a more or less comparable legal burden be imposed throughout the Community, in order to avoid that decisions to establish businesses would not be neutral vis-à-vis this legal matter. The continuous freedom of the States will lead to substantial differences in terms of risks, costs, and liabilities and will ultimately influence if not even distort business decisions.

Once admitted that some form of harmonization should be attempted by the Community, the next issue will be what kind of group law one should try to devise: can the German model be followed, as was attempted in the Ninth Directive?[5]

[3] O.J. L 193/1 (1983).
[4] Doc. No. III/1639/84, reprinted in 14 *ZGR* 444 (1985).
[5] See BUXBAUM & HOPT, *supra* note 1, at 223-224.

The rules on contractual groups have in most of the States been more or less rejected, as being alien to their legal tradition and to their business practices. We will come back to the issue on a later occasion.[6]

As for the *de facto* groups the issue may be different: the draft Ninth Directive proposed that the parent should indemnify its subsidiary once it appeared that it had acted too much in favor of its own interests. By and large this has also been the basis of the German system for *faktische Konzerne*. It seems that it has not worked too well, especially for procedural reasons. The European system would be more effectively framed. But the substantive question remains: how to evaluate the injury caused to the subsidiary? Should it be assessed on a case-by-case basis, or should one also take into account the advantages the subsidiary may derive from its presence in the group? Can one compare long-term advantages with short-term burdens, and vice versa? Except in very blatant cases, this assessment seems extremely hazardous to make, and one may expect that it will not lead, as is apparent from today's published case-law, to any indemnification getting if the parent clearly robbed the subsidiary without unless anything in return, not even the hope for better days.

These arguments urge us to explore other avenues of reasoning. Two of these may be proposed here. On the one hand, some basic rules allowing or disallowing transactions within the group may be clearly spelled out by the legislature. This is, e.g., the case with the limitation on cross shareholdings, or on subsidiaries subscribing the shares of their parents, or parents acting as directors of subsidiaries, and so on. But apart from these, as far as the overall balancing of interests is concerned, it would seem preferable, as a first stage at least, not to set any specific rules, but to leave it to procedural safeguards, to techniques that may contribute to the detection, avoidance or monitoring of the present kind of issues that are basically questions of conflicts of interests. The appointment of independent directors specially in charge of these issues may constitute a valid alternative. Specific reporting and adequate remedies for the protection of the minority or of creditors could supplement this mainly preventive instrument. Other similar techniques of dealing with conflicts of interests may usefully be explored.

Rather than dealing with the substantive issues, procedural devices may be preferable at least in the first stage.

[6] See *infra* at 244 ff.

II. The Need to Harmonize

A. Definition and Regulation of Groups

Edmund Kitch

I first had a problem understanding as an American what the problem is. We do not talk about the problem of groups. All major American corporations have a group structure in the sense that they will be organized as a parent with numerous subsidiaries.

We did historically have a concern about holding company structures in the utility area which led to the passage of the Public Utility Holding Company Act in the 1930s and the reorganization of the holding company structure of the electric and natural gas utilities by the Securities and Exchange Commission. This programme was completed in the 1950s. It arose out of a concern about too much financial leverage through a holding company structure with large minority or even majority public shareholders in the subsidiaries, but effective control by the parent. That concern did not extend outside the utility area.

Now trying to translate the problem of groups to our terminology, as I understand it – and I want to know whether I am getting this right – there are really two issues: one has to do with the position of minority shareholders, the other is the problem of the rights of creditors.

Robert Austin

Apart from the central issues about the duties of directors and dominant shareholders in the group context, and the minority shareholders' and creditors' rights, it seems to me that a clear concept of group relationships and group structure becomes important in a large number of other corporate areas which in Australia, Great Britain and the United States tend to be treated separately from one another.

One can mention some problems about corporate repurchase of shares, insolvency, antitrust, takeovers and amalgamations, which all depend crucially on a concept of group structure. There are probably many more. In fact, the occasions upon which it becomes necessary to look at groups and their structure and internal relationships in order to solve legal problems may well be infinite.

It is interesting that Australian, British and American lawyers do not seem to focus on the group problem as such. It is clear that underlying the problems that arise in all of these areas there are some basic conceptual issues. One is how we define legal personality itself. Related to that, to what extent do we apply strict contractual privity rules treating each entity separately for the purpose of contracting? And fundamentally, what is our concept of control for various purposes?

It seems to me that the question of defining control is now the most pressing issue in company law, at any rate in Australia, although we have to accept the point that control must be defined differently for different purposes. When I read back on the lecture notes that I prepared as a new lecturer in company law in 1973, I am struck with how totally irrelevant the things I spoke about then are to the problems that exist in Australian corporate life today. We in Australia and in other countries who have seen the problems differently have much to learn from European studies of the group problem, although we would all want to emphasize that it is not a single problem but a whole range of issues of law which are tied together by similar conceptual threads.

Eddy Wymeersch

May I just call your attention to an important factual difference between American and European groups? The former are most of the time fully, or majority owned. In Europe many subsidiaries are minority owned, although this shareholding is sufficient to dominate. If the parent owns a small percentage such as 15 to 20%, the practical limits on remedies such as buying-off the minority, or going private are clearly visible.

Klaus Hopt

Could one say that the investors' or creditors' interests are a sort of consumers' interests, i.e. unorganized and mostly unorganizable interests which have to be defended by the State and its law? I would tend to say yes.

If one speculates about the background of the new German group law as developed by the courts, one of the reasons for it was the narrowness of our Stock Corporation Act: this Act with the traditional German group law imbedded in it does not cover for example the group formation process, and of course not other companies than the stock corporation, e.g. the limited liability company or the public limited partnership. Even though the common opinion in Germany is that there are lacunae and that they need to be filled, the legislator has no intention whatsoever really to tackle the problem. He does not feel any pressure from business for doing that, and this is quite natural. Why should groups be interested in being regulated?

So what happens is that investors and creditors go to the courts and get protected by them. Actually we have quite a number of important cases which mark the beginning of a new judge-made law on groups, particularly concerning the limited liability companies group (*GmbH-Konzernrecht*), with all the risks, of course, that such a case-law is not systematic and may really go far apart. But the need to develop such a law is felt, and the courts do not need a pressure group, but just a plaintiff to go ahead.

As for the concept of dominant shareholder, I have some doubt whether the British approach, i.e. setting a clear limit of say 50% shareholdings, is really the solution. In Germany we had such a solution in another context, in antitrust law. But it was just too easy to circumvent it. I would therefore plead for a substantive definition of one kind or another. This is difficult, of course, but a mere shareholding concept does not really work.

As for the German experience with group law, I agree with Prof. Wymeersch's statement[7] that the German Statute does not cover all important points. But there are still three lessons to be learned from the German experience.

The first is a positive one: it makes sense to acknowledge legally the group interest since this is the only way to live up to reality. A law cannot afford, at least in the long run – and this is addressed to the American way of dealing with groups –, to live with a contradiction between law and reality. This would undermine the credibility of the legal order as a whole.

The second lesson is a negative one. It is, that the *de facto* group is probably the most important form of conglomerate, and if German group law has failed, it is because it has failed to get hold of the *de facto* group. The contractual group for those enterprises which choose this form has functioned quite well, no complaints. The problem is that the hypothesis of the German legislator to drive the *de facto* group people into the contractual group system has proven to be unfounded. But this is so because we did not really come to grips with the *de facto* group, and I wonder whether loosening or even forgetting the regulation of the *de facto* group is not definitely the wrong direction. If the legislator does not do anything meaningful about the *de facto* groups, he may as well forget the whole regulation of groups.

We had still another negative experience in Germany. The legislator of the law of groups of 1965 was concerned only with existing groups. Yet in the meantime it has become more and more obvious that regulation must already start at the stage of formation of groups. This of course is hardly new for other European countries. Just take the takeover example. Yet in Germany there is nothing similar, hostile takeovers are virtually unheard of in practice, and because of that we have also failed legally to come to grips with the formation of groups.

Geoffrey Fitchew

On the question of groups, reference has been made[8] to the earlier draft of the Ninth Directive.[9]

That draft was aimed at dealing with two types of problems. First of all, it was put forward – particularly the provisions dealing with the contractual group – allegedly in order to make it easier for groups to be managed as a single economic unit. The *quid pro quo* for that was various obligations in relation to minority shareholders and creditors. The other part of the directive dealt with the *de facto* group which did not opt for contractual

[7] See *supra* at 303.
[8] See *supra* at 267.
[9] See *supra* note 4.

status. But nevertheless the directive would have involved imposing various obligations on the *de facto* group as well.

I agree that there is little or no evidence of any demand from the business sector for contractual arrangements. It does not seem to be a general problem. So we are left with the questions which have been discussed around the table of the protection of minority shareholders and of creditors. I can see the case for arguing that a difficult situation would be created in the Community if the jurisprudence in different Member States relating to the *de facto* group situation diverges and that that could affect the location of businesses over time if the situations become very divergent; and it is for that reason that we have initiated the surveys that are being carried out at the moment as to what is actually happening in Member States' jurisprudence. Within DG XV we have reached no conclusions at this stage. The survey is divided into two parts and has not yet been completed.

The question I would like to raise to the members of this group is really the following, in relation to the problems of minority shareholders and creditors: why is it the case, it is very striking, that only two Member States in the Community have legislated at all on this subject? There is a general agreement around this table that there are problems, or could be problems, relating to the treatment of minority shareholders and creditors. Why is it that there appears to be no demand at the national level to deal with these problems? Is it because the minority shareholders by definition almost are too weak as an interest group or is it because in reality the problems are not all that serious? And what evidence is there of abuses and difficulties arising in the group situation which justify legislation?

Alain Hirsch

Most of us think that harmonization of group of companies law is necessary, and it is relatively rare to see an institution asked to take up some new competence and power being reluctant to do so!

André Tunc

I think it is fair to say that we have in France a full law of groups covering all the aspects of the group phenomenon. When I say law, I do not mean statute. We do not have a statute called *Loi sur les groupes de sociétés*. We do not have in the *Loi des sociétés* a chapter called "*groupes*," but, practically, I think it is fair to say that all aspects of the group phenomenon are presently covered by the law. Of course taxation, accounting, but also duties of directors, *abus de droit*, *abus de fonction*, bankruptcy, and so forth. Part of it is judge-made law and, in my opinion, somewhat vague and unsatisfactory. But, we have statutory rules on cross holdings, circular holding and self-control.

I do not see any aspect of the group phenomenon and of the group problems which is not presently covered either by statute or by judicial decision. Again, jurisprudence should be refined. But, practically, everything is covered in French law. To a certain extent that is a partial answer to Mr. Fitchew's question.

Finally, I fully agree also with Prof. Wymeersch's idea[10] that the group phenomenon should be dealt with by *géometrie variable*, that is to say that various definitions or criteria should be given for various purposes. Nevertheless, again, I think that the idea of a dominance may have a general value. It may not be able to lead us, except perhaps in some cases, to precise rules comparable to the ones which I have criticized in French law.[11] It should lead, however, to guiding principles, some of them relatively precise.

Eddy Wymeersch

Mr. Fitchew's comments on the state of regulation in the Member States describing it as the absence of regulation, puzzle me.

What Prof. Tunc declared is very interesting: we are developing group law in many respects and this as a consequence of the growing attention paid to group relationships in the case-law. Therefore we are practicing group law, and to compare with Molière's Monsieur Jourdain, we are doing so without really knowing. The absence of a formal regulatory system should not hide the real fact that in most Member States there already exist elaborate rules for dealing with the group phenomenon, wheter with respect to creditor protection, or to the determination of minority shareholders' rights.

Today's rules may not be very satisfactory and some further refinement is undoubtedly necessary. The idea that this refinement should be left to the case-law will be favored by many but creates quite a lot of uncertainty, especially for actual group management.

The issue of contractual groups could be taken up again. As mentioned above,[12] in many States the rules of the Ninth Directive with respect to contractual groups are considered to be an element alien to traditional group law techniques.

Until six months ago I also shared this opinion. Today, however, I would be more reserved. It has appeared that within some groups the practice was been developed of spelling out the rules of conduct which the group management will adhere to with respect to management of the subsidiaries in a set of informal internal rules. In this kind of code of conduct the group management delimits the boundaries within which the group interest may lawfully be exercised. These rules may be approved at the shareholder meetings and will constitute the official policy of the group, especially towards its subsidiaries. In Belgium, rules of this kind have been elaborated within a major financial group under the auspices of the *Commission*

[10] See *supra* at 235.
[11] See *supra* at 216 f.
[12] See *supra* at 239.

Bancaire. It means that within the group the strains on the relationship become predictable, that the boundaries of permissible injury to the subsidiaries' interest can be assessed in advance, and that the countervailing advantages flowing to the subsidiary may be expressly put into the balance. The legal value of these rules is largely unknown, but one may presume that the case-law would consider that group action remained within the boundaries of the permissible if it remained within the limits of the *Commission Bancaire* approved code of conduct.

A comparable set of ideas may be developed here with respect to the idea of so-called autonomy of the bank's management, according to which the bank should be managed independently from the directives given by its parent shareholders. Here too, the autonomy principle has often been implemented by way of contracts entered into by the parent and the subsidiary, under the close supervision of the *Commission Bancaire*. Although not comparable to the German rules on contractual groups, one will easily see the possible links that could be developed from this common contractual underpinning.

Also the subject could be broadened to whether and to what extent the parent should be given a right to give injunctions to the subsidiary, a privilege that parent companies do not enjoy in many of today's European company law systems. Therefore the issue should be sorted out whether from the analogy of these two types of contractual infrastructure, any common ground could be found for the purpose of harmonization of the rules on groups at the European level.

Christian Timmermans

Let me just add, to answer the questions of Mr. Fitchew which I found the most essential, that in the Netherlands too, as Prof. Tunc has said for France, there definitely exists a legislation on groups of companies, not only implicitly but also explicitly.

We have some rules for instance in the case of insolvency in which the liability of the directors is increased, by reversal of the burden of proof. In that clause there is a specific section referring to a group relationship, applying this reversal also for a parent company and all those who have in fact dominated the management of that particular company. And there are other examples to be given, not of implicit but of explicit rules regarding groups of companies. Apart from that, we just had that example of the jurisprudence of our Supreme Court in applying the general torts rules; in that jurisprudence you find explicit solutions to protect in particular the creditors of a subsidiary company.

And I think that what I am saying might apply for most of the Member States. So the situation is not really such that only Germany and Portugal have rules on groups of companies.

L.C.B. Gower

First of all, to join the others who have said that it is not true that their country has not got any group laws.

England certainly has, both statutory to some extent and through the Takeover Code with the valuable rules about mandatory bidding, but we will come to that matter tomorrow.[13] And there has been a recent development under the recent Insolvency Act 1986. This introduces the concept of wrongful trading as opposed to fraudulent trading and says in effect that anybody who has been a director or participated in the business at a time when he knew or ought to known that it was most unlikely that the company would escape going into insolvent liquidation, could be ordered by the court to contribute to the debts for the benefit of the creditors when it went into insolvent liquidation. And when it says "directors" it includes "shadow directors" which are defined as any person under whose directions or instructions the directors are accustomed to act. In some Sections of the Companies Act it is expressly provided that you shall not be deemed to be a shadow director merely because you are a parent company, but significantly there is no such exception in the case of wrongful trading, and this is I think the biggest breakthrough that we have yet had under English law. It appears that if a subsidiary goes into liquidation it is going to be very difficult in future for the parent company, because every parent company known to me does get up-to-date financial information from its subsidiaries and unless it can show that the directors of the subsidiary company did not at all act on its parent's directions or instructions it is likely to be made liable in the future. And this is a considerable breakthrough.

We have also got case-law on the extent to which the directors of subsidiaries are entitled to think of the group interest. The trouble with that is that it is purely judge-made law, not very satisfactory or realistic and in practice totally disregarded by most people who only become conscious of it if and when they are taken to court, which happens very rarely in the UK because of the cost of litigation.

And finally why, Mr. Fitchew asked, is there no pressure from the business world for modifications in this respect? The answer so far as England is concerned is that on the whole the business world never presses for changes in the law on the assumption that the devil they know is better than the devil they do not know, and therefore opposes automatically any change. Years and years ago, before the Ninth Directive was ever thought of, there was in fact pressure. I suspect that the reason why it has now died down is because the business world is horrified at the thought that if anything was done it would be the present draft Ninth Directive.

It is dealt with unsatisfactorily and the weakness in the UK is that insofar as some of the parts are dealt with by case-law, the case-law is just not

[13] See *infra* at 375 ff.

observed. The English case-law fairly clearly lays down that the directors of a company must think of the interests of the shareholders of their company; this does not stop them from considering whether to behave in a way which is beneficial to the group might also be beneficial to their subsidiary, but they must primarily consider whether promoting the interests of the group as a whole is going to be of benefit to their company. Directors just do not behave like that. And as I say, they only get caught on the occasions when a case is brought, and some cases have been brought, and I have no doubt that the people who were caught complained bitterly. But, there would not have been enough of them to make sufficient noise to come to the ears of Brussels. But I do think genuinely that the main reason why everybody in the UK has kept quiet about this is because they are fearful that they may be landed with the present draft Ninth Directive, and they would rather have the present situation than that.

B. Methods and Main Issues

L.C.B. Gower

As has been pointed out,[14] in point of fact all major industrial and financial activity is now dominated by groups and most of them are multinational groups. Many of them, unfortunately from the point of view of the EC, are dominated by Japanese and US corporations which is very difficult for the EC to do anything effectively about.

But something, it seems to me, on the group area is essential. I do not see how sensibly – and this is a point made in the *Buxbaum* and *Hopt* book[15] – you can divorce takeovers from groups, because the whole point of a takeover is to produce a group. And therefore, to my way of thinking, the one thing that the EC ought to be concentrating on in the corporate field is doing something about groups.

Now unfortunately the Ninth Directive[16] seems to be a dead duck and even the Germans apparently do not support it any longer as sensible. Nevertheless, it does seem to me that it has two basic principles. One, as I see it, that in certain circumstances the group as a whole of the parent company must accept responsibility for the obligations of its subsidiaries. Secondly, that when a group is created some restraint must be put on the way that the parent can operate all the companies for the benefit of the group, disregarding the interests of minority shareholders in the subsidiaries. And at least I would have thought that something could be done along those lines.

At the moment you have an absurd position in the UK. When the Ninth Directive was originally promulgated, the attitude of the British, I am

[14] See *supra* at 238 ff.

[15] BUXBAUM & HOPT, *supra* note 1, at 188 f and 222.

[16] See *supra* note 4.

ashamed to say, was first of all, and this is very typical, to say: "This is totally unnecessary." Why is it unnecessary? "Well, because groups do not present any problems." Now, that was of course nonsensical, for even the accountants had been saying for some years that something had got to be done about this, and at one time made some pretty extreme proposals about accepting liability for the debts of the subsidiaries. So driven from that they turned around and said: "Well, there may be a problem but this is not a EC problem. We do not need any harmonization here." That is nonsense because groups are precisely the people who are most likely to operate throughout the EC. So our attitude towards anything on this has simply been: "We do not want this, kill it." And it is a very typical British attitude, I am afraid. But this is absurd and as I have said something has got to be done about this, instead of bothering about piddling little things like harmonizing rules about the one-member private limited company, which is the latest proposal.[17] Groups are important and they dominate industry, especially the financial services industry. How are we going to clear up the problems of a single market without some harmonized regulation about groups?

The position in the UK is that there is no liability on the parent company unless you get a guarantee. Parent companies on the whole do not give guarantees. So what you try and get instead is a letter of comfort. Letters of comfort most people have thought are not legally enforceable guarantees. A recent decision has held that they are not legally enforceable guarantees but that they may well be something which, if they are breached, may give rise to a civil claim for the loss suffered. This case is going to a Court of Appeal, I assume, and may be overruled.

Richard Buxbaum

Putting aside the fact that Anglo-American tradition only sees the disaggregated functional aspect of groups but does not see the coherent thing itself, let me break it down first of all into public law issues and private law issues.

It seems obvious to me that while groups are an important phenomenon, it is the public law side of groups that is the primary candidate for federal level constraint rather than the private law side. Now this has already happened. Accounting is a public law matter, and accounting is already to some degree in the group structure at the European level. Taxation of course is a public law matter, and that is there. I do not think we need to worry, Prof. Wymeersch,[18] whether we have unitary standards. Obviously these are functional issues, and the question of what defines a group is driven by different public policies to different definitions. So the fact that we do not have a unitary definition of groups does not strike me as a manko in the area of public law.

[17] Directive adopted in 1989: see O.J. L 345/40 (1989).
[18] See *supra* at 239.

It gets more interesting when you get down from that to the two primary private law aspects of group law (by the way, I put aside codetermination as a separate model), namely, creditor protection and minority shareholder protection.

Gérard Hertig

Just a question about what you just said: why are you making a division between private and public law? What is the scope of that? What difference does it make? Or was it just a matter of speaking?

Richard Buxbaum

No, I am hypothesizing that there is more correlation between a public law issue and the Community intervention than in a private law issue and such intervention. That is a hypothesis. It is perfectly open to challenge. But there are certainly public law issues and that is what I mentioned in the creditors' remedies side, which may not necessarily, for that reason alone, be issues of high priority for the Community.

L.C.B. Gower

Are you saying that creditor protection is on the public law side whereas investor protection is on the private law side? If that is the distinction, then I do not understand it.

Richard Buxbaum

Of course one of the great dilemmas of the modern corporate structure, the growing incongruence between ownership and control, is that so much of what we used to think of as comfortable company law has slipped over into public law through the investor protection side. You have to look at the investor as a consumer in some degree, and while you may have different standards of the degree of consumer protection, it is a public law of consumer protection. Unfortunately it is just different enough from other types, and is still so embedded historically in a private company law structure, that we have been stuck, for some decades I think, trying to work up definitial boundary lines in this area. Obviously much investor protection law is not only public law but is already at the federal level, just as it is in the United States. I was only trying to say that in the case of creditors' remedies we have some similar definition issues.

L.C.B. Gower

Is not there another problem here? In dealing sensibly with some of the aspects on the accounting side, whereby you consolidate published accounts of all the companies concerned, and ignoring at the same time the implications of that, I mean the consequence of this must be to lead creditors and investors to think that the group as a whole is going to support them, whereas this is not true.

Richard Buxbaum

Well, I know lots of banks that do not believe that, but that is different.

Christian Timmermans

Just a small remark on the private/public law distinction as a distinctive criterion to decide for harmonization: product liability would be a nice exception to that.

Edmund Kitch

I want to sound a dissenting note in my capacity as a non-voting observer.

First of all, let me report that as I have listened to the conversation I still have not come to understand the problem which leads to the recommendation endorsed by Prof. Gower[19] that something must be done by the Community about groups. I still do not hear why that must be done.

Let me go further and sing the praises of the holding company, and part of my concern would be that perhaps it is because the holding company is such an important device that people are concerned about it. I think the holding company, the parent-subsidiary relationship, has been one of the great transactional lubricants of the twentieth century. I do not know the European history.

The holding company was not available to our lawyers until 1892 when New Jersey amended its Corporation Code to adopt what was then seen as a fairly radical provision – that a corporation could include among its activities owning shares in another corporation. Prior to 1892, our lawyers had to struggle in an integrated constitutional Union to solve the legal problem of engaging in multistate business activity through a limited liability corporation. The lawyers for Rockefeller – who was one of the pioneers for this form of doing business because of his creation of multiple oil companies operating related businesses in different States – really did not have a very good solution to that problem. There were a number of quite bizarre solutions including multiple State incorporation. We had some examples of corporations which would get themselves incorporated in more than one State with identical charters in order to make it clear that they had authority to operate across State lines.

All this was solved in the United States in 1892 with the amendment of the New Jersey Statute and the creation of a system where a parent could

[19] See *supra* at 248 f.

operate across State lines simply by quite mechanically incorporating subsidiaries in every State. I do not know whether the modern multinational has other origins. I suspect it does, that there are other analogues, but clearly the modern multinational is an extension of that American practice to the world. The structure has the marvelous advantage that it becomes possible for an economic enterprise which desires to operate worldwide to enter the national market and make that portion of its business which is related to the national market subject to the idiosyncratic or unique or special or whatever regulatory requirements of that national market without placing at risk its entire economic position. I have no doubt that there are not many important enterprises which would have entered the markets of many countries, had the condition of their entry been that they had to place all assets worldwide at risk as a condition of entering a single market.

The lawyers have been able to do wonderful and amazing things with the holding company structure, but it is clear that a central theme of what is accomplished is various forms of regulatory evasion or minimization of national power. That is, you expose to the local taxing and regulatory authorities through the subsidiary which is operating within the country only those assets which you choose to place within the subsidiary. Then, you always have the option of withdrawing, should events become unfavorable, from that market at fairly low cost to your total enterprise. That is the useful and economically important aspect of the holding company structure.

I think it is significant that in our history the greatest concern about holding companies has been in highly regulatory environments where the holding company can be used as a device to limit or repel regulatory reach. That is the Public Utility Holding Company Act. And we have a Bank Holding Company Act for the same reason because otherwise the banks could evade restricting features about of our banking regulation through a holding company structure. So there are special legal regimes concerned about holding companies that have been tried for making regulatory regimes effective.

There has also been a general political uneasiness about the holding company, an idea that something is wrong with the holding company. I think the notion is that General Motors should not be able to do business in France and yet escape being subjected to French jurisdiction because the real wealth of General Motors is not capturable by France. General Motors always has the option of turning over the shares of the subsidiary and smiling a regretful smile and saying *au revoir*. The idea is that that is disrespectful of, or defeating of, or an undesirable subversion of, the scope of appropriate national power.

But the other side, of course, is, and I think it is very important, that all these legal systems do regulate these group relationships. The truth of the matter is that the way they regulate them is to enable firms to use subsidiaries. The legal regimes of all the countries, in fact, enable economic enterprises to use parent subsidiaries structures in the form that they choose to use them with very little interference from the law.

What is not clear to me is why that enabling policy of the national legal regime is not the correct one, that is, that what we have seen is a race to the top, to use another metaphor that we have been using, rather than a race to the bottom. If it is a race to the bottom, obviously then some intervention by the EC or someone else to stop it might be desirable; but I think the argument that it is a race to the top, that it has been a transaction facilitating institutional device is quite strong.

It is the benign neglect of the issue of groups that is, in fact, a wonderful thing, and we should be worried if it is going to be brought to the top of the agenda because only mischief can be done. That is the dissenting note that I would like to state.

Christian Timmermans

Others have already tackled the question: what is law on groups of companies? It is indeed rather obscure what we mean by that.

Let me first say that the aspect mentioned by Eddy Wymeersch[20] which is really a candidate for harmonization, is the problem that stringent rules of company law risk being eluded through group relationships, for instance through subsidiaries buying the shares of their holding company. I do not think that is a problem. We all agree that that risk should be excluded by adequate legislation. Once we have the Second Directive on capital protection,[21] which only covers the single public company, it is evident that, to make that function, also group relationships should be included, and I must say that it has not been an omission by the Commission that we do not find such rules in the predraft of the Ninth Directive. It was in an earlier draft, but it has been deleted. But these proposals are still in the drawers of the Commission services, I know. I would plead for that harmonization.

There is another subject when we talk about groups of companies which has not yet been mentioned. It has been presented as one of the arguments to justify harmonization on the European level. It has been said that international groups within the Community have difficulties in functioning, in implementing group policies, because subsidiaries, at least in some Member States, are too independent, or have to be, to respect the local company law rules. Personally I do not think that is a problem at all. I do not see any signals from practice that there is a problem here. Of course you would expect business to protest if there existed any. As far as the and the jurisprudence are concerned, I can only speak for my country and I must say that our company law has perfectly tackled and solved this problem. Insofar as it has not been clearly solved in the books and in the statutes, it has been solved by case-law. In my country case-law certainly takes the

[20] See *supra* at 240 and 229 f.
[21] O.J. L 26/1 (1977).

group situation into account and allows groups to function, even obliges directors of subsidiary companies to take the group interest into account, and if they do not, they may be dismissed. That is a legally justified ground for dismissal. So I do not think that is a reason to harmonize.

Workers' participation is certainly a problem. Prof. Buxbaum mentioned it already.[22] I will not go into that, but the functioning of the regime of workers' participation in a group, and particularly an international group of companies, creates problems. But I think they could be solved, by the European Company Statute if it were feasible to solve the problem adequately in that framework, which is quite problematic. Mr. Fitchew mentioned yesterday[23] a new draft of the Commission for a workers' participation Directive.[24] I am curious to see what the Commission is going to propose taking into account the objections which have been made within the Council regarding the earlier draft. But that could be a framework for tackling this issue of workers' participation, as far as groups are concerned.

Klaus Hopt

As far as priority is concerned it may make sense to start with the Takeover Directive.[25] But the protection cannot stop here. Just look at the German situation where we have practically no, at least no hostile, takeovers. If you want to give protection, you need a market where takeovers are really going on with the beneficial effects attributed to them by some former American theories which in the meantime, as I understand it, are disputed. But even if these theories are right, in Germany this alone is just not doing enough.

Maybe the most important points for the moment are the ones mentioned already, i.e. harmonization of fiduciary duties, corporate opportunity and others. It was said[26] that they are candidates for harmonization – but for harmonization by whom? By the legislator, i.e. EC directives, or by courts? Harmonization of the issue by directives seems somewhat difficult. The factual problems are just too manifold, the legal distinctions developed for solving them are extraordinarily subtle and if in addition to that you begin to combine these fiduciary problems with group situations, then it becomes a quagmire.

Therefore I would submit that at least for the beginning, if fiduciary duties and corporate opportunities are accepted as candidates for harmonization, they should be candidates for harmonization through the courts.

Now despite this basic premise, can anything be done here by directives?

A first possibility would be to try just to harmonize certain principles in the fields. For example, harmonizing a principle of group law saying that

[22] See *supra* at 250.
[23] See *supra* at 21 and 13.
[24] Published in 1989: see O.J. C 263/69 (1989).
[25] Proposals: see O.J. C 64/8 (1989) and O.J. C 240/7 (1990).
[26] See *supra* at 248 ff.

the group interest may all legally be taken into account would be an enabling provision and would make sense to me. On the other side, establishing by way of harmonization that the directors have to take into consideration the interests of let us say the shareholders or the creditors or the workers or still other constituents may not mean very much, because this is too general and would leave all the work to the courts.

A second possibility beyond just harmonization principles could be the one mentioned by Prof. Wymeersch,[27] i.e. we could try to find out procedural devices to be harmonized, and of course there are quite a number of them. I do not want to say this would be the very best way to go, but at least it would be a possible direction. Take for example the outside director. I would agree with most of what Prof. Wymeersch said about him,[28] but still this is the kind of procedural device I am talking about. Or take the consent of the general meeting in certain cases of conflicts of interests, or quorums regulations or the prohibition of a vote for the interested party: all really difficult problems, but still good illustrations of the point.

A final possibility to be mentioned may lie in the remedies question.

Summing up, I think that the result of this search for harmonization through directives in the field would not be completely negative. But still basically much of it would have to be left to the courts, and one would have to think very carefully which parts to tackle by directives.

André Tunc

Prof. Wymeersch has made a number of proposals in Section V, paragraph 2 of his report:[29] I fully agree with them. However, I would go further than he does in paragraph 3.[30] He states that it would be very difficult to work out rules of substantive law as regards the relationships of the companies of a group.

I agree on the difficulty, but I do not think that the task is impossible. I assume that the duties of a parent company should be considered within the general framework of the duties of a dominant shareholder. And, on that problem, I consider as extremely valuable the *Principles of Corporate Governance* drafted by the American Law Institute. You have there 40 pages analyzing the decisions of the American courts and trying to state with as much precision as possible the duties of a dominant shareholder. As for the duties of the directors of a subsidiary, they are also covered in the more general Part V of the *Principles*. I think that in Europe we should pay more attention to this document and see whether we should not import some of its principles.

[27] See *supra* at 233 f.
[28] See *supra* at 234.
[29] See *supra* at 233 f.
[30] See *supra* at 234 f.

Alain Hirsch

Eddy Wymeersch has written[31] that the harmonization of group of companies law should not be so much harmonization of the substance but harmonization of procedures. I think this is a most important and interesting suggestion: to what extent should law of groups be left to courts and private litigation and how much should be dealt with by an administrative body (whether it is a State or a self-regulatory body is secondary)?

His example about Belgium[32] comes from the *Commission Bancaire*, and it is interesting to see that the fields in which law of groups is already effective are securities regulation, taxation, accounting, banking: fields for which administrative bodies are active. And then should law of groups be harmonized only for important companies or also for small groups, private groups, family groups? In this case of course the idea of having an administrative body competent to intervene and inquire is more difficult to accept.

Moreover, a possible harmonization of private international law of companies should concern especially groups of companies, making it possible to apply some laws on groups disregarding the incorporation of the companies.

Christian Meier-Schatz

I share the basic approach of Prof. Wymeersch's paper and agree very much, as a matter of principle, with his procedural (as compared with a substantive) regime.[33] However, I see the same problems of effectiveness with respect to his proposal of independent directors.[34] US as well as European experiences have shown that institutional as well as psychological mechanisms and factors within boards themselves are at work which make it rather difficult to implement an effective internal control by legal rules.

Eddy Wymeersch

You quite understandably raised doubts about the institution of the independent directors: do they exist? And are they really independent? One may try to answer with a reference to the independent auditor.

A couple of years ago, it was often thought that in some Member States there would not be auditors, and that in any event they would not be sufficiently expert nor independent. At present and as a consequence, among other things, of the Eighth Directive,[35] the situation has become much better and the justification of the auditor's function is not put into

[31] See *supra* at 233 ff.
[32] See *supra* at 234.
[33] See *supra* at 233 f.
[34] See *supra* at 234 f.
[35] O.J. L 126/20 (1984).

doubt any more. With respect to the independent directors, the situation is not entirely similar, as these do not yet form a well settled body of practitioners. But traditions may change: does one not already have an institute of independent directors and officers in the UK?

L.C.B. Gower

My experience suggests that it is going to make it very difficult for the EC to work out any workable rules about the regulation of the securities industry and the financial services industry generally, if there is not some harmonized regulation of groups throughout the Community.

At the moment you have the ludicrous situation that if an American company decides to operate in London through an unincorporated department, that will produce one situation that has to be dealt with. If on the other hand it decides to set up a separate subsidiary company, the regulations which will apply to it would be completely different despite the fact that economically the situation is exactly the same. What is the logic in making it different?

In any case, I say it is difficult to draw up any regulations which will apply meaningfully to both situations unless you have got some rules about how you treat groups. I think it is extraordinarily difficult to have satisfactory regulation and I suspect this would apply equally to regulation of other industries as well.

Edmund Kitch

There may be a separate set of rationales not really developed in this discussion for being concerned about groups in the context of highly regulated industries, which may include the financial services sector. Perhaps the European view is that all industrial activities are subjected to intensive regulation and it is really a question of implementing the European regulation, making it effective as applied to the multinationals.

Hartmut Schmidt

I would endorse this. I think there are ways to deal with the problem described by Prof. Gower aside from dealing with groups in general.

Alain Hirsch

Are you both saying that it is not worthwhile harmonizing groups of companies on the EC level, or that it could be worthwhile if it is done reasonably?

Hartmut Schmidt

If I understand Prof. Kitch correctly, he is strictly opposed and my position seems slightly weaker. I said, due to the remark by Klaus Hopt,[36] that if the EC has a regulation that seems to make sense, it may be worth trying it but it should not be a mandatory rule.

C. Protection of Creditors and Minority Shareholders

Edmund Kitch

As I said,[37] as I understand the problem of groups, there are really two issues.

One has to do with the position of minority shareholders in subsidiaries which are dominated by parents, the role and rights of the minority shareholders, and the problem of any duties by the controlling parent and its director agents to those minority shareholders. This is a problem which we subsume under the general issue of the fiduciary duties of directors and controlling shareholders. Here of course the Delaware mechanism comes to the fore for us. The law of the place of incorporation controls these questions of the duties of directors and the large important economic groups in the United States will be organized under Delaware corporation law and with Delaware subsidiaries.

Delaware law is not unsympathetic to the notion that minority shareholders in subsidiaries do have rights which must be respected by the parent and its agents, and indeed I think American lawyers generally have the view that a holding company structure with minority share interests is going inevitably to lead to some difficult legal problems and that there are great advantages in 100% share ownership of the subsidiaries. Then we do not have to worry about the minority interests. And indeed Delaware law through a short-form merger procedure attempts to assist the easy liquidation of minority positions in less than 10% in subsidiaries to get rid of the problem. And I think a lot of American companies simply operate with 100% share ownership.

Now the other wing of the problem that I understand is being addressed under the heading of groups is the problem of the rights of creditors who deal with one subsidiary to reach assets or make claims against the parent or other members of the economic complex. Here our basic approach would be to take the view that the creditor has a claim against the entity with which the creditor has dealt. If the creditor has asked for guarantees or the credit of the parent or some larger obligor, then the creditor gets that. But if the creditor simply dealt with the subsidiary and it turns out that the subsidiary does not have the assets and is taken into insolvency, then that is all the creditor gets. It is possible under some conditions to persuade a court

[36] See *supra* at 254 f.
[37] See *supra* at 241.

that one should be able to go through the limited liability of the subsidiary and reach the parent. "Pierce the corporate veil" is a terminology which we use to discuss these problems. This can be done in situations where the use of the limited liability company has been deemed fraudulent or abusive, often in situations where the forms have not been fully respected and the subsidiary has just been treated as a substitute for the parent.

The resolution of these claims depends upon amorphous legal standards and can be asserted under many different State laws and will be tried in a State court, where the outcome is fairly unpredictable, although I think it is fair to say that those claims do not generally succeed and the limited liability of the subsidiary prevails. You can find some cases to the contrary. The fact that there are differences of stated rationale or administration of that line in the State courts has never bothered anybody in the United States, partly I suppose because the issue will come to a head in bankruptcy court administration where the State law will be applied by a federal court.

Richard Buxbaum

Let me speak first on the minority shareholder protection problem. The issue as I see it, apart from whether you have decent fiduciary rules, is whether you have a prospective or a retrospective review, under whatever standard, of the treatment of the minority shareholders in that structure.

The main problem is that of prospective review, and therefore the main problem is that of a federalized standard, because it seems to me the prospective review lends itself more readily to a unitary federalizable standard than does retrospective review with its heavy emphasis on individual fact situations. The main problem with any prospective standard – and I personally believe this is the main problem with the German approach – is the transition into it; that is to say, how do you adopt a contract by which you turn existing minority shareholders into *rentiers*? Either you give those existing minority shareholders a veto power over the terms of that contract or you do not.

Now it seems to me that drives you right back into an insoluble problem, one which does not lend itself well to a federal approach because it really drives you back to a standard of fiduciary duty that I cannot quite see being prospectively generated. I do not know what the percentage is exactly, but if you have a small minority group, which are below the percentage at which they have a veto power over the terms of the prospective contract (I think I have that right), then of course somebody has to decide whether the terms of that contract are fair, at least in my naive way of looking at it. The minute you get into a factual situation like that, I think you have a difficult candidate for harmonization across boundaries.

So in a way I think the minority shareholder issue is not the issue. The issue is creditors' remedies, that is where I come out at the end. The problem with creditors' remedies, apart from the comfort letter, apart from the question of upstream guarantees, apart from all the traditional issues is:

we need to look at it, I think, as a public law matter because so many creditors are not contractual creditors. It is very easy to think of creditors as having contract relationships with their debtors and therefore being able to take care of themselves, and to overlook the tort claimants, the public claimants, the environmental pollution control claimants as in the American situation, and so on.

Now if that is so, then it becomes in a sense public law. Is it the kind of public law that the Community needs to harmonize or to unify? That I cannot speak to from the outside. It seems to me there are elements in it which go very closely to the equal starting point issues, no distortion of competition and so forth, and there are elements in it which do not. I cannot generalize on it. But I would think that it has to be treated as a public law issue, that is the creditors' remedies side. Whether therefore it needs to be at the European level I cannot judge from the outside.

Christian Timmermans

The issues of protection of minorities and creditors are, I think, the central issues when we talk about groups of companies. I have only one thing to add to what has already been said.

But let me say first that it will of course be interesting to see what this comparative research which has been organized by the Commission[38] will teach us, particularly on the existing devices in the Member States and also on how they are being applied in case-law.

What, in practice, have Member States done and are doing to protect minorities and creditors in a group situation? I think it is extremely important to know what the actual situation in the Member States is, because that will inform us whether there are sufficient procedural devices and what is the impact of these devices in practice. One word on this: I do not think harmonization of these devices as such – I mean the liability clauses – is a feasible thing.

I have great doubts on that, at any rate. In some Member States this is a question of the application of the general rules on tort. Perhaps it will be possible to agree on some very vaguely drafted clauses in a harmonization directive regarding protection of creditors or minority shareholders. But that would mean in practice that the interpretation of such clauses would be a matter for the Court of Justice in Luxembourg and it would hardly be harmonization by directive. What it would amount to is harmonization by jurisprudence. I have great doubts whether that could work in practice and whether that would have an adequate impact in terms of protection.

[38] See *supra* at 244.

Geoffrey Fitchew

In relation to the problem of minority shareholders: if there is takeover legislation[39] which requires the company making the bid to make a general offer at some stage and all the shareholders have the opportunity to accept that offer,[40] if some of them choose not to do so, then is that not a case for saying that they have made their bed and must lie in it thereafter? That is very much an off-the-cuff proposition but I would be interested to have reactions to it.

Christian Timmermans

Would it not be sufficient to protect the minority at the birth so to speak of the group situation, by regulating takeovers? Well, I should say no because if you only do that you leave the minority entirely to the will of the parent company once the group starts to function. Over a number of years however the situation might change completely without at the start there having been any risk of damage for creditors. In such a situation where the group's functioning is causing risks and damage for the creditors, there must be a legal device to compensate for that.

Gérard Hertig

I agree with most of what has been said, so I will make just one remark. If you seek protection of minorities, then you should see that there may be two different kinds of minorities.

One is: you have a minority because you have a joint venture and one company has a dominating position in the joint venture. I would let that pass and say there is nothing to be done about it. The other kind, related to tender offers and mergers and acquisitions, is made of minorities which are private investors and here – this may be a silly idea – we should not provide a specific protection. What should only be done (and it is not easy to do, and I do not know how to do it) is just to ensure that there is a liquid market for the stocks involved. If you do that, you do have the basis for suits afterwards, or at least for selling your stock.

Alain Hirsch

By liquid, do you mean liquid at an adequate price?

[39] See *supra* note 25.
[40] See *id.*, Art. 4.

Gérard Hertig

That is why I said that this is maybe the basis for a suit afterwards: if it is a very insufficient price, then you should try to see why it is an insufficient price and you have at least some data for suing.

Desmond McComb

Well, accountants of course always thought of groups mainly in the context of consolidation and that belongs to this afternoon's topic.[41] But as Prof. Gower mentioned,[42] the profession in the UK has also in the past exerted pressure concerning the liability of parent companies for the debts of subsidiaries. I think probably accountants have got involved in that because of the very obvious inconsistency between their treatment of groups as unified companies for purposes of reporting and then the legal position of a subsidiary which is not even treated as an agent of the group but is treated as a private person for whom the parent has no responsibility.

Now probably that might be an area for harmonization on a European level, though I get the impression that Prof. Buxbaum is not quite of the view[43] that parent companies should be responsible for the activities of their subsidiaries. I think however that many of those aggrieved by the failure of subsidiaries to meet their liabilities often feel that they should be, and whether or not one could say that a subsidiary is an entirely independent legal person or is indeed an agent of the group as a whole is, I suggest, an open point.

Eddy Wymeersch

With respect to the protection of creditors, and of liability of the parent for the subsidiary's debt, you imply that this liability, stated in terms of lifting of the veil or otherwise, has often been based on the excessive influencing by the parent of the subsidiary.

In terms of case-law, this is very true. For general legal purposes, I would warn against this as too broad an idea, whereby the degree of independence is merely used as the yardstick for setting aside the separate existence of the subsidiary as a body corporate. Legally it leads nowhere, or rather everywhere. It may greatly upset the corporate texture, whether by making parents generally liable for their subsidiaries, or by imposing on them an unnatural sense of restraint.

A more refined and effective approach would seem to be the one based on negligent or tortious acts of the parent, as has recently been developed in Dutch case-law, whereby negligent conduct of the parent shareholder was

[41] See *infra* at 286 ff.
[42] See *supra* at 249.
[43] See *supra* at 260.

considered to be a basis of liability against third parties, in the sense that the parent had made the creditor believe that it would continue to sustain its subsidiary although it later refused any further support.

Christian Timmermans

Well, let me say that the recent decision just mentioned by Prof. Wymeersch is, at least in my view, not revolutionary. It is an evolution in the case-law, and indeed the general torts approach is for my country the typical solution for the protection of creditors. This particular case relates to a company in difficulty recently taken over, the parent of which, after having publicized that it would keep the company running and allow its survival financially, withdrew its help a number of months later without informing the creditors. And then one of those creditors went to court and said: "Well, I have been misled in a serious manner and now I claim damages." And that was accepted by the court.

III. Concluding Remarks

Eddy Wymeersch

It is remarkable how large a consensus there has been around this table about the usefulness of having regulations on groups of companies, and on having these rules put into force on an harmonized basis. Would the law of groups of companies be one of the fields about which a general consensus could easily be found? I very much doubt it. Although the law of groups may be an issue about which many people think some form of regulation is necessary, preferably on an harmonized basis, I doubt however whether this common approach would subsist once one starts to discuss about substantive rules of group law.

Many issues have been raised and one is at about the wealth of ideas put forward. The matters raised are too diverse, so one is obliged to pick only a few of them.

Several approaches have been offered for regulating groups, especially of abusive conduct within groups. Some prefer a general approach[44] such as the fraud on the law, the lifting of the veil, and so on. Others more specifically and very much in point mentioned[45] that the time may have come to supplement several rules of today's harmonization directives. The Second EC Directive on capital formation and maintenance[46] could usefully be revised from a group perspective, e.g., to extend several of its rules to a

[44] See *supra* at 259.
[45] See *supra* at 248 ff.
[46] See *supra* note 21.

specific group setting and this in a perspective of groups of companies. I cannot but fully agree with the latter approach.

The major issues involved seem to be the ones of minority and creditor protection.[47] The proposals I have submitted to you concerning the introduction of procedural devices have in general been well received. The approach suggested by Prof. Tunc[48] consisting of the imposition of a general rule on the fiduciary obligation of group management seems very interesting from the intellectual point of view, but will raise difficult issues of implementation, and therefore will result in a legal system mainly evolved by the European Court of Justice, which is not necessarily the most efficient approach. A similar remark could be made with respect to the development of rules on the parent's liability for the subsidiary's debts on the basis of tort or negligence, or other general principles of law, such as the mysterious "lifting the veil," as have been developed in a few Member States. It is preferable to leave the further development of case-law on the basis of these principles to the legal system of the States.

Geoffrey Fitchew

I think after this discussion I remain grateful but open-minded. On this I am speaking personally, as I have on a number of other issues.

First of all, let me say that we have in a number of areas dealt with the group concept already, that is to say in the accounting Directive (the Seventh Directive),[49] to a limited extent in the taxation area where there is a directive that has been on the table for some time, dealing with the taxation of dividends paid by subsidiaries by one Member State to a parent in another Member State, with the limited aim of avoiding double taxation of the dividend in those circumstances. We also have a directive which has already been adopted on the consolidated supervision of banks.[50]

I can certainly foresee that we will need to deal with the group problem in what Prof. Kitch has described as highly regulated sectors,[51] such as banking and securities.

Indeed we are already envisaging an amendment to the directive on the consolidated supervision of banks, precisely to bring in banking groups where the holding company is a non-bank. And I think there are special important problems that need to be answered at the Community level on the application of capital adequacy rules to groups in banking and the financial services sector.

[47] See *supra* at 258 ff.
[48] See *supra* at 215.
[49] See *supra* note 3.
[50] O.J. L 193/18 (1983). For a new proposal, see com (90) 451 SinaP-SYN 306, 22 November 1990.
[51] See *supra* at 257.

But it seems to me that that is conceptually a separate problem which does not necessarily require answers to be given to the minority shareholder and creditor problems which we have been discussing.[52]

On those two problems I entirely accept what everybody said around the table, that in all Member States, even where there is no group law named as such, there has nevertheless been a developing jurisprudence dealing with group relations. And it is because we have been conscious of that and of the risk of divergences developing that we have commissioned this survey which is now going on,[53] and I think we need to wait and see what the results of that are. If it looks as though there are serious divergences of treatment, then we clearly have to consider some degree of harmonization.

But I think it is likely to be a very difficult task. Everybody around the table thinks we should do something, but there is not really a consensus on what it should be.

If we try to deal with it in a substantive way, we have to try to answer the question: "Where does the liability of the parent stop?" And equally in defining what is meant by the right to be able to take into account the group interest. It seems to me extraordinarily difficult to get agreement on that at the European level.

On the other hand, if we confine ourselves to procedural solutions (and I am extremely interested by Prof. Wymeersch's ideas[54] and I think we ought to look into this further), that still leaves open the possibility that the procedural solutions will be applied in ways which give different and divergent results in different Member States. But it certainly is a subject which is clearly on the table.

[52] See *supra* at 258 ff.
[53] See *supra* at 244.
[54] See *supra* at 233 f.

Chapter Seven

Accounting

A. Report: Desmond McComb

As one who is not a legal expert I feel I have been privileged to participate in the discussions on a topic which I am accustomed to consider from an accountant's viewpoint. I have learnt much in the process. One of my reactions on receiving and studying the *Buxbaum* and *Hopt* text[1] was to feel somewhat intimidated by the scholarship of the authors. Specifically it forced me to examine issues of harmonizing corporate financial disclosure from new perspectives, and I have found this to be a rewarding exercise.

Although the *Buxbaum* and *Hopt* comparative study is primarily concerned with "harmonization" through law, I believe there is a particular need to adopt a liberal interpretation of legality in the circumstances which have surrounded the evolution of international concepts of accounting and financial reporting. The authors have shown an awareness of this by, for example, recognizing the significance of quasi-legal codes of conduct such as those issued by the UN and OECD.[2] I have adopted such a liberal interpretation of the law in some of the following sections.

There are three distinguishable strands in the evolving pattern of harmonization of accounting and corporate reporting in Europe, and indeed worldwide. These are:
- business interest
- professional, and
- political.

It can be argued that it is the business interest group – widely defined to include transnational firms, financial institutions and individual investors, all as constituents of the capital markets but the former also as transactors on the international scene – which provides the impetus and the resources for the provision of financial information to external users. This model would conform broadly with the Anglo-American environment. However, it is also the case that government economic planners as in France, and tax

[1] R.M. BUXBAUM & K.J. HOPT, *Legal Harmonization and the Business Enterprise* (Berlin/New York 1988).

[2] *Id.* at 232.

authorities as in France and Germany may provide an impetus for the provision of financial information oriented to their perceived objectives.[3]

A critique of the achievements and/or prospects of the international harmonization of accounting and corporate financial reporting should therefore be viewed in the context of the aspirations of those groups who are committed to, or see advantage to themselves in international accounting harmonization, and the attitudes of the companies, etc. who are called upon to meet the perceived information demands of users (however defined) of corporate financial reports. At the interface between the business interest and the political strands in the harmonization process, it could be implied that some of the dilatoriness and indeed antagonism[4] which has been displayed in member countries of the EC in regard to the implementation of company law directives may be attributed to differences in perceptions of the demand for or need for particular rules or laws. A case in point might be the German reluctance to agree to a directive which would make "The GmbH & Co." subject to the disclosure norms of the Fourth and Seventh Directives.[5]

The professional accountancy strand in this process of harmonization derives its significance in some degree as arbitrator between providers and users of accounting information, but perhaps more importantly as an independent though not disinterested party linking the business interest and political strands.

I. The Business Interest Group

The primary transactors in the business interest group are firms actively engaged in international trade and production, and in particular those firms whose management, financing, production and trading policies are multinational. Such firms are therefore inherently interested in assuring the compatibility of accounting principles and practice within their affiliate companies. However, their ability to operate a homogeneous framework of accounting within their corporate groups is restricted by the generally accepted principles and practices applying in the various host countries.

Problems of this kind are likely to be most marked in those host countries which possess well developed and highly structured national accounting codes and standards, since in these circumstances the transnational company finds itself faced with the need to keep virtually two sets of records, one for group accounting purposes based upon the accounting standards of the home country, and the other to comply with host countries' legal require-

[3] McCOMB, "International Accounting Standards and the EEC Harmonization Program: A Conflict of Disparate Objectives," *Int'l J. of Account.* (Spring Issue 1982).

[4] BUXBAUM & HOPT, *supra* note 1, at 236-241.

[5] *Id.* at 241 ff.

ments relating to tax and public reporting.[6] In this scenario, transnational companies could be seen to have a vested interest in the promotion of harmonization, legal or otherwise, of accounting at an international level.

In this context it is not surprising that since the sixties American generally accepted accounting principles have acquired some level of international visibility. However this suggested role of the transnationals as promoters of international harmonization of accounting should also be distinguished from the posture which they have adopted in regard to proposals for corporate financial disclosure emanating from the UN Commission on Transnational Corporations.[7] In the latter case they have been called upon to provide a uniform level of information about their activities, information which host country governments and others could use to control, discipline, or assist competition against the companies providing the information. Naturally they have displayed little enthusiasm for this type of harmonization.

Buxbaum and *Hopt* would appear to imply that the UN's efforts have been more influential than is perhaps the case.[8] The OECD proposals[9] also do not appear to have achieved much in terms of actual implementation although they have been more favorably received. However, the OECD also acts as a catalyst in bringing together representatives of interested groups from various member countries in order to discuss emerging problems in accounting. A recent such meeting, for example, was convened to discuss accounting for new financial instruments.

In the context of the authors' study it is therefore significant to recognize that a particular "interest group" could be both a proponent and an antagonist of the international harmonization of accounting and financial reporting at the same time. However, in a generalized way I think we can say that companies who engage in international trade are going to be interested in and willing to pressure for international harmonization, but how far they are going to go along those lines is open to doubt. One might also find a parallel here with the attitudes of national legislators towards harmonization. Ultimately, self-interest, whether benevolent or selfish, is going to be a major determinant of attitudes taken, or postures adopted.

From a capital markets' perspective, transnational business firms, financial institutional investors and individual investors have a community of interests in harmonized regulation which may evolve from below or be imposed from above, respectively through private regulators such as stock

[6] ACCOUNTANTS INTERNATIONAL STUDY GROUP, *International Financial Reporting* (Toronto 1975).

[7] UNITED NATIONS CENTER ON TRANSNATIONAL CORPORATIONS, *Towards International Standardization of Corporate Accounting and Reporting* (New York 1982).

[8] BUXBAUM & HOPT, *supra* note 1, at 232.

[9] ORGANIZATION FOR ECONOMIC CO-OPERATION AND DEVELOPMENT, *Guidelines for Multinational Enterprises* (Paris 1976).

exchanges or through laws promulgated by states. The differences in the development of accounting and corporate financial reporting in various countries can be attributed at least in part to the relative strengths of the pressures which each of the above three parties have been able to exert. Arguably, it would not be rational to assume that the disparities which we find between national systems of accounting have come about randomly.[10]

In the context of this admittedly subjective judgment, it can be postulated that some of the arguments for relevance of accounting information can also justify even fundamental differences in accounting principles among various countries. Thus it is frequently suggested that the US/UK investor/shareholder orientation of corporate financial reporting reflects the historical importance of those countries' open capital markets as sources of finance for industrial and commercial investment, whereas the lesser significance of open capital markets and the proportionately greater part played by banks in Germany and France in the provision of investment funds in turn can explain the stronger emphasis placed upon liquidity and solvency, and the more tolerant attitudes taken towards income smoothing.[11] Indeed this latter aspect of accounting has been also favored in Switzerland and Sweden for different reasons.

A question which arises from the recognition of disparate national systems of accounting and financial reporting is whether national differences are fossilized survivors or spontaneously evolving responses to local information demands and needs. Alternatively, the changes which have taken place in the environment of international business may have made it desirable to strive for greater uniformity. The analogy between EC and US state company law and federal regulation of securities markets is of limited relevance to this matter since the individual American states have not had the constraints on capital and monetary flows and interstate trading which up until now have been a commonplace of the European situation, and which have dictated in large measure the financial framework within which European firms conduct their business. Looking forward, however, the recently adopted Capital Liberalization Directive,[12] and the intended removal by 1992 of trade barriers between EC countries may provide a more acceptable, even if imperfect, analogue.

In evaluating the EC harmonization of corporate financial reporting it can also be questioned whether the presumption that there is[13]

> "a substantial connection between the harmonization of company and capital market laws on the one hand, and the advancement of economic integration, as defined in the Treaty of Rome, on the other,"

[10] McCOMB, "The International Harmonization of Accounting: A Cultural Dimension," *Int'l J. of Account.* (Spring Issue 1979).

[11] F.D.S. CHOI & G.G. MUELLER, *An Introduction to Multinational Accounting* 182-183 (Englewood 1978).

[12] O.J. L 178/5 (1988).

[13] BUXBAUM & HOPT, *supra* note 1, at 167.

and which is analyzed further in Chapter 3 of the *Buxbaum* and *Hopt* book, has been adequately related to the national environmental factors which historically have determined the nature of corporate financial disclosure. Doubt about this relation arises whether or not the above presumption is accepted. Do we accept that existing differences in national frameworks of accounting and financial reporting are random events, or are they considered to be environmentally determined? Or if they are both random and environmentally determined, what degree of impact does each factor have? Such an analysis would not preclude a conclusion favoring harmonization, even in the extreme case that differences are wholly environmentally explicable, since it is arguable that these differences will self-destruct in a common market. However, I have failed to find any evidence that the issues concerned have been seriously explored and subsequently incorporated into the Fourth and Seventh Directives,[14] this despite the various options contained in the directives.

Admittedly, the above critique contains an inherent bias, based on the assumption that the "business interest group" produces or demands decision-relevant information, and that this relevance is the primary determinant in justifying the expenditure of resources in producing accounts. If, on the other hand, the primary objective of accounting and corporate financial reporting is to provide information for purposes of macroeconomic planning either by national governments or the European Commission, many of the problems discussed above do not arise. Both micro and macro-objectives exist in most European countries, but with distinct differences in emphasis upon the two. But while discernible self-interest of producers of financial reports will in many cases give rise to some measure of voluntary disclosure to investors and creditors (whether personal, corporate or institutional), it is highly unlikely that information for tax or economic planning by governments will be provided without legal compulsion.

Therefore, once it is accepted that it is necessary for governments or the Commission to access accounting information for planning purposes, it follows that laws to enforce its provision must be enacted, and, in the case of the Commission, that these should be harmonized throughout the Community. However, the companies who were called upon to provide such information and the shareholders, etc., who receive them may regard accounts conforming with, for example, the Fourth and Seventh Directives as being of limited usefulness. It is possible also to envisage a "sub-culture" of unregulated accounts superseding the official accounts as a basis for corporate financial reporting.

The safety valve to prevent such a situation, however unlikely, is the "true and fair" (*image fidèle*) overrider clause in the directives.[15] Countries which have found it difficult to assimilate the implications of the "true and fair"

[14] O.J. L 222/11 (1978) and O.J. L 193/1 (1983).
[15] BUXBAUM & HOPT, *supra* note 1, at 21.

clause can in fact be distinguished not so much by whether they have code law or common law systems but by the relative degree of precedence which their accounting systems have given traditionally to the provision to government-oriented as distinct from investor-oriented information. Thus, the Netherlands, for example, appears to have experienced little difficulty in accommodating the concept of "true and fair" taking precedence over other criteria such as compliance with legal codes. By contrast in France and more particularly in Germany some companies and their auditors have experienced a form of cultural shock in relating to this idea of subjective judgment, however moralist in tone, ranking above the literal requirements of the legal code.

The implication to be drawn is that the scope for harmonizing accounting and corporate financial reporting through legislation is fairly limited. Formal compliance with the Fourth Directive, for example, has provided a limited basis for making ratio comparisons across national frontiers, but the still unresolved problems encountered in the development of the BACH[16] data base have shown that the validity of such comparisons is somewhat doubtful.[17]

II. The Accounting Profession

In many countries of the world, including some in the EC, the accounting profession has a role in the regulation of corporate disclosure.

In the Netherlands the professional influence operates through the medium of the Tripartite Accounting Standards Committee (TASC) set up following the Act on Annual Accounts of Enterprises in 1971. Guidelines on accounting issued by TASC are widely regarded as binding. In the UK and Ireland the profession sets accounting standards through its Accounting Standards Committee (ASC), and enforces their application through its internal disciplinary processes. Many of the UK/Irish standards deal with issues of technical detail, but Standard 10 is by contrast the sole authority for regulating the publication of "The Statement of Sources and Application of Funds."

In situations such as this, the "guidelines" or "standards" create a form of surrogate law. The close relationship which developed in the US between the SEC and the American Institute of Certified Public Accountants – through its Accounting Principles Board (APB), and since 1973 the

[16] EC COMMISSION, *The Fourth Company Accounts Directive of 1978 and the Accounting Systems of the Federal Republic of Germany, France, Italy, the United Kingdom, the United States and Japan* (Doc., Luxembourg 1986).

[17] G.M. SEEFF, "Comparing Business Performance of European Companies Using Harmonized Accounts: Overcoming the Problems," (Paper presented at the Eleventh Congress of the European Accounting Association, Université de Nice 1988).

Financial Accounting Standards Board (FASB), and under which the accounting standards which are the basis of "Generally Accepted Accounting Principles" (GAAP) are virtually underwritten by the SEC – is a further example of professional input to the development of accounting laws. More specific input to the legislative process is provided under Regulation 44 of the Canada Business Corporations Act (1975), which requires that financial statements of companies covered by that Act should be prepared in accordance with the recommendations of the Canadian Institute of Chartered Accountants (CICA) Handbook, thus transforming the profession's rules and standards into company law.

The above examples of professional involvement in the regulation of corporate financial reporting at a national level must not be generalized, however. It is true that in the countries mentioned, the accounting profession has varying degrees of ability to add to the legal regulation of corporate financial reporting, but equally there are other countries, for example Germany, where the profession has a much lower profile in such matters. Nevertheless, it is possible to observe an increasingly direct involvement of the accounting profession in company law development at something more than a simple advisory level, an involvement which commenced in the US in the thirties following the establishment of the SEC, and has spread to many other countries, finding perhaps its ultimate form in Canada.

Buxbaum and *Hopt* refer to this role of the accountancy profession in regard to US GAAP[18] but do not expand the issue thus raised to include comparable professional involvement in the regulation of corporate financial disclosure in Europe and elsewhere. It is unclear whether this is because the accounting aspects of legal harmonization represent only a small part of the authors' overall thesis, or if it is because they regard the development of regulation from below in this instance to be a minor phenomenon in Europe. I would disagree with the latter line of reasoning. It is true that until recently regulation from above has been the dominant approach in European code law countries, with the exception of the Netherlands. However, the period since the seventies has seen a marked growth in self-regulation by European corporations influenced by the desire to access international capital markets. Thus many of the larger Italian companies have had their degree of accounting disclosure determined for some years by the CONSOB (Stock Exchange Control Committee) rules rather than by the legal code.

In fact, all the anecdotal evidence would appear to imply that improvements in corporate financial disclosure tend to be market-directed rather than law-directed. Conversely, it has been those countries with the most prescriptive commercial codes which have tended to be those in which company reports have been least informative to external users. However, by the accident of history, such countries have also been those in which open

[18] BUXBAUM & HOPT, *supra* note 1, at 275.

capital markets have been less important sources of corporate finance, and where therefore there was little pressure or demand for increased accountability. Whether the quality of financial disclosure is predominantly law-determined or user demand-determined is open to question. The latter, however, implies that EC harmonization of corporate financial reporting by directive may not be a very promising route to the achievement of that objective.

The significance of the accounting profession's input to legislation from below , as far as the present study is concerned, relates to its involvement in the harmonization of accounting, at both a regional and an international level. On the strictly European front, this is achieved through the activities of the *Fédération des Experts Comptables Européens* (FEE), who since 1987 has taken over this function from the *Union Européenne des Experts Comptables Economiques et Financiers* (UEC), and the EEC Accounting Study Group. On the international scene, the International Federation of Accountants (IFAC) has been active in the issue of international auditing guidelines, which by their nature have an impact in harmonizing accounting for many technical areas of accountancy practice.

The most notable professional accounting impact upon the harmonization of corporate financial reporting regulation, however, has been made by the "International Accounting Standards Committee" (IASC). Founded in 1973, the IASC represents professional accountancy organizations from more than sixty countries, and its function is to formulate, publish and promote, in the public interest, international standards for financial statements.[19] It seeks to achieve its objectives through the issue of accounting standards, in a manner analogous with the procedures of the American FASB and the British ASC, the member organizations being committed to use their best endeavors to ensure that the standards are met. Such international standards do not necessarily have legal status in the IASC member countries, and the method by which they are applied varies.

In the UK, for example, they are incorporated into the ASC Standards, whereas in France and Germany they have little more than advisory status. In an interesting recent development, however, the Netherlands has indicated that compliance with the IASC Standard on consolidated group accounts would be deemed to represent compliance with the EC Seventh Company Law Directive, thus in effect incorporating it into the legal code. In this case the IASC Standard has been used in a manner comparable with the use of the American Bar Association's Model Company Act by the US state legislators.[20] Many developing countries also have used IASC Standards as a basis for the development and improvement of national standards. In this limited area of company law concerned with accounting

[19] INTERNATIONAL ACCOUNTING STANDARDS COMMITTEE, *International Accounting Standards Committee: Objectives and Procedures* (London 1982).

[20] See BUXBAUM & HOPT, *supra* note 1, at 117-119.

and financial disclosure, it could be inferred that the accountancy profession has achieved the establishment of an international forum for the harmonization of company law in a manner which at a more general level has eluded the legal profession.

Arguably, however, the IASC's efforts have been too widely dispersed over a spectrum ranging from third world countries to those with highly developed economies, so that in some respects the harmonization brought about has been superficial. Of course, such doubts could also be expressed about the effectiveness of the politically motivated policies of the EC in this same field of activity. Nevertheless, despite criticism concerning the value of its efforts, the international accountancy profession is now a potent force in the development of company law and its harmonization at an international level. It seems unlikely that it foresaw this role for itself when the IASC was formed in 1973, but the Committee shows no tendency to withdraw from its new sphere of activity.

III. Political Factors in Accounting Harmonization

The willingness of national legislators to be influenced by and indeed copy accounting, auditing and financial disclosure practices and laws of other countries is not an entirely modern phenomenon. Thus we find evidence in the report of the United Kingdom Select Committee on Joint Stock Companies, 1841-1844, that the members were both interested in, and willing to learn from enterprise organizations and accounting procedures in other countries.[21] Again, in evidence given before the British Company Law Committee in 1961, *Manuel Cohen*, then Chairman of the SEC, stated: "Our new issue regulation is, of course, borrowed from the British Companies Act, 1929."[22] Similarly, the natural inclinations of European colonial bureaucrats to export their legal systems to their subject countries has resulted in harmonized accounting systems reflecting for example French, British or German accounting practices. Even today we find French Government officials active in providing assistance to developing countries who are interested in adopting the OCAM Accounting Plan,[23] which has been adapted from the *Plan Comptable Général.*

Harmonization of corporate accounting and financial reporting therefore has a history based upon zones of political influence, which may continue to provide some guidance in regard to current pressures in this field.

Contemporary political impetus for harmonization of accounting and corporate financial disclosure derives, however, not from nation states but

[21] British Parliamentary Papers (1844) vii.

[22] COMPANY LAW COMMITTEE, Minutes of Evidence, 1961, 19th day, § 6583.

[23] ORGANISATION COMMUNE AFRICAINE, MALGACHE ET MAURICIENNE, *Plan Comptable Général* (Paris 1970).

from supranational organizations. In particular, the international pressures have come from the UN, the OECD, and the EC.

IV. UN and OECD

In 1973 the UN Economic and Social Council (ECOSOC) undertook a study of the effects of the activities of transnational corporations (TNCs) on development and international relations, particularly between developed and developing countries. The Report of the Ad Hoc Intergovernmental Working Group[24] was by no means unanimous, and recommendations on information disclosure by companies were somewhat wide ranging, covering social as well as financial issues. One aspect of the UN study, relevant to both the recommendations and their acceptability by the TNCs to whom they were principally addressed, is that one of the stated objectives of the exercise was:

> "to strengthen the negotiating capacity of host countries, in particular the developing countries, in their dealings with transnational corporations."

Seen in this light the proposals needed a high level of government commitment to their implementation, particularly on the part of the industrialized countries, to achieve their objectives. On the evidence to date that commitment has not been forthcoming. Understandably, as previously noted, the TNCs have not shown any tendency to react positively to the proposals.

In contrast to the UN Commission on Transnational Corporation's emphasis on developing countries, the OECD by the nature of its membership reflects views of the industrialized countries. As a result, the Guidelines on disclosure of information by transnational companies[25] tended to reflect good accounting practice in member countries, but with some emphasis on geographical segmentation of information and intergroup pricing policies. Subsequently, also it has addressed topics such as comparability of accounting standards, group consolidated accounts and foreign currency translation. As with the UN, the guidelines and proposals of the OECD are normative only, since as an organization its power is limited to the influence it can exert by virtue of its status. In general, though reactions to the recommendations made by the OECD have been positive, although it would be difficult to attribute any specific development in the harmonization of international accounting to them.

[24] *Cf. supra* note 7.
[25] *Cf. supra* note 9.

V. European Community

The obvious distinction between the EC and all other groups concerned with international harmonization of accounting and corporate financial reporting is its capacity to legislate directly through regulations or indirectly through directives. It can therefore, at least in theory, impose its policies on Member States. In practice its ability to bring about truly meaningful accounting harmonization throughout the Community is limited by what each country regards as the objectives of corporate financial reporting and the ranking given to those objectives.

Some of the twelve member countries, notably Greece, Luxembourg, Portugal and Spain have had until joining a fairly minimal level of law regarding corporate disclosure, little history of professional auditing and a consequent absence of a well organized, highly educated and trained accountancy profession with which to implement the new laws. The latter is a short-term problem which can, given the provision of adequate resources, be resolved within a relatively short-time scale. Other structural deterrents to harmonization, such as legal systems, levels of industrialization, etc., are likely to be more resistant to change.

In countries with developed systems of corporate financial reporting, the difficulties in implementing directives may be closely related to problems of compatibility with national rankings of objectives of corporate disclosure. The existence of distinguishable national characteristics of accounting systems can in some measure be ascribed to attitudes towards legal regulation of business. The early cases of such regulation tend to be found in the code law countries of Europe, the French Commerce Ordnance of 1673,[26] for example, prescribed the keeping of records of transactions by persons engaged in commerce. Such laws emphasized the function of accounting as a basis for the verification of transactions and proof of claims to property or the existence of liabilities. Subsequently, fiscal laws accentuated this aspect of accounting since verification and proof are of primary significance in tax assessment. The comparative importance or ranking attributed to these functions of accounting is one reason for differences in attitudes towards corporate financial reporting among European countries. The other major explanation for differences relates to the nineteenth century development of the joint stock limited liability company as a popular organizational form for business enterprises. The abuses[27] which followed the availability of incorporation by registration had a profound influence upon accounting, whose primary purpose came to be regarded as providing independently verified reports upon corporations' financial activities to shareholders and creditors, who had a vested interest in the corporation's profitability and solvency, but were external to their management and control.

[26] *Ordonnance du Commerce*, Art. 1-10 (Paris 1673).
[27] BUXBAUM & HOPT, *supra* note 1, at 176.

The distinctions which can be made between the major industrial and trading countries of Europe in regard to their philosophies of corporate financial disclosure reflect the relative impact limited companies made on their economic life, and the manner by which their financing influenced the development of capital markets and financial institutions. Harmonization of corporate financial reporting in these countries requires that differences which are accidental historical survivals be distinguished from those which truly reflect contemporary environmental differences. While the former could be eliminated without loss, the latter must be accommodated if accounting is to be socially relevant.

Arguably, harmonization by directives carries out this selective function since directives enable individual countries to legislate in a manner appropriate to their own financial environment. However, conflict can potentially arise between the company law and capital markets' harmonization objectives based upon the EEC Treaty, Article 54(3)(g), and other national objectives such as the use of accounting as a basis for taxation or economic planning. Thus while the development of common standards of protection for shareholders, creditors and potential investors can rationally allow for national differences in the relative importance of each group, it is arguable that the accommodation of other objectives, however significant in their own right, might run counter to the broad intentions of directives issued in the context of the EC company law and capital markets' harmonization program. In comparing German with US accounting, for example, *W. Busse von Colbe*[28] identifies *inter alia* the factors summarized below which distinguish the German from the US environment of corporate reporting:

(1) minor importance of equity market as a source of corporate funds;
(2) importance of creditor protection because of historical importance of credit finance;
(3) the legal right of German shareholders to dividends of 50% of declared profits, with the consequences of this for corporate capital maintenance;
(4) identity between taxable and reported profits.

The comparison would apply equally to the UK, Ireland, and to some extent the Netherlands. The above factors should not make any appreciable differences to the way in which transactions are recorded in the various countries. They would, however, and this applies particularly to factor (4) above, influence the allocations of revenues and expenses which are inherent in the processes of editing and summarizing raw financial data for the purposes of external financial reporting.

Comparable distinctive environmental factors can be identified in varying degrees in all European countries, and taken to an extreme position it could be argued that accounting harmonization is irrelevant unless accompanied

[28] BUSSE VON COLBE, "A True and Fair View: A German Perspective," in *EEC Accounting Harmonization: Implementation and Impact of the Fourth Directive* (S. Gray & A.G. Coenenberg eds., Amsterdam 1984).

by harmonization of the social, legal, political and economic environment as a prior condition. To some extent, of course, that is what the Commission is attempting to bring about, and many of the implementation problems associated with the accounting directives have reflected the gap between its ideals and the reality of national aspirations within the Community. The authors wisely[29]

> "beg the initial but unresolvable question whether economic reality preordains political reality or vice versa, or whether the two realities reciprocally influence each other."

Equally, I make no attempt to justify the assumption that accounting information provides a basis for economic judgments, and that each Community devises accounting measurement systems which are appropriate to its decision-oriented needs at a particular period in time. However, if that is a valid assumption, it appears to me that it follows that the countries of the EC must accept the imminence of the convergence of economic and political reality within the Community, in order to justify the abandonment of their presumed environmentally relevant accounting frameworks in favor of that set out in the accounting directives. How valid that judgment is at this point in time is open to question.

A. The Fourth Directive

The Fourth Company Law Directive[30] is the cornerstone of the plan to harmonize corporate financial reporting throughout the European Community. It requires that companies should publish annual accounts consisting of a profit and loss account and balance sheet, and establishes minimum information to be provided in the accounts. A choice of four formats for the profit and loss account and two for the balance sheet is permitted. Countries have the option of permitting any or all of the formats when incorporating the directive into their national laws. In practice the choice of balance sheet formats is one of display only, since the same information is provided by each. In the case of the profit and loss account there is again a display option, but also an option of classifying expenses by function, e.g., operating costs, administration expenses etc., or by type of cost, e.g. raw materials, wages etc. Small companies and medium-sized companies may be allowed to provide shorter accounts.

Ostensibly therefore all companies reporting within the European Community should be providing harmonized financial information. However, the directive does not provide any detailed technical guidance on methods of accounting measurement and reporting to be adopted in specific situations, such as are commonplace in the US GAAP. As a result, it is quite possible for two companies in the same industry to produce look-alike

[29] BUXBAUM & HOPT, *supra* note 1, at 7.
[30] O.J. L 222/11 (1978).

financial reports conforming to the Fourth Directive formats, but at the same time to have used incompatible methods of measurement and accounting for identical transactions. This could occur within one country, but is more likely and indeed inevitable where the accounts of companies in more than one country are being compared.

Thus for example two companies in the brewing industry, one in Germany and the other in the UK might each acquire a leased plant. The German company would expense the leasing cost through its profit and loss account, the UK company would normally capitalize the leasing cost. The German company would therefore report a lower amount of profit than its UK equivalent, even though there was no difference in the nature of their transaction. Again, although the directive contains valuation rules these are little more than a general statement of the rules of historical cost or current value accounting. However, without accounting standards specifying how assets and liabilities should be valued, there are many situations in which it is possible for companies to account differently for comparable assets or liabilities.

With regard to assets this disparity of accounting values may also be accentuated by national tax rules or laws. In France, Germany, Italy, Luxembourg, Portugal and Spain income reported for taxation must normally be identical with that reported in published accounts. The effect of this is that the depreciation charge appearing in the accounts will be the amount permitted for tax purposes, however large or small that may be, while the written down value of the asset will reflect that writedown. In the remaining countries whose tax laws or customs make no such demands, the depreciation charged in the accounts is more likely to be based upon the expected useful life of the asset concerned, and in all probability the residual value of such assets appearing in the balance sheet will be higher than would have been the case if the common tax and financial reporting basis had been used.

Across Europe therefore we can find companies which, in full compliance with the Fourth Directive, may account for and report upon assets on the bases of a scale of values ranging from value to the enterprise as a going concern through to value as a residual of cost less amounts written off for tax purposes. Again French companies may be required to revalue assets for tax purposes, German companies forbidden to value other than on written down historical cost, and UK and Netherlands companies permitted in appropriate circumstances to use written down historical cost, replacement cost, and even market value.

In reality therefore even when the Fourth Directive has been fully implemented by all member countries, the European world of harmonized corporate financial reporting will remain something of a scaled-down tower of Babel and international comparisons of corporate performance, although more valid than heretofore, must remain constrained by the limitations of the primary data.

B. The Seventh Directive

Partly because it is based upon and supplemental to the Fourth Directive, the Seventh Directive[31] has engendered less commentary, despite the fact that it took eight years of negotiation before it was agreed. An early issue involved defining the "group" whose accounts were to be consolidated, the choice being either economic dominance or legal control. While the former has intellectual appeal, it was eventually abandoned because of its subjective characteristics. Legal control therefore became the normal basis adopted by the directive, although options reflecting economic dominance criteria were included.

Prior to the issue of the Seventh Directive, some European countries either had no law regarding consolidated group accounts, or where such laws existed, they mandated largely incompatible accounting standards, or as in Germany, required the consolidation of the accounts of domestic, but not of foreign subsidiaries. In this latter case though we find the marketplace effect operating, in that many large German corporations who had international stock market quotations have for some years adopted the practice of consolidating foreign and domestic subsidiaries in their group accounts. Therefore, when fully implemented the Seventh Directive should make available much corporate financial information which until now has been hidden by the diversity of accounting methodologies used.[32]

C. The Eighth Directive

The Eighth Directive[33] establishes standards of education and training which will be required of auditors, and is arguably central to all the accounting directives, both now and in the future, since the activity of a strong and independent auditing profession is an essential factor in the credibility of company accounts provided to shareholders, creditors, employees, and all other external users. The directive is of particular significance in the context of the "true and fair view" overrider clauses of Article 2 of the Fourth Directive and Article 16 of the Seventh Directive, since in future auditors will be required to certify that accounts meet that criterion. The influence of a strong and independent auditing profession could therefore be a potent force for harmonization of corporate financial reporting standards, not least because of the ever present threat of negligence claims against auditors.

[31] O.J. L 193/1 (1983).

[32] S.M. McKINNON, *Consolidated Accounts, The Seventh EEC Directive* (A.D.H. Newham ed., London 1983).

[33] O.J. L 126/20 (1984).

D. True and Fair View

The term "true and fair view" did not appear in the early drafts of the Fourth Directive, but was introduced in the amended draft of 1974.[34]

Its first use in legislation was in the UK Companies Act 1947, and *Flint*, referring to it in a UK context, said:[35]

> "An understanding of the 'view' which is given by company accounts and whether it is a true and fair one, requires some knowledge of accounting, of the purposes for which accounts are prepared, and of the objective which they are intended to fulfill."

The distinctions made as to "purposes" and "objectives" are of particular relevance when the concept of "true and fair" is applied throughout the EC countries, since these, or at least their ranking, can vary widely.

Because the concept had been used since 1947 in the UK, and had been in use subsequently in Ireland and the Netherlands, its use in the accounting directives was readily accepted in those countries. France and Germany, however, which traditionally had emphasized strict compliance with legal codes as the criterion for acceptable financial reporting were faced with a dilemma: Article 2 of the Fourth Directive was quite clearly establishing a higher level goal for the evaluation of the acceptability of corporate reports.[36] In practice compliance with legal requirements for disclosure normally will enable a company and its auditors to regard their accounts as being "true and fair." However, the view that this would automatically follow must be rejected as contrary to the clear intention of Article 2.5. Nevertheless its interpretation is unlikely to be uniform across national frontiers,[37]

> "not only because of the different juridical tradition but also because of the different socio-economic environment of companies."

An ethical problem arises from this, however: in treating "true and fair" as a term of art we are effectively saying that truth is relative rather than absolute.

In the immediate future it is difficult to envisage the concept making a marked impact upon accounting standards throughout Europe. Inherently, however, it possesses the potential for drawing attention to and questioning the currently existing disparate objectives and standards of accounting, which have not been addressed by the accounting directives. In the wider context of the removal of barriers to trade and commerce, and of the Europeanization of financial and commercial institutions (a requisite of a common market), the concept of true and fair reporting could therefore be the catalyst for a fundamental reappraisal of and harmonization of account-

[34] COM(74)191 final (21 February 1974).

[35] D. FLINT, *A True and Fair View in Company Accounts* (London 1982).

[36] *Id.* at 7.

[37] BUSSE VON COLBE, *supra* note 28.

ing and financial reporting in Europe. The accounting directives provide the formal structures for harmonized accounting, but they have not and indeed could not encompass the environmental factors which help explain the existing differences in national systems. Nor can the problem be legislated away by further Community directives or indeed recommendations, although the latter could in appropriate circumstances provide a basis for giving EC status to recommendations on the harmonization of accounting standards emanating from the FEE or the IASC. In the long term, the true and fair overrider concept of Article 2 may, however, provide an argument for leaving further harmonization to market forces within the Community. The accounting directives have been a prime example of legislation from above in the almost total absence of evident social need or demand.

The history of legislating for corporate financial disclosure in Europe has not on balance been such as to provide high expectations for improvement in the quality of corporate information as a result. Rather it is in those situations where market forces have begun to operate, such as the standards imposed by the Italian Stock Exchange Control Committee, that we find user relevant reports being produced, almost in spite of the legal codes.

Nevertheless, by establishing a framework for minimum disclosure standards in the Fourth Directive, and for the publication of consolidated group accounts in the Seventh Directive, it could be maintained that the basis for a European accounting system has been laid, and that the danger of a blocking effect being exercised on future developments in corporate financial reporting has been mitigated by Article 2, and is probably of minor significance. As with all general judgments, however, this one also calls for a *caveat*, arising from the Directive of 8 December 1986 on the annual accounts and consolidated accounts of banks and other financial institutions.[38] While extending the accounting disclosure provisions of the Fourth and Seventh Directives to banks and other financial institutions, this directive enshrined the right of banks to create and maintain secret reserves on the same spurious grounds of public confidence which were used in the UK Companies Act 1948 to justify this privilege. The UK clearing banks have voluntarily abandoned the use of secret reserves since the seventies, and suffered no resulting loss of confidence on the part of the public. Similarly, US banks do not appear to be disadvantaged by conforming to GAAP, and report on the normal basis of an "all inclusive concept of income." The EC directive, however, has effectively blocked the demise of this pernicious use of reserve accounting by banks, when it might have otherwise had a greater probability of being abandoned under the influence of international financial market pressures.

[38] O.J. L 372/1 (1986).

VI. Conclusion

Buxbaum and *Hopt* commence Chapter 4 by stating that:[39]

> "[T]he harmonization process by means of Community directives and to a very small extent also of regulations will without doubt go on continuously, even though slowly and piecemeal."

In relation to accounting directives this process seems most likely to involve industry specific directives, e.g., accounting for insurance companies, since the immediate scope of further refinement of the requirements of the Fourth and Seventh Directives would require a level of political commitment which does not appear to exist currently in the member countries. Whether this reflects a general tendency to draw back from further erosions of national sovereignty, or doubts about the economic benefits of harmonization, or perhaps both, is an open question.

Viewed in retrospect it is difficult to find any convincing economic arguments which can be used to justify a conclusion that accounting harmonization through the legal process of EC directives would be either beneficial or necessary to the growth and development of European corporate economic activity. Certainly there is no significant evidence of demand for such a process emanating from European corporations or investors. Further, insofar as the efficient capital markets hypothesis could be deemed to provide an appropriate model for corporate information retrieval in European countries (which is somewhat doubtful), it would not have led to an assumption that the market required the Community to legislate for its greater efficiency. Indeed when European corporations have been motivated to seek funds on domestic or international capital markets, there is clear evidence of gravitation towards the investor orientation of the Anglo-American model of corporate financial reporting. Thus the Italian CONSOB rules pay more homage to this model than to the more macro-oriented model which had previously been favored by legislators. Certainly other claimants for corporate reports, such as employees and their trade unions, have exercised some influence, but overall it appears that the demand for accounting harmonization was politically motivated on the basis that market harmonization throughout Europe would be more readily attainable if the Commission and member governments had access to harmonized information on corporate economic activity. Such a view favors political intervention in economic markets rather than a "hands-off leave it to market forces" approach. In that it better reflects the politico-economic trends of the fifties and sixties rather than those of the eighties.

It is a fact of history that the momentum for harmonizing corporate financial reporting emanated from Commission thinking and objectives of the sixties. The Fourth Directive in particular is a product, albeit much modified, of that period. Whether there exists the momentum for further

[39] BUXBAUM & HOPT, *supra* note 1, at 271.

evolution of harmonized corporate financial reporting within the framework of directives is doubtful. The length of time taken to reach agreement on and implementation of the Fourth and Seventh Directives suggests that directives are at best a questionable vehicle for achieving harmonization of corporate financial reporting. Of course, a framework is now in place for a moderately coherent system of accounting throughout the Community. Nevertheless much of the uniformity which has been introduced is based upon form rather than substance, with the result that the information content of intercountry and interfirm comparisons is highly flawed. There is little doubt that standards of corporate financial reporting will become more comparable in Europe. That process of standardization had been taking place quite independently of EC harmonization, was largely a result of the growing internalization of capital markets, and was being reflected in the ability of companies to conform to the disclosure requirements of the various international capital markets in which they wanted to trade their equity or loan capital. Interestingly, compliance with the accounting directives would not necessarily enable companies to meet those requirements.

Looking to the future the Fourth and Seventh Directives represent a sunk cost. It is of little importance now whether the desired result could have been achieved more efficiently by other means. What is important is that they should not be allowed to act as a blocking mechanism which would inhibit the evolution of corporate information systems which are an ongoing response to a continually changing market place.

B. Discussion

I. Introductory Remarks

Alain Hirsch

Mr. Bertrand d'Illiers has joined us for this topic. He is presently Chief of the Accounting Division at the *Commission des Opérations de Bourse*. We are very happy to have him with us this afternoon, especially because he has worked during the last year in a very important small team, together with securities regulators and the International Accounting Standards Committee (IASC) towards more harmonized and comparable financial statements.

Bertrand d'Illiers

I am very honored to speak here as I am not at all a professor: I am only a practitioner in the field of harmonization of accounting standards, a modest practitioner among many others; for instance, I have taken some responsibility in drawing up the Fourth Directive,[1] together with Prof. Timmermans and afterwards the Seventh Directive.[2] As a representative for France I participate in both the OECD and the UN working groups on accounting and reporting; thus I have a large experience of harmonization from the top in international organizations. However, previously I have been a bank officer, and have experience of the needs of the business community for comparability of financial statements issued by companies; so that I was much interested in the work performed by the accounting profession at the world level, i.e., by IASC.

I think that my best contribution to your work could be focused on two complementary objectives: first to clarify, from my point of view, the criticism addressed to the Fourth and Seventh Directives by Prof. *Buxbaum* and *Hopt* in their book,[3] by Prof. McComb in his contribution[4] and by several participants in the discussion; and secondly to explain what is new and instructive for us in the present process led by IASC in cooperation with the International Organization of Securities Commissions (IOSCO).

[1] O.J. L 222/11 (1978).
[2] O.J. L 193/1 (1983).
[3] R.M. BUXBAUM & K.J. HOPT, *Legal Harmonization and the Business Enterprise* e.g. at 275 ff (Berlin/New York 1988).
[4] See *supra* at 279 ff.

It has been written and said[5] that the Fourth and Seventh Directives are a case of "failure of harmonization," because the values in the balance sheets and the net profit in the income statements will continue to be different even after full implementation of the directives by all Member States. But uniformity of financial statements was not the objective of the directives; it was comparability of information given in the financial statements, including the notes in which the effects of tax laws must be corrected, the effects of revaluations explained with figures, etc. As for the balance sheets and income statements, it is true that the directives focus more on formats to be respected than on valuation and recognition rules; but I do not think that this weakness is a definitive one, and here I am helped by my experience with the French example: this kind of criticism has been addressed in France to the French "General Accounting Plan" for years, with perhaps exactly the same words.

What the French *Plan Comptable* of 1947 has done is mainly to codify formats, exactly what is now said about the Fourth and Seventh Directives; this kind of action has subsequently proved to be a necessary basis which has permitted in-depth progress, year after year, towards common accounting methods. The superficial harmonization of codified formats has helped the French accountants to learn together how to think more and more in similar ways when putting figures on the lines of the uniform balance sheet. Forty years after the adoption of the 1947 *Plan Comptable*, the evolution of the accounting profession had been sufficient to make them able to implement without difficulties the *Loi Comptable* with its complement for consolidated accounts in such a way that comparability between the financial statements of French companies is not superficial but effective. The harmonization process has been performed with the cooperation of time, not against time.

So, when I read[6] that the EC directives have proved to be a failure as regards the accounting harmonization, I cannot agree at all: such a sentence seems to be a definitive judgement, as if we were at the end of the process – which is not at all the case, for the same reasons as in France with the Accounting Plan of 1947.

What is true is that, first, there are too many options in the directives (I shall come back to that point) and, second, even if the European accounting harmonization process will require less time than the French one, it will be too lengthy in view of the rapid evolution of financial markets towards internationalization: multinational offerings of securities as well as quotations on stock exchanges of companies from different countries require comparable financial information; the politics of developing policy mutual recognition of listing or public offering prospectuses require some sort of mutually acceptable accounting standards, as benchmarks for comparisons if not as uniform rules.

[5] See e.g. *supra* at 279 ff.

[6] See *supra* at 285.

Within the EC, the comparability was possible but not easy on account of the number of options, and it was impossible to suppress them in the short term because the directives apply to thousands of small and medium-size companies, which are eager to keep their national accounting practices and for which international comparability has little meaning. On the world level, non-EC countries were not ready to take the directives as a benchmark... How could IOSCO obtain the possibility of developing internationally the mutual recognition of prospectuses in those conditions?

Another organization existed, on the world level, but it was not an intergovernmental body: IASC had been created in 1973 by the accounting professional organizations of the main industrialized countries, it had drawn up and issued some 25 standards, its membership covered more than 50 countries; it was agreed by the OECD and the UN as a consultative body. Its standards did not try to codify formats or terminology but were mainly aimed at formulating principles of valuation and of revenue recognition; they were generally praised, but they could not be regarded as a set of "international accounting principles" because they included many options – not so many as in the directives, but important ones nonetheless. The compliance with the IASC by two companies was not a warranty of comparability between their accounts.

In that period, the late seventies, the situation of IASC was not a good one: its standards had no legal authority, their implementation in a country depending upon (1) the goodwill of the accounting organization of the country, and (2) the degree of involvement of the accounting profession in the national standard-setting process. Around IASC existed on one side the Generally Accepted Accounting Principles (GAAP) of another most powerful country, the USA, which ignored anything else; on the other side, in Europe, a common set of accounting rules was being drawn up, but the process was hardly known outside a limited circle of specialists, as no tangible testimony of common practice was to be seen. The virtue of the EC "approximation of laws" process, that is parallel harmonization of commercial law, company law and accounting law, was not understood. Prospects of harmonization were remote; when the newly created UN Commission of Transnational Corporations wanted to propose some uniformity of reporting and accounting by transnational corporations (TNCs), the model chosen was, evidently, the US GAAP. The IASC catalogue of standards was ignored in the US, despite (or because of) the fact that in every IAS the US way of accounting was always present, either as the only treatment or as one of the agreed options.

In the beginning of the eighties the conditions were changed in the accounting harmonization field because the US discovered that they were not the only country in the world. First they had discovered that the dollar could be weak; after the oil shocks they had understood that money could spring up in Arabic countries rather than in America and that branches of US banks in foreign countries had no right to ignore the law of these countries. In the field of corporate accounting and reporting US businessmen discovered that their subsidiaries in Europe would soon be obliged to publish consolidated statements according to the future Seventh Directive. It was a scandal to see this developing group of countries claiming to impose some accounting obligation on US companies – but that existed. As the US are realistic, they examined and studied the draft Seventh Directive, they discussed it with EC officers in Brussels, the US official and professional bodies: Treasury, SEC, FASB, AICPA, took interest in EC literature, and finally people in the US became mature enough to discuss and negotiate with people outside.

In that context where several sources of accounting principles were recognized, the US accounting bodies began to find interest in the IASC as a meeting place; for years FASB had ignored it, but in 1985 the US began to be represented on the IASC Board by a retired member of FASB, and gradually the presence of FASB increased in the Consultative Group and then on the Board.

Having become stronger, the IASC Board was able to take a decision which required courage, that is to improve the quality of its existing standards by eliminating all free choices between several allowed treatments for similar transactions. The objective is to allow only one treatment, but that is not always possible for two different reasons: first, when national laws and deep-rooted practices prevent the possibility of rapid change: then a transitional period is necessary, with an "allowed alternative treatment" identified as such; in some cases perhaps an in-depth study of the divergence will show that under the same name there are in fact two different kinds of transaction or situation, and that the alternative is not an illicit free choice but the recognition of two phenomena, which are to be named differently.

Of the 27 existing standards 13 have been scrutinized in that way, just eliminating or reducing the options; some other standards are in the process of a full revision and the remaining ones contain no option. The preferred treatment is not necessarily the one which is conceptually the best, but rather the one which IASC believes to be the most appropriate because a general consensus is more probable in favor of it. When an allowed alternative treatment is adopted by a company, it must reconcile its reported net income and shareholders' equity to those that would have been determined using the preferred treatment.

Comments and suggestions are to be addressed to IASC prior to the end of September 1989, in view of an adoption by the Board in the first half of 1990 with implementation beginning on the 1st of January 1991. The temporary period of admittance of the alternative treatments could be perhaps four years, so that in 1995 it is not impossible that every transnational corporation (I use the UN language) and every company issuing multinational offers of securities, every company quoted on several stock exchanges, will publish financial statements conforming to similar standards, with a minimum of necessary reconciliations in the notes.

If this becomes true, it will show how some new sort of harmonization process can succeed, combining impetus from the top (the securities regulators via IOSCO) and impetus from the bottom (the need for comparability by money-suppliers and the desire for lower administrative costs by managers). But I must stress that I am fundamentally optimistic.

Alain Hirsch

Will an agreement within IASC be reached earlier than 1995? Will the implementation take time because multinational companies will recognize only little by little that it is in their best interest to use these harmonized standards? Just to have an idea, when do you reasonably expect IASC to adopt these revised standards?

Bertrand d'Illiers

The set of standards will be issued by IASC in March 1989 as a preliminary draft. It is the beginning of the process of discussion and so on. Afterwards I do not know exactly which will be the time; perhaps one year later, in March 1990, it could be issued as a standard with perhaps the beginning period 1st January 1991, and afterwards I suppose four more years.

Desmond McComb

Perhaps it should be made clear that these are not new standards. This is largely a process of revising existing standards, approximately 20 old standards which are being updated and modified.

Bertrand d'Illiers

It is not quite clear till now if there will be a charge for companies between conforming to the old standards or adopting the new ones, the revised version of the old standards along with the new ones, or if there will be no charge.

Alain Hirsch

I was asked at lunch what is the bulk of the difference between harmonization in the EC and harmonization under the IASC and IOSCO auspices. The bulk of the difference is that the EC harmonization is a mandatory set of rules applicable through national law to all public companies of all member countries, whereas the rules which are now beeing elaborated by IASC together with IOSCO would be purely suggested rules for companies which want to accept them. If I understand well, the most important incentive for these companies to accept them would be if a number of securities commissions of important countries like the United States, Canada, the United Kingdom and Japan said to them: "If your accounts respect this set of standards, you do not need to do anything more if you want to issue bonds or shares in our country."

Robert Austin

I had one comment as a matter of information. The Symposium may be interested to know of a variation of the Canadian way of treating accounting standards which has developed now in Australia. We have set up by statute an Accounting Standards Review Board. It is therefore a public authority, but the membership comprises representatives of business and the accounting profession. And so the standards of overseas accounting bodies and other models which may come from IASC or elsewhere are translated into the Australian setting through the Accounting Standards Review Board. Once there they are required to be complied with as a matter of legislation subject to an overriding true and fair view requirement.

It is interesting that in other respects today we have been talking about the attempt to harmonize from the bottom or from the top within the EC. If you like, what is happening in the accounting area is to an extent harmonization achieved from the "supertop" in the sense that the pressure is coming internationally, particularly in relation to multinational securities issuance.

II. Aims of Accounting and Harmonization

Edmund Kitch

I just want to comment about the American finance literature on accounting which Prof. Meier-Schatz's paper also refers to.[7] The American perspective on all of these matters has to be understood as exclusively a disclosure perspective. We have a field of tax accounting, but it is viewed as such and we are comfortable with the notion that it is an entirely separate matter.

In American academic circles there is considerable contemporary skepticism about the objective of accounting to produce a uniform system for preparing accounts which results in the presentation of single and definitive numbers. It is clear that this procedure serves a lot of interests of businessmen because it gives them clear guidelines as to what figure to present and protects them from challenges on the ground that whatever the figure they presented it was the false or wrong figure, and of course it is a great convenience to the accounting profession because it also gives them clear guidance.

But the finance literature suggests that the markets value companies based on the information which is obtained from sources other than the accounting statements and that much of the most important information

[7] See *supra* at 81 f.

may be obtained elsewhere and that the straitjacket of any single set of accounting conventions may, in fact, necessarily lead to misleading accounting information as to apply to some subset of the economic enterprises. To take American GAAP, there are obvious problems with the valuation of assets, all based on historical cost that suppresses information and hides it from public disclosure. Any information about the current value of assets is not disclosed.

In the takeover environment the offeror may be after the target because the analysis of the offeror leads him to believe that there are unrevealed asset values in the holdings of the target whose value can be captured by a takeover and subsequent market sale of the assets. But the stock market has not appreciated that valuation because the GAAP disclosure suppresses it and may mislead the public shareholders. Not that the choice of cost versus valuation is necessarily the wrong one, but if you are going to make a choice that you will use across the board, you are never going to end up with statements all of which will not be misleading.

This line of thought even suggests a version of accounting in which you would have sort of multiple methods and presentations, perhaps with attached probabilities. You would have not one earning per share which is, of course, the great safe harbour of the brokers and sellers. You can call up the customer and say: "You should buy his company because the earnings last year were $1.37 per share." But you would have a probability distribution. You could say: "Well, we think that his earnings might have been $1.37 with an associated probability."

Needless to say, that form of communicating the information would be incredibly complex and costly. But it would be more accurate. The finance literature has introduced a note of skepticism in the American thinking about accounting which is just a counter-note to these very admirable and ambitious efforts to move everybody towards a single system.

Richard Buxbaum

I would like to make one note variation on Prof. Kitch's point. I hardly think that is a significant problem as to those companies whose shares have a marketplace and therefore have intermediaries who do the normal type of review and analysis. The further down you get into relatively smaller and illiquid companies, it is true that you can have an information deficit created by categories like the one he mentioned, historical cost versus market value, but I do not think there are many others.

There are some sectors, however, as to which accounting concepts have baffled even the experts; for example, in natural resources and particularly in oil. I would say that it is a source of significant debate in American finance circles to this day, and I mean practitioners more than theoreticians, as to how they really are to understand the valuations of major companies. To some degree perhaps in time there should be a sector-specific concern here or there on these issues.

I think that is also going to be a problem as we get into the extreme securitization of assets that has become a feature of modern life. Just to take one example: nowadays there are many companies which have leased back their assets because financial intermediaries, like specialized leasing companies, make a play on the post-depreciation value that they have available. This kind of structure is extremely difficult to capture in traditional accounting, so that the more you get into a kind of double commoditization of the world – I mean into a kind of securitization of assets – the more we have a different concept that is going to become important.

But finally, and this is really the only legitimate intervention, I would like to ask the two experts a simple question, not a trick question: to what degree does the extreme international structure of the accounting profession through the Big Eight, at least in the OECD countries and related major groups, already create a kind of *de facto* uniformity? Because we seem to have left that out, and yet I have to imagine that there is a unifying function there just through those offices.

Christian Meier-Schatz

I would like to emphasize two points both of which were already briefly mentioned in another context.

I am glad that Prof. McComb stressed the different national orientations of disclosure and accounting rules.[8] But I am not so sure whether they are, as his paper indicates,[9] indeed the product of different tendencies of the various interest groups. I rather see them as a result of fundamental differences in perspective of the various regulatory concepts. If you take, for instance, a look at the policy goals of the disclosure rules in the sixties and seventies in Germany around the Mandatory Disclosure Law *(Publizitätsgesetz)*,[10] you begin to realize that its political objectives were incredibly ambitious. The legislators believed that corporate disclosure would not only inform and protect creditors but also workers and the general public. At the same time, these information rules were thought to install a particular technique of public power control over big private corporations. These objectives expressed, I think, the ideological mood of the time, i.e., the famous enterprise law debate (*Unternehmensrechtsdebatte*). This historical experience may offer some interesting insights for the modern discussion as well. It leads, in particular, to the question as to how such differences in legislative concepts and goals influence the harmonization process in the disclosure field.

Now my second point: I have done some research in the disclosure field myself, and I completely share the skepticism with respect to the informational value of traditional accounting information. There are significant

[8] See *supra* at 277 ff.
[9] See *supra* at 268.
[10] Law of 15 August 1969, BGBl. 1969, 1189.

functional limits with respect to informational purposes of accounting and disclosure rules. And they become even more significant when legislators have more ambitious and broader regulatory goals in mind. This provokes a second question with respect to harmonization of disclosure rules: are there any perspectives in the EC of broadening the informational bases beyond traditional accounting data, for instance by introducing new information instruments?[11]

Gérard Hertig

If you look at any tender offer, you see big differences between the pre-offer market price and what is being offered. Now, all those offerors have people who make analyses for them, very sophisticated guys. How can we explain that for a regular investor we have a market value (with the same people making the same analyses with the same books), and then here comes somebody, a raider, and he says: "I am going to offer twice the price?" From that point of view, one is not so much interested in having accounting statements which are clear for the investor, which have to be true or are even comparable from country to country. The main thing then is for one firm to be able to have, across the world and for all subsidiaries, the same accounting practices.

Bertrand d'Illiers

It seems to me useful to stress the fact that the objective of standard-setting, of improving the quality of standards, of harmonizing, etc., cannot be that the financial statements of a company give "the truth" about its situation and allow the reader to determine the value of the enterprise. What is a reasonable objective is to reduce the uncertainties and ambiguities contained in the accounts by the use of a set of accounting conventions upon which a general agreement has been obtained and from which are derived precise standards. Then the financial statements of different companies will give directly the value of a company, even if not its "true profit" – because that does not exist.

About concepts of value and valuation methods, there is no "truth" to be looked for: an enterprise has not one value which exists before we look for it; this is a chimeric idea: the value of a company, at any moment, results from human decisions. The function of accountants is not to indicate a value but to help the reader to be able to use correctly the data presented in the financial statements thanks to clear accounting principles and precise valuation and profit-recognition methods.

[11] See *infra* at 303.

Hartmut Schmidt

I was brought up with the notion that whenever you talk about accounting of companies, you ought to know what aim you are after, and obviously, as Prof. McComb pointed out,[12] there are many aims and each aim requires a different set of accounting rules. And the discussion just about accounting and standardizing of accounting is a discussion which somehow appears to be not really firmly based.

Time is a scarce resource so I will just make one more comment. If you, for example, believe that the information that is being published ought to be useful for shareholders or for potential shareholders, for investors, then you ought to ask first how they are going to value a company. They have to come up with a value. They have to figure out how much they will pay for that share, let us say 525 francs and no more than that. And how do they arrive at this figure? Obviously, they arrive at it by using valuation models and as you probably know there are a number of valuation models around and they are being improved on and they require different information. If you look at the accounting directives you will not find mentioned the information which serves as an input into these models. Of course you may then look for translation models which translate the accounting information into the information that is useful for the valuation models. Finding out what information investors need is obviously a rather complicated process and it is very unlikely that it lends itself to international groups getting together and establishing rules.

Eddy Wymeersch

I would like to express some reservation with respect to the prevailing regulatory pattern in which the accounting or auditing rules are fixed by the professionals themselves. As Prof. Schmidt just mentioned, accounting is a matter of aims, but I would add: aims are very much a matter of the perspective from which you look at things. Accountants, and this seems normal, will look at the issues from their perspective, which is very often the perspective of their masters, i.e., the management. But in practice accounts are used for a variety of purposes and in varying perspectives. Therefore it seems strange that accounts are drafted with an eye on the objectives of one set of users, disregarding the purposes of other people.

I would advocate that accounting rules be framed by a wider group of people, including all possible users of the accounts. This is already done in the Netherlands where a three-party agreement lies at the basis of the accounting board. It would be useful to have this approach extended at the EC level.

[12] See *supra* at 267 ff.

Christian Timmermans

Two remarks on the exposé of Mr. D'Illiers.[13] Really in these matters the international scale of harmonization is much higher, so to say, than the EC level. If I am well informed, there is, however, another body: the OECD, which is also trying to harmonize to some extent the accounting standards. My question is: will that have any practical impact? Because after hearing your exposé on the IASC and the IOSCO attempts I wonder whether that is not double work.

Second remark: the EC is not represented in this effort to come to an adapted version of the IASC standards in order to obtain within the EC mutual recognition of admission to the exchanges. It is not unimaginable that the outcome of this work would not be entirely compatible with the company accounts directives and particularly with the one on consolidated accounts. Then a legal problem will arise because I cannot imagine that the national authorities will be authorized to admit to the listing according to the IOSCO standards, when these standards would be incompatible with the EC directives. Something must be done there. Would it not be better to involve the Community in a much earlier stage, the more so because the Community has exclusive competence in the field of disclosure and accountancy, as has been recognized even by the Council with regard to the OECD activities?

Bertrand d'Illiers

One observation about the differences between EC directives which apply to hundreds of thousands of companies, and the future set of IASC standards which, so far as IOSCO is concerned, will be mandatory for one or a few hundreds of multinational issuers of securities.

First of all, I do hope that there will not be any important divergence that could impair the whole process.

Let us assume that there will be appropriate compatibility. In this case, I think that the experience we have known in France during the last twenty years with the influence of the COB could teach how things will be in the international field with the standards of IASC: in France, the COB is not a standard setter, it issues only "recommendations" (not mandatory) addressed only to quoted companies (their number is nearly 1,000). But as the recommendations of the COB are regarded by the accounting and auditing profession, by company managers and finance executives, by analysts, as sound and appropriate rules of conduct in accounting, a number of unquoted companies conform their accounting methods to the recommendations of the COB. Why should not the same process occur with the IASC standards, if their quality deserves it, in which assumption I am confident? Perhaps in the year 2000 there will be a two-level sort of international

[13] See *supra* at 286 ff.

harmonization of accounting standards, with national and regional (such as EC) standards for everybody, and the IASC system for large companies with transnational activity.

Klaus Hopt

Overall I would not agree that it would have been a good idea to keep the EC Commission out of the field and to leave the harmonization process to market forces.

Look at the German example. In Germany we have complained for decades that we did not really have a general accounting legislation. Everybody agreed that there was a lacuna to be filled. But the legislator just did not move. It was only by the way of the European harmonization that we got the German "Balance Sheet Directive Statute" (*Bilanzrichtlinien-gesetz*).[14] Of course there are now discussions and critiques as to single concepts and provisions of the statute. This is normal. But the critical point is that, for whatever reason, we would just not have brought about such a statute without the intervention of the Commission.

Christian Timmermans

I would like to make two remarks regarding the report of Prof. McComb.

First of all, a comment on his severe criticism with regard to the Fourth Directive not having given us uniform solutions.[15] I think he is quite right there, but the question is whether that was the objective of the Fourth Directive. I would say that as long as these different solutions following a correct implementation of the Fourth Directive still allow us to know exactly what different system has been applied so that the peculiarities of the solution can be traced through the annual reports, the first objective of the Fourth Directive – that is comparability – remains satisfied. So I think the ambition of the Fourth Directive was really much more modest than trying to achieve uniform solutions. It was much more to achieve comparability, and if the information on the divergent solutions as such is correct, that objective is fulfilled.

My second remark concerns your optimism, Prof. McComb,[16] with regard to the harmonization which will indirectly be achieved through the Eighth Directive on the qualification of auditors.[17] I think in that respect I would be more pessimistic. Because what will happen in fact? The accountants will be taught the implementing legislation and national standards as before. They will be taught very divergent interpretations of the true and fair value principle. And as long as they will remain educated in

[14] Now integrated into the German Commercial Code (HGB), Sections 238-339.
[15] See *supra* at 279 ff.
[16] See *supra* at 281.
[17] O.J. L 126/20 (1984).

the national context, I think more or less automatically these divergences, particularly on the so important true and fair value principle, will continue to exist. So I think that in the end we have to come back to the question of substance of whether harmonization should go further in this respect.

Geoffrey Fitchew

I begin with a confession of a high degree of ignorance of the subject, so I will try to say what I think my accounting experts in the DG XV would have said. I think that we would regard it as rather early to evaluate the impact of the Fourth and Seventh Directives. They have only just come into effect in some Member States and I think I am right in saying that the first accounts being produced in conformity with the Fourth Directive will only be emerging in 1988, in some Member States at any rate.

Desmond McComb

It is only from 1988, I think, that all Member States will be producing accounts in conformity with that directive, although Denmark and the UK have by now produced a five year run of conforming accounts, and Belgium, France, Luxembourg and the Netherlands have also complied for the past two or three years.

Geoffrey Fitchew

So I think it is rather early to evaluate the impact of those. Indeed, as I already mentioned,[18] we are thinking of organizing a conference of both governmental experts and the accounting profession towards the beginning of 1990 to try to make a first assessment of the implementation of the Fourth Directive on the basis of a comparison which we are commissioning of the sets of accounts of a number of major companies in different Member States.

Having said that, I think we would agree with the assessment that the Fourth and Seventh Directives were limited first steps aimed at achieving the degree of comparability that Prof. Timmermans described, but nevertheless a first step which has had a healthy impact in raising disclosure standards in a number of Member States.

The question that we are now beginning to ask ourselves is: do we need to go beyond the Fourth and Seventh Directives and, if so, for what purpose and by what methods? There are really two types of development which would lead us to think that perhaps more will be needed in due course.

One is that, partly as a result of the lacunae in the Fourth and Seventh Directives, there is a risk that the degree of convergence and comparability so far achieved could be put at risk through diverging standards and

[18] See *supra* 33.

through diverging treatment of new developments in the real world, of which perhaps the most notable example is the increasing recourse to various forms of off-balance sheet financing, a development which is of concern to accountants in a number of countries.

The second is the drive towards mutual recognition, both within the Community and internationally, in respect of the accounting information to be provided in connection with listings and with public offer prospectuses. We are working within the Community on mutual recognition. There is already agreement on mutual recognition of listing prospectuses and there is the negotiation in progress on mutual recognition of first public offer prospectuses on which the Council of Ministers agreed a "common" position in December 1988.[19] And there is the work that has been described going on in IOSCO and IASC. We are concerned about the risk that the work in IOSCO in particular could lead to the European voice being drowned by the American voice.

In response to both the two factors that I have mentioned – the risk of diverging standards and the wider international work going on – we are beginning to think that we should perhaps move in two directions. One is to develop more detailed accounting requirements for listed companies. It is clear that the SEC requirements for listed companies are much more detailed than the requirements of the Fourth and Seventh Directives. The second option might be to try to move in the direction of a European Accounting Standards Board which would presumably – as in the UK and the USA – primarily be composed of members of the accounting profession. And there it would be possible, I think, to use Commission recommendations as the instrument for promulgating those standards. That is a non-binding recommendation because my impression is that binding legislation would probably not be an appropriate form of instrument to use for standards of this kind which are liable to need to be adapted with changing circumstances in a very flexible kind of way.

III. Various Other Topics

Klaus Hopt

Very briefly: "true and fair view." I remember the bitter fights about this "foreign Anglo-Saxon" concept we had in Germany. Of course now it is beautifully incorporated into the German commercial law statute. But I tell you, not much has changed. Everything is more or less like before. This is true even in the book: the new statutory text[20] is generally interpreted in the light of the old legal situation. Even less has changed in the actual accounting process. Part of this is because there is really nobody who could

[19] Directive adopted in 1989: see O.J. L 124/8 (1989).
[20] Particularly Section 264, Subsection 2 of the Commercial Code (HGB).

challenge this important practical deviation from European law. So the (apparent) harmonization achieved seems to satisfy everybody. This is one of these instances where one can really say: "What about a homogeneous administration of the harmonized law?"

Apart from this, there is a problem which already arises in the legislative process. I mean the danger of being misled by seemingly the same or similar legal concepts. These are the so-called "*faux amis*" which we all know from translation work. It is not specific to legal harmonization.

Christian Timmermans

Prof. McComb, I have two minor remarks on what you have said in your report about the situation in the Netherlands, and I was quite grateful that you have said something about the situation in my country. First of all, you have observed[21] that the national standards of the accounting standards setting body in the Netherlands are binding. I must say they are only binding in the view of that particular body because the prevailing opinion of the lawyers is that they are not binding. But I agree with you that a different opinion is sometimes presented in the accountancy literature.

A rather interesting incident which you have mentioned[22] is the ministerial decree declaring the consolidated accounts of non-EC groups which conform to the international accounting standards compatible and comparable with the Seventh Directive. That has been for most interested people in the Netherlands a surprising action by the Minister of Justice and there has been severe criticism also by the European Commission – and I think quite correctly because this is in fact not a mere matter of judgement for the Dutch Government: whether the IASC standards conform to the Seventh Directive is really a EC matter.

The legal consequences of that are rather important because according to our Companies Act this will allow an exemption from subconsolidation as long as the consolidated accounts of this third country group conform to the international standards. But if I am well informed, this will be deleted from existing legislation after the protest we have received from the European Commission. So what you have said on the binding effect of the International Accounting Standards under our law is really true, but only for a short time.

Eddy Wymeersch

The legal consequences of consolidated accounts seem to be very limited.

This view is accepted in most if not all legal systems in Western Europe. At least in my country, it is largely accepted today that consolidated accounts have a merely informative function, and have no further legal

[21] See *supra* at 272.
[22] See *supra* at 274.

effects. So, e.g., they cannot be used to indicate the amount of distributable profits, although the question has effectively been raised, expressly referring to the regulations that have been introduced in a couple of American States. Also, it is not admitted that the mere inclusion of a subsidiary in consolidated annual accounts will constitute a basis for rendering the parent liable for the subsidiary's debts. In some circumstances, however, for instance when the subsidiary had a negative net worth and was nevertheless included in the parent's consolidation, this may constitute an indication of the parent's will to support its subsidiary further.[23]

IV. Concluding Remarks

Desmond McComb

Thank you for your very helpful comments upon my paper. While each of you has emphasized particular problem areas I think it is possible to identify certain common themes which have linked some individual comments. Of these the most prevalent have been the related problems of income measurement and asset valuation. Allied to these has been the question of the validity of the historical cost accounting model, and the feasibility of potentially more relevant alternative models such as current cost. National perceptions of goals and aims of accounting and their relevance to the international harmonization of corporate financial reporting was also an issue which some of you addressed. This latter can also be related to national interpretations of the "true and fair view" clause (Art. 2(3)) of the Fourth Directive.

Before discussing these issues I think it is important to emphasize the context of corporate financial reporting to external users within which our discussions are constrained. In other words we are not concerned with what is technically possible, but rather with what is feasible in that context. It is important that we recognize that in this situation accounting information is not a free good. It must be paid for by the reporting corporations, both directly, in that accounting and auditing services are an expensive commodity, and indirectly, in that information disclosed by a corporation may be used by competitors to their own advantage and the reporting corporation's disadvantage. In the latter case it is even arguable that the provision of certain additional information to existing shareholders may operate to their disadvantage. In evaluating the quality of financial disclosure, therefore it needs to be emphasized that we are not concerned with an ideal world of costless information provided to disinterested seekers after knowledge, but rather with one in which information provided to shareholders of a

[23] For further details, see our study "Ondernemingsdiscontinuiteit in groepsverband," in *Ondernemingsdiscontinuiteit* 79-145 (H. Biron ed., Antwerpen 1984).

corporation is also available to the public at large, including corporate predators.

Published financial reports are frequently criticized for their failure to provide sufficient information to enable users to value the accounting entity concerned. Such criticism has validity if it is related to the value which an investor might attach to a shareholding in a particular corporation, compared to market values of alternative investments. Accounting income and valuation measurements are made within the going concern convention under which it is assumed that the entity is going to continue in existence in its present form for an indefinite future period, and an investor should arguably be able to use such information as a guide to an investment decision. Financial reports do not, however, provide information which has direct relevance to values which might be placed upon a corporation in the context of mergers or takeovers, and they are not designed to do so. It is unfortunate then that very real deficiencies in accounting models are often overshadowed by mistaken criticisms made in these situations. Published periodic accounts cannot provide valuations which are relevant to such events since the values arrived at in any individual merger or takeover are specific to that situation, and cannot be estimated out of context.

The usefulness of the historical cost accounting model as a basis for measuring values and arriving at credible estimates of periodic income, and the feasibility of using alternative models based upon current purchasing power has been the subject of much debate and experimentation over the last two decades. Some of your comments[24] have indicated a preference for a current value model, and these would indeed find an echo in much of the academic and professional accounting literature. There are strong arguments in support of this model, based upon a concept of asset value in the context of replacement of productive capacity, and during the period of rising global inflation in the seventies and early eighties it found many adherents. It also became a model for corporate financial reporting in a number of countries, in which current cost accounts were required to be published along with, or in place of, historical cost accounts.

Interestingly, with the fall in rates of inflation worldwide we find that there has also been a decline in the demand for current cost information and evidence that where it was available little use was being made of it by investors or analysts. The much maligned historical cost model seems in fact to have been preferred once inflation had fallen to modest levels. The moral would appear to be that users of accounting reports prefer the greater verifiability and reliability of historical cost accounts to the higher level of relevance claimed to be an advantage of current cost accounting.

Prof. Kitch has draw our attention[25] to claims in the finance literature which would suggest that markets value companies on the basis of information obtained from sources other than accounting statements.

[24] See e.g. *supra* at 292.
[25] See *supra* at 291.

Clearly investors will use all information which is available to them but – despite the frustrations which we all experience with regard to the inadequacies of published accounts – I think it is only fair to say that they represent the main coherent source of financial information about corporate activity. They cannot and should not be expected to be sources of information about, for example, production developments and market conditions.

However there is clearly room, as Prof. Meier-Schatz has implied,[26] for improving the quality of accounting information by broadening and refining the information base.

Prof. Buxbaum has indeed drawn attention[27] to one area of accounting with regard to oil exploration where some highly innovative probability statements have been suggested in the US, and in the UK proposals have been made for value based statements of financial position. It seems unlikely however that these will be incorporated into the regulatory system for corporate financial reporting in the countries concerned. Even less likely is the prospect that they will become the subject of an IASC standard or an EC directive. However, some of the inadequacies which from time to time surface in traditional accounting arise from a failure to appreciate the impact of new industrial processes or novel financing techniques.

Mr. Fitchew has drawn attention[28] to a contemporary problem which exists in accounting for off-balance-sheet financing. These deficiencies relate to the methodologies of accounting rather than to the historical cost accounting model, which is perfectly capable of providing better information on such financial devices. This issue of accounting for off-balance-sheet financing could indeed provide a prime subject for harmonized regulation within the European Community, or through the issue of an International Accounting Standard.

Quite a number of you[29] spoke on the significance for harmonized corporate financial reporting of differences in national perceptions of the aims of accounting and expectations of users of accounting reports in various countries. I would agree that this is probably the most difficult hurdle which has to be crossed in the international harmonization of corporate financial reporting. It has been a particular problem in the context of the European Community, where the aims and expectations have traditionally varied from one country to another. Thus the French *Plan Comptable* had its origins in 1947 as a part of the National Economic Plan. As such it was designed primarily with the information needs of government economists and planners in mind. It has been modified over the years and now has a greater degree of investor orientation, but nevertheless it could not be regarded as being primarily directed to investor/shareholder

[26] See *supra* at 294.
[27] See *supra* at 292.
[28] See *supra* at 299.
[29] See e.g. *supra* at 295 f and 300.

information needs as exemplified by the US/UK model. Again the German model of corporate financial reporting has reflected the unique relationship between banks and industry and commerce and their importance as sources of finance for long-term investment. Also the system whereby a common basis of accounting for tax and financial reporting is required by law in Germany creates a situation in which precedence must be given to compliance with legal codes over all other criteria. As Prof. Hopt has pointed out[30] the German interpretation of the "true and fair" clause in the Fourth Directive has reflected that unique approach.

For all these reasons the scope for harmonized corporate financial reporting in Europe is, I think, limited for the present to the fairly modest objectives referred to by Prof. Timmermans,[31] and I would agree with him that comparability of form is a real step forward. However I should emphasize that if harmonization is to be only at this level it could end up with a delusion of comparability.

I would like to conclude by referring to Mr. Fitchew's comments,[32] if for no other reason than that the EC harmonization is central to our discussion; I have already referred to his comments on accounting for "off-balance-sheet financing" and I accept that issues such as this could be addressed by the Commission through the use of recommendations.

The idea that the Commission might sponsor a European Accounting Standards Board is however one which I would approach with caution. For all practical purposes international harmonization of accounting is a waste of time unless the major industrial countries of the world are part of that process. So I could see a future for a standards board set up under the auspices of the EC, but not one which would try to issue standards simply because it seemed feasible to negotiate them on a European basis. I would rather see the arguments over standards thrashed out at IASC level and then filtered down the line by the European Commission. Perhaps indeed the EC could become an active participant in IASC matters through the FEE, and this would seem a particularly opportune time to do so since the FASB is now at last beginning to show an interest in, and a willingness to cooperate in, the international standard setting process, and has established a close relationship with the IASC. My reason for caution with regard to European standards is that they might encourage an inward looking attitude which would run contrary to the process of international harmonization of accounting which has been gathering momentum since the seventies.

Geoffrey Fitchew

I certainly did not mean to suggest that the European Accounting Standards Board would operate in isolation from or would seek to ignore or act as a

[30] See *supra* at 299 f.
[31] See *supra* at 297.
[32] See *supra* at 298 f.

rival to efforts to harmonize at the international level and I do not think there is any necessary conclusion to that effect that can be drawn. But I think it is important that there should be a strong European voice in the setting of international accounting standards.

Chapter Eight

Capital Market and Securities Regulation in the Light of the Recent British Experience

A. Report: L.C.B. Gower

It is a daunting task to comment critically (as we have been asked to do) on the themes and conclusions of Prof. *Buxbaum* and *Hopt* in their massive contribution.[1] The basic aim of the book (I hope the authors will not quarrel too violently with this summary) is to identify what lessons from the USA's experience in harmonizing the companies and securities laws of its member States could be learnt by the EC in relation to its aim progressively to complete by 1993 a single integrated European market "without internal frontiers in which the free movement of goods, persons, services and capital is ensured."[2] The book's emphasis is therefore on harmonization (rather than on other contemplated means of establishing the single market, such as the removal of restraints on freedom of establishment, freedom of capital movements and freedom to provide services), and on harmonization of company law and capital market and securities regulation (rather than of non-financial services).

My allotted task is to comment, in the light of the British experience, on capital markets and securities regulation. The book handles that topic relatively briefly.[3] It seems clear, however, that the authors regard most of their main conclusions on company and business enterprise law as equally applicable. Accordingly, I start with a few general comments on the book and on those conclusions.

[1] R.M. BUXBAUM & K.J. HOPT, *Legal Harmonization and the Business Enterprise* (Berlin/New York 1988).

[2] Art. 8A of Treaty of Rome, inserted by the Single European Act (*Bull. EC*, Supp. 2/1986) supplementing the original Art. 8.

[3] And in Chapter 2 (*cf.* BUXBAUM & HOPT, *supra* note 1, at 130) almost apologetically:
"This is a field not usually thought of as part of corporation law, but both because of its substantial overlap with the traditional subject and because of its European doctrinal unification with company law in the larger subject of enterprise law its American scope should at least briefly be discussed."

I. General Comments

The *Buxbaum* and *Hopt* book has four chapters. Following an introductory Chapter 1 of 22 pages, Chapter 2 deals in 140 pages with "The American Experience," Chapter 3 in 102 pages with "European Harmonization Efforts," and a final Chapter 4, of 16 pages, helpfully summarizes the main conclusions. An explicit assumption runs throughout, that the Community is a federal institution (albeit an incomplete one) and that the Treaty of Rome is a federal constitution (and indeed, that "at the direct textual level the constitutional acts[[4]] are similar"[5]), and likewise an implicit assumption that therefore it is likely that the long experience of the USA, the father of modern federal constitutions, will be valuable in helping to solve the fledgling Community's problems.

The authors admit that the contrasts between the USA and the EC may be so great as to invalidate these assumptions, and they rightly point out that, even so, their study would have been worthwhile in establishing that contrast.[6] I have never doubted that the American experience will be valuable. But the authors have failed to convince me that the lessons for harmonization which should or will be learnt relate to the resolution of constitutional problems or to the criteria, methods and tools to be employed in achieving harmonization. And it is to these that Chapter 2 is largely devoted.[7] I believe that the value of the American experience will relate instead to the solutions to be achieved in harmonization (especially in relation to capital markets and securities regulation); in other words, the American experience exemplifies what should result from harmonization rather than the methods of accomplishing it or the resolution of constitutional problems met on the way. Having said that, I must attempt to justify it.

A. Constitutional Law

One who does not pretend to be a constitutional lawyer is rash indeed to stray into the territory of those who actually are. But it seems to me that, while the Treaty of Rome establishes the European Community as an international organization which is a *sort* of federal body, it is a sort very different from the USA, and that the Treaty of Rome is a very different sort of constitution from that of the USA or of other federal *States*. Federal constitutions divide legislative competence between the federal organs and the State organs. The Treaty of Rome does not seem to me to do that.

[4] I.e., the Treaty of Rome and the American Constitution.

[5] BUXBAUM & HOPT, *supra* note 1, at 4.

[6] *Id.* at 22.

[7] *Id.* at 164:

"The principal purpose of the foregoing study ... has been to introduce enterprise law to constitutional law in a federal setting."

Instead, it lays down the aims of the Community, enacts directly some of the legal provisions needed to achieve those aims, and confers wide powers on the organs of the Community to legislate to achieve the others. So far as the Single European Market is concerned, the aim is reasonably clear and the powers needed to achieve it seem to be ample, especially now that the Single European Act is in force. I do not know of any proposals in this area which have been abandoned, or of any directives or regulations which have been struck down, on the ground that they were unconstitutional as beyond the Community's powers. Proposals, while in the pipeline, have been opposed as unnecessary or misguided (the UK has constantly done so), but once adopted they have been implemented sooner or later (by the UK sooner than by most others). I would not expect this to change, even if use is made of the increased powers, conferred as a result of the Single European Act, to proceed by measures not requiring unanimity. The only constitutional law problem that I know to have arisen is that certain Member States have used, as an excuse for not implementing particular Community legislation, the alleged fact that under the States' constitutions they have no power to do so. The legal position, however, seems clearly to be that this is not a valid excuse and that the Community has ample powers to ensure that, *de jure*, Community law and Community obligations have supremacy over national laws. If, *de facto*, States adamantly refuse to comply, the only, and chilling, lesson to be learnt from the American experience seems to be that the ultimate solution is civil war, not constitutional law.

Buxbaum and *Hopt* emphasize particularly the relevance of the Commerce Clause of the American Constitution and of the jurisprudence upon it. Admittedly, Europe is faced with the same basic problem as was the USA; namely, how to reconcile the national feelings and pride of the Member States with the needs and aspirations of a wider multinational Community. The Commerce Clause was designed to aid that reconciliation. Perhaps Europe could have learnt more from this clause in deciding upon its harmonization priorities. And, as stressed by Prof. *Buxbaum*,[8] the jurisprudence on it could well be of doctrinal value to the European Court in the evolution of coherent principles concerning the direct effect of provisions of the Treaty on public and private rights. But, except to that limited extent, I remain skeptical about the relevance of American constitutional law to a European harmonization programme intended to be completed before 1993. It may well have greater relevance to other programmes, especially when the Community embarks (successfully, I hope, whatever Mrs. Thatcher may say) on efforts to convert itself from a Common Market to a United States of Europe.

[8] See *supra* at 22.

B. Criteria

In Chapter 1,[9] the authors make the point that, just as the founding fathers of a truly federal constitution ought to have a consistent theory on which to base the criteria determining the division of powers between federal and State organs, so *ideally* ought the Community to have such a theory on which to base decisions on what needs to be harmonized, and what does not. And I expect that they are right in saying that:[10]

> "It is clear that in the European Community of today the institutions responsible for the harmonization of law have not yet even taken up those bits and pieces of any theory which might be helpful to that effort. Instead, they explicitly understand themselves to be political actors, rather than social engineers, and seem more inclined to reach politically feasible compromises at the outset rather than to construct a theoretically optimal dual legislative system in this field."

But, since the authors concede that "it is still unclear whether any existing economic or political theory of integration is already able to offer"[11] such a model, it seems a bit harsh to criticize the hard-pressed officials of the Commission for failing to cobble together "the bits and pieces" of the various models that have been suggested[12] and to try to sell to the Member States the result of their (inevitably lengthy) cerebrations. The British experience of trying to unify English (common) law and Scots (civil) law is that although it is easy to obtain agreement on the optimum solution it is virtually impossible to get agreement on the theoretical basis for that solution.[13] If European harmonization had to await European acceptance of a theoretical model, I suspect that few of us would live to see it.

C. Methods and Tools

I have doubts also about the practicability of importing American methods and tools as an aid to European harmonization. The views of *Buxbaum* and *Hopt* on this aspect of their subject can, I think, be summarized as follows:

(a) So far, the progress of harmonization in the Community has been painfully and disappointingly slow.
(b) It is wholly unrealistic to suppose that the Internal European Market will be completed by the end of 1992.

[9] BUXBAUM & HOPT, *supra* note 1, at 15.
[10] *Id.* at 15.
[11] *Id.* at 15.
[12] *Id.* at 8-14.
[13] On the establishment of the English and Scottish law Commissions in 1965, they agreed that, in the light of the likely accession of the United Kingdom to the EC, among their first projects should be the production of a uniform Code of Contract for England and Scotland. It broke down not because there was disagreement on what the law should be but because it was impossible to agree on the reasoning.

(c) As much, or more, progress is likely to be achieved by an approximation resulting from States' actions (harmonization from below) rather than from Community action (harmonization from above).
(d) The methods employed in the USA should be examined to see whether they could not usefully be employed in relation to harmonization upwards or downwards.

My comment on (a), the first of these propositions, is that although progress has indeed been slow, what is surprising to me is that it has not been slower. Any form of law reform is painfully slow and that which involves harmonization of the laws of States with different legal roots is slowest of all. Considering the inevitable dislocations caused when new Member States have been admitted, I find it remarkable that so much progress has been made.[14]

As regards (b), I agree that it is unrealistic to suppose that the internal market programme will be fully *completed* by 1993. But I think that the book underestimates the head of steam that is now behind the programme in the Commission and the degree of enthusiasm for it displayed by Member States. Cynics may dismiss Article 8A and the Declaration accompanying the Single European Act affirming the political will, as lip-service to a pipedream. But, in this case, that is not this cynic's impression. I detect genuine enthusiasm in informed circles, manifested even in countries where I would least have expected to find it. Clearly, full harmonization to the extent that is *ideal* will not have been achieved, but I think that there is a fair chance that the Community will have adopted most of the measures which are *necessary*, even if all Member States have not actually implemented them by the target date.[15] Clearly, however, that would not be so if the initiative were left to Member States, rather than to Community organs, as suggested in proposition (c). That would take a century or more and even then harmonization to a standard anything like the optimum would be unlikely.

As regards proposition (d), many of the methods and tools which have been employed in the USA, and which are mentioned in Chapter 2 (such as the Restatements and other activities of the American Law Institute, the Model Business Corporation Act of the American Bar Association, and the

[14] E.g., in relation to harmonized prudential regulation of banks, insurance companies and unit trusts, and in company law and in stock exchange listing.

[15] I share the authors' doubts whether most of the unadopted company law draft directives are *necessary* to achieve a single market. Of the two in the pipeline which are least likely to be adopted by 1993, the Fifth and the envisaged Ninth, the latter (on groups) seems to me to be the more vital, but, as the book says, it is not satisfactory in its present form (BUXBAUM & HOPT, *supra* note 1, at 223-224), and the German law on which it is based "is commonly regarded as well-meant, but inefficient" (*id.* at 217). But it will, I think, be difficult to solve the problems which the programme faces in relation to conglomerates unless there is some satisfactory harmonization on groups.

activities of the Commissioners for Uniform State Laws) are admirable – and are widely admired in Europe. But, in suggesting that they might be adopted in the Community, I think that the book fails to give sufficient weight to the differences between the USA and the Community. The United States have a common language and, except to some extent in the case of Louisiana, a common legal heritage.[16] The Community does not enjoy either. This makes a difference to the practicalities that can hardly be exaggerated.

Nor am I convinced that the Community's methods for consultation on proposals differ greatly from, or are less extensive than, those used in the USA. At the Community level the consultations with "experts," officials, ministers and representatives seem to me to be almost too extensive and time-consuming and I would prefer to see a streamlining, rather than a proliferation, of the Community's legislative processes. It is true that consultation with the public and professional bodies in each Member State is largely left to that Member State; but, in the United Kingdom, the Department of Trade and Industry certainly does a good job in this respect (without always getting the response that it deserves). The suggestion that the Commission should organize formal *public* meetings[17] on its proposals is not one which would arouse enthusiasm in the United Kingdom; the British experience is that such meetings are largely a waste of time except, occasionally, as a public relations exercise.

Doubtless the authors are right in saying that, in the USA,[18]

> "the very existence of a federal judiciary that reaches to the level of trial courts in every significant American locality ... in its focus on federal law becomes a resource or magnetic point around which the otherwise centrifugal local profession develops a federal outlook by proxy."

But if they are really advocating the adoption, by the Community, of the dual system of federal and State trial courts in each country, with all the American jurisdictional and other frills, I can only say that I recoil in horror. It is, I would have thought, one of the three worst features of the American legal system,[19] and it is part of the American model which other federal constitutions have rejected.

However, if there is one respect above all others in which America seems superior, it is in the quality and quantity of initial research and in the financial and manpower resources which it is prepared to devote to it. One of the great contributions that the book will make is that it shows what can be done and what insights can result when the research is undertaken as a joint European/American operation.

[16] So do most federal States. Two exceptions are Switzerland and Canada which might in some respects be closer analogues.

[17] See BUXBAUM & HOPT, *supra* note 1, at 287.

[18] *Id.* at 283.

[19] The other two being the civil jury and elected State judges.

II. Capital Market and Securities Regulation

A. The British Experience

In commenting on the authors' treatment of this aspect of their subject, I am instructed to do so "in the light of the British experience." That, I take it, refers principally to two interrelated events: (1) the transformation that has occurred with startling rapidity of the organization and practices of the British capital markets – a transformation which has come to be described (at any rate in the United Kingdom) as *Big Bang* – and (2) the introduction of a comprehensive system of regulation of the financial services industry under the Financial Services Act 1986.

Big Bang was basically an exercise in *de*-regulation, the regulations destroyed being, in the main, restrictive rules and practices imposed not by law but by trade and professional bodies (particularly the Stock Exchange[20]) to protect their members and their near-monopolies. These restrictions had to be removed if the City of London was to maintain and enhance its position as a major financial center and as the European pillar of the developing 24-hour global capital market.

Equally, it had long been recognized that the United Kingdom lacked an up-to-date system of securities regulation affording adequate protection for investors and, in 1981 (when *Big Bang* was still undreamt of) I had been commissioned by the Government to undertake a wide-ranging one-man review and to advise on new legislation.[21] The need for this became more acute once *Big Bang* burst and, by the Financial Services Act 1986, my recommendations were enacted with an alacrity and to an extent which, until then, I had never envisaged as likely.[22] Under the Act it is a criminal offense to carry on in the United Kingdom investment business (an expression widely defined[23]) unless duly authorized. Authorization may be granted by the top regulatory body, the Securities and Investments Board

[20] Its Rulebook had been referred, in 1979, to the Restrictive Trade Practices Court but, by 1983, the case was still unheard. The out-of-court settlement of that reference in 1983 led immediately to the beginning of the transformation completed on *Big Bang Day* (27 October 1986).

[21] For the products of this, see: *Review of Investor Protection: A Discussion Document* (January 1982, HMSO); *Review of Investor Protection: Report Part I* (January 1984, Cmnd 9125); *Report Part II* (May 1985, HMSO) and the Government's White Paper *Financial Services in the United Kingdom: A New Framework for Investor Protection* (January 1985, Cmnd 9432).

[22] Particularly as I had been frankly warned that one of the Government's reasons for choosing a one-man review rather than the traditional 12-man departmental committee was that it would make it easier to reject the report if the Government did not like it.

[23] "Investment" includes shares, bonds, warrants, units, options, futures (financial or commodity) contracts for differences and long-term life insurance; and "investment business" includes dealing, arranging deals in, managing, or advising on investments, and operating a collective investment scheme.

(SIB), the members of which are appointed and may be dismissed by the Secretary of State and the Governor of the Bank of England acting jointly, or obtained through membership of a self-regulatory organization (SRO) recognized by SIB.[24] In the conduct of investment business, firms are subject to the provisions of the Act, to the regulations made thereunder by the Secretary of State or SIB and to the rules of their authorizing body which, in the case of an SRO, must provide investor protection equivalent to the rules of SIB. The system is essentially one of statutory regulation, but with considerable practitioner input and some reliance on self-regulatory bodies for the monitoring of their members' continued fitness and compliance with the rules. This surveillance by the SROs of their member firms is matched by the surveillance of the SROs by SIB.

That brief and over-simplified account of the events and of the resulting legislation must suffice for present purposes.[25] Here I need only to draw attention to what, as I see it, are their implications for the Community's harmonization programme in relation to the single (financial services) European market.

B. Implications for the Harmonization Programme

(1) I was specifically instructed in relation to my Review "to take account of relevant developments in the European Community." Up to 1981, such "developments" had been mainly in the fields of banking, insurance, the listing directives and the (then) draft UCITS Directive. The Commission was only just beginning to plan an extension of its programme into other areas such as the regulation of brokers, dealers, investment managers and investment advisers. Copies of my initial Discussion Document were sent to the Commission and I met with the relevant Directorates and the Secretariat. They assured me that the general lines of the Document were in accord with their thinking.[26] Thereafter I kept in close touch with them by further meetings and correspondence. So, of course, did the Department of Trade and Industry in relation to *Big Bang*, to the Government's White Paper and to the Bill which became the Financial Services Act. Great care

[24] There are at present five recognized SROs plus a member of "recognized professional bodies" (RPBs) through which members regulated by such bodies (e.g. the law societies and the accountancy bodies) can obtain authorization to carry on investment business if that does not constitute a major part of their professional work. RPBs have to adopt rules equivalent to those of SIB.

[25] I gave my personal account of them in a lecture delivered in the Summer of 1987, "Big Bang and City Regulation," published in 51 *M.L.R.* 1 (1988).

[26] They expressed particular gratitude for the Discussion Document which, they said, had enabled them for the first time to understand what the regulatory position was in the United Kingdom and they lamented that they lacked similar reviews of the position in other Member States. But when I suggested that they might commission such studies, they replied that they could not afford it: "Do you not realize that our budget is less than that of the Hampshire County Council?"

was taken to ensure that the Act fully complied with our Community obligations. For example, it provides for automatic authorization of firms not transacting business from a permanent place of business in the United Kingdom, if established in another Member State and formally authorized there under provisions which afford investors in the United Kingdom adequate protection or which satisfy the conditions of a relevant harmonization directive;[27] and it affords further concessions to insurance companies[28] and collective investment schemes[29] established and authorized in another Member State.

(2) Although the *methods* employed to bring about the transformations resulting from *Big Bang* and from the Financial Services Act owed nothing to "the American experience" (and were doubtless deserving of the strictures which *Buxbaum* and *Hopt* apply to the Commission for behaving as "political actors" rather than as "social engineers"[30]), there was nevertheless very extensive borrowing of American solutions. Indeed, the framework of the new regulatory system is based firmly on "the SEC model" (though it was thought politic not to emphasize that), and many provisions of the Act and of the regulations and rules made under it are borrowed from the American securities legislation or from rules of the SEC or NASD. The main respect in which it differs is that greater emphasis is placed on the regulation of those who are engaged in retail marketing of investments and in advising the public on investments.

(3) One result of these developments is that, at present, the United Kingdom has, I would suppose, capital markets better adapted to play a role in the developing global market and freer from restrictive membership and other rules than those of other Member States. However, a combination of pressure from the Commission acting under the anticompetition Articles 85-90 of the Treaty and of self-interest of Member States (the authors' "harmonization from below") might narrow that gap without further Community legislation (unless some Member States see their self-interest as best served by restricting their capital markets to domestic and European activity, abjuring any role in a wider international market).

(4) The other result of the developments is that the United Kingdom now has unquestionably a more comprehensive and sophisticated system of securities regulation than other Member States – some of which have no regulation at all of several areas of investment business. This has consequences which may or may not be helpful to the Commission. If the British solutions are in accord with the Commission's views, it has a model, acceptable to it, to which it could require the others to conform. In this it would obviously have the wholehearted support of the United Kingdom –

[27] Financial Services Act 1986, c.60, Section 31.

[28] Financial Services Act 1986, c.60, Sections 22 and 130(2).

[29] Financial Services Act 1986, c.60, Sections 24 and 86.

[30] See *supra* at 310. But I think BUXBAUM & HOPT would have commended the extent of the consultations.

which the Commission might find a pleasant change from our customary opposition to the Commission's proposals (until they are adopted). It would also have the long-term advantage that it would bring the EC closer to the American model adopted with variations in the major financial centers outside Europe.[31] Such a convergence would help to avoid the danger that an internal European financial market might become insulated by a *cordon sanitaire* from the developing global market, and thus become a stagnant backwater to the detriment of the European economy and European investors. It should also be welcomed by both of the common law Member States, which have found, to their regret, that their corporation and business enterprise law is increasingly diverging from that of other common law countries as a result of company law directives largely influenced by civil law doctrines. That trend is irreversible in relation to company law but it need not be extended to capital market and securities regulation where, conceivably, a single worldwide harmonized system might ultimately evolve.

(5) If, on the other hand, the Commission were to take the view that it is impracticable to harmonize upwards to that extent and instead were to decide to put forward less comprehensive proposals, harmonization would clearly take longer and, if the United Kingdom had to dismantle or truncate the system which it has labored to install over the past seven years, it would face bitter British opposition.

(6) In advocating the adoption of harmonization based on the British version of the American model, I am not suggesting that this version could not be improved upon. The United Kingdom is well aware that it has not yet perfected the system, and any help that the Commission and other Member States can give to improve it will be warmly welcomed. The main criticism voiced in the United Kingdom is that the Financial Services Act and the rules and regulations made under it are excessively detailed, complicated and legalistic. There is some validity in this criticism. It is impossible to prevent law from being legalistic, but British legislation always tends to be excessively detailed and complicated (in a vain attempt to make it "judge-proof"), and in this instance that flaw was aggravated by pressure from various interests within the financial services industry to introduce exceptions and qualifications to meet their peculiar circumstances. Recent EC directives have not wholly avoided that danger,[32] but I am sure that the Commission and other Member States will succeed in avoiding it more successfully than we did under the pressure to get the new system up-and-running in time to deal with the increased conflicts of interests arising from *Big Bang*. Happily SIB is, at present, reviewing the whole of its Rulebook in an attempt to make it more like EC directives are

[31] And which, I would have thought, has already had some influence on developments in the French *Commission des Opérations de Bourse* and the Belgian *Commission Bancaire*.

[32] See *infra* at 317 ff.

supposed to be:[33] i.e. prescription of the ends to be achieved rather than of the detailed means of achieving them.

(7) To my mind an even more serious flaw in the new British system is insufficient built-in flexibility. The experience of securities commissions in other parts of the world, and of the British Takeover Panel, makes it clear that maximum flexibility is essential and that regulating bodies should be empowered to grant "permissions" and to issue "no-action letters." Seemingly the Financial Services Act does not enable SIB to do that.[34] Instead, to deal with exceptional and deserving cases, all it can do is to amend its rules. This it can do speedily in an emergency, but the result is to complicate its Rulebook with still further exceptions and qualifications designed to accommodate a single firm or a unique situation. The Community should avoid this error.

(8) Hence I am suggesting that the United Kingdom now has a well tried model, which it believes it has adapted to suit European conditions in a way which will help to coordinate European capital market and securities regulation with a global market and the internationalization of investments and investment business. If the whole Community is to achieve the needed harmonization by 1992, it might, I suggest, build on that experience. In other words, it should take "one more leaf from the American experience" by using an individual State (the United Kingdom) as one of the "laboratories of the law."[35]

C. Comments on the Authors' Views

1. Overly Specific Directives

Buxbaum and *Hopt* point out that:[36]

> "Many directives and draft directives contain very detailed provisions indeed that leave only a ministerial role to the Member States in transforming them into national law. This is particularly true for much of company and capital market law harmonization."

[33] But often are not; see *infra* at 317 f.

[34] There seems to be nothing to prevent the recognized SROs from framing their rules in the form of "Without the permission of [the SRO] member firms shall not ..." and to some extent they have. This destroys one of the arguments advanced against conferring a similar power (which indeed the DTI had, and usefully exercised under the former Section 14 of the Prevention of Fraud (Investments) Act 1958 (6 & 7 Eliz. 2, c.45)), namely that it would be improper for SIB to exercise such a power since it might deprive investors of their civil remedy for breach of the rules: see *infra* 321 f.

[35] See BUXBAUM & HOPT, *supra* note 1, at 286.

[36] *Id.* at 233.

This is undoubtedly the case, and one could add to the examples they quote the listing directives,[37] which were regarded by the British Government as sufficiently specific to permit their initial implementation by regulations[38] which, in effect, adopted them verbatim as the law of the United Kingdom and repealed or disapplied any inconsistent existing legislation. Although the authors are obviously unhappy about the tendency towards specificity, they rightly say that it "is a legal phenomenon which is commonly accepted practice today."[39]

I personally am not so worried by the increased specificity. Admittedly it has made something of a nonsense of the Treaty's expressed distinction between ends only (directives) and means also (regulations), but I suspect that in many matters in the field of capital market and securities regulation the needed harmonization will work only if it amounts to the nearest approximation to uniformity which is possible without a single Community language. For example, one area which the Commission has identified as demanding harmonization relates to segregation by investment businesses of clients' money. As SIB has found, a multinational financial conglomerate may find itself incapable of complying with the applicable regulations of one country without breaching the regulations of another unless both regulations are identical and not merely harmonized.

In such cases there would obviously be much to be said for proceeding openly by regulations,[40] rather than by directives so specific as to be indistinguishable in substance from regulations. But this, I imagine, the Commission will be reluctant to do in the light of the Declaration, appended to the Single European Act, on the new Article 100A of the Treaty of Rome.[41] And on the whole I think that directives, however specific, probably are preferable to regulations since they enable Member States to translate the wording to make it more consistent with their national laws and practices and more intelligible to their local practitioners.

2. Use of Options

The authors also point out that:[42]

[37] I.e. Directive 79/279/EEC, O.J. L 66/21 (1979), Directive 80/390/EEC, O.J. L 100/1 (1980), and Directive 82/121/EEC, O.J. L 48/26 (1982).

[38] The Stock Exchange (Listing) Regulations (1984 S.I. 716) made under Section 2 of the European Communities Act 1972, c.68. This was not a very satisfactory solution (for reasons summarized in my *Review of Investor Protection, supra* note 21, *Report Part II* at paras 6.13-6.17) and the Regulations have now been repealed and replaced by Part IV of the Financial Services Act 1986, c.60.

[39] See BUXBAUM & HOPT, *supra* note 1, at 234.

[40] Which should also be speedier.

[41] "In its proposals pursuant to Article 100A(1) the Commission shall give precedence to the use of the instrument of a directive if harmonization involves the amendment of legislative provisions in one or more Member States."

[42] See BUXBAUM & HOPT, *supra* note 1, at 234-235.

"In recent years quite the opposite problem has appeared – not that of protecting the Member States against too much intrusion by Community directives, but rather that of securing meaningful European harmonization against the stiff defense of national legal peculiarities. At issue is the phenomenon of harmonization by options."

When, as in the example suggested above, harmonized, but not unified, regulations are likely to cause insuperable difficulties to firms whose business is not restricted to domestic transactions with or on behalf of domestic clients, the use of options is clearly fatal; it amounts not only to settling on "the lowest common denomination of national laws and to camouflag[ing] this by options",[43] but to unworkable harmonization. Conversely, when the directive can be and is one which merely directs the ends to be achieved and not the means, it is difficult to see why options should be needed. The need for them arises when, as seems increasingly to be the case, the Commission decides that the best hope of making progress on effective harmonization is to prescribe both ends and a choice of acceptable means. Here options are the only, and therefore the best, solution so long as they are not excessive in number. This, as I understand it, is the authors' conclusion,[44] and I respectfully agree.

3. Direct Applicability

I also agree with the authors that, in the light of the increasing specificity of directives and the developing jurisprudence of the European Court on direct applicability,[45]

"there is a great potential for individuals, courts and authorities within the Member States to take action to implement the directives even where the States themselves have not enacted implementing legislation."

Indeed this occurs with increasing frequency and is, I would have thought, a far better way of encouraging a "centrifugal local profession" to develop a "federal outlook by proxy" than would be the establishment of Community trial courts in each Member State. It is, however, a somewhat clumsy and unsatisfactory way of encouraging Member States timeously to fulfil their Community obligations, and one which, until they have done so, inevitably leads to possible conflicts between Community and national legislation.[46]

[43] *Id.* at 235.
[44] *Id.* at 235, 236.
[45] *Id.* at 239.
[46] *Id.* at 240, 241.

4. "Blocking" and "Petrifying"

The authors have wise and perceptive words to say on the "blocking" and "petrifying" effects of Community legislation on national legislation.[47] My impression, however, is that these effects are not proving as serious as might have been expected. The Commission, as it seems to me, has shown, to perhaps a surprising degree, a willingness to amend directives, and seems able to do so with considerably greater rapidity than in relation to the original directive. For example the listing Directive 80/390/EEC[48] has already been amended twice since adopted in 1980,[49] and two amending directives have been proposed[50] to the UCITS Directive 85/611/EEC adopted in 1985.[51]

Moreover, the British experience (and, I believe, that of other Member States) has been that the need to implement Community legislation has afforded opportunities, which might not otherwise have occurred, for passing legislation making long-overdue reforms of domestic law.

One of the problems faced in the United Kingdom in relation to law reform is the shortage of Parliamentary time and the resulting difficulty of obtaining a place in the legislative programme. In relation to the measures implementing directives this difficulty was minimized by providing that, subject to various limitations, such implementation could be undertaken by secondary legislation,[52] a power which has been used whenever possible and which partly accounts for our comparatively good record in implementation. But the limitations are such that, in the case of major directives, secondary legislation cannot be used.[53] When that is so, the Government has had to find time for primary legislation; and the Department of Trade and Industry has then been astute to tack on to the Bill company law reforms additional to those required by the directives. Thus large parts of the Companies Acts 1980 and 1981 (the primary purposes of which were to implement the Second and Fourth Company Law Directives[54]) comprised domestic reforms for which Parliamentary time would otherwise not have been found. The same practice is likely to be adopted in a Companies Bill.

[47] *Id.* at 241-243.

[48] O.J. L 100/1 (1980).

[49] A minor amendment by Directive 82/148/EEC, O.J. L 62/22 (1982), and substantial ones by Directive 87/345/EEC, O.J. L 185/81 (1987).

[50] See Directive 88/220/EEC, O.J. L 100/31 (1988), and proposal of 1986, O.J C 129/5 (1986).

[51] O.J. L 375/3 (1985).

[52] European Communities Act 1972, c.60, Section 2 and Sched. 2.

[53] As mentioned above, it was used for the initial implementation of the listing directives but the result was unsatisfactory because para 1(c) of Sched. 2 does not permit conferment by secondary legislation of the "power to legislate by orders, rules, regulations or other subordinate instrument" and the Stock Exchange Council as "the competent authority" needed such power.

[54] Directive 77/91/EEC, O.J. L 26/1 (1977), and Directive 78/660/EEC, O.J. L 222/11 (1978).

Hence we in the United Kingdom would say that up to now Community legislation, far from petrifying our domestic company legislation, has been a positive help in keeping it up-to-date. But, of course, that may change if and when the Community legislation has preempted the whole field.

5. The Role of Self-Regulation[55]

As I understand it, the Commission has no objection to self-regulation or to the employment of self-regulatory organizations in the regulatory system, so long as there are legally enforceable remedies for breaches of rules required by directives or provided by regulations. As already pointed out,[56] under the United Kingdom's new system of authorization for investment business, although authorization can be obtained through membership in a recognized SRO, the organization will not obtain or retain recognition unless its criteria for membership are at least as strict and its rules at least as protective of investors as those of SIB (which is not a self-regulatory body but one which exercises statutory powers delegated to it by the Secretary of State). Moreover the sanctions for breach of the rules, whether of SIB or of a recognized SRO, are severe. Not only may a breach lead to withdrawal of authorization (resulting in the commission of a criminal offense if the firm continues to undertake investment business), but any person who suffers loss as a result of the breach will have a civil remedy.[57] Clearly this fully complies with the Commission's criterion. In relation to takeovers, however, that probably would not be so. At present, takeovers are regulated by a non-statutory City Code, promulgated and administered by a purely self-regulatory Panel which has no *legal* sanctions. However, it now has some legal support, in that SIB's rules and those of the SROs indicate that refusal to comply with the Code or the rulings of the Panel, or continuing to act for clients who refuse to do so, will be treated as evidence of unfitness to carry on investment business. Nevertheless, it seems likely that any EC Directive on takeovers[58] would require the Panel and the Code to be brought fully within the regulatory scheme, with the provision of effective legal remedies against offenders whether or not they are "authorized persons."

Except in two respects, the British insider dealing legislation, now the Company Securities (Insider Dealing) Act 1985, as amended and strengthened by Part VII of the Financial Services Act, seems to go at least as far as

[55] See BUXBAUM & HOPT, *supra* note 1, at 246-250.

[56] See *supra* at 313 f.

[57] Financial Services Act 1972, c.60, Section 62. Note also Section 61 under which SIB may apply for an injunction and restitution order (borrowed from the American "disgorgement order") on behalf of the clients generally, which is likely to prove a more useful remedy.

[58] Proposals for a directive: see O.J. C 64/8 (1989) and O.J. C 240/7 (1990).

any Community legislation[59] is likely to require and, thanks to the new investigatory powers,[60] appears at long last to be pretty effective.[61] The two respects in which it may not comply are that (i) it does not provide expressly for a civil remedy[62] but only for a criminal offense, and (ii) it applies only to dealings on a recognized exchange (widely defined). In contrast, however, with the German *Insider Trading Guidelines*, referred to in the book,[63] it cannot be faulted as failing to provide legal sanctions or, now, as lacking effective enforcement.

Hence, in general, the new British system does not bear those characteristics of self-regulation to which the Commission objects. In fact the self-regulatory element is relatively slight, being relegated to the monitoring of rules and regulations which are statutory in substance and breach of which gives rise to effective legal remedies. This monitoring role is to my mind one which SROs are more likely to undertake effectively than a remoter watch-dog body, whether that be a government department or a statutory commission – a view which the SEC told me that they shared. But it seems clear that no Member State will be allowed to rely on rules or guidelines of a cozy club as implementation of Community obligations.

6. The Role of Administrative Agencies

As the book says,[64]

> "this question comes very much down to the pros and cons of either (i) creating a European securities and exchange commission[[65]] or else (ii) harmonizing and possibly creating national capital market supervisory bodies, which could be in part self-regulating subject to some meaningful state counterpart."

The authors say of (i):[66]

> "Theoretically, it would be conceivable for the Commission of the European Communities to be entrusted with the tasks for such a supervisory body. Politically, however, the prospects for such action are nil."

I agree.

[59] Directive (89/592/EEC) adopted in 1989: see O.J. L 334/30 (1989).

[60] Financial Services Act 1986, c.60, Sections 177 and 178.

[61] In the sense that offenses are more likely to be detected and more offenders charged. But there is, as yet, no evidence that the practice is being stamped out.

[62] But if the offense is committed by an "authorized person" there will be a breach of the rules of SIB or the relevant SRO, and anyone who can establish that he suffered loss as a result of the breach will have a civil remedy under Section 62 of the Financial Services Act 1986: see *supra*.

[63] BUXBAUM & HOPT, *supra* note 1, at 247 ff.

[64] *Id.* at 266. I have inserted the (i) and (ii).

[65] Embracing, I would suggest, the roles of both the American SEC and CFTC; all types of "futures" are investments (even if not "securities") and dealings in them are pre-eminently in need of harmonized regulation.

[66] BUXBAUM & HOPT, *supra* note 1, at 266.

They add:[67]

> "The proposal for a regulatory agency at the European level on the model of the US Securities and Exchange Commission raises similar reservations. Again, the political chances of realization are non-existent."

Again I agree; at any rate if to the second sentence one adds "in the near future." I would not rule it out as a possible long-term development and I do not wholly go along with the statement that[68]

> "it is highly questionable ... whether its manifold peculiarities, could be successfully transferred to the European Community."

As stressed above, the United Kingdom has transferred (we hope successfully) an adaptation of the US model (headed by a body much more closely resembling the Ontario Securities Commission than the SEC itself) to a Member State of the Community.

I completely agree, however, that[69]

> "[d]evelopments in European regulation will most likely take another route, relying on national capital market supervisory bodies,"

i.e. on route (ii) above.

I hope, however, that there will prove to be more uniformity in the nature of these supervisory bodies and of their regulations than the authors appear to think either likely or desirable.[70] Without such uniformity, the operations of multinational financial conglomerates, which already dominate most branches of the financial services industry, will be severely handicapped.

7. Multiplicity of Regulators

Not only have investments and investment business become international but the boundaries between investment business and other financial services are increasingly being eroded. I am dubious whether it will prove practicable to maintain the present general practice of having distinct supervisory bodies for the various branches (e.g. banking, insurance and investment business). The need for exchange of views and co-operation between the various supervisors in each Member State and between them and those in other Member (and non-Member) States is widely recognized and is stressed in the book.[71] But, while they remain separated, will exchange really take place to anything like the necessary extent? I have the gravest doubts; particularly as regards the various national supervisors of different branches of financial services. Effective co-operation between, say the banking supervisors in different countries seems to me to be more likely

[67] *Id.* at 266.
[68] *Id.* at 266.
[69] *Id.* at 266.
[70] *Id.* at 266-268.
[71] *Id.* at 267-268.

than effective co-operation between the banking, insurance, and securities and capital market supervisors even in the same country. Yet, especially since "the Crash of 1987," the need for that co-operation has been recognized increasingly, and both in the USA and the United Kingdom there have been calls for a supra-supervisor.

In the light of the expanding role of banks, it has been suggested that the supra-supervisor might be the banking supervisor. Apart from the political difficulties in bringing that about, I would be reluctant to see the introduction of a further tier in the regulatory structure. Ideally, as it seems to me, the various supervisors of financial services should be united in one body and under one roof. But as yet the only Member State that has gone that far is Denmark[72] – and only since the beginning of 1988 and, of course, only in relation to such branches of financial services as it presently regulates. The United Kingdom, though it has avoided a separation of the securities regulator and the futures regulator, uniting both roles in SIB, has not wholly merged the insurance regulator and SIB;[73] and the banking regulator remains the Bank of England, whose pre-eminence as a regulator is recognized only to the extent that it is treated as "the lead regulator" in relation to overall capital adequacy for all business carried on by banking groups.[74] In the light of the ever-increasing "securitization" of formerly banking instruments this has led to hideously complicated attempts to distinguish "banking business," regulated by the Bank of England, from "investment business," regulated by SIB,[75] and has not avoided the need for banking groups to obtain authorization both from the Bank and, for their investment business, through membership of several different SROs.

The satisfactory solution of these problems may prove to be the biggest headache faced by the harmonization programme.

[72] Outside the Community the only countries known to me that have done so are Norway and Singapore.

[73] The case for doing so in relation to life insurance is stronger than in relation to general insurance, but until the Community implements the long-term policy of forcing a de-merger of existing insurance conglomerates there are difficulties in doing even that.

[74] The Belgian *Commission Bancaire* perhaps comes closer to being a banking-cum-securities regulator?

[75] See Financial Services Act 1986, c.60, Sections 1 and 43 and Sched. 1 and 5.

B. Discussion

I. Introductory Remarks

L.C.B. Gower

I feel very apologetic, because in the first part of my paper[1] I really exceeded my brief. My problem was that having read the *Buxbaum* an *Hopt* book[2] I could find so little to criticize that I was scraping around to see what I could say that would be regarded as critical – as commentators were instructed to be. But it did seem to me that although Prof. *Buxbaum*'s contribution on American constitutional law and the Commerce Clause of the American Constitution[3] was of fascinating interest, it did not seem to me that the American experience was likely to have much relevance so far as the development of the EC harmonization programme is concerned. There are such great differences.

I do not wish to emphasize the fact that the EC is not a State but is merely an international organization because that is not the important thing. And I accept that both the EC and the USA were faced with the fundamental problem of reconciling the national feelings of each of the constituent members with the needs and aspirations of a wider multinational community and that the Commerce Clause was specifically designed to help in that reconciliation, and to that extent it clearly is interesting and useful.

But as things have developed now with all the powers the Commission has to get its way, it did not seem to me that problems of constitutionality are going to play a big part in the future. The chances, it seems to me, of any State or individual striking down a directive that has been adopted or a regulation that has been promulgated on the ground that it is unconstitutional, seemed to me to be so remote that I really cannot see how all the American jurisprudence on the Commerce Clause and other clauses in the American Constitution is likely to play a major part. But as I am no constitutional lawyer I may be completely wrong, in which case I shall happily delete from the published version everything I have said.

Similarly I was dubious as to how far the various admirable methods of law reform that the USA has introduced – such as the Commissioners on Uniform State Laws, the Restatements of the American Law Institute and

[1] See *supra* at 308 ff.

[2] R.M. BUXBAUM & K.J. HOPT, *Legal Harmonization and the Business Enterprise* (Berlin/New York 1988).

[3] See *id.* at 28-62.

so on – can really be transported into the European scene. The language difficulties alone seem to me to preclude much in that direction.

But these are the only points I really tried to make in this part of my paper and I do not think I need to say any more about it. And I apologize for sticking my neck out and I am genuinely humble on this which is not the way I normally am.

What I was asked to do is to speak about these topics in the light of the British experience and that I took to mean in the light of what we in the UK call *Big Bang*, which was an extremely rapid process of deregulation that converted the City of London from a place dominated by old Etonians and operating by pretty primitive methods in many respects almost overnight into a place where the old Etonian tie was no longer the entry card but a MBA from the Harvard Business School. This happened with a rapidity that took everybody by surprise. Happily, I suppose, we were able to couple that with the introduction for the first time of a really up-to-date system of securities regulation which we had never had before. We were working on a pre-World War II Act which was obsolete really before it ever came into operation.

The basic lines of our solution are very much borrowed from the American SEC type of regulation, which of course has spread so widely throughout the world in one form or another. Ours is a slightly idiosyncratic method of doing it. We have not set up a public agency. The top body under our new regulatory system is a private company, but it is a very extraordinary private company because its members and its directors are the same people and they are all appointed by the Governor of the Bank of England and the Secretary of State for Trade and Industry jointly, neither of whom of course is a member of the body at all, but who together in effect can hire and fire all the members of the body.

Before that body, the Securities and Investments Board (SIB) was recognized as the top regulatory body. It had to satisfy the Secretary of State that it had adequate rules in every respect to do the job properly. It also had to satisfy the Director General of Fair Trading that its rules were not excessively anticompetitive. Having done that, the main task of the SIB was to lay down rules and regulations which everybody who is carrying on investment business, widely defined, has to observe after becoming properly authorized, either by the SIB, the mini-SEC or the poor man's SEC as I generally describe it, directly or through one of the self-regulatory organizations (SROs) recognized by that body (there are five such recognized SROs); in addition there are a number of recognized investment exchanges.

One of the interesting and perhaps unusual features of our system is that under it we treat exchanges and SROs differently. To become authorized for investment business, which as I say is very widely defined and includes sellers of insurance and mutual funds and so on, one has to satisfy either the SIB itself, or in practice one of these five SROs; that one is fit and proper. In conducting business, if one does it through a recognized investment exchange, then the rules are easier on the authorized person. In other words, firms are encouraged to use recognized (or designated in the case of foreign) exchanges on the basis that these will have proper reporting requirements and the like so that the strictness of the rules can be somewhat relaxed. To meet the problems of accountants and lawyers who in practice do a considerable amount of investment business as defined in the Financial Services Act, they can become authorized through membership of a recognized professional body. Those bodies will not be recognized for this purpose unless they have amended their rules so that they are equivalent to those of the SROs. And that is what they are now in the process of doing and they have been given interim recognition in the meantime.

The system is now pretty well in full operation, though not completely, because as you can imagine we have had teething troubles in the transition from a primitive system which did not cover many parts of investment business to one which is extremely comprehensive in its coverage. There has been a certain amount of aggro as a result of this, as you can imagine. People are now saying that the rules of the SIB and the rules of the SROs – which have to be at least as good if they are to get recognition – are excessively legalistic and complicated and there is some truth in this, I think. And indeed the SIB has recognized this and is now looking at all these rules and seeing if, instead of laying everything down in as much detail as it has, it can adopt what directives are supposed to be. In other words, to indicate the basic principles and the aims the rules must achieve, with SROs left to fill out the details to the extent that they think necessary.

Now the fact that we have got this system obviously is either going to help or hinder the harmonization programme – I am hoping to hear what Mr. Fitchew thinks about this. If the Commission likes what we have done they clearly have a model they could work on. It has taken us seven years or more, because we started on this operation before *Big Bang* was ever thought of and it was rather a happy coincidence that it was ready at the time. If the Commission is to get harmonized regulation for everybody in fore, I would have thought that there would be some advantages in looking at this as a possible model to follow. It also means of course that if the harmonization that the EC introduces were to require us, who have sweated blood to get this thing through over the past seven years, to dismantle all we have done, implacable opposition may be expected in the UK. On the other hand, nothing would please the UK more if the system was introduced everywhere, whereby at least one could be ensured that people who are authorized in Member States to carry on investment business really are fit and proper, because at the moment we have provided – being good Europeans in this respect – that "Euro persons" (which is the horrible word we have invented to describe people who have obtained authorization in other Member States and satisfied an authority in that Member State that they are properly regulated to carry on business in the UK) shall be automatically regarded as authorized in the UK. But we are I think slightly alarmed in that – well, we are happy at the moment because we do not think many countries have yet been able to satisfy that requirement, because in many cases there is no formal authorization required. As long as that is so, our rules will protect; but the danger clearly is that each Member State will have rather different criteria of what is fit and proper and we should be alarmed in the UK if the formal requirements of fitness and properness, which of course include in particular capital adequacy, were much laxer everywhere else.

That I think is enough to start the ball rolling and I will stop. I have described our system very inadequately, I am afraid, but it is difficult to do it in five minutes.

II. Constitutional Issues

Christian Timmermans

I would like to make a remark about the issue raised by Prof. Gower[4] whether discussing these matters from the EC side is really a constitutional issue. If I remember well, Prof. Gower has written in his paper[5] that the Treaty of Rome really has little to do at first sight with a constitution in terms of division of power between a federation and the State. I agree with him on that. I think that the Treaty as such is not really a constitution; it is completely silent on matters of division of competence. The Treaty attributes in a number of fields powers to act and to legislate to the Community institutions, but the consequences of these powers with regard to the competence of the States are absolutely neglected. The Treaty is silent on that matter.

I think, however, that we could nevertheless call the Treaty in some respect a constitution because of the fairly important contribution of the Court of Justice. It is the Court really that has confronted these questions and given some clear answers. First, the principle of preeminence of Community law which we do not find in the Treaty. In quite a number of fields the Court has drawn a clear line in matters of division of powers: the external field – the *AETR* case[6] was mentioned yesterday[7] – the field of commercial policy where the Court has stated the exclusiveness of the Community power, and there are other examples to be added.

I think therefore that insofar as we can qualify the Treaty a constitution and lawyers can raise constitutional questions about the relationship between national law and Community law, it is because of this case-law of the Court of Justice. And most specifically we find this also insofar as the Court has in numerous cases struck down regulations, mostly in the field of agricultural policy, after having tested the regulation not only against the

[4] See *supra* at 325 f.
[5] See *supra* at 308 f.
[6] Case 22/70, [1971] E.C.R. 263.
[7] See *supra* at 32.

Treaty itself but also against general principles of law: I think this really is a constitutional exercise.

As far as company law and securities markets directives are concerned, I do not think that testing will occur easily. It is nevertheless not to be excluded and particularly not – and I refer to what we discussed earlier[8] – the matter of the blocking effect of the directives. It is quite imaginable that a national court will raise that question before the Court of Justice and the Court will, at least insofar as this dividing line between the national and the Community competence is concerned, give quite an explicit answer in a specific case.

So personally I would not go so far as to say that there is no constitutional issue and that the American experience is not entirely relevant because the constitutional setting is completely different. I think there are similarities.

Desmond McComb

I am very much a layman in this area but there is one example which perhaps Prof. Gower could add to. We normally assume that the United Kingdom has a uniform framework of company law, but in point of fact under the devolution of power Northern Ireland had separate company laws. I wonder if as a constitutional point this has created any problems in the administration of UK company law or if it had implications for example for the *siège réel* to which Prof. Timmermans drew attention.[9]

L.C.B. Gower

You asked whether there was true uniformity of company law in the United Kingdom and mentioned Northern Ireland. Well, though Ireland at one time was a problem in this respect, Northern Ireland now has identical legislation. Slight problems arise as to whether this can be done straight forwardly by making Companies Acts UK Acts or whether you have to pass them first of all for Great Britain and then adopt precisely the same thing in North Ireland. Even that problem now seems to have been solved.

But what is a greater problem in a sense is Scotland, because its common law differs and although in the main the statutory provisions are identical for both England and Scotland, they are not wholly identical. There are various sections which apply only to Scotland and this is particularly so in connection with company charges and the like. The floating charge which is an English invention, and I think a valuable one, was unknown in Scotland and was introduced by statute. So was the law relating to receivers. The result of this is that at the moment you have two sets of provisions relating to these, much better ones for Scotland because clearly thought out.

[8] See *supra* at 151 f, 217. See also *supra* at 200 ff, 236 and 320 f.

[9] See *supra* at 149 ff; see also *supra* at 133 ff.

So we still do not have complete uniformity in the United Kingdom. There is that problem but it is not a terribly serious one except in certain things, particularly in connection with mortgages and charges.

Klaus Hopt

On the constitutional issues, I would agree very much with Prof. Timmermans. I do not think I have to develop that further.

Then very briefly to the methods and tools you mentioned, Prof. Gower.[10] Of course you are right that there are many differences between the United States and Europe. But at least one has tried to go similar ways. In Germany the Max-Planck-Institute in Hamburg has started with a project based on a restatement like approach. I understand that Drobnig and Lando have made good process. Of course the results remain to be seen and particularly in practice. But the experience was much better than many of us had actually expected at the beginning, when the concept was presented at the European University Institute in Florence in the late '70s.

L.C.B. Gower

Would not you agree that you could not use that as a device for getting the single European market finished by 1992? Because after all, this is what it is all about.

Klaus Hopt

I would never claim this. But the problems we discuss here are on a much broader time frame. Therefore restatements may very well be one of the many tools and devices we have been talking about, and as such I think may have a meaning for European integration.

Then I would like to take this opportunity to mention "the formal public meetings" you thought[11] we had recommended. There seems to be a misunderstanding. We did not mean large public conventions, but legislative hearings as we use in the national parliaments. Indeed we have used them in Germany during the last 10-15 years with good results. The danger we have felt is that these hearings may sometimes be a bit manipulated, i.e., the legislative body may use them as a fig-leaf, calling in just those experts who can be expected to state what the legislator wanted them to say. Then of course such a hearing is not very meaningful. Our *plaidoyer* in the book[12] was to use this not only in the parliamentary process, but also for bodies with similar functions, i.e., for quasi-legislators. One should give more thought in that direction.

[10] See *supra* at 310 ff and 325 f.

[11] See *supra* at 312.

[12] See BUXBAUM & HOPT, *supra* note 2, at 287.

Geoffrey Fitchew

Perhaps I could, since Prof. Hopt has raised the question of public hearings, just make a comment on that. The Parliament does organize public hearings. For example one is going to take place in the Legal Affairs Committee on the Tenth Directive at the end of September, and I suspect such hearings will increasingly be a feature of the Parliament's work. The Commission already consults very extensively in a semi-public way and I would not have thought that there was much need to go beyond what takes place on that.

I was not entirely sure from the *Buxbaum* and *Hopt* book[13] whether you had in mind that the Council could organize public hearings, but I see no prospect for that whatsoever because although what the Council does is part of the legislative process, it is so in a very peculiar way, in that the act of legislation is at the same time an act of international negotiation between the sovereign States. There is no way in which international negotiation is going to be thrown open to the public.

André Tunc

I would like to make only a remark on the value of the American experience. I assume that the backgrounds of the American experience and the European experience are quite different for a number of constitutional reasons, which have been mentioned,[14] but also for the importance of harmonization from below.

The latter has played a great role in the United States. I do not see how something comparable could occur in Europe. The Max-Planck-Institute will certainly do something valuable in a not too distant future. But that cannot be compared to what has been achieved by the American Bar Association, the American Law Institute or the American universities which give, as you know, a general view based on national case-books. We have nothing comparable in Europe. So there are in the United States powerful centripetal forces certainly which do not exist at present in Europe. I cannot offer any figure, but it is certainly a tiny minority of French *avocats*, who, even apart from the language barrier, would be able to have a useful discussion with their English or German brethren. The general law background which exists in the United States just does not exist in Europe.

L.C.B. Gower

First of all, could I just say that the main criticism, as far as I was concerned, seemed to be that I had overstated my case. I generally do. But I did not overstate it, I think, quite as much as some people have suggested. The whole of my approach was based on the assumption – and if this is wrong,

[13] See *id.* at 287.
[14] See *supra* at 325 f and 328 ff.

then I grovel – that what *Buxbaum* and *Hopt* were trying to do was to identify the lessons of the US experience in harmonizing companies and securities laws of its member States which could be learned by the EC in relation to its aim progressively to complete by 1993, "a single integrated European market without internal frontiers." I certainly did not want to deny that there is a possibility of constitutional problems arising in connection with the EC. If one State wanted to withdraw from it, then clearly constitutional problems would arise. That has got nothing to do with the harmonization needed to complete the Common Market by 1993, or so it seemed to me.

But I remain on the whole uncontrite about what I said because I entirely accept Prof. Buxbaum's point[15] that, as I said myself, so far as the solutions which we seek to adopt are concerned there are great lessons to be learned from the United States of America. And similarly – and I think this was a point he was making – in connection with the priorities we could learn much from America. All I was doubting[16] was whether the jurisprudence on the Commerce Clause was really going to be of real relevance to this particular narrow issue, and unless you tell me I am talking absolute balls (there are no ladies here, I can use this expression) I would not propose to delete what I have said.

III. The EC and the British Experience

A. Big Bang as a Source of Inspiration

Christian Timmermans

I have one remark to make and that is that the message of *Big Bang* at any rate got through to Amsterdam, as you know, and our Stock Exchange authorities have introduced a quite impressive reform, in order to prevent that trade be diverted from the Amsterdam market. So it seems to work in that respect, I would say.

André Tunc

Prof. Gower suggested[17] that the British scheme could be a model for European countries. I am pleased to say that in France it has been considered to a great extent as a model, not to be copied but as a source of inspiration. The COB – Mr. d'Illiers will correct me if I am wrong – has created a working group under the chairmanship of Mr. Brac de la Perrière on problems of ethics for financial intermediaries, and the group has considered with great attention the English experience and also suggested

[15] See e.g. *supra* at 183 ff.
[16] See *supra* at 325.
[17] See *supra* at 315 and 327.

that some rules of ethics should be general and then should be adapted to the various financial activities.

On the other hand, if the general scheme is the same as in England and if the philosophy of the rules is the same, a difference may arise as regards the implementation of the rules. We were somewhat frightened by the volume of British rules and we tried to stick to principles, to enunciate guidelines rather than go into details.

L.C.B. Gower

That is what SIB is trying to do now.

Hartmut Schmidt

I think that the process of development Prof. Gower described for the United Kingdom is exactly what I would call harmonization by market and which others[18] may call the fear-and-greed mechanism. He pointed to the market pressures and there had to be a sufficient answer, and there were well-tried American solutions that helped to formulate it, and all came about with great speed. I think, if I may say so – I worked for the Office of Fair Trading prior to *Big Bang* when they prepared their Restrictive Practices Court suit, and therefore looked into the situation – it took a bit longer than it appears from your paper. I think the Wilson Committee work was important to prepare the ground for the later changes.

The adoption process in other European countries may also take 10-15 years though things have been speeding up lately as was pointed out already.[19] This harmonization by market seems to work in Amsterdam, Copenhagen, France. Germany is certainly very much affected and I think this is a process which will bring about a certain level of uniformity though no real uniformity. Everybody tries to improve on what the other has done. You tried to improve on the American model and we are trying to improve on the UK model, and I think this is the way the process should work.

Klaus Hopt

Much has been said, so I can be reasonably brief. Prof. Gower, I admire the new English system. On the other hand, to have it as a model for Europe is somewhat difficult.[20] Just to transfer the whole system to the European level can hardly be the solution. Just to duplicate it in all nation States cannot be the solution either. So what I do not see yet is a possible demarcation line, particularly since the system appears as a unity and since I think it is working as such and is conceived as such. So I wonder how the model can

[18] See *supra* at 17.
[19] See *supra* at 332 f.
[20] *Cf. supra* at 315 and 328.

be useful for our European discussion, and I would be grateful if Mr. Fitchew could give some hints on where he thinks that structural splits could be made and on how to divide different parts of the model for the Community and for the Member States without endangering its functioning as a whole. At the moment I have no idea how that could really work.

Geoffrey Fitchew

What I think might be helpful is to try to describe first of all the existing situation from which we start in Europe and second what the Commission is trying to do in its legislation now; I will try and pick up various points made round the table in doing that.

First of all, the *Big Bang* in London is certainly being followed by a series of big bangs in other Community financial centers. Prof. Timmermans has already mentioned the example of Amsterdam.[21] There has equally been reform and modernization at the Copenhagen Stock Exchange. There have been major changes proposed and already under way in Paris, in particular in permitting banks to purchase an *agent de change* who can operate on the Paris Stock Exchange. Legislation has been passed in Spain and Portugal and changes are under contemplation in Italy and in Greece. Germany to some extent stands outside this process and it could be described as being a late starter, but nevertheless it could equally be said that in many respects the universal banking system in Germany already contains many of the things that have taken place elsewhere.

Motives for all these changes. We come back[22] to fear and greed, in particular the fact that several countries found that a growing proportion of transactions in their shares were taking place on the London market. Obviously also the worldwide liberalization of capital movements has been a major factor.

Nevertheless we still start within Europe in a situation – particularly in relation to securities markets, perhaps less so in relation to banking markets – with a variety of different systems, in particular a variety of differences about who can do what. In one Member State, Germany, securities business is almost exclusively the privilege of banks and they are supervised for that purpose by the banking authorities. In other Member States banks are still limited in their capacity to engage in securities business. There are limitations certainly, I think, in Belgium and Italy, and there have been such limitations, although moves to eliminate them are under way, in France and Spain.

Apart from that, the monopoly of brokers if you like, there is also in several Member States the concept that securities transactions should take place through a single exchange. There is not a multiplicity of exchanges.

[21] See *supra* at 332.
[22] See *supra* at 17.

There is off-exchange trading but there is in several of those States only a single exchange.

Now the Commission's objectives in this area. In the early eighties there was the idea of creating a single European securities market. That idea in that form is probably dead and I think it is actually very unlikely that the end result of the European integration process will be a single European market in the sense that the New York Stock Exchange or the London Exchange could be regarded as a single market. What I think there will be is several overlapping markets. There will be shares of major countries which are listed on and quoted across and traded in on a large number of exchanges, and in the case of the more important companies they will be traded worldwide. There will be European companies which are big enough to be quoted on all the European markets, but there will nevertheless remain identifiable local markets, I would have thought.

So what we are aiming to achieve are three things. First of all freedom of capital movements which has already been agreed on in the Community.[23] Second freedom of establishment and third freedom to provide cross-frontier services for all the main types of transaction operator in the banking and securities markets, and that means that we have to define the terms and conditions on which people or corporations would be authorized to engage in these activities.

Before coming to our proposed legislation, I think I should digress to say that there is clearly a potential for conflict between the European legislation and the UK legislation in these areas. This could arise, if the authorization criteria in the conduct of business rules that we propose are significantly different. But there is actually a potential for conflict already, even in the absence of any Community legislation. There is potential for conflict because of the fact that the UK authorities and the UK legislation are seeking to impose authorization in conduct of business rules on branches of foreign firms, and to some degree on firms offering services into the UK without having a branch. And there are clearly established criteria laid down by the European Court, which govern the extent to which an individual Member State is permitted to do that.

In particular the Court has said that rules of that kind must not be discriminatory, that is obvious; second, that they must be objectively justified; third, that there should be no duplication between rules laid down in one jurisdiction and rules laid down in another jurisdiction; and fourth, that the rules laid down should not be unduly burdensome, that the rule of proportionality should operate. The Commission has to look at the UK's authorization rules (and those of any other Member State) with these points in mind.

I think also that any individual Member State may have encountered significant problems in seeking to apply its own conduct of business rules, in particular capital adequacy rules to the branches of overseas banks and, *a*

[23] See O.J. L 178/5 (1988).

fortiori, in applying them to firms doing cross-frontier business into their markets.

These difficulties underline the importance of getting something agreed on a Community-wide basis and ultimately on a global basis as well.

I now turn to the two directives, one of which we have already proposed and the other on which we are working.

We have produced a proposal for a banking directive which impinges significantly on the securities area. This is the Second Banking Coordination Directive which was issued at the beginning of 1988.[24] This introduces the idea of a single banking licence which would be valid for either setting up a branch or providing cross-frontier services, and at the end of the directive there is an Annex of activities for which the single licence would be valid. Clearly if you have the concept of a single licence, you have got to be clear what the licence is valid for, and this directive covers all forms of securities activity in both the primary and secondary markets. It is quite clear therefore that the Commission is proposing to remove any kind of Glass-Steagall prohibitions which may exist within the Community. In principle it seems to me that it, because cross-frontier provisions of services is involved, potentially creates the basis on which a NASDAQ type system could be introduced within the Community.

I should now say a word about the investment services directive which we are still working on and aim to produce by the beginning of 1989.[25] This essentially seeks to create the same kind of single licence for non-banking operators in the securities market in relation to such activities as broking, dealing and portfolio management.

In the case of both directives the key questions which we are having to ask ourselves are those which I have listed in my paper,[26] namely what are the key supervisory or prudential rules which we should harmonize, how detailed should the harmonization be, and how should the responsibilities be divided between home country and host country supervisors.

The view which we have taken is that there should be common rules relating to fitness and properness not only of the operators but of major shareholders and some degree of surveillance of major shareholders; second, there should be capital adequacy rules. Both those two sets of rules can only efficiently and properly be administered by the home country supervisors. But in connection with the investment services directive we are looking at a whole range of conduct of business rules related to investor protection essentially, to the relationship between the provider of the services and the client – where a variety of solutions are possible regarding the division of responsibility for subjects such as compensation schemes, reporting of transactions and the degree of information to be provided for clients in

[24] Directive adopted in 1989: see O.J. L 386/1 (1989).

[25] Proposal published in 1989: see O.J. C 43/7 (1989). See also the amended proposal published in 1990: O.J. C 42/7 (1990).

[26] See *supra* at 9.

relation to business being carried out. It is quite conceivable that we will say that some of these rules should be the responsibility of the host country supervisor rather than the home country supervisor.

Just a short word on capital adequacy. In connection with the banking directive there is a parallel proposal for dealing with credit risk (harmonized solvency ratio)[27] which is very close in substance and detail to the recommendations from the Cooke Committee. It has become clear to us that we will also need to make a proposal specific to securities activities dealing with market risk[28] and there will be a number of difficult questions to be answered about the relationship between these two rules and who should supervise the application of these rules to banks which are engaged in securities activities as well as in traditional banking.

B. Setting of Rules and Enforcement

Robert Austin

My comment relates to Prof. Gower's suggestion[29] that harmonization may involve the expansion into Europe of the Financial Services Act. It is a piece of legislation which is fascinating to all of us, not least in Australia.

My impression, when Prof. Gower started the enterprise was that it was to be seen essentially as an interim solution. He thought that politically it was not feasible to establish an SEC in the United Kingdom. It was therefore necessary for him to look at a more complicated solution, and certainly (with respect) a more complicated solution came out of that process. Instead of having a system in which the securities regulator is a statutory authority directly issuing rulings to govern the industry, we have a system of standard rules set by SIB but subject to the facility for self-regulatory organizations to issue their own rules. The effect has been considerable complexity and perhaps a risk of a lack of direction in relation to such difficult problems as capital adequacy requirements. It seems to me that the system is so structured that it is very difficult to solve these sorts of problems, and so I personally would like to see the Financial Services Act as an interim solution even now, even as it is getting started. It seems to me that it is a part of a process of evolution which may in the United Kingdom eventually lead to something in a different form.

If we say that the Financial Services Act is part of a process of evolution, Prof. Gower's suggestion must be that this process of evolution can be extended into Europe. Now I take it he is not suggesting that the self-regulatory organizations which have been structured to some extent artificially in the United Kingdom should be extended to become European self-regulatory organizations. The suggestion presumably is that there

[27] Directive adopted in 1989: see O.J. L 386/14 (1989).
[28] Proposal published in 1990: see O.J. C 152/6 (1990).
[29] See *supra* at 315 and 328.

should be a similar establishment of self-regulatory organizations for each separate country. That would be an added dose of complexity, because each of the twelve EC nations would have five, or more than five, self-regulatory organizations, each dealing with one another and each dealing with their respective SIBs. I wonder how that would work and whether it might not be necessary, if we see this whole structure as an evolutionary process, to try to accelerate the evolution a little bit beyond that point.

Hartmut Schmidt

Prof. Gower, you mentioned in your paper[30] that you would like to see securities regulation and banking regulation under one roof. We also looked at this and Prof. Giersch and myself came to the conclusion that those countries that do not have one roof have the better securities markets and better financing for their industries. One agency should develop the securities market and another agency should be in charge of banking. Aside from this I go along with your suggestion that in addition there should be self-regulatory organizations.

Edmund Kitch

First, let me try to speculate about what the central problems are for the European Community based on what I know about the history and current structure of the American system. I think you have to assume that the vision of the Community is a vision that assumes that the industrial enterprises will finance themselves from private sector financial instruments. If you are talking about State finance of enterprise and so on, all these problems become unimportant.

If that is the structure that you want for the financing of commercial enterprises, then it is obvious that an efficient market for trading in those instruments is a very desirable feature of that arrangement. I think it also seems clear that this is an activity where there is what economists would call economy of scale, that is, there are tremendous advantages in having a single unified market in which everyone participates all the time because of the depth that market gives you and its enhanced stability and reduced transaction cost. So I would think the vision here would be that there would be the emergence of a large and important public market in securities in Europe in which all firms throughout Europe would participate on an equal basis. If the institutional conditions necessary for that could be created you would then have a public securities market in Europe which would be as large or as important or more important than the securities markets in the United States and that would be a good thing, I think, not only for Europe but for the world.

[30] See *supra* at 323.

Also, it seems that the technology of market organization has now arrived at the point where on the mechanical side one can see how this can be done rather easily. That seems to me to be the NASDAQ model of trading where you have the possibility of competitive market makers who can simply enter the market without changing their physical location by accessing a sophisticated communications system. So you no longer are faced with what would otherwise be a rather difficult political problem of deciding where this market is going to be located. Is it going to be put in London so that all the associated services, income and so on, benefit the English or is it going to be located somewhere in Germany and so forth? It can be located anywhere and thus you no longer have to fight over that question.

Well, then the question becomes: why is not the technology the end of the problem? Obviously, people can purchase these terminals. Groups through cooperation can agree on standards and conditions for the system. I take it that the problem in the operation of an exchange is that you have to be careful about who has access to these exchange communication facilities because they are always open to various strategies of short-term manipulation. Someone can enter into this market and place orders for which they do not have the financial backing and so on in order to manipulate prices and throw these markets off. You have to make sure that the transactions that have been reported in this system are genuine economic transactions, by real sellers and buyers. Otherwise, you will see a lot of manipulation and it will make the market unreliable.

Then, in my mind, the question becomes: can this not be easily solved simply through membership requirements, that is, whatever quasi-private European body or quasi-public European body was operating this system could simply have a set of conditions for "membership" in the system which would be non-discriminatory by nationalities. Any German or French or English firm that could meet these standards and would agree to accept this system could join it. And why would that not be the end of the problem and present any particular governmental difficulty? I take it, given the fact that the English have a slight institutional time advantage, that this might very well just work out from London. The English would make their facilities available to firms in other countries under conditions that they would set and they would be accepted in the other countries and this system would become a European system.

But the problem is that a private body, or even a national UK body, may not really have sufficient enforcement and investigatory powers to make these membership agreements effective. It may not be able to audit sufficiently; it may not have the backing of an ultimate criminal sanction and of systems of public investigation and sanctions, and a private agreement without that may not be enough. After all, the SROs in the United States are backed up by the public investigatory and enforcement authority of the SEC.

If you need public reinforcement for the system in the end, I find it very difficult to see how this European market can emerge short of some kind of supranational agency. I have great difficulty imagining the creation of twelve parallel regulatory agencies which would then all closely cooperate on everything and remain parallel. That seems to me a very difficult dance and one that would not make sense for some of the smaller countries, at least I cannot quite see the answer to that.

So, I just wonder, if the idea is to have an equivalent to the New York Stock Exchange in Europe, which would be done through NASDAQ technology, whether in the end you do not in some sense have to have a European SEC, and that means something really different from harmonization. If that has to be a part of the picture, then it is a different kind of problem. Whether that is so or not, I do not really know.

André Tunc

On the problem of a European regulatory agency. The prospect of such an agency seems politically impossible at the present time; however one should not completely rule it out for a not too distant future. When one considers the genius of swindlers and their ability to use international financial commerce, one may hope for a series of international scandals which would shake reliance on national regulators.

Geoffrey Fitchew

I think it is implicit from what I have said[31] that I entirely endorse Prof. Tunc's view that the European Regulatory Agency is politically and administratively out of the question for the moment, and we will have to operate on the basis of cooperation between securities market supervisors. That is still at an embryonic stage in comparison with the banking supervisors. We are seeking to encourage it. We have set up a Committee of senior security market supervisors.

One point I should mention which relates to something that Prof. Kitch said. As the investment services directive is envisaged at the moment, it would lay down the conditions for access of securities businesses to exchanges in different Member States; but the UK legislation also deals with the question of who can set up exchanges and indeed also with who can set up and operate clearing houses. Our proposal does not at present deal with that and I think that is likely to have to come rather later.

Eddy Wymeersch

I very much wanted to take up Prof. Gower's very interesting developments of the creation of an European SEC.[32] As far as I can remember, this idea has been floating around for a very long time now, probably even before the

[31] See *supra* at 335.
[32] See *supra* at 323 f.

Segré Report of 1966 where I saw its first mention. Both Prof. Gower and Prof. Austin[33] indicated that there may be intermediary levels of reasoning between the full federal type of regulation and the exclusively local or national one. One wonders if we in the EC are not already heading towards an original solution, with a three level system.

The general policy making today already takes place at the European level: it is done by way of harmonized instructions to the lower level, the Member States. Here the Single European Act creates new possibilities to set up specialized organizations in charge of formulating these policy directives. At the State level, implementation and local adaptations to the harmonized rules take place. The further application of the rules to the real world is left to numerous specialized organizations, government bodies or SROs. This three level system of operation is more in conformity with the European tradition which is one of diversity in harmony, not one of uniformity.

L.C.B. Gower

Some people seem to think that I was advocating that there should be a European SEC. If anybody thinks that, I was not. I think that as a long-term objective it might be a good thing because markets now are certainly not limited to national or regional boundaries, and I can see this happening ultimately. But, I agree with the *Buxbaum* and *Hopt* book,[34] it is unattainable at this stage. All I was saying[35] is that I do think it would be worth looking at a regulatory system which is broadly on the UK lines because it is not just the UK that has this, this is what America has done, Japan has done, Singapore, Hong Kong, Canada, Australia have done, and I think it has considerable merits. That is all I can say.

I think on the whole a self-standing body is likely to be a better regulator than a government department, which seems to be the other alternative.

Richard Buxbaum

It is just interesting speculating on the idea of the SEC as a model – but of course that is our independent regulatory agency structure and it is a unique, in-between form.

[33] See *supra* at 337.
[34] See BUXBAUM & HOPT, *supra* note 2, at 266.
[35] See *supra* at 327 f.

IV. Various Other Topics

Gérard Hertig

I have two remarks. First about the cost of the system.

I was amazed when I heard Prof. Schmidt seeing it as regulation by the market.[36] I do not know if you are familiar with SIB regulations. We receive them in Geneva. I cannot understand them and you could not either. They are so complicated that it is very difficult to follow them.

Hartmut Schmidt

The SEC regulations are very complicated, and the New York Stock Exchange regulations are very complicated, but they are very good.

Gérard Hertig

And now let us see the result of it. I heard recently that small investors are not interested in the financial intermediaries any more because it is so costly to comply with the system. Hence, starting with the point that most or a lot of rules have to do with protecting small investors, in the end, although well protected, these do not invest any more. So why regulate in that sense in the first place? I do not think that the system as such is not good, but that it is implemented in a far too detailed manner, and for that reason I do not think it would be a very good model for general use. I would be in favor of something much more simplified and I guess that Sir Kenneth Berrill has seen the effect of that.

My second point is a minor one; it has to do with compensation. I do not think that the SIB or anybody else should act in favor of the consumer. If you look at the American experience, you see that first of all they have a system called *parens patriae* which does not work that well; and if you tell me that the SEC can do some work for recovering funds, you have also to see that as quickly as they have recovered profits from somebody, tax operators are coming in and saying: "No, do not give that to the investors but to us." So I do not see the use of this. And even if you say that that is not the case, I think that it would be better for the authorities to regulate and to supervise the system rather than looking for disgorgement of profits.

Klaus Hopt

A remark about Section 61 of the new British Financial Services Act.[37] I found fascinating the idea that a public authority should enter the private fields and be able to act as a receiver for private investors with private law means, i.e., the idea of an ombudsman with civil remedies. Yet this goes well beyond what we have traditionally been used to. Traditionally in our fields

[36] See *supra* at 333.
[37] See also *infra* at 367.

we have regarded remedies as an annex of substantive regulation. But maybe now things are turning around.

In any case this is one of the phenomena I mentioned yesterday,[38] namely the interrelationship between substantive law and procedural law which cannot be ignored by harmonization. Of course if we really go beyond our substantive corporate, securities and banking laws and venture right into the middle of procedural law, then we have a whole new topic for research and possibly for action.

L.C.B. Gower

On Section 61. I was surprised that Prof. Hertig said that he did not think this was a good idea at all, or that the Revenue would somehow step in and collar the whole thing and make it disgorge. That I think is a misunderstanding. We have borrowed the American disgorgement system. What this means is that SIB can bring proceedings in the court asking for an injunction restraining a firm's misbehavior and/or getting an order for disgorgement. Now what certainly happens in the United States, as I understand it, is that in 99 out of 100 cases never actually get to court but are settled out of court. We assume and hope that this is what will happen to a large extent in the UK. But whether it is done through the court or whether it is settled out of court, the money that is collected certainly will not be regarded as a profit, by SIB or anybody else, that the Revenue can get its hands on. It belongs to the people on whose behalf it has been collected.

V. Concluding Remarks

L.C.B. Gower

It has been a most interesting and informative discussion, I think we will all agree. I am particularly grateful for what Mr. Fitchew told us about the lines along which the Commission is thinking.[39] It is difficult to know where one starts on this.

Prof. Austin, I think, was criticizing our system[40] on the grounds that it relied too much on self-regulation and not enough on statutory regulation. Is that a fair statement of what you said? If so, that I think is a misunderstanding. A great emphasis was placed, in the debates and arguments about all this, to pretend that we are introducing a system which was as self-regulatory as possible. In point of fact, our system does not rely on self-regulation now to any serious extent. The rules and the regulations are in effect statutory rules because SIB's rules clearly are statutory and all the SRO's rules have in substance to be equivalent to SIB's rules.

[38] See *supra* at 222 f.
[39] See *supra* at 335 ff.
[40] See *supra* at 337 f.

The object of not centralizing the whole thing in SIB was because it was felt that this could weaken the system. And this was certainly something that was pressed upon me very strongly by the SEC themselves. They said: "So far as the monitoring role is concerned you must decentralize it." At the time I was talking to them, they still had SECO dealers that they have now got rid of, but they said: "This is where we are weakest. For God's sake, have a system whereby monitoring the SROs is decentralized because they are closer to the ground, they are closer to the things that are going on."

What I had envisaged really was that SIB would lay down its rules in the way that directives ought to be drafted and that then the SROs would produce their rules which would be designed to amplify this and if possible make it more "user friendly," to use the expression that was used. That has not happened. What has happened is that SIB has produced rules in enormous detail. Prof. Hertig is perfectly right, I can well understand that he says[41] he cannot understand a word of them. They are too detailed and SIB recognizes this and is now trying to make its rules more "user friendly" and to make statements of aims rather than means in the hope that this will encourage the SROs to do likewise as far as possible.

Well, I am not advocating for one moment that you should follow our present excessive detail. A problem in the UK is that we always legislate in far too much detail. There is a historic reason for this, that people who are drafting legislation think they have got to make it judge-proof! As a result our companies legislation is enormously large compared with any civilized country. For God's sake do not follow that.

But I do think that there are merits in a system whereby you have a top regulatory body, and it does not seem to matter whether you make that body an ordinary company, or form it by directly incorporating it under statute. The great beauty of the way we have done it is that it has solved a real problem which most other securities commissions suffer from, namely they have to keep within a budget prescribed from outside and cannot use any surplus to improve their services. Another advantage of the SIB system is that the whole thing is paid for by the people being regulated and they in turn of course pass it on to some extent to their customers and clients. The result is that probably investment will be slightly more expensive for some people but certainly much cheaper for the institutional investors who, in the UK, are now dealing on far better terms than they were before. The small private investor probably is being charged slightly more than he was before. But as long as you spread the cost around a bit, it does not seem to be harmful.

It is certainly not true to say, as Prof. Hertig did,[42] that private people are no longer investing. As a result of the Crash of 1987, they are probably not investing directly in stocks and shares with the enthusiasm that they had

[41] See *supra* at 342.
[42] See *supra* at 342.

before, and one will see how far this really has had a lasting effect when the next privatization issue comes out. It certainly had pretty calamitous consequences on the B.P. privatization in the middle of the Crash. But small investors are certainly continuing to invest in a very big way through mutual funds, and through insurance-linked investments, and clearly there has been in the UK a four- or fivefold increase in the actual numbers of *direct* investors over the last few years. How far that will continue despite or as a result of the Crash I do not know.

But as I say, under our system we have got the whole thing paid for by the people being regulated and by the people being protected indirectly, and SIB can use the revenue thus created to improve its services. It does not have to keep within a prescribed budget. This rather shocked the Labour Party who said that this was going too far but it is an enormous advantage. In many years, I think I am right in saying, Prof. Buxbaum, the SEC actual revenue has been considerably larger than all its expenses and it would dearly have loved to use it to improve its services, instead of which it had to hand it back into the Treasury. SIB does not have to do that and that is an enormous advantage.

It has meant for example that it can employ people on something nearer to what they would earn in the City than if it had to keep within civil service salary scales. We have not gone over the board as anybody who is employed by SIB will probably not get a salary as great as he could get if he went to say one of the city firms, and indeed he won't. But he will get something nearer it than if he went into the civil service.

And if you say that this is awful, here is a body which is under no control, that is not true because ultimately if the Government considers that SIB is behaving recklessly or excessively, it will exercise its considerable powers because the whole of the Board can be dismissed by the Secretary of State for Trade and the Governor of the Bank of England.

One final point. One of the things, I think, that distinguishes SIB from other securities commissions is that it has less to do on the side of primary issues than do most other commissions. That is because as a result of implementing the EC listing directives, the Stock Exchange became "the competent authority" for the purpose of the listing directives and it remains the competent authority for that purpose. The Stock Exchange has a dual role. It is both the organizer of the market – the market in listed securities and indeed in some other securities as well – and also the competent authority for the purpose of listed issues. And that is not a role which SIB itself does. SIB has a role in connection with non-listed issues but they are at the moment relatively unimportant. There was a growing over-the-counter market much of which has been destroyed, and probably rightly because the abuses that were going on in it were in some cases pretty severe.

Chapter Nine

Worldwide Legal Harmonization of Banking Law and Securities Regulation

A. Report: Alain Hirsch

I. Introduction

(1) I read with great interest the excellent and stimulating book by Prof. *Buxbaum* and *Hopt*.[1] I would prefer not to discuss the points with which I agree, but rather to present some differing views on legal harmonization, without claiming that they are better than those of the authors.

(2) Until recently, the relations between banking and securities regulation were distant in most countries. Belgium is the most important exception: the same supervisory body, the *Commission Bancaire*, has been entrusted with banking supervision and the supervision of the securities primary market for more than fifty years!

However, the relations between the two fields are now apparent, with the "globalization" of financial markets: the banks are increasing their securities business and many securities companies engage in some banking or para-banking activities. Even in the United States, where the separation of securities and banking has been especially strict,[2] it is now vanishing. It has practically disappeared in most countries, with the exception of Japan.

Therefore, it is useful to examine jointly the harmonization of banking law and of securities regulation.

[1] R.M. BUXBAUM & K.J. HOPT, *Legal Harmonization and the Business Enterprise* (Berlin/New York 1988).

[2] See, e.g., the regulations of the Banking Act of 1933, 48 Stat. 162, which are also popularly known under the name "Glass-Steagall Act." The statute is codified as amended in scattered Sections of 12 U.S.C.

II. Differences in National Regulations and the Aims of Legal Harmonization

(1) *Buxbaum* and *Hopt* write that, in Western industrialized countries, the goals of company law and of capital market law are similar and subject to no ideological conflict.[3] (However, they also write that "the differences between national company and capital market laws are not superficial ... but reach deeper," involving "complex interaction with other legal areas, such as procedural, tax, commercial, insurance and labor law.")[4]

I agree that the goals of most banking laws are very similar. The differences are rather technical, certainly less important than for company law. In most countries, the relative importance of banking law for society is similar. Therefore, I would suggest that international harmonization of banking law is in principle a relatively easy task.

On the other hand, the fundamental approach to securities regulation is still very different from one country to another. In the United States, securities regulation is considered an important social objective, justifying substantial administrative efforts and strong sanctions. The American authorities have even decided to cooperate quite closely with some offenders, in order to discover further (and hopefully more serious) violations of securities regulations. In some countries this policy is considered even more questionable than tolerance of insider trading.

In the United Kingdom, securities regulation was not considered a central objective until recently. It remains to be seen what the political and social importance of the Financial Services Act of 1986[5] will be, and, in particular, how much the UK authorities will take into account the international development of London as a financial center, and avoid promoting and applying rules that are too strict.

In Continental Europe, securities regulations do exist in some countries, for instance France, Belgium and Italy; however, they do not have anything like the same importance as in the United States. In Germany and Switzerland, as well as in many other countries, securities regulations are rather minimal and are not considered as being an important social and political goal; this may change in the near future.

Finally, apart from the traditional goal of securities regulation (investor protection), a new goal (avoiding systemic risks) is emerging as very important in many countries, especially after the "October crash of 1987."

Therefore, I believe that the harmonization of securities regulations will be a much more difficult task than that of banking law.

[3] BUXBAUM & HOPT, *supra* note 1, at 174.

[4] *Id.* at 192.

[5] See RIDER *et al.*, *Guide to the Financial Services Act 1986* (Bicester/Chicago 1987).

(2) *Buxbaum* and *Hopt* write that the aim of harmonizing company and capital market law in Europe is not clearly established.[6] Some insist upon the political aspects of such harmonization. Some think that harmonization is necessary to allow free exchange of financial services. Some argue that international freedom of financial services is already very well developed: legal harmonization would rather be a response of the legislators and regulators to the increasing "internationalization" of financial activities.

According to this point of view, with which I personally agree, legal harmonization is also often welcomed by the finance industry, to avoid the distortion of competition for multinational banks and securities companies. For their part, the regulators understand that any national regulation of financial activities cannot be wholly effective for multinational enterprises. For the protection of investors, of depositors and of the international financial system itself, only internationally coordinated and harmonized financial regulation can be really effective.

Here, the US experience is interesting. The United States thought, until recently, that they could independently regulate their banking and securities industry, without taking much account of the international context: today, they accept that this is becoming increasingly difficult.

III. The Methods of Harmonization

(1) Considering especially company law, but also capital market law, *Buxbaum* and *Hopt* analyze and compare different methods of legal harmonization:
- harmonization by laws, especially by "directives,"
- harmonization by official "recommendations,"
- harmonization by legal models (as in the United States),
- harmonization by self-regulation,-- harmonization by case-law,
- harmonization by administrative agencies.

For banking and securities regulations, the last method is the most important.[7] Substantial progress may be made by informal means of cooperation and mutual persuasion among the different national agencies. In this respect, the experience of international cooperation among banking supervisors (Committee of the Bank for International Settlements (BIS), Basle) is remarkable. Such informal cooperation could be, in practice, even more important than the formal harmonization of rules.

Of course, some basic harmonization of rules would also be very useful. However, in many cases, the development of harmonized self-regulation would be more useful and indeed easier than legal harmonization. In a field changing so rapidly, self-regulation is in principle a better tool, because it can be adapted and modified easily. Furthermore, it may be politically easier

[6] BUXBAUM & HOPT, *supra* note 1, at 193-204.

[7] *Cf.* also *infra* at 354.

to harmonize self-regulation than to harmonize laws adopted by each national parliament. Therefore, it seems very paradoxical that the European Communities should rather favor legal regulation and not generally consider that self-regulation is a valid means of implementing directives. It is not at all certain that laws are better applied in practice than self-regulation; the nature of the sanctions is not a good test for judging the practical effects of rules.

(2) *Buxbaum* and *Hopt* suggest that harmonization could be limited to international activities (which is often the same thing as big business), excluding national activities. I fully agree with their suggestion for banking and securities regulations, although it may be difficult to distinguish between national activities and international activities, especially since the latter are occasionally conducted by small enterprises. Efforts to harmonize regulation for all activities would either be blocked by small business[8] or be circumvented by industry (as happened in the case of company law with the increase in the number of private companies to avoid the harmonized rules on public companies, or in the case of securities regulation with the creation of a second or a third market, in part to avoid the stringent harmonized rules of the first (official) market). For purely national financial activities, legal harmonization is unnecessary or even harmful: different national laws might as well continue to apply.

Most important financial activities are already conducted worldwide. Consequently, I suggest that the main efforts of legal harmonization for international financial activities should be made on a worldwide basis, for all financially developed markets. Regional harmonization (especially in the European Communities) may prepare worldwide harmonization. If such regional harmonization is not made, it may be that worldwide harmonization in financial regulations will be decided in practice by three countries only: the United States, the United Kingdom and Japan. Furthermore, regional harmonization in the European Communities may be important politically, for all national financial activities, especially if Europe is to be politically considered as one country.

IV. The Objectives of Harmonized Banking Law and Securities Regulation

(1) The aims of banking laws and of securities regulations are in principle very different.

Banking laws aim at preventing bank failures, so that banking depositors are not at risk. One assumes that banking depositors are not in a position to make their own judgement upon the financial strength of their bank. For economic and social reasons, people should be encouraged to put their

[8] BUXBAUM & HOPT, *supra* note 1, at 277.

savings in the banks, who invest them again for the benefit of the economy. Consequently, banking laws imply direct supervision of banking organizations and activities, to ensure that they are reasonably safe.

On the other side, buyers of securities are supposed to be able to gauge for themselves the quality and the risks of the securities offered in the primary or the secondary market. Securities regulations are not intended to provide any guarantee as to the quality of the securities, but mainly to provide for appropriate disclosure rules so that each investor can make his own judgement and take his risks independently.

(2) However, in the real world, the need for protection of banking depositors and of investors in securities is not always so clearly differentiated.

In particular, for securities regulations, it is now admitted that the small private investor needs a very different protection from that of the large professional institutional investor. Indeed, most securities regulations increase the practical importance of this fundamental distinction.

In many countries, the small private investor is not in a very different position from the small banking depositor. For instance, a traditional banking depositor may be induced to buy short-term bonds issued by his bank, keeping the full protection of the banking law. With the same protection, he may buy long-term bonds from his bank, or indeed from other banks. Then, there does not seem to be much difference between buying bonds issued by the State, by some municipal organization or by a very important industrial company. The probable next step could be to buy some shares in a conservative mutual fund. In countries with a universal banking system, the banks would advise their clients to do so and would do all the broking. Under this process, it is not at all certain that the private client will have understood that, at a certain point, he is suddenly totally "at risk" and has to evaluate the risk himself. Moreover, banking laws do not protect the depositors from the risk of inflation... and many laws on mutual funds do provide for some basic quality in the assets.

On the other side, in banking supervision, disclosure rules may also play an important role in preventing the banks from taking excessive risks.

Consequently, the aims of banking laws and of securities regulations are less divergent than it would appear at first sight.

(3) Harmonizing banking laws and securities regulations also implies harmonizing the definition of banks and the definition of securities.

As for banks, it is striking that the investment banks (or securities houses) are not regulated by banking laws, although in some cases (especially for the important American and Japanese institutions) they are undertaking many activities which are very similar to banking.

As for securities, the main problem is to decide whether commodities are or are not to be considered as securities. One will perhaps have to consider that some new products are now offered to investors, especially real estate, works of art, etc., for which also some disclosure rules could possibly be useful.

(4) One of the most important differences between banking law and securities regulation is that, in the latter, the detection and the repression of fraud (especially insider trading, but also wrong or insufficient disclosure for new issues, stock manipulation, fraudulent prices in secondary markets, etc.) are of great importance, whereas this is not the case for banking law.

This is probably one of the reasons why the harmonization of securities regulation is more difficult, since the definition of fraud is difficult to harmonize. Furthermore, there are great differences as to the importance of the administrative efforts to be made for detecting and punishing such frauds.[9]

(5) For banking laws, rules for the organization and the financial strength of the banks are essential. However, the same is true for brokers (investment banks, securities houses): although the rules are generally quite different, the protection of banking depositors and of investors raises similar problems.

In both fields, strict capitalization rules have been developed, in sharp contrast with company law. Moreover, proper organization of financial intermediaries is necessary, so that they can themselves evaluate the risks they are proposing to their clients. Proper internal and external controls are essential. Important shareholders should not have an undue influence upon the management. Consequently, both in banking and in securities regulation, strict rules for the organization of financial intermediaries have been developed, going far beyond any comparable rules in company law.

In both fields, there is also a need for rules of conduct in relations with clients. However, these rules are much more important for securities regulations than for banking laws: the rules concern not only the acceptance of deposits, but the advice given to clients, especially for buying or selling securities (know your client, know your product, conflict of interests, etc.).

(6) In company law, although groups of companies play a very important role, it has not yet been possible to develop a proper legal framework for them. The only complete legal regulation of groups, which has been developed in Germany, is not satisfactory.[10] Any harmonization for groups of companies is therefore extremely difficult.

In contrast, banking law is very concerned with banking groups. However, the aim of the rules is completely different. In company law, the general aim of the rules is to protect the creditors and the shareholders of the subsidiaries and consequently to insure that the existence of a group is not detrimental to their interests. For the banks, it is acknowledged that, in practice, it is in their direct interest not to "abandon" a subsidiary in difficulties. Consequently, the rule is to take into account the fact that any risk incurred by a subsidiary must be taken to concern also the banking group as a whole and particularly the parent bank. This principle has by now induced most countries to supervise international banking groups on a

[9] *Cf. supra* at 348.
[10] See BUXBAUM & HOPT, *supra* note 1, at 188.

"consolidated basis:" the supervisory authority for the parent bank also keeps an eye on the other banks in the group. Obviously this "consolidated supervision" is not exactly the same in each country, but harmonization has already begun and will continue.

The same development has not yet taken place for the supervision of securities companies, although it is just as necessary for them as for the banks. National regulatory efforts in this direction would probably not be effective: therefore, harmonization should be envisaged soon and might not prove too difficult.

For the financial conglomerates, i.e. financial groups with banks, securities houses, insurance firms, etc., no firm view has yet been taken by the supervisory authorities upon the possibility of a "consolidated supervision." Of course, the financial conglomerates oppose this tendency, arguing that they can organize a clear separation between their different financial activities, ensuring that the risks incurred by one of these activities do not affect the others; however, it is difficult to believe that this separation could be organized without, at the same time, jeopardizing the "synergy effect" which is the aim of the financial conglomerates.

(7) In a broader economic context, both banking law and securities regulation should help to protect the national and international financial system. The importance of this objective has been clearly recognized, as regards banking supervision, for over ten years, but has only recently been accepted for securities regulation. During the "October 1987 crash," central banks recognized that the liquidity problems of securities markets (and of the financial intermediaries active in such markets) could be very detrimental to the international financial system in general, and they felt obliged to provide the necessary "liquidity," directly or through banks. Even if the central banks want to avoid a formal responsibility for the securities markets and for the solvency of securities houses, it is certainly very much in their interests to ensure that major accidents in this field are avoided. As the interests of all central banks here are parallel, international harmonization and cooperation should not be too difficult, and has already begun, especially within the OECD.

(8) Finally, for banking laws and for securities regulations, it is important to note that these prudential rules are often in conflict with a policy of free competition and deregulation. In principle, free competition induces banks and securities houses to take more risks and even to advise their clients to take more risks. In many cases, the aims of both sets of regulations are consequently in some contradiction. The balance to be reached differs from one country to another. Some harmonization, in this field also, is probably unavoidable.

V. Implementation of the Harmonization

(1) As *Buxbaum* and *Hopt* write,[11] harmonization is only important if it affects the real world and not only the "law in books." Obviously, this is true for all laws, although lawyers are reluctant to admit it.

In this context, I suggest that, in all economic regulation, excessive requirements induce individuals and enterprises (even State enterprises!) to try to get around the regulations. In financial activities, this "getting around" is especially likely to succeed through "internationalization," taking advantage of differences among the national regulations. The remedy would be not only international harmonization and cooperation among authorities, but also self-restraint by national laws and regulators, who should agree to regulate only when it is necessary and useful. This is sometimes overlooked, especially in "over-regulated" countries, like the United States.

(2) As regards company law, the question of how the rules are to be applied in practice is a very difficult one, especially because the case-law is (with the exception of the United States) not very extensive.

As regards banking law and securities regulation, administrative agencies play an important role in implementation. This is especially true of international legal harmonization, because each administrative agency has contacts with the others and may discuss with them the application of the laws, in general or in particular cases. Even without any international authority to promote a common interpretation and application of the law, the dialogue between authorities may be very efficient, because each authority is aware that it would be detrimental to its function if each national authority were to apply different interpretations to similar rules.

(3) A difficult question is whether private litigation should be an important factor in the application of securities regulation (for banking law, this aspect is not important).

Private litigation plays an important role in the United States. The role it will play in the United Kingdom is still open and is the center of controversy (see Section 62 of the Financial Services Act). Private litigation does not play an important role in securities regulation in any other European country.

In principle, it is not very logical to adopt rules of conduct, and then to provide that the violation of such rules would not give any private right to litigate to the clients who might be injured. However, *Buxbaum* and *Hopt* show that private litigation has its limits and may "distort objective implementation of the law."[12] I agree, in principle, that the proliferation of private litigation in this field is not in the general interest. In particular, it would be harmful if financial intermediaries were out to protect themselves from private litigation rather than to serve the best interests of their clients.

[11] *Id.* at 250.
[12] *Id.* at 214.

A specific problem, in this respect, is the way in which a number of investors (or banking depositors) who claim to be injured may litigate jointly, as in the United States (class action). If this is not permitted, private litigation will not play an important role in practice, because the amounts in dispute for one individual are generally too small to justify the expenses of litigation. In any case, it is better to avoid the grave drawbacks of the American system, in which the initiative of litigation is often taken by the attorneys, in their own interest.

VI. Perspectives on Legal Harmonization in Banking and Securities Regulation

(1) In their conclusions, *Buxbaum* and *Hopt* write that, in Europe, harmonization by way of "directives" will "go on continuously, even though slowly and piecemeal."[13] They note that securities regulation seems to deserve a high priority, without suggesting, however, that harmonization in this field will be more successful.

As far as banking law is concerned, I suggest that harmonization will proceed rather quickly and in a more or less global way. This could succeed especially if (as in the "BIS Committee" but not in the EC) harmonization is concentrated upon multinational banking activities. As regards international worldwide banking activities, harmonization at a European level is only efficient insofar as it allows and prepares for worldwide harmonization.

As regards securities regulation, harmonization is not yet very extensive. However, the practical need for harmonization is so great that progress should come. But, again, harmonization should be concentrated on international activities, without trying to include all national activities. In this field, European attempts at integration could be especially useful for preparing worldwide harmonization.

(2) In banking and securities regulation, legal harmonization is certainly important, but less important than for company law. Its judicial role will be very limited: cooperation between administrative agencies will be more important. As regards securities regulations, self-regulation could play a very important role and be easier to harmonize than national laws.

(3) *Buxbaum* and *Hopt* wonder whether, as in the United States, each European State should not remain free to adopt new national regulations, playing the role of "laboratories of the law."[14] This could be an important defense against the danger of "petrification" of harmonized law. But it would also be a danger to harmonization itself, unless such new national

[13] *Id.* at 271.
[14] *Id.* at 286.

regulations covered only new activities, not yet envisaged by the harmonized law.

VII. Before Harmonization: What Banking or Securities Laws Are Applicable?

The harmonization of banking law and securities regulation is a long and difficult process. Even within the European Communities (let alone worldwide harmonization!), such harmonization will still take a long time. Consequently, with different national laws still in force, it is very important to determine the national laws applicable to international banking and securities activities.

This question is a part of international administrative (economic) law, which at the moment is far less developed than international private law. It would be very useful to have at least some common principles internationally admitted in this field. My sole ambition here is to encourage further research in this complex field, without yet undertaking the presentation of any firm set of solutions.

For banking law, this question has been under examination for over ten years, especially within the Banking Supervisors Committee of the BIS. For securities regulation, it has not yet been examined from an international viewpoint, especially taking into account the globalization of the markets and new technologies.

A. Banking Laws Applicable to Multinational Banks

(1) If a bank has some activities abroad, *without there being a branch or a subsidiary*, it is generally admitted that the banking law of the bank (head office) is applicable. This is so because banking law (as opposed to securities regulation) is concerned with the organization and solvency of the banks, not with their relations with their clients.

However, most legislations restrict the ability of a foreign bank to do business within the country, without establishing a branch or a subsidiary, so that the practical importance of this principle is not very broad.

(2) If a bank has a *branch* abroad, such branch will be included in the supervision of the head bank's supervisory authority. Consequently, the banking law of the seat of the head bank is applicable in principle (there are some exceptions!). This is logical, because the branch is nothing other than a part of the head bank itself: all assets and liabilities of the branch are assets and liabilities of the head bank.

Nevertheless, the local banking law of the branch will also be applicable, with some exceptions (especially taking into account the fact that the solvency of the branch alone is generally irrelevant in practice).

Astonishingly, it does not seem that this application of both banking laws to branches raises difficulties in practice.

Within the European Communities, the intention is to allow European banks to have branches in all Member States, with the sole application of the banking law of the head bank (draft for a Second Banking Directive[15]). It remains to be seen whether, from a competitive point of view, it will make sense to have such a sharp distinction between branches (subject only to the head bank's banking law) and the subsidiaries (subject mainly to the local banking laws), although economically branches and subsidiaries play a very similar role.

(3) Although a *subsidiary* is often economically very similar to a branch, the legal situation is very different. Here the principle is the application of the banking law of the subsidiary, which is legally an independent bank.

However, in fact, it is hardly acceptable for the parent bank to leave one of its subsidiaries insolvent; in most cases, a parent bank will support its subsidiaries, even without any legal duty to do so, so long as its own existence is not endangered.

It follows that, for the supervisors of the parent bank, the risks assumed by its subsidiaries are considered to also affect the parent bank. This is the main reason for the "consolidated supervision" of banking groups, by which at least part of the law of the parent bank (especially the rules for capital ratios) are applicable to the group as a whole (and consequently indirectly to its subsidiaries).

(4) The scope of application of banking laws to "*financial conglomerates*" is still very uncertain. A "financial conglomerate" is a financial group of companies, including banks, whose parent is a holding company. Just as a branch may be economically very similar to a subsidiary, a financial conglomerate may be very similar to a banking group. The question is whether (and within what limits) banking laws (but which ones?) could be partly applicable to the group as a whole or whether the fact that the parent of the group is a holding company and not a bank excludes any kind of "consolidated supervision."

This difficult problem must first be solved nationally and there are no clear views yet on the subject. It may well be that the solution should differ, depending on the relative importance of the banks within the financial conglomerate.

B. Securities Regulation Applicable to Multinational Securities Houses

(1) The regulations applicable to securities houses (also called broker-dealers or investment banks) are partly concerned (like banking laws) with the organization and the solvency of the company, but also with the relations between the company and its clients (conduct of business rules). Consequently, the problem of the applicable law is different.

[15] O.J. C 167/32 (1989). Directive adopted in 1989: see O.J. L 386/1 (1989).

(2) If a securities house *does business* abroad, but has no branch or subsidiary there, the law of the securities house home office is clearly applicable. In addition, the local law would often be applicable to the home office's relation with its local clients. This would certainly be the case if the securities house were seeking clients locally; it should normally not be the case if the clients (normally not very numerous) have taken the initiative of contacting a foreign securities house and requesting its services.

(3) If the securities house has a *branch* abroad (which does not seem frequent in practice), the local law would normally be fully applicable to any such branch. It seems that the law of the head office would only apply for the rules concerning the organization and solvency of the branch (because this could affect the clients of the head office), but not for the "conduct of business" rules.

(4) If the securities house has a *subsidiary* abroad, this subsidiary would be fully governed by the local law. In striking contrast with banking law, securities regulators have generally not developed any concept of "consolidated supervision," so that the supervisory authorities of the parent securities house are not concerned with the organization and the business of their subsidiaries, and indeed receive no information about them. This situation is clearly unsatisfactory, insofar as (like for banks) an important international securities house can hardly leave one of its subsidiaries insolvent or even in financial difficulties without putting its own credit in danger. It is certain that, in one way or another, securities regulation should be applied to groups of securities houses.

C. Securities Regulation Applicable to Multinational Transactions (in Particular International Computerized Trading)

(1) The traditional view is that national securities law is applicable to all *transactions executed in the markets of the country concerned*. In practice, this was a good and easy solution at a time when all markets were clearly national or even regional. Today, with globalized international markets and with the extraordinary advances in technology, *it is not always easy to say in which country a specific securities transaction takes place* (and this will be more difficult to ascertain in the future).

With the development of electronic markets, the situation will become more complex. It may well be that the London Stock Exchange will permit foreign brokers to have electronic terminals, allowing them to deal directly on its international market (SEAQ International). The same brokers may, at the same moment, buy or sell the same shares on another electronic market, which can be related to another stock exchange or even possibly to no official stock exchange at all.

If an electronic market is organized outside any traditional stock exchange, possibly common to a number of institutions of different countries, which securities laws will be applicable?

Moreover, short of a system which allows automatic execution of the transactions (and possibly, in future, automatic clearing and settlement), it will not always be easy to draw the line between an electronic information organization and an electronic market.

Even for the primary markets, the situation will become more and more multinational. The Euromarket is already an important primary market not clearly related to any one country. If "direct selling efforts" are made in one or several countries, one can admit that the issue is taking place in each of these countries. But it may well be that, in the future, some issues (especially by well-known companies) could be made without any "direct selling efforts," simply through information given through electronic means. Even today, this information may be given through international newspapers or television.

(2) It follows from the foregoing that *the traditional idea that securities regulation applies to all transactions done "on the markets of the country" will soon be obsolete and impracticable for a number of multinational transactions.*

I do not at all claim to have a valid alternative to suggest. But I believe that securities regulators, the industry and securities lawyers should look for adequate solutions to this problem of international administrative law. What follows are only very preliminary ideas, essentially for generating discussion.

My general propositions are the following:

(a) If issuers or broker-dealers are soliciting investors by "*direct selling efforts*," it is quite normal and acceptable that these transactions should be governed by the securities law applicable in the country of residence of the investors. This is a traditional solution, which could well be maintained (with possibly some exceptions for professional and sophisticated investors).

(b) If, on the contrary, an investor is spontaneously taking the *initiative to buy or sell securities abroad*, without being solicited by "direct selling efforts," I see no reason to apply the securities regulations of the country of residence of such an investor.

(c) For securities traded multinationally, the application of *a number of different securities regulations*, depending on the market where the transactions are taking place, is often *inadequate*. One should try to agree to some reasonable solution whereby only *one securities law should be applicable: normally the law of the main marketplace for such a security*, which will be, in most cases, the same as the law of incorporation of the company whose securities are traded: the *principle of "leading securities regulation."*

(d) In principle, each securities regulation is applied by the national securities commission. In other words, the principle of "leading securities regulation" corresponds to the *principle of the "lead regulator."*

However, for the application of any national securities regulation abroad, international cooperation among securities commissions should be organized: first, to assist the "lead regulator" and second, to ensure that the main principles of the foreign jurisdictions concerned are respected.

(3) For the *primary markets*, *if "direct selling efforts" are made*, this will normally be done through securities houses established (at least through a branch) in the country of their clients. Indeed, such "direct selling efforts" are often forbidden to securities houses without local establishment. In this case, the local securities laws (in practice the laws of the residence of the intended clients) should be applicable, as has traditionally been the case. Possibly, an exception could be made if only professional or sophisticated investors are solicited, without any retail to private clients.

More difficult are the cases of issues made *without "direct selling efforts."* (I would include here issues promoted through international newspapers (without specific edition for each country) or through international television advertisements, etc.) Should we not, in such cases, consider that the client decides spontaneously to buy a new issue abroad? In this case, I suggest that the securities law of the "main market" of the securities (in most cases the law of the place of incorporation of the issuing company) should apply. Such an investor is accepting to take the risks of buying a foreign security, with all the political, economic, financial, and monetary risks of such a security. Why should he not also bear the "risk" of the securities regulations of this foreign country?

Indeed, I would even suggest that a company should not be allowed to organize a issue without respecting its own securities regulation. In other words, it seems to me difficult to justify allowing an American company to make an issue of securities abroad without respecting the SEC rules. Foreign investors should know that they have the same protection if they buy American securities, quite irrespective of the place of the transaction. Moreover, abuses abroad may well have consequences on the American market for the same securities. This would not prevent a company from organizing an issue from a certain place (for instance New York or London), voluntarily submitting its issue to the rules of such place, in addition to its own national securities regulation.

(4) What should be the securities law applicable to the *secondary markets*, especially if we think of electronic markets with terminals in many countries?

If such a market is organized by a traditional stock exchange, in a specific country, the securities regulation of such country could apply worldwide. In other terms, any firm wanting to trade on a terminal should be licensed by the country of the stock exchange and submit itself to the jurisdiction of that country (e.g., the case of Globex).

Obviously, this would theoretically allow the organization of an electronic exchange based in a country without any securities regulation. It would be up to the securities regulators of the broker-dealers to forbid them to enter into such a system.

The most difficult question will be raised by the organization of an electronic exchange by a number of different national institutions. Such a development could certainly be useful and the regulators should be ready to have an acceptable solution for such an event. It may be that such a development will begin in Europe, possibly with harmonized rules; in this case, the regulator could be either a "lead" national regulator, appointed in common by the relevant countries, or possibly a new European regulator, if this appears more practicable.

(5) For securities regulations concerning *fraud* (especially insider trading, manipulations, etc.), I also suggest that a single system should be adopted even for securities traded in a number of different places. It does not make sense to apply different rules, because a fraud committed anywhere will influence the trade in the same securities in other places.

For instance, if a share is traded on three different stock exchanges (e.g., New York, London and Tokyo), any dysfunction in one of the markets (not to speak of insider trading or manipulation) will affect the transactions for the same shares on the other markets. In the same case, if a foreign investor wants to buy or to sell such shares, he will certainly not instruct his broker to do it on a particular market, but under the best conditions. Consequently, it is not clear that it makes sense to decide simply that the market in New York is governed by American law, in London by English law and in Tokyo by Japanese law.

I do not see why it would be difficult to apply American insider rules to transactions on American shares in Switzerland; and on the other hand, I do not see any sense in applying English rules on insider trading to Swiss shares traded in London (unless this is their "main market").

(6) For the "*takeover*" of a company whose securities are traded in more than one country, it again seems irrational to apply different rules for the takeover of the same company, especially as the rules in different countries are not only different, but often contradictory.

In principle, one should once again apply the regulations of the "main market" of the target company. The securities regulator of this country should be the "lead regulator," cooperating with the securities regulators of other countries in which a substantial market in the shares of the target company exist, but without applying in principle the rules on takeovers of such countries.

As the discussion of my contribution in Lugano has shown, the problem discussed in the last chapter is the most challenging of my report and the solutions proposed are the most controversial. Since that discussion (and partly with the benefit of the same discussion) I have improved and refined my paper. I have decided, however, to keep most of the discussion in this book, even if I have now already taken into account some criticisms and modified my proposals accordingly.

B. Discussion

I. Securities Regulation: Internationally Applicable Law

Christian Timmermans

Prof. Hirsch, you propose[1] that the law applying to issues should be the law of the issuing company. The example you give[2] is not so disturbing but I could imagine other examples which could be quite disturbing. Could that not cause a race in laxity? Now your answer probably would be: "Well, we would have to be strict on the definition of the real office, of what is the head office of the company concerned." But if a group has a financial company and incorporates that company in a country where the conditions regarding issues are really fairly lenient, I do not think that even the most strict criterion in this respect can help us. But I would like to hear your views on that.[3]

L.C.B. Gower

The conflict of laws problems here are acute already, as SIB found when making its rules. They are particularly intractable in relation to groups which is one of the reasons why I am so keen on harmonization in that area. You raise a very interesting point, it seems to me, Prof. Hirsch.

Robert Austin

First, in relation to Prof. Hirsch's paper, which bristles with interesting issues, I want to focus only on the conflict of laws problems.[4] I would like him to develop in due course[5] the point that Prof. Gower made[6] as to whether there ought to be a distinction between branch offices and subsidiaries. What are Prof. Hirsch's thoughts where there is a cross-shareholding relationship between securities firms operating in two or more countries without there being a holding company and a subsidiary involved? Say you have a firm such as Goldman Sachs investing in a broking

[1] See *supra* at 358 ff.
[2] See *supra* at 360.
[3] See *infra* at 372 f.
[4] See *supra* at 356 ff.
[5] See *infra* at 371.
[6] See *supra* at 323.

firm in London, but perhaps holding a little less than a 50% interest or perhaps a little more: how would his rule work out in that situation?

Prof. Hirsch says[7] that it would be absurd, and I quite agree, to treat differently a branch office of Goldman Sachs in London and a subsidiary of Goldman Sachs operating in London, and he says:[8] "They should be treated the same." The question I would like to raise for general comment is: "Yes, but in which direction?" This is a fascinating area. I agree entirely that there is a difficulty because of the way markets are operating in the age of modern technology, and I see it as a particular difficulty for bodies like the SEC to continue to apply such outdated regulatory principles as the "coming to rest abroad" principle. The concept of a security coming to rest anywhere is just nonsensical. But what the SEC is now doing, without going to the extremes that Prof. Hirsch has suggested,[9] is to issue no-action letters which produce a "factors" approach. You weigh up various considerations and you make a balancing judgement about which market the issue is most closely connected with. In the short run it may not be possible to be more specific than that.

André Tunc

I was most interested in Prof. Hirsch's proposals. I was however slightly frightened by the idea of applying American security regulations on a worldwide basis.[10] But I see that I was not alone in being afraid of the idea that such a complicated regulation could apply everywhere.

Christian Meier-Schatz

Time constraints induce me to make only one short comment on what is probably the most revolutionary proposal of Prof. Hirsch,[11] namely his head office principle as a conflict of laws rule.

I think that the proposal itself is very interesting not only because of the fascinating perspective of having a US circuit court for Europe or even for the rest of the world, but also for a couple of other reasons. I see, for instance, some functional similarities with influential principles of administrative supervision. In addition, some economic arguments could be made for integrating the legal risk into the product itself. However, I have some reservations and ask myself whether this approach is not effective only when some harmonization has already taken place.

More specifically, I see two difficulties. From the buyer's perspective, there are probably substantial information problems. I do not think so

[7] See *supra* at 357 f.
[8] See *supra* at 358 f.
[9] See *supra* at 359 f.
[10] See *supra* at 360.
[11] See *supra* at 359.

much of, e.g., US law or UK law. But as soon as one gets a wide variety of more exotic issue laws then we face, even from a sophisticated investment perspective, severe informational problems. This is especially the case if you intend to also include rules of conduct.

The second point relates to the seller's side which has already been mentioned by Prof. Timmermans. I do not know how appropriate an assumption is that not only fictitious but real operational issuing activities could be started from low standard countries. That may *de facto* not be a realistic perspective but at least it reopens the question of the race for laxity. Again, the proposal is itself highly interesting and, of course, takes into consideration the new technologies and the internationalization of securities markets. But I perceive a tension between, on the one hand, conflict of laws rules in a transition period towards more harmonization and, on the other hand, conflicts of laws rules which themselves are functionally based on a certain degree of already harmonized laws.

Eddy Wymeersch

Does Prof. Hirsch's proposal[12] not risk being counterproductive? As a purchaser of shares I will be afraid of buying American shares at the risk of being exposed to an SEC investigation or even worse, to be put, possibly by mistake, on some or other black list, especially if I am unwilling to cooperate with their investigations. Also, dealing in these shares may expose me to the liability rules and measures as applied in the United States. If you want to apply Rule 10b-5 to European investors dealing in American shares on a European stock exchange, you will probably render the market in these shares more onerous, and not comparable to the markets in European shares. But the question deserves to be further scrutinized and the approach certainly opens up interesting perspectives.

Prof. Hirsch pointed to the importance of the rules of private international law in securities matters.[13] But there is more: there are first the conflicts between the rules of trading in the different electronic trading systems. These rules, often embedded in the electronic programs, are real rules of law and are quite difficult to find, and even more difficult to harmonize. If I am trading in one system, my order will remain valid until the next hour, while in the other it will remain stored until executed. If packages of orders are transmitted between systems, matters will be even more complex. One may also think, e.g., about the question when an order is executed, or which acceptance will have to receive priority if several acceptances are routed to the same offer at the same moment.

Some order should be established in this diversity, and it probably will not be possible to reason along the traditional lines of the conflict of laws rules, but some specific, uniform minimum system will have to be devised.

[12] See *supra* at 359 f.
[13] See *supra* at 358 f.

One small note: I have seen that UNCITRAL has put this item on one of its agendas for future consideration. But would it not be useful for the EC to put a similar subject on one of its future work schedules?

A further point relates to conflicts of laws: usually rules of conflict deal with private law. With the internationalization of the markets, one finds that more and more rules of conflict between public law systems are necessary, i.e., rules that attribute the responsibility for certain parts of the regulatory system to one of the different national bodies that could claim some sort of responsibility, but maybe also will bear some sort of liability. Here again new procedures will have to be worked out.

Hartmut Schmidt

From a user of a market viewpoint, mainly that of an issuer, I think it is paramount that he has a choice, that he can select those systems which give him, given the investment project of the company, the highest proceeds from the instruments he is issuing. This may require for example that he go to the Netherlands Antilles for tax reasons though he is not interested at all in having anything else to do in the Netherlands Antilles; he may like to use the primary market system, for example, of the United Kingdom and therefore he is interested that UK securities law applies to his issue. And any solution that solves these conflict problems that Prof. Hirsch mentioned and that takes away these important choices would be I suppose very detrimental to securities regulations.

Gérard Hertig

Regarding Prof. Hirsch's paper, I would very much be in favor of that idea of localization with the issuing corporation.[14] Prof. Hirsch already floated that idea last June; here you are very kind to him, because then it was an uproar. But the more you think about this idea the better you find it. Prof. Wymeersch has just given a good example. He said: "If I am buying American shares here in Switzerland or in Europe, I do not want American rules to apply." But at the same time I am sure that if you buy American shares on the New York Stock Exchange through your broker here in Europe, it does not make any difference to you. It is just a telephone call differently routed and you would not mind having American rules applying in such a situation. It is a global market. And I think that is the point.

Klaus Hopt

I do not believe in the issuing law approach. I have just made a study for a major bank group on prospectus liability. How this works in practice is that the bank group wants at the same time to keep its market and enter new

[14] See *supra* at 359.

ones. These are the market forces we talked about yesterday.[15] Given this goal the bank group must, in its own interest, adopt the most protective rule, because to distinguish between the American, German and other issuing markets does not make sense to it any more. But if it sticks to the most demanding rule, then it has served at the same time all the other markets also. Overall this may be even less costly in the international scene.

On the other hand, if you take smaller and less serious issuers, under an issuing law approach, they could very well have a subsidiary somewhere which launches the operation under the lax rules of that country. Then either you accept this and you have the race for laxity, as mentioned,[16] or you want to do something about it and then we are again back to our financial group law discussion.[17] Just right in the middle.

Geoffrey Fitchew

On the question of the choice of law, I speak as a non-lawyer with great hesitation but I would just like to throw out two ideas.

First of all, there is the Rome Convention on applicable law[18] which will become effective, I think, when one more Member State ratifies it. So it is actually quite likely to come into force. Now the Rome Convention excludes both the insurance and negotiable instruments but the rules in the Rome Convention would apply to the provision of financial services other than those two exceptions, and I think in general it would tend to give a lot of weight in many cases to the applicable law of the client rather than that of the operator of services.

In relation to the primary market and the issue of new securities, it seems to me that there must be a distinction to be made between the instrument itself and the services provided in connection with the marketing of the instrument. The Rome Convention would apply to the services provided in connection with the marketing of the instrument but not to the instrument itself. In relation to the instrument itself, presumably one of the more important questions will be the prospectus requirements, and the prospectus requirements, subject to whatever mutual recognition arrangements are negotiated, would be the responsibility of the market or markets where the issue is being placed. I do not know how far those two thoughts go to suggest solutions to this problem. I would be interested in any further discussion on it.

[15] See *supra* at 248 ff.
[16] See *supra* at 362.
[17] See *supra* at 252 f and 264 f.
[18] O.J. L 266/1 (1980).

II. Securities Regulation: Role of Private Litigation

Olivier Guillod

It is true that American lawyers are much more aggressive, I would say, in pursuing litigation, but there are now many American lawyers coming to Europe through the big law firms and they have established subsidiaries in Brussels, in Paris, London, Rome and so on. I wonder whether the presence of all these American-trained lawyers now in Europe could have some impact on the litigation issue.

L.C.B. Gower

Prof. Hirsch referred to Section 62 of the Financial Services Act,[19] and perhaps I could just comment on that. This provides that a breach of the rules of SIB or an SRO gives rise to a civil remedy. That caused somewhat belatedly something of an uproar, very largely for the reasons which have just been pointed out where people were scared that – now London is full of litigious American lawyers – these are going to tell their clients to sue everybody under the sun. In other words, I do not think the English firms were particularly worried that their English clients would be likely to rush into civil litigation but they thought that the big American firms might do so and that the American lawyers might encourage them.

I think myself this is a bit of a nonsense. The reason why people litigate in the United States is because they have very different rules about the cost than we have in England and they have contingent fees and so on. It seems to me that once the American lawyers realized – as I am sure they realized long since – that litigation is very expensive and the dangers considerable in the UK, it is unlikely that there will be a rush of individual civil litigation.

But a much more important thing, I think, is that the Act also provides in Section 61 that SIB can take action, can apply for injunctions and a restitution order (this is borrowed lock, stock and barrel from the American disgorgement procedure). This avoids most of problems of the class action, because it is in effect a public body litigating on behalf of the people who have been ripped off. This, I think, is the important Section.

Section 62, I personally would not want to see scrapped, but Section 61 is the one that I think is important.

Richard Buxbaum

I just take the liberty of interjecting that on this litigation issue, at least so far as the major broker-dealer and customer situation is concerned, as compared with investment fraud, the American move to arbitration has practically swept that field since the Supreme Court has authorized

[19] See *supra* at 354. See also *supra* at 342 f.

arbitration of these disputes; and I think that this, too, has changed the picture and the image significantly. At least, as I say, as to the customer's litigation against the intermediaries, to distinguish that from the investor's litigation against the issuer or secondary party.

Edmund Kitch

On the questions of litigation, I take it that the traditional lawyer's solution to these problems has been to try and give each issue of a security a distinctive national identity, so you had an American issue and then you do an issue in London and you keep them separate. I take it that Prof. Hirsch's underlying vision is again that it ought to be possible for international enterprises to do a single issue which would be offered worldwide, all in one transaction. Obviously, if you did that today, for instance, you would end up with class actions in the US district courts, in which part of the certified class would be all the rest of the worldwide purchasers.

Our legal profession would love to have those cases, and I assume the issuers are not about to give them to our lawyers. I find interesting Prof. Hirsch's suggestion[20] that the purchasers buy not only, the issuer but its legal system. The purchase of a security in an American company buys into the American legal system as well. There suddenly flashed into my mind a vision of a new US district court for Western Europe where securities claims brought by Europeans under this theory could be heard. I mean, if you are going to buy into the substance, then you might buy into the procedure as well – right? And so, then the European buyers would go to the court, it would sit in London, and give these American firms in London something to do. You file your claim there under the US federal rules of civil procedure, with a class action and so forth.

If that is not what you are going to do and you are just talking about traditional conflict rules, then I do not know enough to see how this would work out. Can we imagine a case in a German court involving the applicability of Rule 10b-5 and the German judge struggling with that?

André Tunc

Prof. Hirsch has raised the problem of the place which should be recognized for private litigation.[21] I can give some information on this point.

In France the trend is certainly to encourage litigation: litigation by the individual parties or by a small group of shareholders. Class action has also been considered for a number of years. It was even recently introduced in a bill, but finally withdrawn. The Government and the COB also considered encouraging the formation of associations of shareholders. But it is a very difficult problem. There are some associations but they may not be entirely

[20] See *supra* at 360.
[21] See *supra* at 354 f.

public-minded. The COB, I think, would have liked to have associations of shareholders of Suez, of the *Société Générale*, of the big companies which have been recently privatized. So far, nothing has been done. On the other hand, progress has been made on something comparable to Section 61 of the Financial Services Act, that is to say the power of public authorities to apply to the court in the interest of the shareholders. The COB has recently received some powers to act for the benefit of the normal shareholder. The COB and the *ministère public* can also request the appointment of an *expert de minorité*. There is this trend towards encouraging private or public litigation in the interest of private persons. For the time being, we are not afraid that we may go too far.

III. Various Other Topics

Olivier Guillod

I fully agree with most of the options Prof. Hirsch submitted as to a worldwide regulation and as to a uniform regulation for all financial services. I am only wondering whether it is really realistic to expect a unique worldwide regulation to be agreed on one day.

And if it happened, coupled with self-regulation, I wonder whether it would not be a means to protect the already established markets in the world and to exclude other markets which could arise in the future.

Christian Timmermans

GATT seems to have the ambition to put financial services on the agenda, and has done it already to some extent in the final resolution of the Punta del Este Conference. The follow-up is not quite clear, but if this is going through it could have some consequences, not so much I think in achieving harmonization, as in obtaining consensus on non-discrimination principles in this respect. It would be interesting to have a reaction from Mr. Fitchew because the Commission has, as far as I know, taken a stand on this.

Geoffrey Fitchew

My view is that the GATT negotiations on financial services are likely to be very limited in their scope in comparison with what we are doing within the Community, and therefore I do not think there is any great potential of conflict with that. The reason why they will be limited in their scope is the absence of freedom of capital movement in a very large part of the world, in particular among developing countries. In the absence of freedom of capital movements the concept of cross-frontier provision of financial services more or less does not exist, and I think for that reason the focus of negotiations in relation to financial services in GATT will be on the exercise of the right of establishment.

Gérard Hertig

One of the "weak" points in Prof. Hirsch's paper, I think, is when he says[22] that you can harmonize on the international level and that national situations can be left to the States. I do not think that in the financial services market you have so much to do with "pure" national situations. For example, you have an asset manager in Geneva, who has a client in Italy and who may buy stocks in New York. Is that a national situation or an international situation? Hence, it is very difficult to find a dividing line between national and international operations.

Klaus Hopt

Prof. Hirsch, you mentioned[23] that a viable delimitation could be not to have European harmonization for purely national activities. This sounds very appealing. It is okay for company law. It is already much more difficult for banking law. But I do not see how this can reasonably be done for securities regulation for the same reasons you mentioned, i.e., the factual connection of the different national securities markets.

In addition to your first suggestion, you mentioned in brackets that also small business in general could be excluded from harmonization at the European level since in most cases it is purely national. I doubt that this is really the case. In Germany, small enterprises – really small ones, not corporations, but GmbH and even commercial limited partnerships – are to a high percentage multinational companies. So I think the division between smaller and larger companies would be arbitrary in our context. Of course the interstate commerce differentiation is embedded in the Treaty of Rome, and EC antitrust law and national antitrust law are divided along this line, and for a new European merger control regulation[24] a differentiation according to size is discussed. Maybe it works there. But as far as our fields are concerned I just doubt it.

A final remark. Little thought has been given up to now to securities frauds, manipulation, stabilizing, etc., and what harmonizing efforts to make there. I think the market operations are getting more and more complex and at the same time harmonization becomes more and more important. In the banking law field, up to now, we have tried more to develop rules for institutions, i.e., for banks. But as to securities fraud we are really in the middle of the market, and in order to get hold of it rules for

[22] See *supra* at 350.
[23] See *supra* at 350.
[24] Regulation adopted in 1989: see O.J L 395/1 (1989).

the market are needed. These may be much more difficult to develop and to enforce.

IV. Concluding Remarks

Alain Hirsch

I think that because of time constraints I have to limit myself to a very few comments on the conflict of laws rules problems. What I would like to say is the following: I am not saying that the conflict of laws rules which I have proposed are excellent or easy to implement, or anything of the kind. What I am saying is that the conflict of laws rules which are presently generally adopted are working less and less well and will be more and more inefficient as time passes, and therefore new ones should be looked at. And what I am suggesting is that the ones which I am proposing could be the basis for a reflection – many adjustments, obviously, being possible. For instance, adjustments as to whether some enterprises should be allowed to make choices of law, to choose more stringent law or possibly even less, or as to whether there should be some evolution of the conflicts of laws rules, depending upon the degree of harmonization, as Prof. Meier-Schatz has said,[25] etc. But let me just illustrate my proposal with a few examples.

Number one: conflict of laws rules relating to the enterprises themselves, that is investment banks and broker-dealers. What I am suggesting is only that the present situation, in which the broker-dealers are subject to the rules of the State in which they exercise their activity is no longer workable: if you have free financial services, you do not know where they are exercising their activity. If you say that they are exercising their activity where their client is located and this would be (but I do not think it is) the consequence of the Rome Convention,[26] then the lawyers have obviously really done their job and industry is dead. But that is certainly not the ideal.

Obviously my proposal implies a minimum of key elements harmonization. It means that for countries in which there are no minimal requirements on any activity, any kind of advertisement would just be prohibited. But I do not think that it is possible to regulate on financial strength from the point of view of a number of different legislations and from the point of view of a number of different agencies. And, I would suggest, the same is true for the organization of business competence and conflicts of interests, and that leads to the conduct of business rules. If you say that the conduct of business rules are a separate matter, even for groups of companies (for the sub in London, the sub in Paris and the sub in Munich of the same group), this means that you have no conflict of interests rules at all. That is what I am suggesting. And I think that in the EC legislation the list of activities still

[25] See *supra* at 364.
[26] See *supra* at 366.

governed by the so-called host countries (which nobody knows what they are) is still too long – although I understand that there are political and practical reasons for that.

Example number two: the problem of the market. The example of my friend Eddy Wymeersch,[27] as Gérard Hertig has said,[28] is just lovely. Does it make sense that if I buy an American share in New York, in London, in Zurich or in Tokyo the situation will be different?

I suggest that most clients – of course we assume they are most sophisticated chaps – do not know where they buy their shares. They ask the Union Bank of Switzerland (UBS) to buy an ITT share and UBS buys that in New York, Tokyo or London (and tomorrow, in any scheme of computerwise buying, nobody will know where it was bought). UBS knows, of course, but the client does not know; it is a pure coincidence.

And if you have a buyer and a seller, where is the order to be executed? If I am in Switzerland and I buy an American share and if the seller, by pure coincidence, is a Japanese, I frankly do not know where the market is. So I think that the "market place" is not an economic reality and a legal useful thing any more – even if, of course, it still exists nowadays in many instances. The New York Stock Exchange still exists. What I am suggesting is that the importance of these things is disappearing.

And to go on, it does not make sense if the SEC can prevent insider trading on the New York Stock Exchange, but is unable to prevent insider trading on American shares on the Tokyo Stock Exchange, even if the shares are bought and sold by Japanese. This directly affects the American markets. Up to now, the SEC has never said that it would do that, and there is no legal basis for fighting against insider trading or manipulation of American shares by foreign buyers and foreign sellers on foreign markets. But up to now this has seldom happened. I suggest that agencies will have to do such fighting and every country has to recognize it is a legitimate thing that they should do that.

Conversely, I have the greatest difficulty in admitting that the United States should fight for Swiss, German or Italian shares even if they are "traded" in the United States. I do not think that an American buyer should be more protected if, again, he is "buying" his shares in the United States or in Switzerland. He does not know where they are bought anyhow.

For the issues, the situation is a little less advanced than for the markets, because today the issues in most cases are, and I said that in my paper,[29] still sold by so-called direct efforts of broker-dealers calling, writing, making advertisement and having direct relationships with their clients. And I understand that as long as this is done the place of these direct efforts is important; but its importance is diminishing.

[27] See *supra* at 364.
[28] See *supra* at 365.
[29] See *supra* at 359.

Prof. Kitch said[30] that somebody could have the idea of making multinational offerings issued in many countries at the same time. It is not only an idea, it is a well-known fact for Euro-Bonds and, since a few years ago, for Euro-Equities, and it will become more and more true. Again, it is not yet the case, but you can easily imagine that tomorrow prospectuses will just be put into the computer and be at your disposal worldwide without any direct efforts, that all professionals in the world will see these prospectuses at the same second and buy for their mutual funds and so on. And now tell me where is the place of issue? I do not know, and I suggest to you that tomorrow nobody will know what the place of issue will be. And that is why I am just saying: let us try, of course, to harmonize some key elements, and doesn't it make sense to say that the head of the company is just a less arbitrary, less uncertain point of contact than the so-called place of issue?[31]

Of course, that does not solve all the problems of the race for laxity or of the race for stringency. Let us look at all the details afterwards. I am only suggesting that if we begin with the place of issue and the place of the market, we begin at the wrong end of the story; then all the small problems, very important, will be just more difficult to solve.

Just one more word. I think we should not be afraid for instance of the American legislation being applied more. That is not at all true. Obviously it will mean quite rightly that any European buyer of an issue or on the market will be protected by American law. What is abnormal with that? I find it very abnormal that a same company should issue shares in the United States and in Europe under completely different rules. I think that the same company should have similar rules applicable to all its securities throughout the world. What I find funny is, as somebody said,[32] this famous "come to rest" theory by which in a very hypocritical manner the SEC tries to protect the American from buying foreign shares but allows him to buy after some time, when it appears that it is too costly to apply the "come to rest" theory, and issues a no-action letter. It is just a dead theory.

Geoffrey Fitchew

Just a last point on the conflict of laws problem. I think perhaps that when I read Prof. Hirsch's paper I maybe misunderstood his proposition. The Rome Convention to which I referred[33] relates to the applicable law of contracts, of course. I think I misunderstood. What you really are talking about is the division of responsibility in relation to supervisory rules primarily, it seems to me.

[30] See *supra* at 368.
[31] See *supra* at 362 ff.
[32] See *supra* at 363.
[33] See *supra* at 366.

Alain Hirsch

Including the private effects of so-called public law rules for protecting the investor outside of the pure contract like Rule 10b-5 and so on and so on.

Chapter Ten

Takeovers

Discussion

I. Introductory Remarks

Geoffrey Fitchew

What I propose to do is to make a few introductory remarks about the incidence of takeovers in the European market and why there are pressures to produce a directive on takeovers,[1] then to say in a rather summary way what I think our directive is likely to contain, and then to raise a number of issues for discussion.

The first point then is the incidence of takeovers, in particular contested takeovers in the Community. Until fairly recently takeovers and in particular contested takeovers have not been a very widespread phenomenon outside the United Kingdom. I think it is probably even now true to say that 90% or more of takeovers both contested and otherwise are within the UK market. There are a variety of reasons for that. Perhaps I will just highlight three of them.

First: in many Member States the securities markets were underdeveloped. There was not a sufficiently liquid market and companies in any case relied to a greater extent on bank financing than on financing through equity issues. Second: absence of disclosure in some markets. I have had a remark, made to me by a previously chief economist of the New York Stock Exchange, that American companies were deterred from seeking to make takeovers in some European markets because they did not know what they were buying. Third: in some European markets the predominance of banks and insurance companies in the shareholding structure. Over the last few years and particularly since the announcement of the White Paper programme,[2] the number of cross-frontier takeovers within Europe – both Community Europe and Europe in a wider sense – has significantly increased and the expectation is that the trend will continue and there will

[1] Proposals for a Takeover Directive: see O.J. C 64/8 (1989) and O.J. C 240/7 (1990).

[2] See *supra* at 4 ff.

be more contested takeovers. As a result of liberalization of capital movements also there is a much greater cross-frontier holding of shares in the companies of other Member States. Those are the basic considerations which are behind the commitment to produce a Community directive on takeovers.

Recently, there has been considerably greater interest shown by the press and by the business community in having a Community directive on takeovers, and that is the result in particular of the *Société Générale* affair in Belgium[3] and of the successful Nestlé bid for Rowntree in the United Kingdom. Both of these events led to a good deal of press comment, in particular in Belgium and France, about the desirability of regulating these matters at Community level. Although there has been that degree of interest shown in the press, there has been surprisingly little discussion either in the press or elsewhere of what the objectives of any Community directive should be, still less of the detailed contents. I think the best way to describe the situation is that there is quite a widespread feeling, at any rate in some Member States, that there is not a "level playing field" in some sense, either within the Community or between Community countries and third countries. I will come back to this question of what the objective of Community legislation should be after I have described what I think the likely contents of our directive are going to be.

First of all, we will certainly want to include in the directive rules relating to disclosure, that is to say the information to be provided in the form of an offer document by the bidding company and the information to be provided also by the target company.[4] I think we are likely to say also that the target company should be obliged to ask for an independent assessment to be made,[5] but obviously for fairly clear reasons we would not want to oblige the directors of the target company to make a recommendation. They are free to do so, obviously, but it seems to me to be impractical to require them to make a recommendation.

Going beyond disclosure rules, the other issues which we are discussing amongst ourselves are first of all the obligation question, the obligation to make a public offer and the setting of a threshold after which there would be an obligation to make a public offer.[6] There is also in the same area the question of whether once an offeror has acquired a very high percentage of shares, 90-95%, there should be an obligation on him to make an offer relating to the total outstanding shares. That is one area of the issue.

Second, the principle of the equal treatment of shareholders of the target company. The principle of equal treatment, as I think has already been commented,[7] is already contained in the Second Company Law Directive[8]

[3] See *supra* at 203 ff.
[4] See Art. 7, 10, 11 and 14 of the proposed directive.
[5] See Art. 14(2) of the 1989 proposal, defeted in the 1990 amended proposal.
[6] See Art. 4 of the proposed directive.
[7] See *supra* at 159.

and in the Listing Particulars Directive.[9] I think it is very likely that we would want to include in the directive on takeovers either a general proposition, along the lines of the Second Directive, that in takeover operations the principle of equal treatment of shareholders should be observed,[10] or we might want to go beyond that and lay down a number of more specific instances where the equal treatment of shareholders should apply, perhaps the most obvious one being that where a offeror in the course of a bid acquires shares on the market at a price higher than that contained in his bid, he should be obliged to raise his bid to the price that he has paid,[11] and a number of other possible applications of the rule of the principle of equal treatment of shareholders.

Next, there is the question of defensive measures. I think that at this stage of the Community development we would want to lay down the proposition that the target company should not be permitted, once a bid has been launched, to engage in measures designed to frustrate the bid, in particular through the issue of additional shares, without the explicit agreement of the body of shareholders.[12] The British Takeover Panel I think has a list, which is not necessarily exhaustive, of the types of frustrating measures which are subject to that rule. I think that is probably the limit to which we want to go at this stage. I do not think that at this stage we would want to go further and say that certain types of defensive measures could not be undertaken at all, even where there was the agreement of the shareholders.

I think finally we would want to lay down requirements regarding the minimum and maximum periods for the acceptance of the offer[13] – a minimum period in order to allow the shareholders to have adequate time to decide whether to accept an offer, a maximum period in order to avoid the uncertainty associated with a bid from hanging over the target company for too long.

There are a number of other issues which we may or may not want to tackle, but I think those are probably the core of the measures that we are looking at.

(The draft/amended draft Takeover Directive published in 1989/1990[14] in fact cover all the issues listed above.)

The disclosure rules that we will put forward would also be likely to require the bidder to include in his offer document a statement of his intentions regarding the development of the company and the position of the salaried employees.[15]

[8] O.J. L 26/1 (1977). See Art. 42.
[9] O.J. L 66/21 (1979). See Art. 42.
[10] See Art. 3 of the 1989 proposal, deleted in the 1990 amended proposal.
[11] See Art. 16 of the proposed directive.
[12] See Art. 8 of the proposed directive.
[13] See Art. 12 of the proposed directive.
[14] See *supra* note 1.
[15] See Art. 10(1) lit. l of the proposed directive.

Two other issues. One which I know Prof. Wymeersch would like to discuss,[16] that is whether the government should retain the right – either within the Community in relation to takeover bids from other Member States or at least in relation to bids coming from third countries – to intervene to prevent takeovers other than on merger and monopoly grounds. I think that everyone would clearly accept that it is legitimate for governments to intervene to raise questions about a takeover on antitrust grounds. Virtually I think all the Member States do that, and there is now a fairly well established process of asking the same questions at the Community level as well at any stage in the procedure, and I would not comment on the mergers issue further. But there remains the question: should governments have the right to intervene on other public order grounds?

Linked with this question, is the celebrated problem of reciprocity which has been raised by the Nestlé bid. In the United Kingdom and other Member States there have been a large number of commentators who have said that it is or should be illegitimate for a company coming from a country such as Switzerland to be able to make a takeover bid for companies within the Community unless the same rights exist on a reciprocal basis. Now I think there is considerable confusion over this issue. In general this problem arises in respect to the use of so-called defensive measures, that is to say, the difficulties which occur both in Switzerland and elsewhere, indeed in a number of Member States in the Community, arise because companies are free under company law to organize their shareholding structure in such a way as to make takeovers extremely difficult, and it is rather rare for this to be a matter of intervention by the national government or to be discriminatory. In most cases these kind of defenses can be used, and are used, both against the domestic bid and against the foreign bid. I think there may be discriminatory rules in one or two countries, but the general situation is, as I have described it, that this is a matter of choices available under corporate law in different countries rather than governmental intervention on a discriminatory basis. It would seem rather difficult for the Community to insist on reciprocity in a situation in which that reciprocity does not already exist within the Community itself. It is clear that the incidence and use of defensive measures of this kind diverges very widely within the Community. Even within the United Kingdom, which is relatively the most open market, there are quite a large number of important companies which have arranged their shareholding structure in such a way as to make bids very difficult.

L.C.B. Gower

The Savoy Hotel.

[16] See *infra* at 381.

Geoffrey Fitchew

That is the most topical case, but Reuters is a very interesting example, and the use of such measures in the Netherlands and Germany is very widespread. That seems to be the only case for intervention in respect to the reciprocity clause, in respect of measures taken by national governments on a discriminatory basis.

Richard Buxbaum

This information is a matter of a five or six minute additional setting of some scenes simply from the American perspective. A couple of these are themes of federalism, translated from the American Nation-versus-State issues to the European scene and a couple are rather vague and more future than currently oriented financial points.

I would like to start with one of the latter. I think one of the most intriguing problems for regulation and policy formulation in the next while is going to be the problem of transition. That is to say, the takeover question is part of a larger issue, oddly enough, namely, that of the conversion of national financial markets to one European air. This is to some degree the conversion of national firms to a different form in which, as was stated,[17] equity financing is expected to play a larger part, in which direct investment by savers is expected to play a larger part, and in which the opening of Europe to international primary and secondary purchasing and trading means a change in the composition of the investor structure, with an increasing institutional investor arrangement, and so on and so forth.

Now, it is interesting to reflect on one not totally analogous experience but one experience of that sort. My impression in Australia was that the first wave of takeovers indeed was in a sense efficiency-inducing, that it woke up a sleepy enterprise management and enterprise control-bloc ownership structure, but that in a second wave more serious questions can be raised about the efficient capital market and efficient control market hypothesis which fuels so much of the American discussion. I do not either accuse or commend Europe for being Australia, but to a degree I think an analogous problem of transition or of a phased situation is going to be an issue here. Whatever is done in the way of policy formation needs to reflect on the fact that you are not going to have the same scene and therefore are not going to have the same policy throughout this period. I found this to be a very complicating factor if you are starting right at the outset with considering how to structure a merger and takeover policy. That is obviously a very quick and in a sense fuzzy point but I think it is worth making.

A second point that the American experience taught and that I do not find much controversy about here is that you cannot separate the jurisdictional

[17] See *supra* at 375.

control of the takeover bidder's regulation from jurisdictional control of the incumbent target management response, and obviously Mr. Fitchew has just made that point. That of course means that there will be a new impetus to harmonization of company law on the European scene. I do not think that this is the tail wagging the dog, but I do think this is in fact one of the most important reasons for company law harmonization. The American shift, the way American company law has been evolving in the last decade driven by the takeover movement is simply phenomenal. Not only our State-versus-federal visions of relative competence, but also the substance or concept of what company law is all about has undergone a sea change in the last decade in the United States. Therefore it not only would not surprise me, it would commend itself, that an entirely new impulse to company law harmonization or centralization is an issue to be faced as a result of this phenomenon.

A third point I think worth making is that the concept of shareholder sovereignty as an organizing principle, first, cannot be separated from the underlying question of what is your philosophy about takeovers, that is, your public policy view of takeovers; and secondly, it is in its own right an extremely slippery and difficult concept to operate with. Our experience with the division of competence between management and shareholding bodies as to the question of early emplacement of potential antitakeover measures is very problematical; e.g., as to delegation of authority under the concept of blank stock authorization, so that an issuance of stock is in a sense authorized by shareholders but is in no real sense conceived of in the context in which it is later to be taken. This raises so-called agency problems, such as why shareholders vote for what some people might think of as measures that are not in their own interests, or the institutional investors' internal conflict of interests between their advisors who vote the portfolios and their beneficiaries and so on. These are enormously difficult institutional issues to which straightforward concepts of shareholder sovereignty really do not provide good second-order answers. So those two things must be on the table.

Finally, although it is part of my second point, there is this question of basic philosophy; and I will put aside the issue of third country versus intra-EC differentiation, and mention only the public order exception problem within the EC. I would simply say that the overall question of what is your view of whether takeovers are good for the economy in my personal judgement – and it is by no means shared widely – ought to be separated from company law and securities market law. It is a quite different public issue. It is a very unsatisfactory one because it is a very politicized one. It is essentially a political question and to try to castrate it by putting it inside the framework of company law or securities regulation with its efficiency-driven concepts is probably an illegitimate thing to do in the long run. This depends a little bit on whether you think the French Revolution ought to be fought over again; and whether, *raison d'Etat* being dead, we should also kill *raison d'entreprise*, and ask who it is that controls the judgment of what is good for us when it now comes to the black box of large firms and their political power. Those are very vague, very big issues, but in any event I do think they have to be tackled. I do not believe that the question of whether takeovers are good for us can really be seen only within the confines of the specialist versions of company law, capital market law and securities regulation.

Eddy Wymeersch

The foregoing developments invite me to report about a feeling that exists in some of the Member States, if not in all of them, about the necessity for the public authorities to control at least to some extent transactions that have a fundamental adverse impact on their economy. In many places there is an uneasy feeling about these wild manifestations of capitalism, that have sometimes been called the "unacceptable face of capitalism." Are these takeovers good for the economy, do they really contribute to the strengthening of the enterprises, or are they based on short-term considerations of private power and wealth, on fear and greed as Mr. Fitchew indicated?[18]

Beyond these issues one finds that some thought is also given to questions of economic sovereignty, questions of safeguarding the regular supply of goods and materials essential to the economy such as petroleum, electric power, defense contractors, of valuable fundamental research, and so on.

The present Belgian Government has announced that it will consider steps to safeguard the so-called "strategic interest" of the economy. The Government plans to supervise the transfer of substantial assets, whether by way of private sales of shares, takeovers or otherwise, and this without regard to whether the purchaser is a national or not. These transactions would have to be subject to Government approval. There is a feeling that some sectors like electrical power supply, which is privately owned in Belgium, should be subject to this type of regulation.

One could compare this with the situation in other States, where these activities are exercised by public bodies, or by the recently privatized industries in which the government has retained a golden share.

On the other hand, one may wonder whether this type of control would not be a reasonable price for having an open and free market for company control within the EC. Would these government-imposed restrictions not be a valid alternative to the present wave of defense techniques whereby companies introduce heavily poisonous pills so that they cannot be taken over whatever the price paid for the shares? These private techniques put a visible burden on the price of the shares and therefore are inimical to the interest of small shareholders. They will constitute, in the longer term, a sleeping pill for inefficient management. I would personally prefer a free and open market for corporate control, on which the rules of conduct, e.g., for takeovers, would be strictly regulated, along with some form of government supervision for those cases in which the strategic or fundamen-

[18] See *supra* at 17.

tal interests of the State are really involved. Also this would prevent the subterfuge of having to refer the transaction to some cartel body, in order to have it cooled off.

II. The Merits of Takeovers

Hartmut Schmidt

I disagree very much with Prof. Buxbaum[19] that takeovers are an indicator of expanding equity markets in Europe. I think just the contrary is true. The merger movement has probably contributed to the decline of equity financing in the United States, and the first thing we may say is: "Well, in view of our much lower equity ratios we are already there, therefore we may not need that many mergers." This would be superficial. I would tackle it very differently. I would say, at least for Germany, that our low equity ratios are due to taxes and due to the fact that we have a creditor-controlled economy. This may provide, Prof. Buxbaum pointed this out,[20] a rather efficient management control mechanism for bread-and-butter operations. I think it is a mediocre mechanism. If you have innovative industries, where a higher risk is involved, there you should have a strictly shareholder controlled economy, at least in some sections. And when I am listening to all the comments being made here, I am very afraid that there will be much less equity around because if some of these proposals come through, this would amount to an expropriation of shareholders. They would never be able to get the yields which you could hope for before these regulations, and it may go so far that a critical mass of public equity financing may disappear. There is very little public equity financing around in most of the European countries, and if there is a takeover guideline which adds to the burdens on public equity financing, I would expect two effects. We would have more non-public companies. Everybody who wants to have a decent yield on equities would try to hold non-marketable equities. That would be one possibility. Or, even worse, the critical mass of equity financing would disappear and this would pose a threat to the economic system as we know it because in principle we rely on corporate control of the shareholders.

This is my first thought about this. There are of course other items, for example shareholder voting. Defensive measures ought to be prevented. But where do you start with prevention? Shareholder voting in Germany is designed in such a way that unfriendly takeovers or takeovers without the consent of banks will not happen. And there are the other related questions, governance questions, which would have to be looked at piece by piece. In general we must be aware that the shareholders should be able to gain

[19] See *supra* at 379.
[20] See *supra* at 379.

significantly from takeovers, and any devices that take away this opportunity are dangerous for the long-term development of Europe.

Edmund Kitch

Let me strike a somewhat different note. First of all, I would just report that in the American literature there has been a lively discussion about the merits of takeovers and there has been an argument that they are a wonderful check on inefficient managements and an important market disciplining device. I find that literature quite inconclusive and myself believe that the other devices which create incentives for managerial efficiency are quite effective, and that takeovers alone are not terribly important one way or the other. Also, of course, with the opening up of the Common Market, you should expect transactions to occur whose purpose is to reorganize the structure of firms in order to make them effective competitors in the new market environment. But I do not think takeovers are a particularly necessary and important form in which those transactions have to occur. There are lots of ways in which those transactions can occur other than by contested takeovers, and they do not have to be one of the transactional options.

If part of the agenda is to increase public shareholding as an institutional arrangement in the Common Market and you start from a position where you have a lot of companies which do not have public shareholding and you think that the managements of those companies are going to be playing a large role in the decisions whether or not to commence public shareholding, I would think those managements would be concerned whether or not it is an implication of public shareholding and that their position would become subject to the risks of contested takeover bids. So it would seem to me from that point of view you could argue that a regulatory environment which said that it is a necessary coincidence of having a public market that contested takeovers can occur might deter the movement to the public market by the firms.

As I understood the proposals that have been talked about,[21] they really would not affect that problem. I gather that any set-up or structuring of the shareholders' rights which occurs prior to the making of the bid would not be affected by the directive so that the management could decide at the time they chose to move to a public shareholder form to imbed in the structure of their company antitakeover protections. I also agree that the form of public intervention which says to shareholders, once shares have been traded, that the rules of the game are now going to be changed by unilateral State action and potential purchasers are to be excluded, is a kind of move which would send some tremors through the shareholder community because it causes a loss of shareholder options and hence wealth.

[21] See *supra* at 375 ff.

III. Shareholder Sovereignty

Robert Austin

Over the last decade, Australia probably has had more takeovers *per capita*, if I can put it that way, than any other country in the world, and certainly the regulation of takeovers has been a central policy concern in our field. We have not moved in the way that the Belgians are proposing to move.[22] Our concern has been with ensuring an aspect of shareholder sovereignty. The basic policies are to ensure that the target shareholders have adequate information, adequate time and equality of opportunity – not equality of treatment but equality of opportunity.

Originally, in the late 1970s, we sought to give effect to those principles by what was called then a "black letter" code. The code went through several stages of drafting, each draft being longer than the one before it. At the very final stages, before implementation of the code in 1979, it was proposed at a conference which I attended that there should be added to this black letter code a series of discretions in our National Companies and Securities Commission (NCSC), discretions to exempt a party from the code, to modify the code in its application to a party and, most importantly, to declare an acquisition or conduct relating to a takeover to be unacceptable notwithstanding its compliance with the black letter system. That suggestion was implemented and the result was that our black letter system was there on the statute books but subject to, if you like, review by the Commission in a particular case. Thus the focus has been on the Commission producing guidelines as to how it will exercise its discretions in this area with the black letter code basically as a starting point.

Christian Timmermans

Shareholder sovereignty is a slippery concept. I think it cannot apply in the European context for dogmatic reasons, if they are accepted: the company is not only a tool of shareholders but also an autonomous institution. I refer to the institutional approach of the company as such. That complicates enormously the issue and I must say that in my country, at least with regard to companies with workers' participation, it is said: "Well, we removed control from shareholders to a complicated board structure in order also to take into account workers' interests amongst others; so can we now accept that in cases of unfriendly takeovers the power of decision will again be given entirely to the shareholders?"

[22] See *supra* at 381.

Desmond McComb

Just reverting to Prof. Timmermans' statement about the other parties to a takeover bid, not all countries have the same attitude towards the blocking effect of labor. But I think there is a very strong argument for long-term loan creditors having a blocking power in relation to takeover bids. I do not mean an absolute blocking power, but the overall sovereignty of equity holders is not an entirely justifiable approach in the context of a takeover situation.

L.C.B. Gower

Sovereignty of shareholders. I would like to ask Mr. Fitchew what that means exactly. If that means that the shareholders must be free to decide for themselves whether they will sell or not sell their shares on a bid, okay. If however we carry sovereignty of shareholders so far as to say that as long as the shareholders in general meetings can be persuaded to vote for something which will make it certain that there never will be a takeover bid or that the takeover bid that has been made will be unsuccessful as a result of the defensive measures taken, then in that sense it seems to me that sovereignty of shareholders has no meaning because in most cases the board, so long as they can obtain the support of the institutional investors, will inevitably get what they have proposed.

Geoffrey Fitchew

What is meant by the term "sovereignty of shareholders." Most of the measures which we are thinking of putting into our directive are aimed at the protection of the shareholders' position. That is really all, I think, and they certainly do not go beyond that to the rather far-reaching proposition that shareholders must be the only parties concerned who decide on the acceptability of a bid, because clearly in certain Member States the workers' participation and the workers' rights bear on that problem.

IV. Self-Regulation and the Takeover Panel

L.C.B. Gower

The British system at the moment is entirely outside the framework of the new legislation (Financial Services Act). The Takeover Panel is a genuinely self-regulatory body. I did not want it that way.

In the Report commissioned by the British Government[23] I suggested that it needed more teeth than it had got and that it should be brought within the

[23] See *supra* at 313.

new framework, very much on the lines that Australia has adopted[24] which seem to me to be the ideal one and one which I would have thought, if we adopted it too, would be acceptable to the Commission on the basis that it has its own legal sanctions. When I was preparing the Report, I had many discussions about this with the then Chairman of the Panel and the then Chief Executive, and I persuaded them that they would be happy to go along on those grounds. Unfortunately there was then a change of chairmanship and the chief executiveship which goes around and the new team ultimately decided that they did not want to go along that route and wanted to remain completely out of the system. And they were left out. SIB asked that there should be a provision in the Financial Services Act to enable the Panel to be brought in if the need arose; SIB thought the Panel would have to have more legal powers than it had. The Panel said: "No no, God forbid, we must remain entirely outside." Then there came the *Guinness* affair where they felt they had been ineffective. At this stage discussions took place between the Panel, SIB and the Department of Trade, as a result of which it was agreed that SIB's rules would in effect require authorized persons to observe the Takeover Code and the rulings of the Panel and a "cold shoulder" rule which said that an authorized person should not act for anybody in connection with a takeover if he knew that they were not prepared to obey the Code or the Panel. And that is the position as it stands at the moment.

Can I just ask a final question: if I understand well, the future directive on takeovers will be a harmonizing directive and not a minimum standards directive; in other words, the rules you lay down will have to be applied and you cannot go further in one direction or another?

Geoffrey Fitchew

You asked whether it would be a harmonizing directive or a minimum standards directive. I think those are not two mutually exclusive categories.

First of all, any directive is a harmonizing directive normally. I cannot remember whether the Court has said that we can propose directives even where no legislation existed in any Member States. There certainly does not have to be legislation in very many Member States for us to operate, so the directive will be harmonizing in that sense; but I think that it is likely that it will state principles and quite a lot of the detail would be left to Member States to fill out.

L.C.B. Gower

Supposing you decided not to put in anything about mandatory bids, would that prevent the UK from continuing to have its provisions about mandatory bids?

[24] See *supra* at 384.

Geoffrey Fitchew

No, in that sense it would be minimum. And equally in relation to the more detailed point of the minimum periods for shareholders to decide on a bid. I think we would not prevent Member States from having a longer period,[25] and of course there is clearly no single right answer.

Robert Austin

I would like to make a remark on whether it is better to proceed by legally binding rules in this area or by something akin to a takeover panel.

Australia has toyed with the idea of a takeover panel for a decade. Generally it has been thought that the British model is not translatable to Australia because so much of our activity exists in Sydney and Melbourne with a degree of interstate rivalry, and we have nothing equivalent to the City of London with all the internal constraints on operations that the City can impose. And so what we first decided to do was to give our national Commission some very broad powers to conduct hearings in conjunction with the exercise of its powers to declare acquisitions to be unacceptable.

What has happened is that in many contested takeovers in the last decade there has been an NCSC hearing at which the parties appear represented by counsel. In 1984 it was declared by the High Court of Australia that Commission proceedings would not comply with the rules of natural justice if the Commission made public statements which affected the business reputation of parties. Nowadays hearings take place in private, but they are hearings in which the NCSC is both the policeman and the judge, because the result of the NCSC instituting a hearing is that it accumulates information and then it makes a decision as to a declaration of unacceptability.

The current proposal in the context of the Commonwealth Bills to which I have referred,[26] is to modify that structure in a way that Mr. Fitchew might find interesting. The proposal is to set up something which we will rather misleadingly call a "Panel" but it is not like the British Takeover Panel. It will be a statutory body and its powers will include powers to issue injunctions and other orders, so it is a very much stronger body than the British Takeover Panel currently is. The composition will be of market experts such as lawyers and merchant bankers, and brokers perhaps. It will be essentially a part-time committee but always on call available to so act swiftly in those areas. The power to declare an acquisition or conduct in a takeover to be unacceptable will be vested in the Panel. The Commission will in effect be the prosecutor before the Panel. If the Commission is worried about what is happening in relation to a takeover it will take

[25] *Contra*: Art. 12(1) of the proposed directive, but with the possibility of an exception to be granted by the supervisory body, Art. 12(2).

[26] See *supra* at 177 f.

proceedings before the Panel. The Panel will operate informally and swiftly, and there will be a right of appeal on questions of law. It will operate in private. The proposal produces something of a midway point, I think, between the British Takeover Panel's informality and the kind of black letter structure which we started out with.

V. Defensive Measures

Christian Meier-Schatz

A brief comment on the future EC directive on takeovers or on what you suppose to be in this directive. Seen from an American point of view, I like very much what I would call a regulatory equilibrium.

One fundamental problem of the US takeover rules is the regulatory disequilibrium under two aspects. The first relates to the formal addressees of the legal provisions. While bidders are regulated at the federal level (Williams Act), management operates predominantly under State law rules. But the disequilibrium goes beyond formal aspects of federalism and touches upon the substance of the legal rules themselves. The US has a relatively comprehensive regulatory regime for bidders but only a very loose judicial framework with respect to defensive tactics of management.

I am perfectly aware of the eminent difficulties to regulate in any abstract manner defensive maneuvers. And yet I welcome the Commission's attempt[27] to include such management defenses in one way or another in its directive. One may ask whether to cover only post-offer measures is a functionally adequate approach, because pre-offer devices are probably not only more widespread but structurally more significant. Yet this question, of course, affects the fundamental relationship between management and shareholders. And then indeed, as already stressed by Prof. Buxbaum,[28] we approach the question as to whether company law harmonization has not to be seen in an entirely new light with respect to the most recent takeover phenomenon.

Christian Timmermans

Two remarks on defensive measures. The first is whether Article 52 EEC Treaty could not be used in a particular situation by unfriendly bidders from other Member States, who would say: "Well, you have so completely closed off your national market by these protectionist devices that in fact you are disrupting the internal market, you are blocking the exercise of the right of establishment." In fact these takeovers are to be qualified as an exercise of the right of establishment, and I refer to what Mr. Fitchew said

[27] See *supra* at 377 f and note 12.
[28] See *supra* at 380.

on the specific tests developed by the Court of Justice,[29] proportionality included. Such tests could be applied in these cases too, and particularly in case of governmental intervention. I do not think that on the face non-discriminatory measures would always stand the test of Article 52. There could be a case of disguised discrimination. There is an opening, Article 56, but it is very narrow and I do not think that, for instance, it would justify measures to protect the national cultural sector etc. It is extremely narrow, but there is an opening.

André Tunc

I just would like to underline the importance of the pre-takeover defensive measures. I think that if the Community is not willing to impose the rule of one-share-one-vote (or, at least, to strongly restrict privileges of voting power), it will be very easy for any board, in some countries, to avoid any takeover by holding a few shares with a large voting power.

Geoffrey Fitchew

The discussion around the table has indicated the divergence of view which exists between the Member States on the problem of defensive measures, because Prof. Tunc has just suggested that we really must have a rule of one-share-one-vote and that is clearly not reconcilable with the kind of concerns that Prof. Wymeersch has.[30]

Eddy Wymeersch

My dilemma is that one in fact has to choose between very restrictive private or company law defense mechanisms, and a public law protection. The former exist already or have been allowed in most of the European States. These techniques have made the companies in these States almost unassailable. Although they very effectively restrict the freedom of establishment, I have not seen any objection raised by the Commission as to their existence.

On the other hand, one could have some form of public law instrument that would only focus on the overall public interest. Provided the instrument is not used in a discriminatory way, I would rather prefer the former type of protection to the latter. Also by allowing public law control, one can safeguard the free functioning of the market for corporate control, which the companies, in the absence of effective alternatives, will be extremely willing to render impracticable.

[29] See *supra* at 335.
[30] See *supra* at 381.

Chapter Eleven

Legal Harmonization and the Business Enterprise Revisited

Richard J. Buxbaum and Klaus M. Hopt

I. The Case for a Transatlantic Comparison in the Light of "Europe 1992"

Time deepens perspective; and in the case of fast-moving events even a short timespan can be useful in achieving this effect. That is the case with the subject and the volume under discussion.[1] Our original sense of the progress of Community and national political actors in realizing the goal of a completed Common Market was shaped by our sense of the pace that marked the decade of 1975-1985. By the time the manuscript finally left our hands in mid-1987, the first signals for the acceleration of that process were about to be given, and the publication date of Spring 1988 coincided with the arrival of the bandwagon, "Europe 1992," on the stage of public consciousness.

The date of the Conference at which that time shift was discussed and whose products are the contents of this volume, September 1988, coincided with the appearance of the first Community-level legislative fruits of that new impulse: the new generation of drafts of banking and financial services directives, of finalized accounting and financial disclosure regulation, of promises of an imminent takeover directive, and of the first glimpses of a new version of the long-frustrated *Societas Europaea*.[2]

The present contribution is being written as a thorough airing of the validity and viability of these proposals is underway. Undoubtedly, by the time these various presentations appear in print, yet other shifts in fact and in perspective will have occurred. Such is the hectic pace of this half decade.

[1] R.M. BUXBAUM & K.J. HOPT, *Legal Harmonization and the Business Enterprise* (Berlin/New York 1988).

[2] *Cf.* EC COMMISSION, "Proposal for a Council Regulation on the Statute for a European Company," O.J. C 263/41 (1989). For more details, see *infra* at 404 ff.

We emphasize this issue of pace and of subjective perspective because of the question implicit in several of the presentations in this volume and explicit in some of the discussions that took place at the Conference at which they were presented; namely, whether the events and hopes gathered around the "Europe 1992" slogan require a reassessment of our original evaluation of the achievements, problems, and processes of European legal harmonization in the sector of enterprise law.

II. The 1992 Movement: Towards a New State of Federation

A. The New Mood

Macropolitical analysis does not lie within our or our Conference colleagues' competence. Still, some overview, however sketchy, of the political reasons for the attraction of "Europe 1992" and of the dynamism inherent in that rubric is needed if only to disclose the starting position from which we come to our views concerning the interaction of that phenomenon with the more technical and legal aspects of European integration. In this preliminary *confessio*, it will be useful to separate the political sense or role of governmental and of private actors.

B. Political and Economic Reasons for the Change

In the largest and vaguest sense, the historic concern of the Europe of the Nine with the democratically bottomed political stability of the Western part of the Continent was a primary determinant of this reinvigoration of the European Community. The Iberian Peninsula had just emerged from its decades of dictatorship, as had Greece from its shorter *junta* epoch. The post-1956 ferment of Central and Eastern Europe, increasingly active since the mid-eighties, with its indications that more reshaping was expectable there, did its part. The political aspects of the economic emergence of Japan, as evidenced by the reactions it engendered in the originally less insulated United States, also contributed to the sense that a politically more encompassing and economically more potent European Community coincided with an enlightened national interest in several of the major nation states of the Community.

In a different sense both the public and the private sector actors (state and firm) reacted to the window of opportunity presented by the failure in fact and in nerve of socialist alternatives to liberal economic organization and by the reflection of that failure in the composition of the national governments. The possibility of emplacing a liberal economic order on that wider Europe invigorated the drive towards the completion of this larger Community, especially as it legitimated the national executive and legislative participation in that movement. Finally, the political leadership of the Community, particularly in the Commission, for its part and for its reasons encouraged and facilitated this development.

Out of this historically unique congruent behavior of the three major relevant groups – that is, national public, national private, and Community actors – a new political ability to complete a politically and geographically augmented Common Market developed.

C. Long-Term Expectations

This origin of the drive for "Europe 1992" has some important theoretical and practical consequences for our more narrow concern with the legal integration of the enterprise sector. In the first place, this view suggests that much of the expected Community legislation in this sector will be liberal and facilitative. This by no means precludes a substantial increase in the production of harmonization legislation at the Community level; on the contrary, in this complex sector the introduction of a liberal economic order represents a substantial change of direction for much of the antecedent and hereafter continuing if subsidiary national legislation. In addition, corporate, capital market, and stock exchange sectors are complex fields and require a substantial legal and regulatory underpinning even of such liberal regimes. "Liberal" and "deregulated" are not synonyms here, as American securities regulation demonstrates.[3]

In the short run, this development has the effect of empowering the Community institutional level of competence to a degree hitherto unavailable, but at the same time condemning it to exercise that new competence in a *laissez-faire* direction. For the time being, while (and assuming that) a liberal economic philosophy dominates the political and even the intellectual landscape, this congruence of interests not only warrants a reasonable stability for legal developments in this sector at the European level, but even assists in the necessary evolution of a critical level of political legitimation there. This legitimation should help Community legislative institutions weather the inevitable divergence of underlying economic views among national actors that inevitable changes in the economic and political climate necessarily will occasion from time to time.

This frame of values and reference also has external implications. The most important is the question of inwardness versus openness – the "fortress Europe" question. If the correlation of Community with liberal economic order suggested by our view of the new situation has merit, then it also has consequences for this much-mooted issue. Neomercantilism may have to be the response of the nation state, at least of the European nation state, to the Japanese challenge; but it is the purpose and function of a strong European Economic State to maintain itself successfully in this pending

[3] See VERLOREN VAN THEMAAT, "Die Rechtsangleichung als Integrationsinstrument," in *Zur Integration Europas, Festschrift für C.F. Ophüls* 243 (W. Hallstein & H.-J. Schlochauer eds., Karlsruhe 1965).

Concert d'Univers as a liberal order. If that is so, then the European Community will be not a fortress but a member of a liberal hegemony; that is, of a European/American hegemony strong enough to bring the Japanese mercantilist superpower to a recognition of the benefits of a trilateral liberal hegemony.

III. Economic Models and Political Choices: The Debate

A. Introduction

Within this frame of values and this frame of expectations, it was our original purpose to describe the process of legal harmonization of economic integration as it was occurring in Europe both in the context of the historical (and directly current) American experience, and in the context of applicable economic theory leavened by political processes of development and consensus-building. The enlightening discussion at the Lugano Conference, reflected in the foregoing position papers and in the debates themselves (also paraphrased above), understandably focused less on the comparative experience than on the comprehensiveness and validity of these political and economic contexts. Just as theory more than information was our original subject, so these discussions, too, turned more to the theoretical challenge than to any informational deficit in our original presentation.

B. Economic Theories and Their Claims

Specific issues or connections between economic theories and substantive as well as institutional developments will be discussed in Parts III and IV below. For the present, it is the larger if preliminary question of the value of economic theory or models to the harmonization process that first occupied the Conference participants and that should first be addressed. Two issues surfaced and need brief review: the role of public finance theory missing from our original discussion; and the value of any economic theory of integration to public policy questions.

1. Public Finance Theory in Particular

While our book discussed public choice theories, especially the theory of regulatory competition,[4] it did not, as especially *Fitchew* noted,[5] separately treat its mirror image, public finance theory. In fact, that effort had been made by one of us in an analysis of constitutional problems arising out of

[4] BUXBAUM & HOPT, *supra* note 1, at 8 f. For a comprehensive review of the recent literature, see the contribution of MEIER-SCHATZ, *supra* at 61 ff.
[5] See *supra* at 2.

US doctrinal developments in the (dormant) interstate commerce area;[6] and perhaps we should have been kinder to its usefulness to our joint enterprise.

Public finance theory, especially as applied to the policies of state units within a federal system, typically divides the fiscal (and, perhaps by extension, other monetary) policies of a government into those that function to support stabilization goals, redistributive goals, and efficiency/allocative goals respectively. In its original, fiscal-policy setting, the first two goals typically are judged to be best carried out by the central authority of a federal regime, because of the risk that mobile resources (especially capital but to a lesser degree also human; i.e., labor resources) will enter or leave a subordinate polity in order to benefit or escape from the shifts in relative burdens that either goal may generate. A progressive income tax may be defeated by the withdrawal of capital, a progressive welfare program by the influx of needy persons.[7]

The legal regimes under discussion in our book and in this Conference, however – not only company and enterprise legislation but also capital market, banking, and other securities regulation laws – have the goal of supporting the efficient allocation of resources. To the extent these laws are needed at all (and some would contend that the state can best support allocative efficiency by letting private forces contend without let or hindrance), they are needed because they are the social infrastructure of a market economy. As such, they may, perhaps, not become available through private regimes because they are positive or negative externalities; that is, it is to no private party's benefit to expend resources to supply them when they will be used, without expense, by competitive or other free riders.

As was said in that earlier study,[8]

> "the basic purpose of the fiscal federalism studies associated with this approach is ... the ... modest though instrumentally ... important one of considering division of powers problems separately within each functional category ..."

The case on which that approach was tested, interestingly enough, was the case of hostile takeover bids and defensive responses to them. In that study, the conclusion was reached that only exorbitant extraterritorial ambitions of a subordinate polity could be questioned under this "*fiscal federalism*" version of public finance theory; in other words, only here did economic theory support a constitutional challenge against such exorbitant subordinate legislation.[9]

[6] BUXBAUM, "Federalism and Company Law," 82 *Mich. L. Rev.* 1163-1181 (1984).

[7] *Id.* at 1169.

[8] *Id. ibid.*

[9] *Id.* at 1178-1181.

With a European *Community Takeover Directive* now a distinct possibility,[10] it would be appropriate to subject the draft currently under discussion to this theoretical analysis. That analysis, however, is only relevant to test a Member State's effort to legislate a role for bidders or target companies or their management that would be antithetical either to a proposed directive or to the Treaty of Rome *per se*. It is not available to test the draft directive unless and until that document were to authorize a Member State to exercise a substantial degree of extraterritorial power, and to exercise it in a way that would significantly inhibit takeover bids; i.e., inhibit the inflow of "foreign" capital to that state. If and when that situation were to arise, the analysis in Part V/C of Chapter 2 of our previous volume[11] would apply *mutatis mutandis*.

2. Economic Theories in General

A second, more general theme of the economic-theory discussion at the Conference was not a critique of the economic theories reviewed in the book. Rather, there was a rejection of the implicit expectation aroused there that economic theory should or at least could be meaningfully exploited to yield more or less direct policy conclusions for the political instances of the Community and the Member States in this enterprise legislation arena.[12]

That is a tonal, not a substantive issue. We may indeed be read to have created a strawman; to have made claims on behalf of economists that they would not make for themselves, only to dash those claims the more emphatically. Our belief that we did not do so is not demonstrable by us; it can only be evaluated by the individual reader, provided that the reader also read the sources we cited. It will surprise no one that the "competition" school of economic theory associated with *Scitovsky*[13] and *Balassa*[14] states its own prescriptive claims a good deal less assertively than the "public choice" school associated with *Buchanan*[15] and *Kitch*.[16] It therefore also should not surprise that our reaction to these two major schools, on this aspect of prescriptive or predictive claims, was itself somewhat differentiated.

[10] EC COMMISSION, "Proposal for a Thirteenth Council Directive on company law concerning takeover and other general bids," O.J. C 64/8 (1989), amended O.J. C 240/7 (1990). For more details, see *infra* 408 ff.

[11] BUXBAUM & HOPT, *supra* note 1, at 130 ff.

[12] This issue was taken up by FITCHEW, *supra* at 2, SCHMIDT, *supra* at 55 ff, and KITCH, *supra* at 36 ff.

[13] T. SCITOVSKY, *Economic Theory and Western European Integration* (London 1958; repr. w./intro. 1984).

[14] B. BALASSA, *The Theory of Economic Integration* (London 1962); same, ed., *European Economic Integration* (Amsterdam 1975).

[15] J. BUCHANAN, *The Demand and Supply of Public Goods* (Chicago 1968).

[16] KITCH, "Regulation and the American Common Market," in *Regulation, Federalism, and Interstate Commerce* 9 (A.D. Tarlock ed., Cambridge, Mass. 1981).

C. The Political Frame of Reference and Its Theories

The second major critical debate of the Conference emerged from the perspective of the Commission as a political actor. It suggested, if we paraphrase *Fitchew*'s points appropriately,[17] that for various reasons theoretical considerations of the kind we originally proposed were of little practical sense. The descriptive and even the heuristic value of these types of theories, at least as a guide to practical dealings, was too limited to be directly useful as political coinage. Most are species of normative rather than of positive economics, whereas what is important for practical purposes are the personal and social preferences of the relevant decision makers. And even were a particular economic theory able to make a statement about whether a particular sector were better treated at the federal than at the state level, this would not demonstrate that the delineation between both levels happened to correspond to the line between European Community and Member State competence. However, we do not in the end find this line of criticism persuasive either.

1. Europolitical Pragmatism Versus Integration Theory?

Many observers of the EC Commission's harmonization efforts, particularly those whose Archimedean fulcrum stands outside Europe, find Brussels' work occasionally somewhat too pragmatic and excessively focused on the short-term goal of acceptance of its normative proposals by the Council and the Parliament. It would surely be too harsh to criticize these efforts simply as political "muddling through," since this concentration on what is politically possible may well be unavoidable. The art of the possible may be even more difficult to practice in Brussels than it is in London, Paris, or Bonn, since the international dimension, with its additional consensus-seeking difficulties and imponderables, is piled on top of the already difficult national level of negotiation and power-brokering.

On the other hand, in very recent times it has become clear that to talk in terms of what is, or is not, politically feasible is to oversimplify. Much that did not seem feasible in Europe before the "Europe 1992" movement has in the meantime been attacked in part with quite successful results. This is true for example for the European Merger Control Regulation of December 21, 1989, which will be in force on September 21, 1990.[18] Even the work on the *Societas Europaea*, which for decades was the example of a subject with irreconcilable conflicts of interests and permanently frozen integration efforts, has been revived with considerable promise, astonishingly thanks in

[17] See *supra* at 1 ff and 16 ff.

[18] EEC No. 4064/89, O.J. L 395/1 (1989). On this regulation, see for example KOCH, "Die neuen Befugnisse der EG zur Kontrolle von Unternehmenszusammenschlüßen," 1 *EWS* 65 (1990), and NIEDERLEITHINGER, "Grundfragen der neuen europäischen Zusammenschlußkontrolle," 1 *EWS* 73 (1990).

part to the encouragement of national industrial interests.[19] This suggests the conclusion that a superficial fixation on the feasibility of each next harmonization guideline or integration measure is not the only thing, and often not even the most relevant thing, as compared with the right direction, the right field, and the simple virtue of persistence.

Above all, however, one cannot simply ignore decades of effort to provide a scientific basis for policy analysis[20] and advice with a casual reference to sound English (or other) pragmatism.[21] It is of course a commonplace observation that the excessive expectations often placed, in the sixties and seventies, in an academically well-founded political economy or economic political science have foundered since. Yet the new soberness does not suggest that the field of scholarly policy analysis has become a wasteland. Even if the priority of policy over expertise is again clearly recognized, it is often the experts who are at least developing the political options for discussion.

An important historical reason for the longstanding dominance of pragmatism in the Commission may lie in its relatively recent creation and in the hesitant transfer of national political discretion and of personal and material resources to Brussels. National ministries, which today control the largest part of at least non-political legislative activity (and of course this is even more true of the national legislator), both within their domain and externally, through their relations with other national centers like central banks, economic research institutes, and economic and other expert bodies, enjoy totally different opportunities to carry out the preliminary staff work essential to legislation. Much more use is being made of these resources today than ever before.[22] In this way, "academic policy advice" has been able to establish itself over many years even without a weighty theoretical component.

It is true that individually impressive examples, such as the *Cecchini Report*,[23] have also appeared on the European scene, but so far these are

[19] See *infra* at 405 ff.

[20] See for example GUTOWSKI, "Zur Theorie und Praxis der unabhängigen wirtschaftswissenschaftlichen Politikberatung," in *Hamburger Jahrbuch für Wirtschafts- und Gesellschaftspolitik* 9-24 (1983); A. GOERLITZ & R. VOIGT eds., *Rechtspolitologie und Rechtspolitik* (Pfaffenweiler 1989); R. MAYNTZ ed., *Implementation politischer Programme II* (Opladen 1983). For the intercultural difficulties, *cf.* BLANKENBURG, "Indikatorenvergleich der Rechtskulturen in der Bundesrepublik und den Niederlanden," 6 *Zeitschrift für Rechtssoziologie* 255-273 (1985); H. WILENSKY, *Organizational Intelligence* (New York 1967).

[21] FITCHEW, *supra* at 1; LINDBLOM, "The Science of 'Muddling Through'," 19 *Pub. Ad. Rev.* 79 (1954).

[22] For example BUNDESMINISTERIUM DER JUSTIZ ed., *Erster und Zweiter Bericht der Kommission für Insolvenzrecht* (Cologne 1985 & 1986).

[23] EC COMMISSION, *Research on the Costs of Non-Europe* (Cecchini Report, 16 vols., Brussels 1988); see also PADOA-SCHIOPPA, *Efficiency, Stability and Eq-*

only first efforts, which because of political rivalry and hard budgetary realities have not (yet?) been able to establish themselves widely. If this observation is accepted as valid, the reference in Commission circles to the primacy of political action, even without solid foundations in economic theory, loses its persuasive force at least so far as these foundations are indeed available at the current levels of knowledge.

2. Regulation at What Level: National, European, Global?

The objection that the economically optimal regulatory level does not necessarily coincide with the demarcation line between the Community and the Member States may well be valid in any given case. In any event, it can only be contradicted with difficulty. Nevertheless, it does not lead us anywhere. It may turn out that there are things which are no better dealt with at the European, rather than the State level. However, even then one would have to try and decide where the matter would best be resolved, if it remained in doubt; alternatively, whether it was better to offer a cooperative solution, with a division of regulatory competence or a cooperative regulatory mechanism. None of this is anything new in the theory or the practice of federalism.[24]

More frequent will be the determination – especially in bank and capital market law – that a global solution would be even better than a European one; e.g., in the area of international free trade in banking services and in the international regulation of banking. In that case the alternative does not lie between regulation on the best, i.e. global level or no regulation, but in the search for the best possible level. And just in this case the clear choice would be a regional solution (harmonization of banking law under the Cooke Committee recommendations[25] and inside the EC) coupled so far as possible with (at least partial) multilateral regulation (e.g., as by a US-UK agreement[26]).

The criticisms discussed above were directed at the economic frame of reference we had chosen for our inquiries, and our view of political integration. They are immanent criticisms. In contrast, possible external critiques were not articulated in any detail at Lugano.

uity: a Strategy for the Evolution of the Economic System of the European Community; a Report (Oxford 1987).

[24] P.M. SCHMIDHUBER, "Der Föderalismus in der Europäischen Gemeinschaft," in *Problematik der Ausnahmenbereiche im Kartellrecht* 107 ff (XXI. FIW Symposium, Cologne 1988).

[25] For example BANK FOR INTERNATIONAL SETTLEMENTS, COMMITTEE ON BANKING REGULATIONS AND SUPERVISORY PRACTICES (*Cooke Committee*), *International Convergence of Capital Measurement and Capital Standards* (Basle 1988).

[26] See for example MURRAY-JONES, "The US/UK Proposal on Capital Adequacy," 6 *Int'l Fin. L. Rev.* 20-25 and 27-30 (1987).

Perhaps the most weighty of these, one that in the last two and a half years has attained particular significance and attention, is briefly reviewed in the following passage, though like so many other problems of European integration it had not been the target of our study except as a general frame of reference. It has been identified as the question of "social dumping."

The question is whether the social "network" gained over decades of struggle in some Member States, above all West German labor and social rights, can be retained in a Europe of 1992 – and, if it can, how. The problem was posed in politically assertive terms by the German labor unions during 1988. It was taken up for domestic political reasons by a politically weakened government and transferred to the European political scene via the Council of Ministers.[27] We review it as the first of our responses to the Conference's review of the legal and political strategies appropriate to the attainment of a viable Europe of 1992.

D. The Social Dimension

1. The Effort to Maintain the "Social Achievement"

Most extreme is the original demand of the German unions to prevent social subtractions of any kind, guaranteeing this state of affairs through harmonization at the highest legal and political level.[28] In the meantime, it has become obvious that such a harmonization effort is neither economically sensible nor financially achievable, and that the achievement of this demand at the international political level is not to be thought of. At its core this type of demand could only superficially be characterized as an example of "European solidarity," arising because of a concern about the interests of workers in the less developed economies of certain other Member States. Rather, the demand is intended to prevent the "loss" of workplaces in highly industrialized Member States with a high level of social protection to less industrialized ones with a lower level.

These less industrialized Member States could not finance such a "social import," and as a result, would lose many of the advantages of the newly liberalized markets which have in the meantime become economically indisputable. Social protection in this absolutist sense, therefore, is a breach of solidarity just in this area of development politics. Even in a social-political sense, it is not appropriate to represent only the interests of a few

[27] EG KOMMISSION, "Die soziale Dimension des Binnenmarktes," *Soziales Europa* (Special issue 1988); DELORS, "Die soziale Dimension des Europäischen Binnenmarktes," (Ansprache anläßlich der Anhörung der SPD-Bundestagsfraktion am 2. Mai 1988), in *EG Binnenmarkt, Welche Chancen und Risiken zeichnen sich ab* (EG Kommission ed., Bonn 1988); W. DÄUBLER *et al., Sozialstaat EG? Die andere Dimension des Binnenmarktes* (Gütersloh 1989).

[28] E. BREIT ed., *Europäischer Binnenmarkt: Wirtschafts- oder Sozialraum* (Bonn 1988) and DÄUBLER, "Grenzüberschreitende Fusion und Arbeitsrecht – Zum Entwurf der Zehnten Gesellschaftsrechtsrichtlinie," 41 *DB* 1850 (1988).

national workforces. Rather, an integration process should also focus to a considerable extent on the workforces of other, and especially of less developed, Member States. These however, would only lose through a labor law and social law harmonization of this sort at the highest constitutional level.

2. Towards a Free Market for Labor?

In contrast with this approach, the academic economic position today points increasingly to the danger of a cementing of current positions through labor law and social law.[29] This controversial, as well as difficult, problem cannot be resolved here more or less *en passant*, even if the general assertion that labor law and social law make the workplace more expensive and thus have a certain relation to unemployment and the export of jobs is, as such, incontrovertible.

On the other hand, the general economic views which are at the base of our book[30] cannot be directly or simply transferred to the world of labor. While capital is a mobile factor, labor is already constrained in its mobility at the national level, let alone at the international level. There may be a certain amount of labor mobility in certain industrial and service sectors, such as modern high technology industries, or for certain highly specialized groups, such as certain liberal professions. This mobility can only be encouraged. The ambitious programs of the Community, e.g., to foster foreign language learning or, through the ERASMUS program, to increase study in foreign countries, are milestones along this path. But one cannot, no matter how extreme the effort, expect to create a general labor mobility appropriate to the demands of the markets, at least not one that vaults over language, national and cultural boundaries.

The example of the guest worker does not demonstrate the contrary, since it does not involve normal allocation processes at either end of this workforce's movements. If one is to say anything further about the problem of the integration of the world of labor and the social world, and of the harmonization of social law and labor law, one must first examine thoroughly the particularities of the labor factor in the European context. So far as can be seen, no such study has yet been made. Even a transcendent critique based on this social dumping issue needs to be based upon this kind of scientifically well-founded frame of reference in order to be persuasive and successful.

[29] See KRONBERGER KREIS, *Mehr Mut zum Markt* 218 ff (Frankfurt 1984) and also same, *Mehr Markt schafft Wohlstand* 99-135 (Frankfurt 1987).

[30] See BUXBAUM & HOPT, *supra* note 1, at 7 ff.

3. The Task of Legal Harmonization and the Workforce

Thus it only remains, at this time, to describe the direction in which, in our judgement, the solution must be sought. The issue is the securing of a certain base level of labor and social protection, which, as an analogy to shareholder and investor protection, has both an individual and a functional protective component.[31] This is not to deny that such harmonization at some, however structured, "middle" *niveau* generates similar problems, though of a lesser intensity, as does harmonization at a higher level.[32] Nevertheless, Article 100A(2) of the Treaty of Rome – which excludes the decision-making process needed for law unification pursuant to Article 100A for decisions concerning the rights and interests of workers – demonstrates that the Contracting Parties were aware of the special nature of this complex question and, in general, wrote this particularity into the Treaty. However, a generally phrased, non-binding declaration of social basic rights will certainly not be sufficient to honor this special situation.

In specific terms it will, in all probability, be unavoidable to embark in a way similar to corporation law, through the national protective norms, until an acceptable European measure of labor and social protection has been reached. The role of procedural mechanisms, which was variously emphasized in our book and at the Lugano Conference, for the solution of problems whose desirable substantive regulation is either not known or not (yet) susceptible of consensus, would be worth study in this field, too. This way unions, work councils, codetermined directorial bodies and supervisy councils and other organs would also be assigned roles in the identification of this area of labor and social protective for a European or harmonized national law.

IV. The Ongoing Process of European Legal Harmonization

A. Free Markets or Harmonization?

1. The Phenomenon: Free Markets and Harmonization

In considering "legal harmonization and the business enterprise," one comes across a surprising and (at first glance) apparently contradictory phenomenon, namely, that the idea of liberalization and deregulation is one of the motive forces of the "Europe 1992 movement," a movement which demonstrates a basically new relationship to legal harmonization. Legal harmonization should no longer be a precondition for liberalization; rather, the latter, through competition among systems (even among legal systems)

[31] K.J. HOPT, *Der Kapitalanlegerschutz im Recht der Banken* 334 ff (Munich 1975).

[32] BUNDESWIRTSCHAFTSMINISTERIUM, *Soziale Dimension der Europäischen Gemeinschaft* (Studien-Reihe 60, Bonn 1988).

should, on the contrary, render a substantial part of the legal harmonization previously deemed necessary, superfluous. However, it is actually demonstrable that legal harmonization has significantly increased since the breakthrough of this idea. One could even say, rather pointedly, that in the fields of company, bank and capital market law not much progress in harmonization could be imagined without the idea of liberalization and deregulation. This contradiction is demonstrated by the fate of the EC directives or draft directives concerning insider trading law or takeover bids.

2. Possible Reasons for the Combined Phenomenon

One may speculate about the grounds for this situation. One answer would be that the grand idea of deregulation has proved itself to be thornier than expected in its practical implementation – not only because particular interests attack each deregulatory measure that concerns them as being unacceptable, but also because at the level of detail it becomes evident that a modern industrial society needs predictability; is beset with individual and collective egoism and with the temptation to free-ride; and that in consequence normative regulation becomes, to some degree, unavoidable.[33] This can be shown, then, even in the field of cross-border normative regulation and harmonization.

The varying economic and legal stages of development, at which different Member States and their legal orders are located, may be an additional ground for this unexpected development. Say that one country already has a particular rule – e.g. concerning tender offers and takeover bids – and another does not. Or that one country will try to go ahead with a rule, while another tries to manage without one. In that case, the principle of "country of origin" should suffice to determine which system will prevail "in the market" as the better. But this approach assumes that other framework conditions are more or less the same. In fact, however, it often happens that particular problems either have not yet seemed to require regulation in one country, or that they may not even have yet appeared in fact. Furthermore, many regulations seek to achieve not only an economic, but a sociopolitical or other purpose, which cannot be left to the market alone to achieve. Thus, it is readily evident whose interests remain frustrated in the absence of an effective legal structure for affiliated enterprises and parent-subsidiary relations. If one does not simply wish to sacrifice them, then even if we take a free market as the basis for integration, it still remains necessary to provide at least a certain degree of protection of these interests in cross-border transactions as well.

[33] *Cf.* H.F. ZACHER, S. SIMITIS, F. KÜBLER, K.J. HOPT & G. TEUBNER, *Verrechtlichung von Wirtschaft, Arbeit und sozialer Solidarität, Vergleichende Analysen* (Baden-Baden 1984); for a similar version in English, see G. TEUBNER ed., *Juridification of Social Spheres* (Berlin/New York 1987).

Finally, the readiness of all affected parties, especially industry and commerce, to accept more harmonization on the way to "Europe 1992" than they had been willing to accept through many previous years also rests in part on the idea that a free market in Europe has now generally prevailed. In previous years industry and commerce were primarily interested in furthering their interests within the national legal order, and were able to use longstanding experiences and contacts for this purpose. The law-formation process at the European level is in comparison much more difficult and uncertain and thus signifies rather a danger than an opportunity, and now the interests of industry and commerce under the new European political realities are different. Now it is important to pursue or protect certain aims like security of transactions and investments, assurance of ability to raise capital and to exploit labor resources on the European level – which means, in many cases, to do so by means of harmonization. Much legal unification is also explainable in terms of, or at least congruent with, this interest position.

One qualification, however, needs to be made to this evaluation. The logic of this argument rests on the acceptance of the common European internal market and it is worth asking whether this acceptance does not rest in great part on the good macroclimate which has already lasted a surprisingly long time. At least, it is much easier to persuade Member States to transfer their competence in the field of corporate and capital market law harmonization to the Community; and it is much easier to defend such a transfer in the political sense so long as no fundamental economic problems arise with system maintenance and system redistribution – but such problems certainly would arise in a European depression of any duration. Therefore the "bootstrap" question is whether the economic and political integration process we have now reached is already so advanced that the transfer of competence could neither legally nor factually be rescinded, either totally or in a still significant degree, by the Member States. Only the future will tell.

B. The State of Actual Harmonization in Company, Capital Market and Banking Laws

The development of harmonization in the fields of company law, capital market law and banking law in the European Community has progressed extremely rapidly since the appearance of our book. Therefore, it might seem to make sense at this point simply to provide a detailed supplement to the book's preliminary table of contents concerning the state of harmonization in 1987.[34] Nonetheless, a simple amplification will not do. Rather, it would be necessary to present a completely new table of contents because of the numerous shifts, from prepared directives to proposed directives and from proposed directives to accepted directives. In the meantime, however, a whole array of compilations and collections has been published to which

[34] See BUXBAUM & HOPT, *supra* note 1, at 250-258.

reference can be made at this point.[35] Therefore, in what follows we prefer to focus briefly on some particular centers of gravity in these developments.

1. Company Law

In the case of company law, as we predicted,[36] no progress towards the proposal of a Fifth Directive concerning structural problems of the publicly held corporation is discernible. The problem of codetermination by employees seems now, as earlier, insurmountable. On the other hand, after almost fifteen years of stagnation, battle positions concerning the proposed Statute on the European Stock Corporation (Societas Europaea) of 1975 have now been drawn up. Following its memorandum of July 15, 1988, the Commission did risk a new run at the problem in July 1989,[37] apparently with some encouragement from industry, and undoubtedly further encouraged by the appropriate legal position adopted by the European Parliament. Many of the pros and cons which were traded back and forth in the '70s have simply become obsolete: not so much because of their intrinsic merits – or so insider reports from Brussels seem to imply – as because a new generation has begun to grapple with these matters and in a certain sense has more or less discovered them anew. It seems that the stumbling block, labor codetermination, is not to be removed but smoothed over.

Models are to be available for selection by the national legislator: the German model of codetermination in the Supervisory Council; the French and Belgian model of codetermination through a separate organ representing the personnel of the enterprise; and a codetermination model based upon contractual arrangements between labor and management as for example exists in Sweden.

[35] For a comprehensive survey, see M. LUTTER, *Europäisches Gesellschaftsrecht* (3d ed., Berlin, in print for 1991); VERBAND ÖFFENTLICHER BANKEN ed., *Kreditwirtschaftlich wichtige Vorhaben der EG* (No. 5, April 1990); BUNDESVERBAND DER DEUTSCHEN INDUSTRIE ed., *Was bringt der EG-Binnenmarkt* (2d ed., Cologne 1990). For a coverage of the developments in different areas, see, e.g., BEHRENS, "Das Gesellschaftsrecht im Europäischen Binnenmarkt," 1 *EuZW* 13 (1990); HOPT, "Legal Harmonization on the Way to Europe 1992: Banking and Capital Markets," 4 *B.F.L.R.* 309 (1990); SCHMIDHUBER, "Binnenmarkt 1992 – seine Auswirkungen auf Finanzdienstleistungen und Kapitalmarkt," *Versicherungswirtschaft* 798 (1989); D. HOFFMANN, *Banken- und Börsenrecht der EG* (Baden-Baden 1990).

[36] See BUXBAUM & HOPT, *supra* note 1, at 271.

[37] EC COMMISSION, "Proposal for a Council Regulation on the Statute for a European Company," O.J. C 263/41 (1989), and EC COMMISSION, "Proposal for a Council Directive complementing the Statute for a European Company with regard to the involvement of employees in the European Company," O.J. C 263/69 (1989). For a survey concerning this development, see KOLVENBACH, "Statut für die Europäische Aktiengesellschaft," 41 *DB* 1837 (1988).

This is thought of both as a means to blunt the complaint of "social dumping," and as a defense of the social achievements to date, with a flexible elective option that corresponds to national and social particularities. The contradiction that appears between the progress made in this regard and the lack of progress in the case of the Fifth Directive is only an apparent one. In the latter case the issue was compulsory codetermination for all national corporations, though with some choice under various models; whereas the choice of the legal form of *Societas Europaea* is, after all, a voluntary one (the only mandatory points are the participation of companies from more than one Member State and the required minimum capital of ECU 100,000). Whether the choice of this legal form will be attractive for companies coming from Member States that do not have codetermination, however, is doubtful. In this case one would have to enhance the attractiveness of the *Societas Europaea* through tax benefits, as the European Parliament has at least contemplated doing. In addition, the competence of the *Societas Europaea* to be an active partner in collective bargaining agreements would have to be explicitly provided for.

The harmonization of company law is further being continued through the proposal for a Twelfth Directive of May 1988, amended in June 1989,[38] concerning the introduction of the single-member private company in all Member States. In many of these states this would be a significant relaxation of many requirements in the status quo. The draft directive, however, still contemplates the use of protective devices, such as the disclosure concerning purpose and subject matter of the company, the written determination of the resolutions and decisions of the sole member in that capacity in lieu of a members' meeting, and in principle the liability of the sole member for the obligations of the company, if the former is a legal rather than a natural person. This last restriction has aroused considerable disquiet in the Federal Republic of Germany. The Institute of Chartered Accountants in Düsseldorf has gone so far as to complain of a substantial intrusion into the well-structured enterprise law. The real objection, however, is probably a different one: the obligation makes little economic or legal sense. Limited to the formal concept of sole ownership, the provision suggests its own evasion: as happened under French law, one would then see 99%-owned, rather than wholly-owned, subsidiary companies.

The harmonization of accounting law remains an ongoing problem.[39] As we originally described it in our book, the Fourth and Seventh Directives of 1983, and their transformation into national law (e.g. in the Federal

[38] Since enacted, EC COUNCIL, "Twelfth Directive of 21 December 1989 on company law concerning single-member private limited companies," (89/667/EEC) O.J. L 395/40 (1989).

[39] *Cf.* generally ORGANISATION FOR ECONOMIC CO-OPERATION AND DEVELOPMENT, *Harmonisation of Accounting Standards* (Paris 1986); see also GROSSFELD, "Gemeinsame Grundlagen des Europäischen Bilanzrechtes," 41 *Wpg* 419 (1988).

Republic of Germany through the Law of 1985 concerning balance sheet directives[40]) on the whole seemed to complete the harmonization process, if one excepts the special problems of bank and insurance balance sheets which needed a special treatment. In contrast, already in those early years the problem of the incorporated partnership (GmbH & Co.), which was specifically excluded from this harmonization, created difficulties. Having taken account of its electoral clientele, the German government looked to like-minded colleagues in the Council of Ministers for a relaxation of the harmonized balance sheet law requirements for small and middle-sized companies, and found them. A proposed Directive of October 24, 1988, tending in this direction, is presently under discussion.[41] It is questionable whether it is in fact legitimate to force such a contrast between a small business policy and the dictates of disclosure for enterprises. On the whole, legal protection weakened through insufficiencies in disclosure is not only a burden on creditors, but in the long run makes it hard for these enterprises themselves to provide adequate information for their own guidance. In fact, many private companies, whether in anticipation of planned relaxation of requirements or through simple boycott of harmonized balance-sheet law, simply do not provide the public disclosure of annual financial statements which are already required. This fact, noticeable in many countries and especially in the Federal Republic of Germany, creates problems, both for European law and its policy underpinnings. In the Federal Republic of Germany, according to a federal survey of the courts of registry conducted in January 1989,[42] only an average of 7% of all private companies have turned in their financial statements to the commercial register. The Federal Ministry of Justice fears the reaction of the Commission and a worsening of the former's negotiating position concerning the small business directive. The Justice Ministries of the individual *Länder* therefore began their own survey of these registry courts in May 1989; their first results show the same tendency. In our book[43] we characterized the failure to implement and impose sanctions as a particular problem of European law; this example shows that the problem is now more pressing than ever.[44] The possible fine of up to DM10,000 which German law[45] provides for failure to obey this provision, so far as can be ascertained, has never yet been imposed.

[40] Bilanzrichtliniengesetz, 19 December 1985, BGBl. I, 2355.

[41] EC COMMISSION, "Proposal for a Council Directive amending Directive 78/660/EEC on annual accounts and Directive 83/349/EEC on consolidated accounts with respect to the exemptions for small and medium-sized companies and to the drawing up and publication of accounts in ECU," O.J. C 287/5 (1988). In June 1990 a common position was reached by the EC Council.

[42] Wirtschaftsmagazin "Impulse" 4/1989.

[43] BUXBAUM & HOPT, *supra* note 1, at 212-214, 264-269.

[44] As to the possible role of the courts in this context, see STEINDORFF, "Gesellschaftsrecht, EG-Richtlinien und Art. 177 EWGV," 33 *AG* 57 (1988).

[45] Sections 325, 335 Handelsgesetzbuch [HGB, German Commercial Code].

2. Capital Market Law

At the intersection of company law and capital market law lies the proposed Directive concerning takeover bids. This proposal, for a Thirteenth Directive in the field of company law concerning takeover bids, has been under discussion since its publication on February 16, 1989.[46] In terms of coverage, it lies more in the sector of capital market[47] than of company law. Since the substance of this proposal was discussed in detail at the Conference,[48] it will suffice here to emphasize two major points.

First, despite much speculation it remains unclear why takeover bids have played only a minor role, and hostile ones almost no role, in the Federal Republic of Germany, compared with, for example, the situation in Great Britain or even France. One aspect of the answer no doubt lies in the obvious reference to the role of the German universal banks. An equally important role however is played by employee codetermination law, and by the financial disclosure mandated in law and available in fact in the Federal Republic, which is inadequate when compared with its level in the United States or in the United Kingdom. At the 1989 Multinational Banking Conference, held in Frankfurt in May of that year, leading German representatives of the banking sector even ascribed to codetermination an important, enterprise-maintaining function, a remarkable comment, given the bitter battles accompanying its introduction and carried all the way through to the Federal Constitutional Court until 1976.[49] Finally, a certain role is played by the specific capital-maintenance and other creditor-protection provisions of German company law. This last aspect is particularly significant in the cases of management and leveraged buyouts.[50] In the light of this background, it is to some degree surprising that the German industrial and financial sectors continue to reject the proposed directive concerning takeover bids so vigorously. It would seem that they wish to retain all options and alternatives as a belt-and-suspender policy. It is additionally important to recall two elements that are not addressed by this proposed directive.[51] The first is that of (legitimate) defenses against hostile

[46] See *supra* note 10.

[47] BUXBAUM & HOPT, *supra* note 1, at 254-256.

[48] See *supra* at 375 ff.

[49] *Cf.* HOPT, "New Ways in Corporate Governance: European Experiments with Labor Representation on Corporate Boards," 82 *Mich. L. Rev.* 1338 (1984).

[50] For details, see HAUSCHKA & ROTH, "Übernahmeangebote und deren Abwehr im deutschen Recht," 33 *AG* 181 (1988); LUTTER & WAHLERS, "Der Buyout: Amerikanische Fälle und die Regeln des deutschen Rechts," 33 *AG* 1 (1989); PELTZER, "Hostile Takeovers in der Bundesrepublik Deutschland," 18 *ZIP* 69 (1989).

[51] The draft directive is treated in more details for example by GRUNEWALD, "Was bringt der Vorschlag einer 13. EG-Richtlinie über Übernahmeangebote für das deutsche Recht?," 43 *WM* 1233 ff (1989); BAUMS, "Übernahmeregeln in der Europäischen Gemeinschaft," 10 *ZIP* 1376 ff (1989); ASSMANN, BASALDUA, BOZENHARDT & PELTZER, *Übernahmeangebote* (Berlin 1990); HOPT, "Übernahme-

takeover bids. In the long run, a harmonization of this side of the takeover battle will also be unavoidable as an element of integration policy. It is here, after all, as the American experience demonstrates, that individual states too easily develop the unhealthy tendency to provide local enterprises with excessive protection, especially against takeover bids emanating from other states.[52]

In this connection, the issue of reciprocity becomes important as well. The provision originally suggested, concerning reciprocity in relation to bidders from different countries, has been omitted from the published version of the proposed directive. The Commission justifies this approach on the ground that since the Member States authorize corporations to use a large number of defensive measures, a regulation concerning reciprocity at the level of the Community would be premature.[53] This raises basic questions concerning reciprocity, questions which cannot be answered at this stage or in this place. At the least, however, it is important to note the discrepancy thereby arising between theory and actual practice. Whereas, on the one hand, academic scholarship and theories of economic law characterize reciprocity requirements as basically harmful to integration efforts, experience derived from the international banking and stock exchange sectors, especially in their contacts with Japan, demonstrates that reciprocity can also lead to the opening of markets. The real question is whether such a function can adequately be fixed in a normative sense by law.

In our book[54] we also discussed in detail the second major problem, that of insider trading. It is commendable that in the meantime the longstanding resistance of German political and economic sectors to a European solution of this problem has broken down. Moreover, if only because of the pressure created by the majority voting potential pursuant to Article 100A of the Treaty, a more sober evaluation has now developed: if not of the phenomenon itself, at least of the international consequences which would ensue if the Germans continued to go their own way. The revised proposal of the Directive concerning insider trading was accepted on July 18, 1989, by the Council of Ministers[55] with some modifications proposed by the European Parliament, and has in the meantime been submitted to that Parliament for its approval, which was given on November 13, 1989.[56]

angebote im europäischen Recht", in *Festschrift für Rittner* (Munich, to be published in 1991).

52 ROMANO, "The Political Economy of Takeover Statutes," 73 *Va. L. Rev.* 111 (1987); MEIER-SCHATZ, "Europäische Harmonisierung des Gesellschafts- und Kapitalmarktrechts," 41 *WuR* 84 ff and 106 ff (1989).

53 COM(88)823 – SYN 186, 16 February 1989, sub I.13.

54 BUXBAUM & HOPT, *supra* note 1, at 246-249.

55 EC COUNCIL, Common Position – SEK (89)fin. – SYN 85, 20 July 1989.

56 EC COUNCIL, "Directive of 13 November 1989 coordinating regulations on insider dealing," (89/592/EEC) O.J. L 334/30 (1989).

Given the recent date of its promulgation, we are obliged to reserve a detailed evaluation of the directive for another occasion.[57]

The Block Trading Disclosure Directive of December 12, 1988,[58] has also been promulgated, albeit with resistance from some Member States, especially that of the Federal Republic of Germany. A considerable gain in transparency and disclosure has been gained through the placement of the reporting obligation at 10%. Up to now, at least, it seems that parts of the German financial sector have still not understood as clearly as they ought to the significance of this decisive change in company law disclosure requirements regarding the acquisition or disposition of a material participation in a listed company.

3. Banking Law

Of all general developments, that concerning banking law[59] has been the most breathtaking. For example, the Liable Funds Directive was promulgated as early as on May 5, 1989,[60] and the Second Banking Law Harmonization Directive on December 30, 1989;[61] at the same time also the Directive concerning the solvency coefficients for credit institutions was enacted.[62] It is interesting that in this sector the principle of reciprocity was insisted upon for the admission of credit institutions from third countries, leading to significant controversies and fears especially in the United States and in Japan. The specifics of the implementation of this reciprocity requirement, on the other hand, remain uncertain and open to date.

Other initiatives also are still pending. Thus work is continuing on an expansion and stiffening of the Consolidated Bank Supervision Directive of June 13, 1983;[63] further, in January 1988 the Commission submitted to the

[57] See HOPT, "The European Insider Dealing Directive," 27 *C.M.L. Rev.* 51 (1990); same, "Europäisches und deutsches Insiderrecht," 20 *ZGR* (Spring issue, forthcoming 1991); K.J. HOPT & E. WYMEERSCH eds., *European Insider Dealing* (London, to be published in 1991).

[58] EC COUNCIL, "Directive of 12 December 1988 on the information to be published when a major holding in a listed company is acquired or disposed of," (88/627/EEC) O.J. L 348/62 (1988).

[59] BUXBAUM & HOPT, *supra* note 1, at 257 f.

[60] EC COUNCIL, "Directive of 17 April 1989 on the own funds of credit institutions," (89/299/EEC) O.J. L 124/16 (1989).

[61] EC COUNCIL, "Second Directive of 15 December 1989 on the coordination of laws, regulations and administrative provisions relating to the taking-up and pursuit of credit institutions and amending Directive 77/780/EEC," (89/646/EEC) O.J. L 386/1 (1989).

[62] EC COUNCIL, "Directive of 18 December 1989 on a solvency ratio for credit institutions," (89/647/EEC) O.J. L 386/14 (1989).

[63] EC COUNCIL, "Directive of 13 June 1983 on the supervision of credit institutions on a consolidated basis," (83/350/EEC) O.J. L 193/18 (1983). New proposal published in 1990: COM (90) 451 final – SYN 306, 22 November 1990.

Council of Ministers a modified version of the proposal for a Bank Rescue and Liquidation Directive of December 23, 1985.[64] The narrow definition of "credit institution" in these banking law harmonization directives has rendered it necessary to promulgate separate directives concerning securities firms. For that reason, on January 3, 1989, the Commission submitted to the Council a proposal for a Directive concerning the provision of services in this sector;[65] and supplementing this, work is proceeding on a first proposal for a Directive concerning capital requirements and risks in connection with securities transactions.[66]

V. General Conclusion and Outlook

It would be unnecessary and pointless to recapitulate the foregoing recapitulations, or to summarize the already summary descriptions of events and progress since 1988. More important is the reemphasis of basic points that remain valid even in this era of new vigor and faster pace for legal integration and harmonization.

The first and foremost point is that harmonization of law is not an aim in itself. It either serves underlying values and underlying goals or it does not. Of course, law is in a sense an end in itself, as well as a social phenomenon and a cultural expression. The failure to resolve the crisis of modernity, *the* challenge of this century, may or may not be a failure of law;[67] "failure" to *harmonize* Europe's law, without more, is not.

The diversity within the legal regime of a European Community, a diversity of history, language, *Lebenswelt*, and system, is greater than the diversity within the legal regime of that civil society known as the United States. Values and goals of peace, prosperity, liberty, equality, mutual toleration, and openness to the "external" world are expressed, *inter alia*, in law. Whether harmonization or divergence of particular laws serves these goals, however, is an issue as specific as it is critical. Even within today's context – one far more positive and energetic than existed even half a dozen years ago – there is no single solution to that problem.

[64] EC COMMISSION, "Proposal for a Council Directive on the coordination of laws, regulations and administrative provisions relating to the reorganization and the winding-up of credit institutions," O.J. C 356/55 (1985), and "Amended Proposal," O.J. C 36/1 (1988).

[65] EC COMMISSION, "Proposal for a Council Directive on investment services in the securities field," O.J. C 43/7 (1989) and "Amended Proposal" O.J. C 42/7 (1990).

[66] EC COMMISSION, "Proposal for a Council Directive on Capital Adequacy of Investment Firms and Credit Institutions," O.J. C 152/6 (1990).

[67] WIETHÖLTER, "Ist unserem Recht der Prozeß zu machen?," in *Zwischenbetrachtungen: Im Prozeß der Aufklärung, Festschrift für J. Habermas* 794 ff (A. Honneth *et al.* eds., Frankfurt/M. 1989).

Much harmonization that is consistent with these goals can be and should be expressed through channels more important than those of economic life (and its law). The growing together of cultural and intellectual life may be more important to those ultimate social values postulated above than a company code; an ERASMUS program of university study,[68] trans-Atlantic as well as intra-European, more expressive of that shared effort than a book on company codes; a pan-European or trans-Atlantic (or Pacific) academy of sciences more useful than a code research project.

One final point. We suggested earlier[69] that, even within the law and within the specific legal sector we have discussed, harmonization "from below" may be at least as important as formal harmonization directed "from above." This was further confirmed by some of the topics discussed at the Conference, such as accounting firm mergers and the growing ease of inter-jurisdictional enforcement agency cooperation. We continue to believe, and believe ourselves confirmed therein by the discussions in this volume, that much of importance is happening and much of importance remains to be achieved in this regard. We venture to predict that these developments will intensify now that liberalization of capital markets and of financial services is descending on Europe; and that through these developments a sound and stable second pillar of support for the European Community and its legal framework will be erected over the next few years.

As the predominantly economic European Community moves towards a "Europe" that can accommodate (if not necessarily assimilate) its other, especially its formerly socialist, European neighbors, its legal system will have to accommodate a wider range of individual state variations, especially in the economic realm, than is the case even today. That is all the more reason to see legal harmonization in the broadest possible context, and especially always to remain conscious of its instrumental character, of its role in supporting the primary values and goals of these European polities.

[68] For the state of progress reached in the Community action programme on student mobility see the recent report adopted by the EC COMMISSION on March 16, 1989, Doc. COM(89)119 final.

[69] BUXBAUM & HOPT, *supra* note 1, at 111 ff.

Index of interventions

FSC
www.fsc.org
MIX
Papier | Fördert
gute Waldnutzung
FSC® C083411

Kolibri 360 GmbH
Ferdinand-Jühlke-Straße 7
99095 Erfurt, Deutschland
produktsicherheit@kolibri360.de